Lecture Notes in Computer Science 6906

Commenced Publication in 1973
Founding and Former Series Editors:
Gerhard Goos, Juris Hartmanis, and Jan van Leeuwen

Jose M. Alcaraz Calero
Laurence T. Yang   Félix Gómez Mármol
Luis Javier García Villalba
Andy Xiaolin Li   Yan Wang (Eds.)

Autonomic and Trusted Computing

8th International Conference, ATC 2011
Banff, Canada, September 2-4, 2011
Proceedings

 Springer

Volume Editors

Jose M. Alcaraz Calero
Hewlett-Packard Laboratories, Stroke Gifford, BS34 8QZ, UK
E-mail: jose-maria.alcaraz-calero@hp.com

Laurence T. Yang
St. Francis Xavier University, Antigonish, NS, B2G 2W5, Canada
E-mail: ltyang@stfx.ca

Félix Gómez Mármol
NEC Laboratories Europe, 69115 Heidelberg, Germany
E-mail: felix.gomez-marmol@neclab.eu

Luis Javier García Villalba
Universidad Complutense de Madrid (UCM), 28040 Madrid, Spain
E-mail: javiergv@fdi.ucm.es

Andy Xiaolin Li
University of Florida, Gainesville, FL 32611-6200, USA
E-mail: andyli@ece.ufl.edu

Yan Wang
Macquarie University, Sydney, NSW 2109, Australia
E-mail: yan.wang@mq.edu.au

ISSN 0302-9743   e-ISSN 1611-3349
ISBN 978-3-642-23495-8   ISBN 978-3-642-23496-5 (eBook)
DOI 10.1007/978-3-642-23496-5
Springer Heidelberg Dordrecht London New York

Library of Congress Control Number: 2011935115

CR Subject Classification (1998): D.2, C.2, D.4, H.3-4, K.6

LNCS Sublibrary: SL 2 – Programming and Software Engineering

Typesetting: Camera-ready by author, data conversion by Scientific Publishing Services, Chennai, India

Printed on acid-free paper

Springer is part of Springer Science+Business Media (www.springer.com)

Preface

This volume contains the proceedings of ATC 2011, The 8*th* International Conference on Autonomic and Trusted Computing: Bringing Safe, Self-* and Organic Computing Systems into Reality. The conference was held in Banff, Canada, during September 2–4, 2011, and was organized by St. Francis Xavier University in cooperation with the 13*th* IEEE International Conference on High Performance Computing and Communications (HPCC 2011) and the 8*th* International Conference on Ubiquitous Intelligence and Computing (UIC 2011).

Nowadays, systems are becoming more and more complex in terms of heterogeneity, size, functional requirements, design and architecture. Autonomic computing (AC) focuses on achieving self-manageable computing and communication systems. Such systems aim to perform an autonomic management of the maximum functionality of the systems without human intervention or guidance making easier the system management tasks. Autonomic systems may also be trustworthy to avoid the risk of losing control and retain confidence that the system will not fail. Trusted computing (TC) aims at making computing and communication systems predictable, controllable, dependable, secure, private and protected and definitively trustworthy.

ATC 2011 provided a forum for scientists and engineers in academia and industry to exchange ideas and experiences in developing AC/TC communications and systems, theories, models and architectures, services and applications. We believe that all of the presented papers not only provided novel ideas, new results and state-of-the-art techniques in this field, but also stimulated future research activities in the area. In addition to the 17 accepted refereed papers, the proceedings include Gregorio Martinez's keynote addressing the "Enhancing OpenID Through a Reputation Framework."

We would like to take this opportunity to thank numerous people whose work made this conference possible and ensured its high quality. We would like to thank all Program Committee members and external reviewers for their excellent job in the paper review process. We wish to thank the authors of submitted papers as they contributed to the conference technical program. Thanks to the Advisory Committee for their continuous advice. We are also in debt to the Publicity Chairs for advertising the conference, to the Local Organizing Committee for managing all conference organization-related tasks, and to the St. Francis Xavier University for organizing the conference. We are also grateful to Chunsheng Zhu for his hard work on managing the conference website and submission and review management system. Finally, we would like to thank the Steering Committee for their undoubtable effort in orchestrating all the people involved in making this conference a successful event.

September 2011

Jose M. Alcaraz Calero
Laurence T. Yang
Felix Gomez Marmol
Luis Javier García Villalba
Andy Xiaolin Li
Yan Wang

Organization

The 8th Internation Conference on Autonomic and Trusted Computing (ATC 2011) was organized by St. Francis Xavier University in Banff , Canada, September 2–4, 2011, in cooperation with the 13th IEEE International Conference on High Performance Computing and Communications (HPCC 2011) and the 8th International Conference on Ubiquitous Intelligence and Computing (UIC 2011). ATC 2011 was technically sponsored by the IEEE Technical Committee on Scalable Computing (TCSC).

Executive Committee

Honorary Chair

Christian Muller-Schloer   University of Hannover, Germany

General Chairs

Mazin Yousif   IBM, Canada
Manish Parashar   Rutgers University, USA
Gero Mühl   University of Rostock, Germany

Program Chairs

Andy Xiaolin Li   University of Florida, USA
Yan Wang   Macquarie University, Australia
Jörg Hähner   University of Hannover, Germany

Program Vice-Chairs

Jose M. Alcaraz Calero   Hewlett-Packard Labs, UK
Felix Gomez Marmol   NEC Europe, Germany
Luis Javier García Villalba   UCM , Spain

Workshop Chairs

Xiaodong Lin   University of Ontario, Canada
Naixue Xiong   Georgia State University, USA

Steering Committee

Laurence T. Yang (Chair)   St. Francis Xavier University, Canada
Jianhua Ma (Chair)   Hosei University, Japan
Theo Ungerer   University of Augsburg, Germany
Jadwiga Indulska   University of Queensland, Australia
Daqing Zhang   Institute TELECOM SudParis, France
Hai Jin   Huazhong University of Science and
                          Technology, China

Executive Committee (cont.)

Advisory Committee

Hartmut Schmeck (Chair)	Karlsruhe Institute of Technology, Germany
Jeffrey J.P. Tsai	University of Illinois at Chicago, USA
Chin-Chen Chang	Feng Chia University, Taiwan
Jean Camp	Indiana University, USA
Jurgen Branke	University of Warwick, UK
Raouf Boutaba	University of Waterloo, Canada
Wolfgang Reif	University of Augsburg, Germany
Zhong Chen	Peking University, China
Tadashi Dohi	Hiroshima University, Japan
Tharam Dillon	Curtin University of Technology, Australia

Publicity Chairs

Damien Sauveron	University of Limoges, France
Xingang Liu	Yonsei University, Korea
Mianxiong Dong	University of Aizu, Japan
Hao Chen	University of Florida, USA
Jiehan Zhou	University of Toronto, Canada
Agustinus Borgy Waluyo	Monash University, Australia
Senol Z. Erdogan	Maltepe University, Turkey
Carlos Westphall	Federal University of St. Catarina, Brazil
Wenbin Jiang	Huazhong University of Science and Technology, China

Panel Chairs

Zhen Liu	Nokia Research Center, China
Srinivas Sampalli	Dalhousie University, Canada

Award Chairs

Chunming Rong	University of Stavanger, Norway
Sajid Hussain	Fisk University, USA

International Liaison Chairs

Zhong Chen	Peking University, China
Junzhou Luo	Southeast University, China
Roy Sterritt	University of Ulster at Jordanstown, UK
Bin Xiao	Hong Kong Polytechnic University, Hong Kong
Hui-Huang Hsu	Tamkang University, Taiwan
Juan Gonzalez Nieto	Queensland University of Technology, Australia

Industrial Liaison Chairs

Nagula Sangary   RIM, Canada
Martin Gilje Jaatun   SINTEF, Norway

Local Chairs

Alice Ying Huang   St. Francis Xavier University, Canada
Shizheng Jiang   St. Francis Xavier University, Canada
Andy Yongwen Pan   St. Francis Xavier University, Canada

Web Chair

Chunsheng Zhu   St. Francis Xavier University, Canada

Program Committee

Mohamed Ahmed   University College of London, UK
Dave Bakken   Washington State University, USA
Patricia Arias Cabarcos   Carlos III University, Spain
Julio César Hernández-Castro University of Portsmouth, UK
Alva L. Couch   Tufts University, USA
Nigel Edwards   Hewlett-Packard Lab, UK
M. Carmen Fernandez Gago   University of Malaga, Spain
Antonio Maña Gomez   University of Malaga, Spain
Luis Miguel Vaquero Gonzalez Telefonica R&D, Spain
Nathan Griffiths   University of Warwich, UK
Jinhua Guo   University of Michigan at Dearborn, USA
Peter Gutman   University of Auckland, New Zealand
Sy-Yen Kuo   National Taiwan University, Taiwan
Miroslaw Kutylowski   Wroclaw University of Technology, Poland
Mario Lischka   NEC Laboratories Europe, Germany
Jorge Lobo   IBM Research, USA
Esteban Egea Lopez   Polytechnic University of Cartagena, Spain
Pedro Peris-López   Delft University of Technology,
                                 The Netherlands
Fermin Galán Márquez   Telefonica I+D, Spain
Florina Almenarez Mendoza   Carlos III University, Spain
Martin Middendorf   University of Leipzig, Germany
Marco Cassassa Mont   Hewlett-Packard Lab, UK
Frank Ormeier   Otto von Güricke University, Germany
Manuel Gil Perez   University of Murcia, Spain
Ronald Petrlic   University of Paderborn, Germany
Andrea di Pietro   University of Pisa, Italy
María Naya-Plasencia   FNHW, Switzerland
Ruben Rios del Pozo   University of Malaga, Spain
Dhiraj K. Pradhan   University of Bristol, UK

Program Committee (cont.)

Jason Reid	Queensland University of Technology, Australia
Isaac Agudo Ruiz	University of Malaga, Spain
Khaled Hamed Salah	Khalifa University of Science, United Arab Emirates
Martin Serrano	Waterford Institute of Technology, Ireland
Kuei-Ping Shih	Tamkang University, Taiwan
Christoph Sorge	University of Paderborn, Germany
Stella Spagna	University of Pisa, Italy
Juan E. Tapiador	University of York, UK
Juergen Teich	University of Erlangen-Nürnberg, Germany
Fatih Turkmen	University of Trento, Italy
Osman Ugus	Hamburg University of Applied Sciences, Germany
Theo Ungerer	University of Augsburg, Germany
Guilin Wang	University of Wollongong, Australia
Huaxiong Wang	Nanyang Technological University, Singapore
Jun Wei	Chinese Academy of Sciences, China
Dirk Westhoff	Hamburg University of Applied Sciences, Germany
Rolf Würz	University of Bochum, Germany
Dong Xiang	Tsinghua University, China
Yang Xiang	Deakin University, Australia
Zheng Yan	Aalto University, Finland
Baoliu Ye	Nanjing University, China
Lu Zhang	Peking University, China
Huanyu Zhao	Oklahoma State University, USA
Deqing Zou	Huazhong University of Science and Technology, China

Table of Contents

Trusted and Secure Computing

Reliable, Secure and Trust Applications

Enhancing OpenID through a Reputation Framework

Félix Gómez Mármol[1], Marcus Quintino Kuhnen[1],
and Gregorio Martínez Pérez[2],[*]

[1] NEC Laboratories Europe, Kurfürsten-Anlage 36, 69115 Heidelberg, Germany
felix.gomez-marmol@neclab.eu, marcus.kuhnen@neclab.eu
[2] Departamento de Ingeniería de la Información y las Comunicaciones,
University of Murcia, 30100 Murcia, Spain
gregorio@um.es

Abstract. OpenID is an open standard providing a decentralised authentication mechanism to end users. It is based on a unique URL (Uniform Resource Locator) or XRI (Extensible Resource Identifier) as identifier of the user. This fact of using a single identifier confers this approach an interesting added-value when users want to get access to different services in the Internet, since users do not need to create a new account on every website they are visiting. However, OpenID providers are usually also being used as a point to store certain personal attributes of the end users, which might be of interest for any service provider willing to make profit from collecting that personal information. The definition of a reputation management solution integrated as part of the OpenID protocol can help users to determine whether certain service provider is more or less reliable before interacting with it and transferring their private information. This paper is providing the definition of a reputation framework that can be applied to the OpenID SSO (Single Sign-On) standard solution. It also defines how the protocol itself can be enhanced so OpenID providers can collect (and provide) recommendations from (to) users regarding different service providers and thus enhancing the users' experience when using OpenID.

Keywords: Single sign on, Reputation, OpenID, Web services, Identity management.

1 Introduction

Providing effective authentication solutions is a key part to successfully deploy any service provider nowadays. That implies as a minimum to identify individuals in that provider and to control the access to the different resources and services being provided by it.

Even if these authentication approaches can be based on well-known technologies such as login/password, smart cards, digital certificates or biometric information, among others, it is usually happening that different service providers

---

[*] Corresponding author. Tel.: +34 868 887646, Fax: +34 868 884151.

J.M. Alcaraz Calero et al. (Eds.): ATC 2011, LNCS 6906, pp. 1–18, 2011.

belonging to different companies or organizations are managing their own identifiers and mechanisms to authenticate their users. This is leading to users creating new accounts on almost every website they use and even in certain cases avoiding websites because they should be creating yet another identifier (e.g., username and password).

OpenID [1] is an open technology standard that provides a solution to this problem. As such it is defined as a mechanism allowing the use of a single account to sign in to different service providers. In this proposal, the user only has to enable her current existing account for OpenID access and then provide any OpenID-enabled service her unique OpenID identifier. With this identifier the service provider sends the user to the OpenID provider so she can be authenticated there and then get access (after successfully authenticated) to the service.

The wide use of this approach as well as the information that certain service providers are requesting from the users are making OpenID providers the right place to store certain private attributes of the end user. Those attributes are also needed when taking certain decisions in the service provider so the access can be provided (or denied) to particular resources. Such access may depend on the role of the user, the domain where she is coming from, her age, etc.

However, as this private information is directly exchanged between the OpenID provider and the service provider via a set of OpenID extensions and the user is not having direct control on this exchange under certain circumstances, there is a clear need to extend the OpenID standard to provide more control on such exchange. Several approaches can be considered, being reputation management a promising option. It can provide end users with certain key information before starting an OpenID authentication process (and attribute release) with an unknown service. Users can then decide whether they are willing to exchange this personal information with that service or not, based on the interactions that other users had in the past, i.e., based on the reputation that this service provider is having among different users.

This paper is providing a detailed definition of a reputation framework designed to be integrated with OpenID. Moreover, it is describing how the OpenID protocol can be enhanced so the OpenID provider can collect recommendations from different users on a given service provider based on their interactions with it. Our work also describes how these recommendations can be aggregated appropriately and provided to the user before she starts interacting with a service.

The remainder of the article is organized as follows. Section 2 provides a common nomenclature as wells as the description of the particular problem being addressed as part of this research work. Then, in section 3 we describe both the functional and non-functional requirements for developing a reputation framework, while in section 4 the OpenID protocol enhancement needed to deal with this reputation framework is presented. Section 5 shows the reputation framework itself, which has been designed for enhancing the users' experience using the OpenID technology. Later, section 6 provides the main references and related works, while in 7 the main conclusions and lines of future work are described.

2 Problem Statement

For consistency throughout the remainder of the paper, we present next a basic glossary of the terms used within the OpenID environment:

- **User** or **end-user**: The entity that wants to assert a particular identity.
- **Identifier** or **OpenID**: The URL or XRI chosen by the end-user to name the end-user's identity (for instance, http://felixgm.myopenid.com).
- **Identity provider** or **OpenID provider** (**IdP** or **OP**): A service that specializes in registering OpenID URLs or XRIs and providing OpenID authentication (and possibly other identity services).
- **Relying party** (**RP** or **SP**): The site that wants to verify the end-user's identifier; other terms include "service provider" or the now obsolete "consumer".

Once we have defined the meaning of those terms and the role of each player, figure 1 depicts an overview of how the OpenID protocol works. Let's say Alice wants to watch a film online, so she accesses the service provider (relying party) offering such service. However, the film that Alice wants to watch contains explicit violent scenes and she must therefore prove she is an adult in order to get access to it.

Then, instead of registering and creating a new account in such RP, Alice wants to use her existing OpenID already registered in a certain OP. Thus, Alice is redirected to the OP she has indicated and logs in. Hence, the RP has access to Alice's identity information stored in the specified OP (like for instance, age, e-mail, credit card, etc) and, after checking she is an adult, the RP actually provides the requested film.

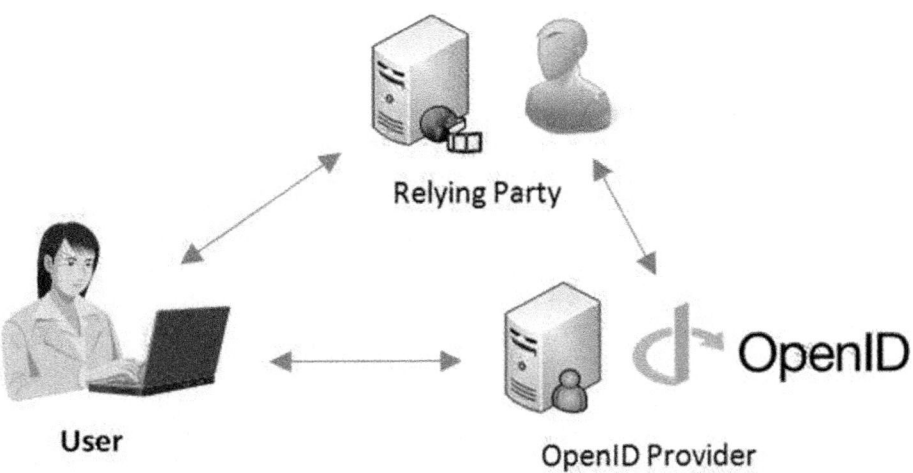

Fig. 1. Scenario definition: single sign-on through OpenID

Nevertheless, despite its several advantages, based on a market survey [2], 97% of the users today in the Internet would like their OpenID providers to offer a way of assisting them with trustworthy information about the relying parties (services that they use). Such reputation information would lead to smarter and more accurate decisions from users when deciding which relying parties to interact with, while preventing them from having transactions with malicious or fraudulent RP, which would be, in turn, identified and isolated.

Spiteful relying parties might misbehave and misuse users' personal information like e-mail address for spamming, or credit card number for charging unexpected expenses, amongst many other dishonest operations. Therefore it is crucial to promptly and accurately detect their unreliable behavior and share this information in the form of a low reputation value within the community, in order to warn other (maybe unwary) users.

3   Requirements Analysis

This section identifies the functional as well as non-functional requirements for developing the envisioned reputation framework for the OpenID SSO system. As in any other study of this category, the requirements represent a list of trade-offs that have to be analyzed and evaluated when building such a system. First, we address the functional requirements that are relevant to the framework. These are:

1. **Majority Rating Evaluation:** Since we want to aggregate possible rating values of the users of the services for calculating the reputation of the relying parties, our framework should provide reputation information about the relying parties, based on the majority of the raters.
2. **Time awareness:** Not only the majority has to be considered, but the framework should consider as well that old ratings should be treated as less important than new ones. Therefore the framework should consider the instant when the recommendation ratings were provided to the relying parties.
3. **Incorrectness awareness:** The framework should consider the possible incorrect feedbacks provided by either malicious users [3] or simply users that by mistake provide wrong rating values to the relying parties.
4. **Users' preferences awareness:** The framework should provide a mechanism that allows users to look for services based on their preferences. That means, the framework should provide a mechanism where the users can express their preferences with regard to the provision of each service.
5. **Privacy/anonymity:** The framework should provide a mechanism allowing users to rate service providers anonymously. Only the OpenID provider should know about the digital identity of the user. This should be protected from the relying parties which receive the recommendation information. We believe such mechanism will give an extra incentive to the users for providing feedback information about the relying parties that they have interacted with.

Moreover, we foresee the following non-functional requirements as the most relevant in order to provide a reliable reputation framework on top of a SSO system like OpenID.

1. **Scalability:** When designing the system, we have to take care of the rate of recommendation inputs and queries made on the system. A centralized or distributed solution might have different implications regarding scalability issues. It is therefore important to bear in mind the potential bottlenecks of the architecture that might also constitute a single point of failure.

2. **Reliability of the transaction:** We believe that, for certain specific situations (like those with a very high frequency of transactions), a reputation system might not provide a 100% reliable transactional support for users' recommendations input. It should rather consist of a best-effort solution based on messages to be exchanged between the different peers. We foresee a high load of interactions; therefore, a 100% reliable transactional support might give additional delay or even block the system.

3. **Performance:** On the one hand, we claim that best effort mechanisms like the exchange of messages are appropriated for such a system. On the other hand, we think that the system should have a high performance. Thus, it should support a lot of applications requests at high rates. For example, a popular OpenID provider, which is accessed by a lot of users, will also have to communicate with other OpenID providers in order to exchange reputation information with them. Such exchange of information needs to have a high performance because otherwise the user experience will be degraded. Hence, this performance requirement fits with the reliability requirement that claims that the transaction should be message best effort based.

4. **Reputation model:** The system should support different reputation models, since we believe those models will be improved, due to lot of research happening in this area. Therefore, it is important for the framework to be able to support different reputation models on the fly through a reputation model plug-in framework.

5. **Portability of data exchange:** The framework should allow data describing the reputation information of the relying parties to be exchanged across the different trust management frameworks. At the current state of the art, there is no protocol between OpenID providers allowing the exchange of information between them. Therefore, the framework requires a protocol and a standardized model for reputation data that can be exchanged between OpenID parties [4].

6. **Compliance with laws and regulations:** Since these SSO protocols might deal with very sensitive and private users' information, any enhancement over them must keep the compliance with current related laws and regulations. Moreover, such compliance with regulations will improve the users' perception of security in the system and, therefore, their willingness to adopt it.

4   OpenID Enhancement

Figure 2 represents the sequence diagram corresponding to the regular operation of the OpenID protocol.

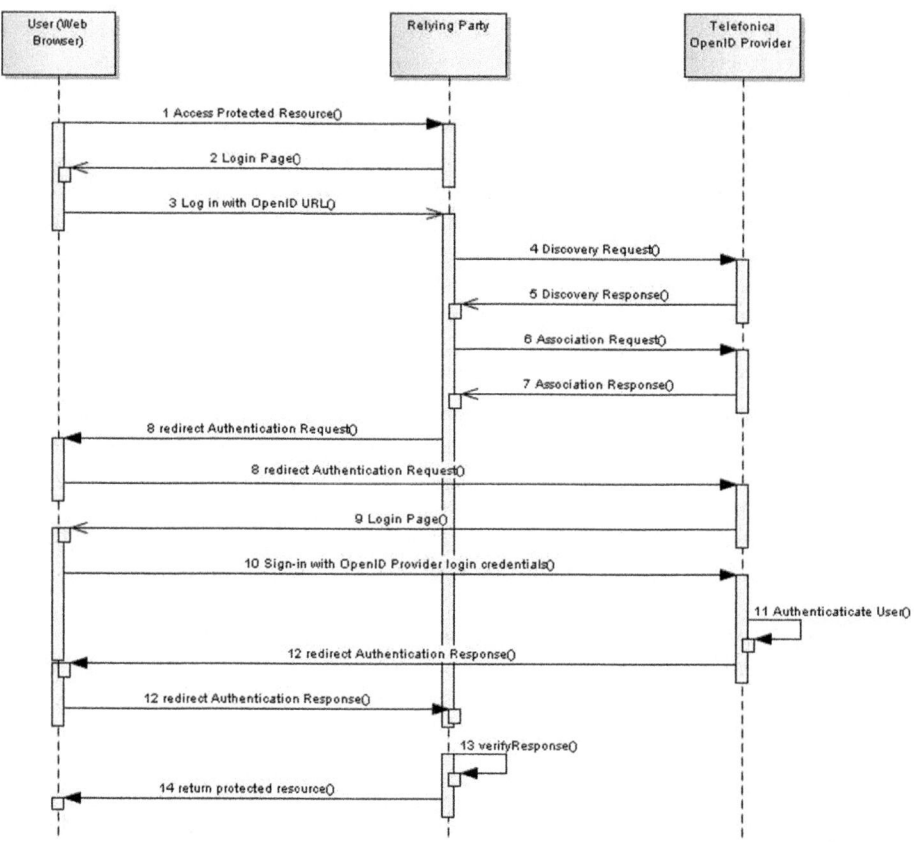

Fig. 2. OpenID protocol: sequence diagram

The main aim of our work is to enhance such protocol so that the specified OpenID provider is able to collect recommendations about the selected RP, and aggregate them appropriately in order to provide the user with a useful and reliable reputation score about the RP.

Thus, figure 3 shows an enhanced flow mechanism of an OpenID based SSO system. The principal goal of the reputation framework is depicted in step 9.4 of the sequence diagram. In this particular step, the framework gives the user of such a system the possibility to receive reputation information about the relying party that he/she is accessing.

Furthermore, once the service has been actually delivered, the user has the opportunity to evaluate the RP and provide her feedback to the OP (step 14.4). Such information will be in turn used by forthcoming users, to keep the most updated reputation value reflecting the current behavior of the RP.

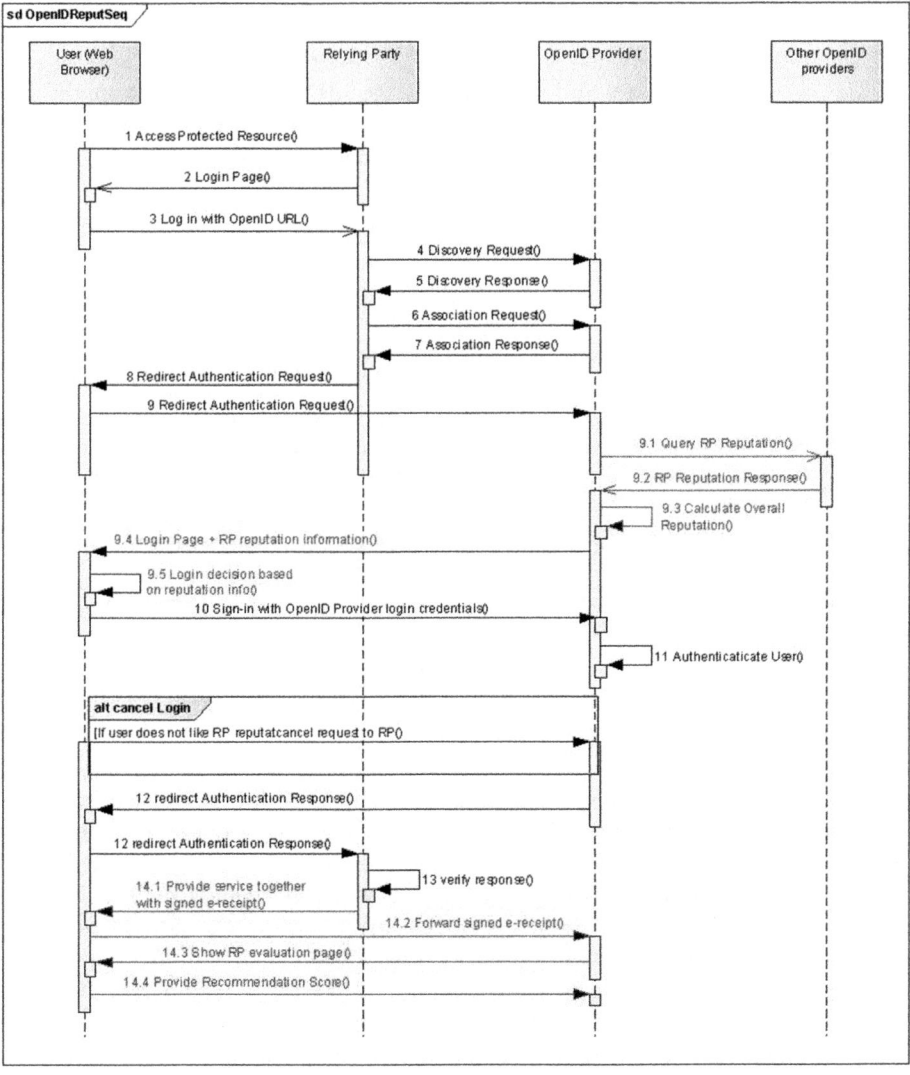

Fig. 3. OpenID protocol enhancement: sequence diagram

5 Reputation Framework

This section shows the reputation framework designed for enhancing the OpenID users' experience when accessing a relying party. It will describe each one of the components [5] constituting the whole architecture.

5.1 Gathering Recommendations

The first issue to solve when the specified OP wants to compute the reputation of the selected RP is to find those other OpenID providers that might have information (i.e., recommendations) about that concrete RP. To this end, we have designed the next subscription/notification mechanism.

Dynamic Publish/Subscribe Mechanism. As soon as one of the end users of an OP wants to access a certain RP for the first time (the OP has never had any transaction with such RP in the past), then the OP sends a subscription request to that RP. Every RP keeps a list with the most recent OPs that have had an interaction with each of them (and therefore might have recommendations/opinions to provide about such RPs).

Thus, the RP will notify all the OP providers subscribed to it when this list of potential recommenders is updated. However, in order to avoid an excessive flooding and overhead, such notification will take place with a certain frequency. Moreover, this frequency will dynamically change throughout the time.

Hence, this list of OP providers will be sent to the subscribed OPs only when it contains Δ (Delta) new entries. The actual value of Δ will determine the real frequency of the notifications. Thus for instance a value of $\Delta = 1$ would mean that every time a new OP is inserted in the list, such list would be sent to all the subscribed OPs. A value of $\Delta = 10$, for instance, would mean that such list of OPs would not be sent to the subscribers until 10 new entries are inserted in the list.

In order to dynamically adapt such value to avoid unnecessarily flooding the system with non-needed messages, while keeping subscribers updated when such information is really necessary, we have thought of the following mechanism (as shown in Figure 4). Every time a user accesses a certain RP through her OP, the value of Δ would decrease, increasing this way the frequency of notifications, since more users are interested in such RP and therefore the OP needs to have the most up-to-date information as possible. However, if nobody requests the services of such RP, the associated Δ would increase (decreasing the frequency of notifications), since the OP then does not need to be continuously updated with the latest sources of recommendations for such RP.

Additionally, Δ would be bounded by a minimum value (to avoid an excessively high frequency of notifications). On the other hand, it should also have a maximum value. This value, when reached, should cause the OP to remove the subscription to that RP, since any of the users of such OP is no longer interested in such RP (see Figure 4).

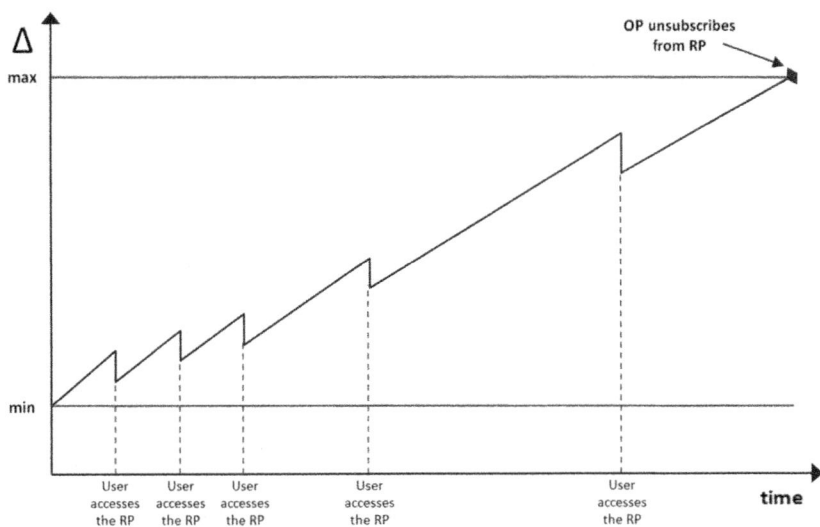

Fig. 4. Dynamic updating of Δ

User-Tailored Recommendations. In order to accomplish with the users' preferences awareness requirement described in section 3 and to provide customized and user-tailored reputation information, each query for recommendations issued by the OP comes with the preferences of the end-user (in an anonymous way) related to the provision of the final service (with regards to price, quality of service, delivery time, etc).

Thus, a higher weight $(\omega_{user,U_{OP_i,j}})$ will be given to those recommendations $(Rec_{U_{OP_i,j}}(RP))$ coming from a user $(U_{OP_i,j})$ whose service preferences $(Pref_{U_{OP_i,j}})$ match with the end-user ones $(Pref_{user})$, since both share predilections or priorities and therefore the opinions of the former might be very valuable for the latter.

$$\omega_{user,U_{OP_i,j}} = f_1(Pref_{user}, Pref_{U_{OP_i,j}})$$

Weighing Aggregated Recommendations. As to fulfill the incorrectness awareness requirement (see section 3), when querying the OpenID providers for recommendations about the RP, the queerer provides a weight factor, ω_{OP_i}, representing how much reliable the information given by other OpenID providers is. Depending on this weight factor, the OpenID providers can treat information provided more or less relevant for the overall calculation of the relying party reputation.

This weight factor ω_{OP_i} should be calculated based on the difference between the end-users' final satisfaction with the received service and the aggregated recommendation provided by each OpenID provider.

$$\omega_{OP_i} = f_2(Sat_{user}, Rec_{OP_i}(RP))$$

Forgetting Factor. Time awareness requirement shown in section 3 entails assigning a higher weight to most recent transactions (and, consequently, their corresponding users' recommendations), in contrast to older ones, which might be considered less important. Thus, we are able to more accurately predict the actual current behavior of the given RP. Therefore, each recommendation $(Rec_{U_{OP_i,j}}(RP))$ is additionally given a weight $(\omega_{t,Rec_{U_{OP_i,j}}}(RP))$ which is obtained as follows:

$$\omega_{t,Rec_{U_{OP_i,j}}}(RP) = f_3(t, time(Rec_{U_{OP_i,j}}(RP)))$$

where t is the current instant of time, while $time(Rec)$ is a function returning the time when recommendation Rec was provided.

5.2   Dynamically Interchangeable Reputation Computation Engine

So once the designed OP receives all the recommendation information from other OpenID providers (step 9.2 in Figure 3), it has to aggregate it properly in order to compute the final reputation value for the relying party $Rep_{OP}(RP)$.

This reputation computation component should take several elements into account when calculating such score, namely: the recommendations of other end-users belonging to other OpenID providers $(Rec_{U_{OP_i,j}}(RP))$, the weight given to each of those recommendations based on the matching of users' preferences $(\omega_{user,U_{OP_i,j}})$, the weight associated to each OP, measuring the reliability of its recommendations (ω_{OP_i}) and the so called forgetting factor $(\omega_{t,Rec_{U_{OP_i,j}}}(RP))$.

$$Rep_{OP}(RP) = h(\omega_{OP_i}, \omega_{user,U_{OP_i,j}}, \omega_{t,Rec_{U_{OP_i,j}}}(RP), Rec_{U_{OP_i,j}}(RP))$$

As an example of a possible generic definition of function h in order to compute reputation scores, we can consider the following one:

$$Rep_{OP}(RP) = \tag{1}$$

$$\bigoplus_{i=1}^{n} \left(\omega_{OP_i} \otimes \left(\bigoplus_{j=1}^{N_{OP_i}} \left(\omega_{user,U_{OP_i,j}} \odot \omega_{t,Rec_{U_{OP_i,j}}}(RP) \odot Rec_{U_{OP_i,j}}(RP) \right) \right) \right)$$

where n is the number of OpenID providers giving recommendations, N_{OP_i} is the number of users providing recommendations under OP_i, $\oplus$ is an aggregation operation, and $\otimes$ and $\odot$ are multiplicative operations that should be specified.

Yet, despite the example of reputation computation shown in equation (1), the reputation calculation engine of our reputation framework should be designed in such a way that it supports multiple reputation computational models. Those computation models should be exchanged easily so that the framework can adapt to different scenarios on the fly, based on current conditions or circumstances (computation or network resources, storage resources, number of feedbacks, etc), as shown in Figure 5.

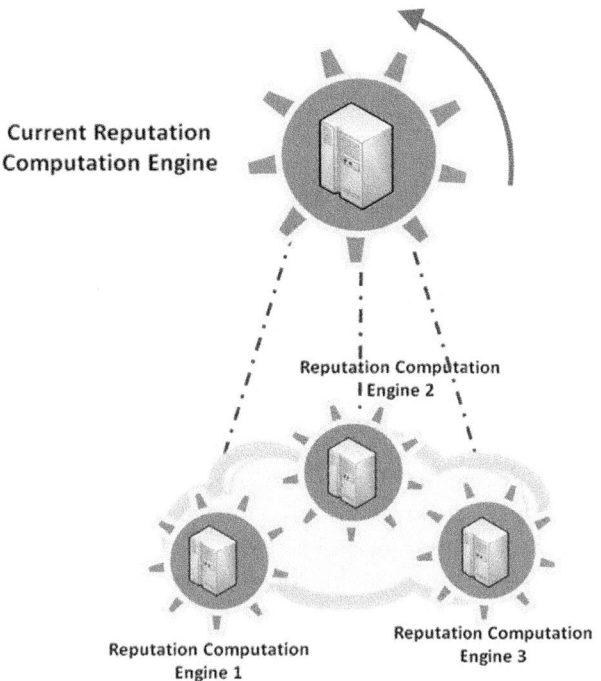

Fig. 5. Dynamically interchangeable reputation computation engine

The framework would therefore seamlessly select the optimal reputation computation engine depending on the current conditions of the system, with the aim of adapting to those dynamic circumstances and to provide the user with the more accurate reputation scores at every time, without degrading the performance of the system or the user's experience.

5.3 Performing the Transaction: e-Receipt

Once the selected OP has calculated the reputation score about the RP (step 9.3 in Figure 3), it shows the end-user a login page together with this reputation value (step 9.4 in Figure 3). In case the user decides to trust the RP according to its reputation, such RP is authorized to access the user's identity information stored in the chosen OP required in order to actually perform the service provision.

Thereafter, the service is actually provided by the RP to the end-user (step 14.1 in Figure 3). However, in order to prevent certain kind of attacks [3] (as we will see later), together with the service, the RP also provides a digitally signed electronic receipt [6] to the end-user, as a proof of service delivery. This e-receipt is a cryptographically generated token issued by the RP, with a unique identifier, that permits to track a specific performed transaction.

5.4   Collecting Users' Feedback

The last step consists of the user providing his/her final recommendation about the service received from the RP. To this end, the e-receipt received together with the service is then forwarded by the user to the selected OpenID provider (step 14.2 in Figure 3), proving this way that the transaction with the RP actually took place at the end. By doing like this, we avoid the possibility of a (malicious) user submitting recommendations about a RP with whom he/she did not actually have a transaction.

Having received the e-receipt from the user, the chosen OP shows a page to the user for introducing his/her satisfaction with the service provision made by the RP (step 14.3 in Figure 3). There are several alternatives to trigger this feedback webpage, namely: through an e-mail set by the OP to the user, when the user logs out, or next time the user logs in, amongst others.

Messaging Middleware for the Recommendations Database. The framework should also consider that many users of the same OP might try to submit their recommendations simultaneously, leading therefore to a performance as well as scalability issue which could damage the users' experience (as seen in section 3).

To tackle this problem, we propose to add a messaging layer (see Figure 6), located between the OpenID provider and the recommendations database, which is able to accept messages in an asynchronous way. Thus, the recommendations inputs should be sent to the messaging middleware without waiting for an acknowledgement in order to mitigate the blocking time caused by the network round trip time delay and the connection to the database.

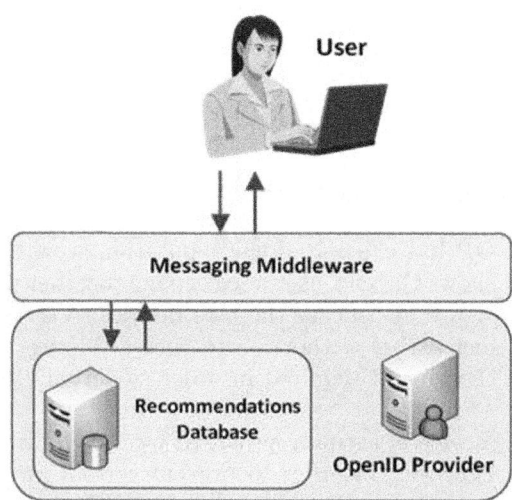

Fig. 6. Messaging Middleware for the Recommendations Database

Sampling Transactions. Moreover, in those scenarios where the number of transactions is highly frequent, it might not be feasible to track all of them, especially if there are limited or constrained resources. For those specific cases, a sampling mechanism could be implemented (as shown in Figure 7). This mechanism would consist of not recording absolutely all the transactions performed, but a sample of them. We would obviously face here a trade-off between scalability and accuracy of our proposal (the more frequent the sampling, the more accurate, and vice versa).

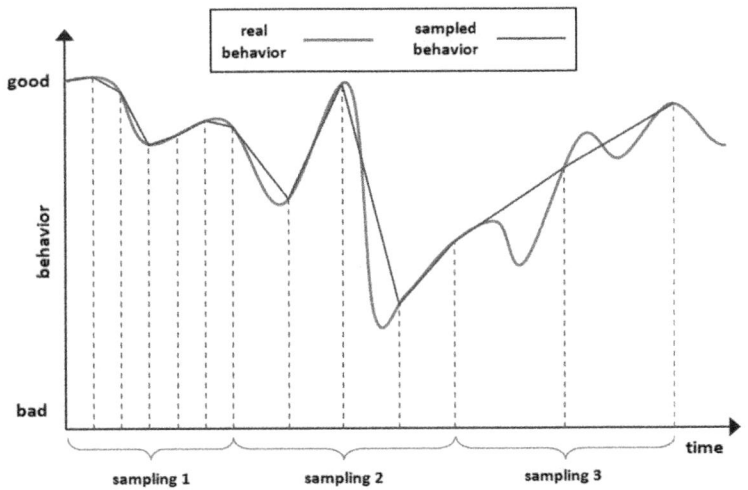

Fig. 7. Sampling transactions

5.5   General Overview

As a summary, next we present the steps to be followed by our proposal, as depicted in Figure 8.

1. Alice wants to watch a film at RP1
2. Alice is redirected to OP1 in order to log-in and therefore share her Open ID with RP1
   (a) If OP1 is not subscribed to RP1, OP1 sends a subscription request to RP1.
        i. RP1 replies with the list of OPs that have interacted with RP1
   (b) If OP1 was already subscribed to RP1, then RP1 decreases the value of Δ associated to OP1
3. OP1 has the list of other OPs that have interacted with RP1 (either because it was previously subscribed and already got it, or because it obtained it in step 2.(a).i. Therefore, OP1 sends a request to each of those OPs, asking for their respective recommendations about RP1. It also sends "anonymously" the preferences of the end-user (Alice in this example)

4. Each queried OP replies with a tailored recommendation based on the received preferences of the end-user
5. OP1 collects and aggregates all the received recommendations
6. OP1 applies the selected reputation computation mechanism and provides a final reputation score about RP1 to Alice
7. Alice then decides, based on such reputation value, whether to trust the RP1 and go on with the process, or finish/cancel here the whole transaction
8. If Alice trusts the RP1, then her profile is shared and sent from OP1 to RP1, where she is now logged-in.
9. RP1 provides the service to Alice, together with an electronic receipt. The RP1 also updates his list of recommenders, including OP1. If applicable, according to the current value of Δ, the OpenID providers subscribed to RP1 are notified with the updated list of recommenders.
10. Alice assesses her satisfaction with the received service and provides a recommendation about RP1 in her OP1, presenting the electronic receipt obtained in step 9.
11. OP1 updates its data base of recommendations about RP1
12. OP1 updates its reliability weights associated to other OPs

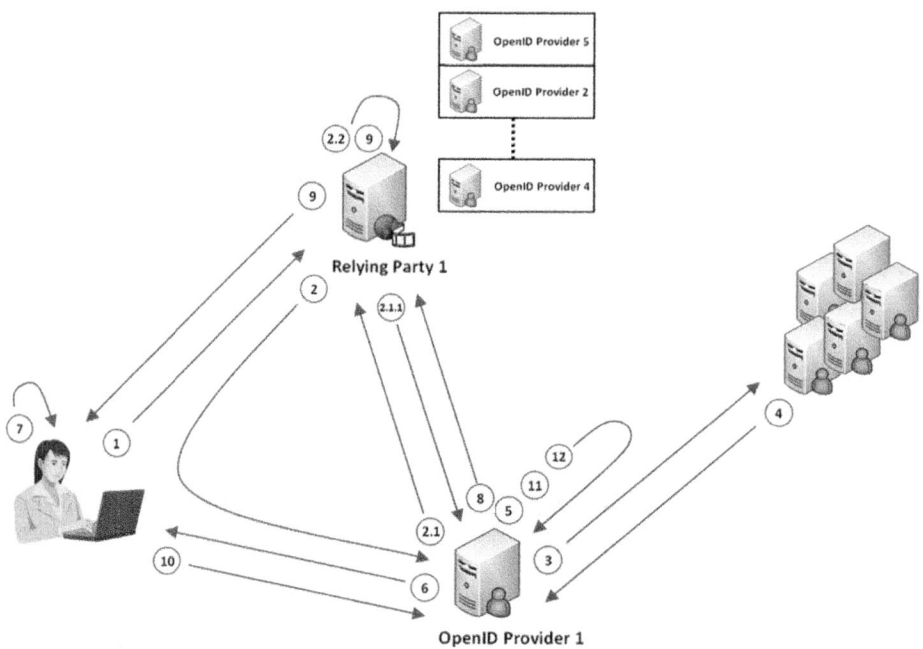

Fig. 8. General overview of the reputation framework

6   Related Work

Reputation management systems for distributed and heterogeneous environments have been studied since a while [7,8,9]. Moreover, reputation frameworks have been proposed in different contexts, e.g., P2P file sharing [10,11,12,13] and reputation enabled Service oriented frameworks [14,15,16,17]. Thereafter, the next trends that we could analyze is the application of reputation frameworks for enhancing authentication systems and the proposal of distributed reputation frameworks. This section describes in more detail the work done in this specific area and contextualizes our work within this field.

The TRIMS framework [18] applies a trust and reputation model aiming to guarantee an acceptable level of security when deciding if a service in a different domain is reliable for receiving user's personal data. That means, it applies reputation techniques for enhancing the privacy of the users when exchanging attributes between services, in a multi-domain scenario. Each domain relies on its own past experiences with the other domain being evaluated. Those experiences are weighted in order to give more or less importance on the final result.

Following the idea of the TRIMS framework, AttributeTrust Framework [19] deals with the trust of relying parties when requesting user's attributes during internet transactions. They address the problem by aggregating user's attribute in defined Attribute Providers and then perform policy based trust negotiations for evaluating trust in the attributes. They proposed a reputation model for calculating confidence values that result from confidence paths leading from the relying party to the attribute providers. The reputation models is resistant to the common attacks known in reputation systems.

[20] introduces a flexible reputation system framework to augment explicit authorization in a web application. The authors argue that explicit authorization frameworks implemented with access control lists (ACL), capabilities, or roles (RBAC) require a such high overhead to the administrators for manually granting the user's specific privileges, and therefore cannot scale for internet type of applications. The framework supports multiple computation models for reputation. However, different from our framework, its focus and design choices targets reputation calculations for human subjects. For example, the framework helps to decide which users' identifiers should a service provider support. Moreover, it is a centralized framework and also does not consider opinions of other users because of the complexity that user's opinions bring to the system. It is an objective reputation system based on measurements.

[21] proposes a distributed reputation and trust management framework where trust brokers exchange and collect information data about services. By doing so, individual users only need to ask their brokers for accessing reputation information. They claim that because of the distributed nature of the brokers it impossible to collect the information of all brokers. In the authors' vision, every user would have a online trust broker, which would collect reputation information for them. The personal brokers are then hierarchically organized for the information distribution. The approach is based on a global database that has information about all servers. Therefore, there is a centralized component in this

distributed approach that can also bring a single point of failure and all the other drawbacks common to centralized systems.

Analyzing the above cited works, we came to the conclusion that to the best of our knowledge, there is no related work targeting a distributed reputation framework applied on top of the Single Sign On OpenID protocol that can provide to the users reputation information about the relying parties prior to their interaction. We claim that such distributed framework on top of the OpenID protocol can enhance the user experience when dealing with SSO in the internet. What we achieve here is a single framework providing SSO and reputation information at the same time.

7   Conclusions and Future Work

In the current Internet there are many service providers, being most of them intended to provide appropriate services while some others are not so well intended. In this context, it is interesting for any end user to have mechanisms to determine how trustworthy a particular service provider is, so she can decide if she wants to interact with it or not. It is particularly interesting if this service is requesting some personal information of her (email address, bank account, age, etc.) before granting access to any of the resources the service provider has.

This is a problem that should be addressed before starting the interaction with the system, i.e., before sending the end user attributes to the service provider. To this end, IdM solutions need to be adapted with particular mechanisms enabling the provision of certain meta-information to the user on the particular service provider being accessed.

One of the SSO-enabled IdM solutions most widely developed nowadays is OpenID. A lot of service providers and certain key IdM providers are including this standard solution as part of the authentication and basic access control services provided to their end users. However, OpenID in its current definition can be used by a malicious service provider to gain access to the private attributes of users and make profit with them.

To provide end users with valuable reputation information on the different service providers, this paper is defining a reputation framework and how it can be applied to an extended version of the OpenID protocol. In this way, this paper is describing a solution helping to mitigate this problem. It is based on the idea that users can provide a recommendation level on a particular service and it is later being aggregated by the OpenID provider and provided to any other potential user that might be interested to interact with the same service provider in the future. With this help, authors are provided with a mechanism intended to increase their level of satisfaction with the OpenID system.

As future work we are currently working on the implementation of this solution as well as on performing experiments in different scenarios. Moreover, we are also analysing different reputation computation models, so the different pros and cons can be determined.

Acknowledgment. This work has been partially funded by the project "Secure Management of Information across multiple Stakeholders (SEMIRAMIS)" CIP-ICT PSP-2009-3 250453, within the EC Seven Framework Programme (FP7), by the SEISCIENTOS project "Providing adaptive ubiquitous services in vehicular contexts" (TIN2008-06441-C02) funded by the Spanish Ministry of Science and Innovation, and by a Séneca Foundation grant within the Human Resources Research Training Program 2007 (code 15779/PD/10). Thanks also to the Funding Program for Research Groups of Excellence granted by the Séneca Foundation with code 04552/GERM/06. Authors would also like to thank Makoto Hatakeyama for his helpful comments.

References

1. Recordon, D., Reed, D.: OpenID 2.0: a platform for user-centric identity management. In: Proceedings of the Second ACM Workshop on Digital Identity Management, DIM 2006, pp. 11–16 (2006)
2. Sakimura, N.: Coping with information asymmetry. In: Identity Management Conference, SESSION G: Managing Risk & Reducing Online Fraud Using New Security Technologies, pp. 1–14. OASIS, Washington, US (2010)
3. Mármol, F.G., Pérez, G.M.: Security Threats Scenarios in Trust and Reputation Models for Distributed Systems. Elsevier Computers & Security 28(7), 545–556 (2009)
4. OASIS. Open reputation management systems (ORMS) (2008), http://www.oasis-open.org/committees/orms
5. Mármol, F.G., Pérez, G.M.: Towards Pre-Standardization of Trust and Reputation Models for Distributed and Heterogeneous Systems. Computer Standards & Interfaces 32(4), 185–196 (2010)
6. Piotrowski, T.: E-receipt verification system and method. US Patent, US 0120607 A1 (June 2003), http://www.freepatentsonline.com/20030120607.pdf
7. Mármol, F.G., Pérez, G.M.: Providing Trust in Wireless Sensor Networks using a Bio-Inspired Technique. Telecommunication Systems Journal 46(2), 163–180 (2011)
8. Mármol, F.G., Marín-Blázquez, J.G., Pérez, G.M.: Linguistic Fuzzy Logic Enhancement of a Trust Mechanism for Distributed Networks. In: Proceedings of the Third IEEE International Symposium on Trust, Security and Privacy for Emerging Applications (TSP 2010), Bradford, UK, pp. 838–845 (2010)
9. Omar, M., Challal, Y., Bouabdallah, A.: Reliable and fully distributed trust model for mobile ad hoc networks. Computers and Security 28(3-4), 199–214 (2009)
10. Mármol, F.G., Pérez, G.M., Skarmeta, A.F.G.: TACS, a Trust Model for P2P Networks. Wireless Personal Communications, Special Issue on Information Security and data protection in Future Generation Communication and Networking 51(1), 153–164 (2009)
11. Wang, Y., Tao, Y., Yu, P., Xu, F., Lü, J.: A Trust Evolution Model for P2P Networks. In: Xiao, B., Yang, L.T., Ma, J., Muller-Schloer, C., Hua, Y. (eds.) ATC 2007. LNCS, vol. 4610, pp. 216–225. Springer, Heidelberg (2007)
12. Huang, C., Hu, H., Wang, Z.: A Dynamic Trust Model Based on Feedback Control Mechanism for P2P Applications. In: Yang, L.T., Jin, H., Ma, J., Ungerer, T. (eds.) ATC 2006. LNCS, vol. 4158, pp. 312–321. Springer, Heidelberg (2006)

13. Marti, S., García-Molina, H.: Identity crisis: anonymity vs reputation in P2P systems. In: Proceedings for the Third International Conference on Peer-to-Peer Computing (P2P 2003) Linköping, Sweden, pp. 134–141 (September 2003)
14. Bansal, S.K., Bansal, A., Blake, M.: Trust-based dynamic web service composition using social network analysis. In: IEEE International Workshop on Business Applications for Social Network Analysis (BASNA 2010) (December 2010)
15. Hang, C.-W., Singh, M.P.: Selecting trustworthy service in service-oriented environments. In: The 12th AAMAS Workshop on Trust in Agent Societies (May 2009)
16. Malik, Z., Bouguettaya, A.: Reputation bootstrapping for trust establishment among web services. IEEE Internet Computing 13, 40–47 (2009)
17. Paradesi, S., Doshi, P., Swaika, S.: Integrating behavioral trust in web service compositions. In: Proceedings of the 2009 IEEE International Conference on Web Services, ICWS 2009, pp. 453–460 (2009)
18. Mármol, F.G., Girao, J., Pérez, G.M.: TRIMS, a Privacy-aware Trust and Reputation Model for Identity Management Systems. Elsevier Computer Networks Journal 54(16), 2899–2912 (2010)
19. Mohan, A., Blough, D.M.: AttributeTrust - a framework for evaluating trust in aggregated attributes via a reputation system. In: Proceedings of the 2008 Sixth Annual Conference on Privacy, Security and Trust, pp. 201–212 (2008)
20. Windley, P.J., Daley, D., Cutler, B., Tew, K.: Using reputation to augment explicit authorization. In: Proceedings of the 2007 ACM workshop on Digital identity management, DIM 2007, pp. 72–81 (2007)
21. Lin, K.-J., Lu, H., Yu, T., Tai, C.-e.: A reputation and trust management broker framework for web applications. In: nternational Conference on e-Technology, e-Commerce, and e-Services, pp. 262–269. IEEE Computer Society, Los Alamitos (2005)

Concept of a Reflex Manager to Enhance the Planner Component of an Autonomic/Organic System

Julia Schmitt, Michael Roth, Rolf Kiefhaber, Florian Kluge, and Theo Ungerer

Department of Computer Science
University of Augsburg
D-86159 Augsburg, Germany
{schmitt,roth,kiefhaber,kluge,ungerer}@informatik.uni-augsburg.de

Abstract. The administration of complex distributed systems is complex and therefore time-consuming. It becomes crucial to evolve techniques to speed up reaction times and support embedded nodes. Higher mammals use reflexes to ensure fast reactions in critical situations. This paper devolves this behavior to the organic middleware OCμ. Within this middleware an Automated Planner is used to administrate a distributed system. A new component called Reflex Manager is responsible to store its solutions. If the system reaches a state, that is similar to an already known one, the Reflex Manager uses its knowledge to quickly provide a solution. Conflicts between plans from the planner and the Reflex Manager are resolved by comparing and switching plans. Finally we discuss possible generalizations of our ideas.

1 Introduction

Embedded devices are hidden in many everyday items, having the ability to communicate with each other. Together with classical devices like PCs they form distributed systems with a large number of participating components. The administration of such complex systems with heterogeneous participants is very difficult and time-consuming. The Autonomic Computing [5] and the Organic Computing (OC [1]) initiatives aim to solve this problem by applying the self-x features self-optimization, self-configuration, self-healing and self-protection to such systems.

The problem of controlling complex systems can also be seen as a planning problem. The system is in an initial state at the beginning and shall be in a goal state after some time. But planning can be very time-consuming.

Also in nature many processes are very time-consuming. But some things happen really fast. If a deer recognizes an unpleasant noise it will run away immediately. Another example is the human reaction. A person can reflect on a particular problem for hours. But if he stumbles and falls he puts up his hands within milliseconds to protect himself. This behavior originates from reflexes.

J.M. Alcaraz Calero et al. (Eds.): ATC 2011, LNCS 6906, pp. 19–30, 2011.

Natural reflexes happen without thinking about the problem or planning the solution. Evolving this technique on computing systems leads to artificial reflexes. The system can therefore react faster to a problem. To show how this approach can be applied we illustrate it on our OCµ middleware [17]. OCµ features an Organic Manager that runs on each node of a distributed system. Within the Organic Manager we use an Automated Planner to implement self-configuration, self-optimization and self-healing [19]. In this paper we will present as part of the Organic Manager the concept of a Reflex Manager that integrates natural reflexes into the middleware to speed up reaction times of the Organic Manager. Additionally the Reflex Manager can replace the planner on resource-restricted nodes without planning capabilities. It stores plans from the planner and can reuse them if a similar problem occurs.

In section 2 we discuss similar approaches. We briefly introduce our middleware OCµ in section 3. In section 4 we give a closer look to the planning step in OCµ. The Reflex Manager and its functionality is presented in section 5. Section 6 addresses the execution of plans. Potential generalizations and limitations of our approach are discussed in section 7. Section 8 summarizes the paper and gives an outlook to future work.

2 Related Work

Automated planning and nature-like behavior are wide research areas, however realizations within a middleware are rare. Nevertheless some middleware systems exist which feature organic behavior.

Mamei and Zambonelli developed the TOTA approach [9]. They realize self-organization by supporting adaptive and uncoupled interactions between agents. TOTA uses tuple-based communication. Messages have rules determining their propagation over the network.

CARISMA [12] realizes self-configuration and self-optimization with an emphasis on real-time capability. It is a service-oriented middleware. Based on local information each service needs to provide a quality rating for a given job. The middleware decides which service executes a job by using an auction system. It also starts or shuts down service agents.

The Artificial Hormone System (AHS) middleware [21] is designed for embedded environments. It is inspired by the hormone system of higher mammals. The AHS middleware concentrates on mapping tasks to processing elements. Hormones are realized as messages. Each processing element calculates a value to rate its fitness for executing a task. The element with the highest value receives the task. If more tasks have to be distributed this procedure is repeated.

ORCA [10] is an organic robot control architecture. ORCA is based on a hierarchical system architecture including several control units. It aims to improve the system behavior and adapts to malfunctions without a formal model. ORCA uses supervised learning to control the self-organization of the system.

Within the CAR-SoC project [8] a two-layered approach is used to control hardware and software components of embedded control units in a car. Each component accommodates a possibly partial MAPE [7] cycle with simple rules in the planning stage. On top of these modules one global MAPE cycle is implemented. In the planning stage it uses classifiers to choose an action. It does not create or learn chains of actions.

Our work focuses on general purpose systems, that do not provide real-time capabilities like CARISMA, ORCA and partly AHS. Additionally we do not expect every service to care for the self-x features itself or to provide functionalities to the middleware like a quality rating. In AHS and TOTA many additional messages are created. We try to reduce network traffic to support components with restricted resources. In CARISMA and AHS each task is assigned separately. Distributing multiple tasks at once is not regarded.

ORCA uses a training set to train the control unit and does not learn from the running system. Our system can execute multiple actions and our Reflex Manager learns at runtime. Especially if the system reaches already known states we want to execute a solution without repeating the whole process of finding a solution.

We use our Reflex Manager to store plans and use them if a similar system state occurs. Unlike plan reuse proposed by Nebel and Koehler [11] we do not manipulate existing plans.

There exists a variety of bio-inspired approaches to realize self-x properties. Trumler [20] developed a self-optimization algorithm which is inspired by the human hormone system. A self-protection algorithm based on the immune system was introduced by Pietzowski et al. [13]. Iwasaki et al. [6] proposed an adaptive routing algorithm by mimicking enzymatic feedback mechanisms in the cell. They optimize the communication in the network to reduce delay time. Each of this and many other approaches only focus on few self-x properties without regarding relations between them. In OCμ we use an automated planner to realize self-optimization, self-configuration and self-healing at once. More details on OCμ can be found in [17,19].

An approach consisting of two stages is presented within the Organic Control of Traffic Lights project [16,14]. A Learning Classifier System (LCS) [4] chooses actions online to control traffic light signals. As second stage an evolutionary algorithm on some powerful nodes creates offline new classifiers and evaluates them in a simulated environment. Our Reflex Manager works on the running system and not offline. Additionally in LCS only a single action is chosen to be executed while in our approach a plan can consist of more than one action.

3   OCμ and the Organic Manager

OCμ [17] is an organic middleware which is enhanced by an Organic Manager per node. The Reflex Manager extends our Organic Manager. Figure 1 shows the basic architecture of an OCμ node. The main middleware functionalities are implemented by the left part. Seen from the Organic Manager on the right it is a *system under observation and control (SuOC)* [15].

Applications are separated into services, which can be distributed over the network. *EventMessages* are used to communicate between services. The *Event*

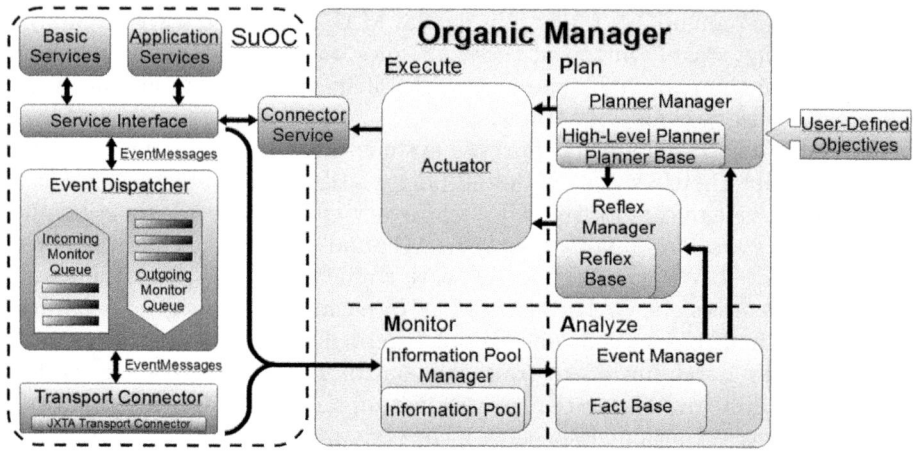

Fig. 1. OCμ architecture

Dispatcher finds the accurate recipient of a message. Without affecting the sender or receiver of the message, data can be piggy-backed on messages by monitors. The *Transport Connector* delivers the messages to the target node. It can support different communication platforms. Each node stores monitor information about the system and passes it to the *Information Pool Manager*. The manager is responsible for deciding whether monitored data is stored in the *Information Pool*. The Information Pool Manager also triggers the *Event Manager*. The main objective of the Event Manager is to transform the raw information into facts. From these compacted facts the *Fact Base* is created. The Event Manager triggers the *Planner Manager* and the *Reflex Manager*. A user can create *User-Defined Objectives* to add goals to the planner. The *Planner Base* contains basic data for the planner. A *High-Level Planner* creates plans if triggered by the Planner Manager.

We developed a *Reflex Manager* to reuse plans created by the planner. Plans are stored in the *Reflex Base*. If the exact or a similar problem reoccurs the stored plan is surpassed to the *Actuator*. The *Actuator* executes plans it receives from the Reflex Manager and the Planner Manager. It can handle unequal plans by comparing and switching between them if necessary. It can use the *Connector Service* to communicate with the middleware.

4   Planning in OCμ

We use the Organic Manager to realize three self-x features. In the following we will explain the general meaning [7] of each one and how we realize them in OCμ.

- **Self-configuration:** When a new component, e.g. a node, joins the system, it will configure itself automatically. It will do this by following high-level policies. In our context, a component is a node running OCμ. After starting such a node it establishes all basic and desired services by itself. A user or service can define desired services by adding objectives. These objectives are added to the planner.

- **Self-optimization:** During runtime all nodes try to make themselves more efficient, so the whole system can achieve a better state. Within OCμ we focus on reaching a balanced workload.
- **Self-healing:** When failures occur, a valid state will be reached again after a short time. In OCμ we can detect the breakdown of a node and consider this as a failure [18]. Then the Organic Manager will lead the system to a valid state.

We decided to combine these three self-x properties into the Organic Manager, as they are strongly related to each other. Each of them works by starting, stopping or relocating a service. So they can use the same actions.

An Automated Planner automatically finds a sequence of actions, leading from an initial state to a goal state. We use JavaFF [3], where a heuristically guided forward search is used to create a plan. We use the Planning Domain Definition Language (PDDL) [2] to describe the input and output of planners as it has become a de facto standard language for describing planning tasks. The effects of an action can be used to model side-effects and hence are already known when creating a plan.

In OCμ we use information about the own node, the network and each service for planning. Each one has a set of values to describe its state. We translate these values into PDDL. The planner can take three actions: It can start, stop and relocate a service. A service can be started or stopped on the local node or on a networked node. This is important for the self-configuration and self-healing. A service can only be relocated from the local node to a networked node. Each node has the goal to reach a workload similar to other nodes. This leads to a self-optimized system. We implemented two different planning models and evaluated them in [19].

5 Reflex Manager

To store plans from the Automated Planner the Reflex Manager needs an appropriate storing structure. We decided to use a key/value-structure where the plans are the values. The key represents the initial state of the system, given by the facts from the Event Manager. We want to stay flexible, e.g. if a new service is introduced at runtime. To describe the state of the system we use a variable set of keywords. Each keyword has a vector of values to describe the monitored information. The name of a service can e.g. serve as a keyword. Its vector consists of the number of instances running locally, system wide and whether the service is relocatable. Another keyword is dedicated to the local node. Among other values the vector contains the workload of the local node. In general these structure can be described as follows:

- $k \in K$ a keyword for one vector from a set of keywords K
- $s_k \in \mathbb{R}^{n_k}$ a vector of n_k real numbers for each keyword k
- $S = \{s_k | k \in K\}$ a state of the system, stored by the Reflex Manager
- $C = \{c_k | k \in K\}$ the current state of the system

To compare stored and current states we introduce the following metrics.

$$|S - C| = r + \sum_{k \in S \cap C} \sqrt{\sum_i^{n_k} (s_{k,i} - c_{k,i})^2} \tag{1}$$

The second metric uses a weighting factor $\lambda_{k,i} \in \mathbb{R}$ that assigns a vector $\lambda_k \in \mathbb{R}^{n_k}$ with $k \in K$ to each keyword.

$$|S - C|_\lambda = r + \sum_{k \in S \cap C} \sqrt{\sum_i^{n_k} \lambda_{k,i} (s_{k,i} - c_{k,i})^2} \tag{2}$$

The value $r >= 0$ increases the distances between S and C. If the keywords of the compared states match exactly $r = 0$. Otherwise there are some possibilities to choose r, depending on the used strategy:

- $r = 0$ if an extra keyword in S or C is insignificant
- $r = \infty$ if an extra keyword leads to a completely different state
- $r = \sum_{k \in (S \backslash C \cup C \backslash S)} \alpha$ One extra keyword increases the difference by a fixed value $\alpha > 0$

To compare the metrics and show the influence of r we will use an example. Let's assume the following vectors are possible:

$$v_{\text{localNode}} = (\text{workload, number relocatable services})$$

$$v_{\text{network}} = (\text{average workload, workload change })$$

$$v_{\text{Service}} = (\text{accumulated number, number running locally, relocatable})$$

The Reflex Manager stored two states: S and $\tilde{S}$. The current state is C.

$$C = \{c_{\text{localNode}} = (60, 8), c_{\text{network}} = (50, 0.1),$$
$$c_{\text{ServiceA}} = (20, 5, 1), c_{\text{ServiceB}} = (10, 8, 1)\}$$
$$S = \{s_{\text{localNode}} = (50, 8), s_{\text{network}} = (40, 0.2),$$
$$s_{\text{ServiceA}} = (20, 5, 1), s_{\text{ServiceB}} = (10, 8, 1)\}$$
$$\tilde{S} = \{s_{\text{localNode}} = (60, 8), s_{\text{network}} = (48, 0.2),$$
$$s_{\text{ServiceA}} = (10, 0, 1), s_{\text{ServiceC}} = (6, 6, 0)\}$$

The state S differs from state C slightly regarding the workload of the local node and the average load. The state $\tilde{S}$ has no measurements regarding ServiceB, instead it has information about ServiceC. Additionally only 10 instances of ServiceA are running.

Before comparing the results of the metrics, we need to set the λ values in the weighted metric. They are used to rate the influence of one particular difference on the whole result.

$$\lambda_{\text{localNode}} = (0.3, 1)$$
$$\lambda_{\text{network}} = (0.3, 1)$$
$$\lambda_{\text{Service}} = (1, 1, 1)$$
$$\alpha = 10$$

By using these values for λ we weaken the influence of the workload distance. Table 1 shows the difference between the stored and the measured state using both metrics. When using the metric in formula (1) and $r = 0$, state $\tilde{S}$ is chosen, although state S fits better. But with the weighted metric state S is closer to C than $\tilde{S}$. If $r = \infty$ system states with different keywords will never be similar. There can be many service types and therefore keywords. In this case many stored states will be useless when compared to the measured state C as the keywords are not equal. A better alternative is to add a fixed value for each not matching keyword as done in the last row of table 1.

Table 1. Example: Distance between states by using two metrics

	$|C - S|$	$|C - \tilde{S}|$	$|C - S|_\lambda$	$|C - \tilde{S}|_\lambda$
$r = 0$	200.01	129.01	60.0.1	126, 21
$r = \infty$	200.01	∞	60.0.1	∞
$r = \sum_{k \in S \setminus C \cup C \setminus S} \alpha$	200.01	149.01	60.0.1	146, 21

We decided not to store every new plan for state S. Instead we store plans, if no plan for a similar state exists already.

6   Actuator

The actuator receives plans from the Reflex Manager and the Planner. We can distinguish three cases

1. The Planner surpassed a plan first.
2. The Reflex Manager was first and the plan is already executed.
3. The Reflex Manager was first and the plan is partly executed.

In the first case it is most likely that the Reflex Manager had no plan for the current situation. Thus the Actuator can just execute the plan. In the second case the plan from the Reflex Manager is already executed. We do not expect the Actuator to do a rollback as this would provide additional programming effort and is in general not possible. Instead the problem is solved in the next planning cycle.

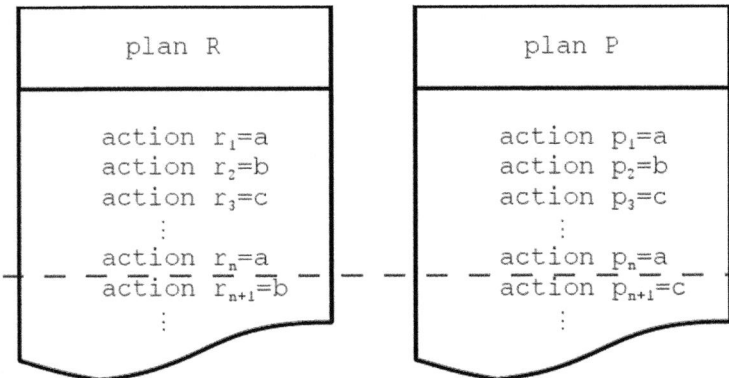

Fig. 2. Comparing plans

Our main focus is to resolve the following situation arising from the third case: The Reflex Manager and the Automated Planner are triggered. The Reflex Manager is faster and sends a plan R to the Actuator. The Actuator executes the plan. Then it gets a plan P from the Automated Planner. The Actuator stops the execution and compares the plans. Each plan consists of actions from an action set A. We can see R and P as an ordered set of actions. Action r_1 to r_n have already been executed. Lets assume there are three actions $A = \{a, b, c\}$.

In the best case the actions already executed match exactly the first n actions of the plan P from the planner as indicated in figure 2. This means $r_1 = p_1, \ldots, r_n = p_n$. In this case we can directly switch to plan P and execute the actions $p_{n+1}, \ldots$.

If no conditional effects are used, another case can be resolved. A conditional effect is e.g. the following phrase:

```
when(raining) (cloudy = true)
```

If no conditional effects are used the following problem can be resolved. The already executed actions match the first actions from P, but have another order as shown in figure 3. Each action $\{r_1, \ldots, r_n\}$ matches to one element of $\{p_1, \ldots, p_n\}$.

In this case the second and third actions from plan R are permuted in plan P. As both are valid plans we can deduce two facts:

- The effect of action b does not destroy the precondition of action c because of plan R.
- The effect of action c does not destroy the precondition of action b because of plan P.

The order of these two action is obviously not fixed. So the Actuator can switch to plan P.

In both examples the Actuator stopped after executing action r_n. If the plan P came later and r_{n+1} also already would have been executed, the plan could not be switched. The Actuator would then execute plan R.

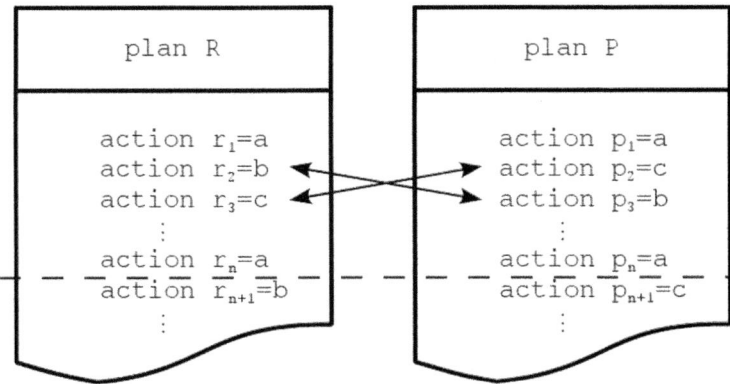

Fig. 3. Permuted actions

Especially the storing of long plans, or plans created in complex planning environments can lead to increased reaction times. Lets assume plan R has 50 actions and it needed 10 seconds to create it. Even if the initial state does not match the current state perfectly, its execution will lead the system to a better state. Then only few actions are necessary to reach the goal state.

7 Discussion

Although we showed our approach by using OCμ a generalization of our idea is possible. We will discuss the possibilities and limitations of the approach in the following. The general idea of storing plans and reuse them in similar situations is especially promising when the generation of a plan needs much time and resources. Nevertheless our approach needs memory space to store the plans.

For the Reflex Manager the plans do not need to be produced by an automated planner. The plans can also be generated by other tools. The only limitation is that the system state must be transformable into the structure which is described in section 5. The key, which is used by the Reflex Manager to store plans, is very flexible. The keywords and its corresponding vectors can be chosen freely. States can consist of different keywords and the keywords don't need to be identical. If an automated planner is used then the PDDL objects can serve as keywords and the corresponding PDDL predicates and functions as values.

As long as the initial state can be coded this way, the metrics presented in section 5 can be applied. We use the metrics to measure the similarity between two states. So we can execute plans which were created for similar states. Depending on the underlying problem it may not be useful to execute a plan which was not created for the exact same state. In this case the metric in formula (1) can be used together with a threshold of 0. Then only plans are chosen which were created for the exact same system state. If plans for similar but not equal initial states can be applied, better results can be achieved by using the second metric (formula (2)).

The Actuator is designed for plans consisting of a chain of sequential actions. In OCμ this is a total ordered plan from the Planner or Reflex Manager. Planning tools which create plans each consisting of only a single action are not suited for our approach. Beside this the switching between plans with equal actions at the beginning should be possible. If the actions are in a different order then the plans can only be switched if no conditional effects are used.

8   Summary and Outlook

In this paper we presented a nature inspired approach to speed up planning times and support embedded nodes. To administrate a large distributed system we use an Automated Planner. The Reflex Manager stores plans from the planner. The Reflex Manager uses a set of vectors and keywords to store the initial system states. It compares the current state with stored ones and chooses a plan if a similar state is already known. We showed two metrics to compare states. The first one is based on the Euclidean distance. The second metric can weaken or strengthen the influence of particular differences on the whole result. The weights need to be specified at design time. The results of the second metric reflects the similarity between states more accurately than the results from the first metric. The idea of our Reflex Manager can be generalized as long as the system state can be coded in our key structure.

The Actuator executes plans from the Reflex Manager and the Planner Manager. If it gets a plan from the planner while processing one from the Reflex Manager it will stop and compare the plans. If possible it will switch to the plan from the Planner Manager. The concept of our Actuator needs a chain of actions forming a plan to be generalizable.

When using the second metric the weighting parameter λ needs to be known. We will investigate techniques to learn λ at runtime. We plan to evaluate our approach and to measure the speed up of reaction times.

The Reflex Manager compares plans by using a metric. Afterwards it decides if a stored plan is sent to the Actuator. We will investigate possible choices of a threshold value to decide if a state is similar enough to send the corresponding plan to the Actuator. We plan to compare fixed and adaptive thresholds and different possibilities to learn the threshold.

References

1. Organic Computing Initiative (2011), http://www.organic-computing.de/spp
2. Ghallab, M., Nationale, E., Aeronautiques, C., Isi, C.K., Penberthy, S., Smith, D.E., Sun, Y., Weld, D.: PDDL - The Planning Domain Definition Language. Technical report (1998)
3. Hoffmann, J., Nebel, B.: The FF planning system: Fast plan generation through heuristic search. Journal of Artificial Intelligence Research 14, 253–302 (2001)

4. Holland, J.H.: Adaptation in natural and artificial systems. MIT Press, Cambridge (1975)
5. Horn, P.: Autonomic Computing: IBMs Perspective on the State of Information Technology, also known as IBM's Autonomic Computing Manifesto. IBM Corporation, 1–39 (2001)
6. Iwasaki, A., Nozoe, T., Kawauchi, T., Okamoto, M.: Design of Bio-inspired Fault-tolerant Adaptive Routing Based on Enzymatic Feedback Control in the Cell: Towards Averaging Load Balance in the Network. In: Frontiers in the Convergence of Bioscience and Information Technologies, FBIT (2007)
7. Kephart, J.O., Chess, D.M.: The Vision of Autonomic Computing. IEEE Computer 36(1), 41–50 (2003)
8. Kluge, F., Uhrig, S., Mische, J., Ungerer, T.: A Two-Layered Management Architecture for Building Adaptive Real-Time Systems. In: Brinkschulte, U., Givargis, T., Russo, S. (eds.) SEUS 2008. LNCS, vol. 5287, pp. 126–137. Springer, Heidelberg (2008)
9. Mamei, M., Zambonelli, F.: Spatial computing: The TOTA approach. In: Babaoğlu, Ö., Jelasity, M., Montresor, A., Fetzer, C., Leonardi, S., van Moorsel, A., van Steen, M. (eds.) SELF-STAR 2004. LNCS, vol. 3460, pp. 307–324. Springer, Heidelberg (2005)
10. Mösch, F., Litza, M., Auf, A., Maehle, E., Großpietsch, K., Brockmann, W.: ORCA – towards an organic robotic control architecture. In: de Meer, H., Sterbenz, J.P.G. (eds.) IWSOS 2006. LNCS, vol. 4124, pp. 251–253. Springer, Heidelberg (2006)
11. Nebel, B., Koehler, J.: Plan Reuse versus Plan Generation: A Theoretical and Empirical Analysis. Artif. Intell. 76, 427–454 (1995)
12. Nickschas, M., Brinkschulte, U.: CARISMA - A Service-Oriented, Real-Time Organic Middleware Architecture. Journal of Software 4(7), 654–663 (2009)
13. Pietzowski, A., Satzger, B., Trumler, W., Ungerer, T.: Using Positive and Negative Selection from Immunology for Detection of Anomalies in a Self-Protecting Middleware. In: Hochberger, C., Liskowsky, R. (eds.) INFORMATIK 2006 – Informatik für Menschen, GI edn., Bonn, Germany. Lecture Notes in Informatics, vol. P-93, pp. 161–168. Köllen Verlag (2006)
14. Prothmann, H., Rochner, F., Tomforde, S., Branke, J., Müller-Schloer, C., Schmeck, H.: Organic control of traffic lights. In: Rong, C., Jaatun, M.G., Sandnes, F.E., Yang, L.T., Ma, J. (eds.) ATC 2008. LNCS, vol. 5060, pp. 219–233. Springer, Heidelberg (2008)
15. Richter, U., Mnif, M., Branke, J., Müller-Schloer, C., Schmeck, H.: Towards a generic observer/controller architecture for Organic Computing. In: GI Jahrestagung (1), pp. 112–119 (2006)
16. Rochner, F., Prothmann, H., Branke, J., Müller-Schloer, C., Schmeck, H.: An Organic Architecture for Traffic Light Controllers. In: Informatik 2006 – Informatik für Menschen. Lecture Notes in Informatics (LNI), vol. P-93, pp. 120–127. Köllen Verlag (2006)
17. Roth, M., Schmitt, J., Kiefhaber, R., Kluge, F., Ungerer, T.: Organic Computing Middleware for Ubiquitous Environments. In: Organic Computing - A Paradigm Shift for Complex Systems, pp. 339–351. Springer, Basel (2011)
18. Satzger, B., Pietzowski, A., Trumler, W., Ungerer, T.: A Lazy Monitoring Approach for Heartbeat-Style Failure Detectors. In: International Conference on Availability, Reliability and Security, pp. 404–409 (2008)
19. Schmitt, J., Roth, M., Kiefhaber, R., Kluge, F., Ungerer, T.: Using an Automated Planner to Control an Organic Middleware. In: Fifth International Conference on Self-Adaptive and Self-Organizing Systems (accepted for publication, 2011)

20. Trumler, W.: Organic Ubiquitous Middleware. PhD thesis, Universität Augsburg, Germamy (2006)
21. von Renteln, A., Brinkschulte, U.: Implementing and Evaluating the AHS Organic Middleware - A First Approach. In: 13th IEEE International Symposium on Object/Component/Service-Oriented Real-Time Distributed Computing (ISORC), pp. 163–169 (May 2010)

Safe Runtime Validation of Behavioral Adaptations in Autonomic Software

Tariq M. King[1], Andrew A. Allen[2], Rodolfo Cruz[2], and Peter J. Clarke[2]

[1] Department of Computer Science
North Dakota State University, Fargo, ND 58108, USA
tariq.king@ndsu.edu
[2] School of Computing and Information Sciences
Florida International University, Miami FL 33199, USA
{aalle004,rcruz002,clarkep}@cis.fiu.edu

Abstract. Although runtime validation and verification are critical for ensuring reliability in autonomic software, research in these areas continues to lag behind other aspects of system development. Few researchers have tackled the problem of testing autonomic software at runtime, and the current state-of-the-art only addresses localized validation of self-adaptive changes. Such approaches fall short because they cannot reveal faults which may occur at different levels of the system. In this paper, we describe an approach that enables system-wide runtime testing of behavioral adaptations in autonomic software. Our approach applies a dependency-based test order strategy at runtime to facilitate integration and system-level regression testing in autonomic software. Since validation occurs on-line during system operations, we perform testing as part of a safe approach to adaptation. To investigate the feasibility of our approach, we apply it to an autonomic communication virtual machine.

Keywords: Validation, Self-Testing, Autonomic Software, Adaptation.

1 Introduction

Autonomic computing (AC) describes systems that manage themselves in response to changing environmental conditions [9]. The popularity of the AC paradigm has led to an increase in the development of systems that can self-configure, self-optimize, self-protect, and self-heal [7,9]. These self-* features are typically implemented as *Monitor-Analyze-Plan-Execute* (MAPE) loops in autonomic managers (AMs). AMs monitor the state of managed computing resources, and analyze the observed state information to determine if corrective action is required. When undesirable conditions are observed, the AM formulates and executes a plan to remedy the situation. There are two levels of AMs: *Touchpoint* – directly manage computing resources through sensor and effector interfaces, and *Orchestrating* – coordinate the behavior of multiple AMs [7].

Some self-* changes may involve adapting or updating system components at runtime, a process referred to as dynamic software adaptation [24]. Dynamic

J.M. Alcaraz Calero et al. (Eds.): ATC 2011, LNCS 6906, pp. 31–46, 2011.
© Springer-Verlag Berlin Heidelberg 2011

adaptation in autonomic software raises concerns regarding reliability, since new faults may be introduced into the system by runtime changes. Runtime validation and verification are therefore expected to play a key role in AC systems. However, a 2009 survey on the research landscape of self-adaptive software stated that "testing and assurance are probably the least focused phases in engineering self-adaptive software" [18]. Although this has improved slightly within the last two years, it is evident that research on testing autonomic software continues to lag behind other areas.

Few researchers have tackled the problem of runtime testing in autonomic software [3,10]. King et al. [10] introduce an implicit self-test characteristic into autonomic software, referred to as *Autonomic Self-Testing* (AST). Under AST, the existing MAPE implementation is used to define test managers (TMs), which monitor, intercept, and validate the change requests of autonomic managers. TMs can operate according to two strategies: *Replication with Validation* (RV) – tests autonomic changes using copies of managed resources; and *Safe Adaptation with Validation* (SAV) – tests autonomic changes in-place, directly on managed resources. Until now, investigation into AST has concentrated on developing and evaluating prototypes that implement localized runtime testing, according to the RV strategy [11,15,20]. Developing these prototypes revealed that RV is a viable AC runtime testing technique, which can be employed when copies of managed resources are easily obtainable for testing purposes [15,20]. Details on the approach by Da Costa et al. [3] are provided in the related work section.

In this paper, we extend previous work on AST by overcoming two of its current limitations. Firstly, we address the need for system-wide validation in autonomic software through the description of a runtime integration testing approach. Our approach views the autonomic system as a set of interconnected, *Self-Testable Autonomic Components* (STACs), and emphasizes operational integrity during the runtime testing process. Secondly, we investigate AST of a real-world autonomic application for which it is expensive to maintain test copies of managed resources. Our application motivates the need for SAV and system-wide AST, and is used as a platform for investigating their feasibility. The rest of this paper is organized as follows: Section 2 provides related work. Section 3 describes our testing approach. Section 4 presents a detailed design for STACs. Section 5 discusses the prototype, and in Section 6 we conclude the paper.

2   Related Work

Runtime validation and verification as an integral feature of autonomic software has received little attention in the research literature [3,10,25,26]. The approach described by Da Costa et al. [3] is most closely related to our work. It presents the Java Self-Adaptive Agent Framework + Test (JAAF+T). JAAF+T incorporates runtime validation into adaptation agents by directly modifying their MAPE control loops to include a test activity [3]. Self-testing under JAAF+T is localized within agents, and as described is not feasible at the integration and system levels. Furthermore, the authors do not address how the integrity of system operations is enforced during the self-test activity.

Stevens et al. [20] developed a prototype of an autonomic container to demonstrate the idea of runtime testing in autonomic software. An autonomic container is a data structure with self-configuring and self-testing capabilities. The purpose of developing the application was to provide a simplistic, lightweight model of how autonomic software operates, and use it to investigate the Replication with Validation (RV) strategy [10]. Ramirez et al. [15] later extended the autonomic container, and applied it to the problem of short-term job scheduling for an operating system. Like its predecessor, the self-test design of the autonomic job scheduler was based on the RV strategy. To the best of our knowledge, the autonomic communication virtual machine presented in this paper is the first prototype to implement Safe Adaptation with Validation (SAV) [10].

Zhang et al. [25] proposed modular model checking for runtime verification of adaptive systems. They harness a finite state machine to check transitions between variations points in the software. To address the problem of state space explosion, they confine model checking to those aspects of the system affected by the change. In a similar fashion, we use dependency analysis to reduce the number of test cases that need to be re-run after an adaptive change. The work by Zhao et al. [26] presents a model-based runtime verification technique that can be applied to autonomic systems. More specifically, their approach targets component-based, self-optimizing systems that dynamically exchange components. The on-line model checker by Zhao et al. [26] is interleaved with the execution of the autonomic system, and shares technical challenges with our work. In general, model checking may offer a viable alternative to the research problem in cases where runtime verification is preferred over testing.

3   Testing Approach

Autonomic software may be viewed as a set of composable, interacting, autonomic components that provide localized self-management through sensors and effectors, while being environmentally aware and connected via a system-wide control loop [16]. The component-based perspective of autonomic software is widely accepted and cited in the literature [12,14]. Furthermore, the increasing trend towards Service-Oriented Architectures, Web and Grid Services, and Cloud Computing suggests that the component-based paradigm represents a pragmatic approach for building these next-generation software systems.

In this section, we describe an approach that facilitates system-wide validation of behavioral adaptations in component-based autonomic software. The boundaries of self-testing are delineated by analyzing dependency relationships between the adaptable components and other components in the system. Any component that invokes an adaptable component is considered to be within the firewall of change, and is therefore made self-testable. We now provide an overview of our approach, and describe its major steps through a workflow, algorithm, and state-based model.

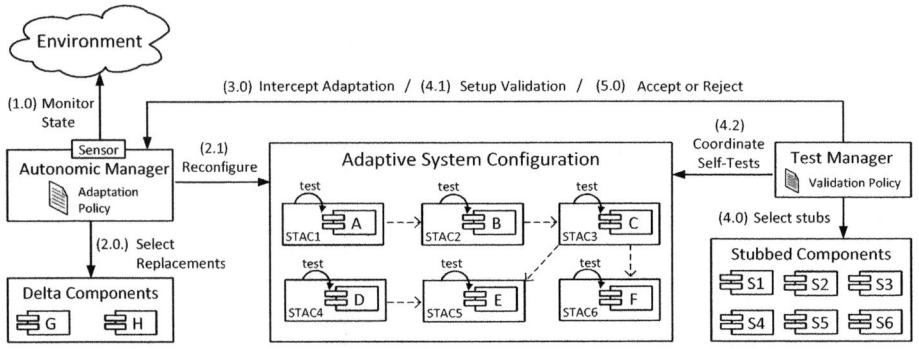

Fig. 1. System-Wide Validation of Behavioral Adaptations using STACs

3.1 Overview

Our approach views the adaptive portion of the autonomic software as a set of self-testable autonomic components (STACs). STACs encapsulate the dynamically replaceable baseline components of the system, which represent the software services being managed (e.g., a local service, web service, or off-the-shelf component). If an autonomic change replaces a baseline component with a delta component that has never been used within the context of the application, self-testing is performed as part of its integration into the system.

Figure 1 presents our system-wide architectural perspective for autonomic software using STACs. Our architecture focuses on validation scenarios in which a baseline component is replaced by some delta component that conforms to the same service interface. Such behavioral adaptations are frequently realized in the implementations of adaptive software, and are directly supported by many component-based software development frameworks [22]. Boxes A through F in Figure 1 represent six baseline components of the autonomic software, which have been made self-testable by enclosing them in STAC1 through STAC6. The arcs labeled test denote the ability of each STAC to perform runtime testing on the application services of its baseline component. Predefined test cases for the application services are be stored within the STAC. Delta components (bottom-left of Figure 1) are represented by a set of components that are dynamically discoverable via a service registry or knowledge repository.

The workflow of our testing approach, as relates to Figure 1, is described as follows (starting from the top-left): An Orchestrating Autonomic Manager (AM) continuously monitors the system environment (1.0) and analyzes its state according to a predefined adaptation policy. In response to environmental changes, the AM selects the replacement components (2.0), and dynamically reconfigures the system (2.1). If runtime validation is required, an Orchestrating Test Manager (TM) intercepts adaptation and generates a test plan (3.0). The TM then selects any stubs (4.0) that may be required for testing, and passes them to the AM in a request to set up the validation process (4.1). Lastly, the

TM coordinates a series of self-tests (4.2) using the STACs, and evaluates the results to determine if the adaptive change should be accepted or rejected (5.0).

We have refined the self-test coordination activity, identified in workflow step 4.2, into Algorithm A.1. Our algorithm incorporates a graph-based integration test order strategy [2].

Algorithm A.1. Self-Test Coordination using STACs

For each delta component D_i being integrated:

1. Replace the baseline component targeted in the adaptation with D_i.
2. If D_i calls other components, replace the callees with stubbed components; and invoke a self-test on D_i.
3. Generate an integration test order (ITO) for D_i to minimize the number of stub re-configurations required during D_i's integration.
4. Use the ITO from Step 3 to invoke a series of adaptations and self-tests until all of the previously replaced callee components have been integrated.
5. Perform dependency analysis to identify the components that call D_i; and invoke self-tests on them in reverse topological order.

3.2   Illustrative Example

To illustrate the behavior of the algorithm, we now apply it to an adaptation scenario. Our scenario involves the baseline component C from STAC3 in Figure 1 being replaced by the delta component H. In this case the algorithm produces the following list of actions:

> Action 0. Replace C in STAC3 with H
> Action 1. Replace E in STAC5 with S5
> Action 2. Replace F in STAC6 with S6
> Action 3. Execute STAC3.selftest
> Action 4. Replace S5 in STAC5 with E
> Action 5. Execute STAC3.selftest
> Action 6. Replace S6 in STAC6 with F
> Action 7. Execute STAC3.selftest
> Action 8. Execute STAC2.selftest
> Action 9. Execute STAC1.selftest

During Action 0 the system replaces the baseline component C with the delta component H, and the self-testing process is initiated. Actions 1–3 set up and execute self-tests on H using stubs S5 and S6. The stubbed configuration allows the behavior of H to be validated in isolation, as depicted by the arc labeled Unit and the stereotypes labeled <<stubbed>> in Figure 2a. Actions 4 and 5 remove the S5 stub and validate the interactions between H and one of its actual dependents E (Figure 2b). Similarly, Actions 6 and 7 realize an integration test between H and its dependent F through replacement of the stub S6 (Figure 2c). At this point the system has reached its target configuration. Actions 8 and 9

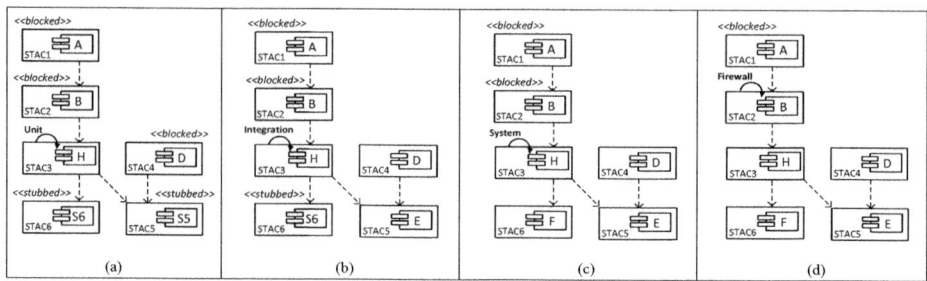

Fig. 2. Illustrative Example of Unit, Integration, System, and Firewall Self-Tests

conclude the self-testing process with the firewall regression test phase which validates each caller component affected by H's integration. This involves first performing a self-test on component B (Figure 2d), and then component A. The stereotype <<blocked>> in Figure 2 indicates the partial disablement of caller components for the purpose of runtime safety.

3.3   State-Based Model for SAV

Recall that Safe Adaptation with Validation (SAV) tests adaptive changes to autonomic software in-place, during the adaptation process [10]. The strategy is based on the idea of *safe adaptation* [24], which ensures that the adaptation process does not violate dependencies between components, nor interrupt critical communication channels. Figure 3 presents a state-based model for our system-wide testing approach according to SAV. It extends the model by Zhang et al. [24] with: (1) test setup activities via a refinement of the resetting, safe, and adapted states; and (2) test invocation, execution, and evaluation activities by adding a new validating state.

Before SAV begins, the system is in the running state where all components are fully operational. An Orchestrating TM then sends a reset command to an Orchestrating AM, which moves the system into the resetting state. During the reset, the system is in partial operation as the AM disables functions associated with the adaptation target (*AT*), and stubbed dependencies (*SD*). Upon completion, the system is in a safe state where the adaptation target is replaced by the delta component, and the system begins adapting for unit tests.

Once all callees of the delta component have been stubbed, the system transitions to the ready for unit tests state. The TM then sends a test command and the system enters the validating state, where test cases are executed. If unit testing is successful, the system moves to the adapting for integration tests state. Stubbed callees are replaced by actual callees one at a time, with a test command issued after each replacement. In other words, the system alternates between adapting for integration tests and validating, until the interactions of callees with the delta component have been tested.

After reaching the target configuration, the system moves from validating to the ready for firewall tests state. The TM then invokes the final set of test

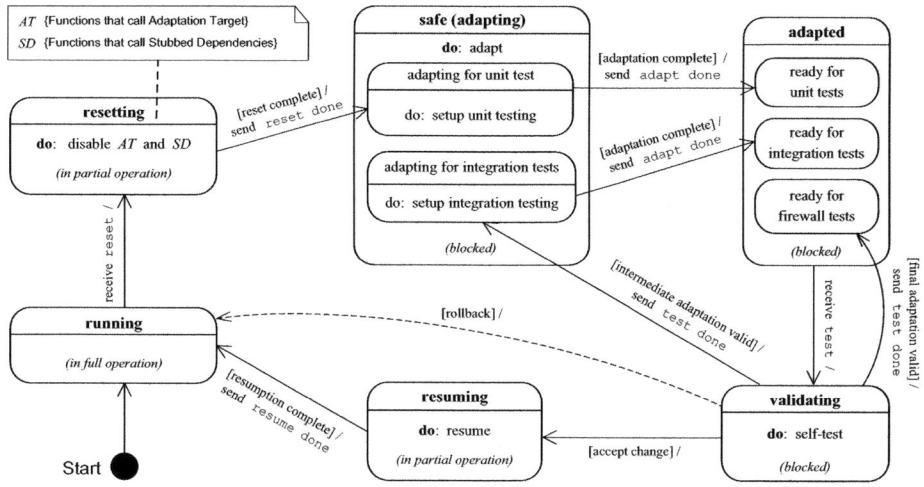

Fig. 3. State-Based Model for Safe Adaptation with Validation

commands. If the firewall tests pass, the delta component is accepted and the system enters a `resuming` state. During resumption, the AT and SD functions are unblocked and then the system returns to a fully operational `running` state. At any point during unit, integration, system, or firewall regression testing, the TM can reject the adaptive change and rollback to the previous configuration (dotted transition in Figure 3).

4   Self-Testable Autonomic Components

In this section we formalize the notion of a self-testable autonomic component (STAC), and provide a detailed design to support STAC development. As depicted in Figure 4, a STAC is defined by a 5-tuple (T, A, R, I, K) where:

T is a finite set of test managers which are responsible for validating self-management changes to resource R

A is a finite set of autonomic managers, disjoint from T, which perform self-management of resource R

R is a computational or informational resource which provides application-specific services to its clients

I is a finite set of interfaces for client services (I_S), self-management (I_A), runtime testing (I_T), and maintenance (I_M)

K is a knowledge repository containing artifacts such as policies (K_P), test cases (K_T), and test logs (K_L)

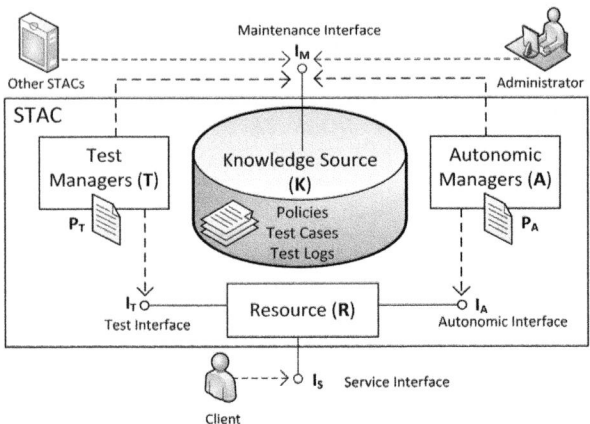

Fig. 4. Elements of a Self-Testable Autonomic Component

4.1   Managers

A reusable design of the test managers (T) and autonomic managers (A) is shown in Figure 5. Both types of managers use a generic design that extends the work in King et al. [11] by: (1) incorporating safety mechanisms for suspending and resuming managers; (2) adding support for updating the internal knowledge via an external knowledge source, and (3) abstracting common logic out of the monitor, analyze, plan, execute (MAPE) functions.

The `GenericManager` class, shown at the top-right of Figure 5, is the main controller class that coordinates the manager's activities. The generic manager may invoke an internal knowledge component or an external knowledge source, as indicated by the interfaces `InternalKnowledge` and `KnowledgeSource` respectively. The key operations provided by the generic manager include: `activate` – sets a specified behavioral policy p as being active in the internal knowledge; `manage` – starts or resumes the MAPE functions; `suspend` – temporarily pauses the MAPE functions for safety or synchronization purposes; and `update` – retrieves new or updated behavioral policies from an external knowledge source.

The template parameter `Touchpoint`, represented by the dotted boxes in Figure 5, is a place-holder for the class that implements the self-management or self-test interface used by the manager. Instantiation of the `GenericManager` requires the fully qualified class name of this `Touchpoint` class, and the name of the sensor method that will be used to poll the managed resource. The package `edu.fiu.strg.STAC.manager.mape` in Figure 5 shows the detailed class design of the MAPE functions of the generic manager. Each function derives from the abstract class `AbstractFunction`, which implements common behaviors such as: (1) initialization, suspension and resumption of the function; and (2) access to data shared among the functions.

Function independence is achieved through programming language support for multi-threading, as indicated by specialization of the `Thread` library (top-left of Figure 5). Once a MAPE object is initialized, its control thread con-

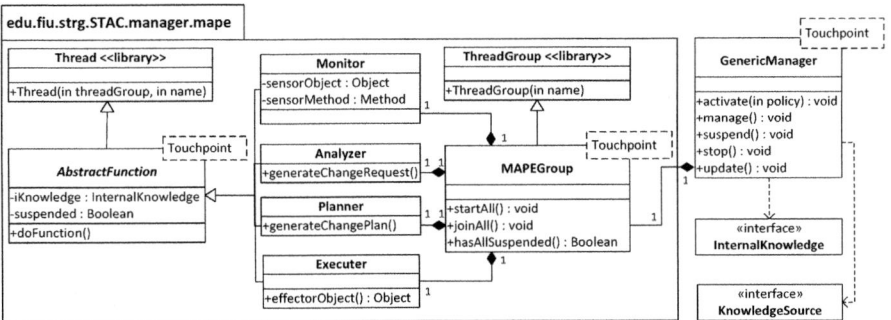

Fig. 5. Extended Design of Generic Manager with Runtime Safety Mechanisms

tinuously invokes a function-specific implementation of the abstract method doFunction(). For example, a monitor's doFunction implements state polling of managed resources, while an analyze doFunction compares that state against symptom information. The boolean variable suspended in AbstractFunction denotes whether or not the function has been temporarily paused. Access to data shared by the functions is through the variable iKnowledge, which implements the InternalKnowledge interface.

The concrete MAPE implementation is represented by Monitor, Analyzer, Planner, and Executer classes (center of Figure 5). Both the Monitor and Executer incorporate reflection-oriented programming techniques to avoid hard-coding the qualified method names of sensors and effectors. Sensors and effectors can therefore be updated at runtime, which allows them to be made consistent with the resource even after structural adaptations. All MAPE threads within the manager can be manipulated as a single unit. The class labeled MAPEGroup in Figure 5 contains the synchronization logic for initializing, suspending, and resuming a collection of MAPE threads. Some programming languages provide built-in support for thread grouping and synchronization, as indicated by the ThreadGroup library.

4.2 Internal Knowledge

Figure 6a shows the design of the internal knowledge of the generic manager. The KnowledgeData class (top-center) realizes the interface InternalKnowledge, which is used by the MAPE functions to access shared data. The key attributes of the KnowledgeData class are: touchData – holds the current state information of the resource R captured by the monitor function; symptoms – represents a set of conditional relations used by the analyze function to determine if R is in an undesirable state; and changePlans – contains an action, or sequence of actions, generated by the plan function in order to transition R back to a desired state.

Individual symptoms are defined by the conjunction of relations between different state variables and corresponding values. As shown at the left of Figure 6a, a Symptom is composed of one or more StateMapping objects. Each

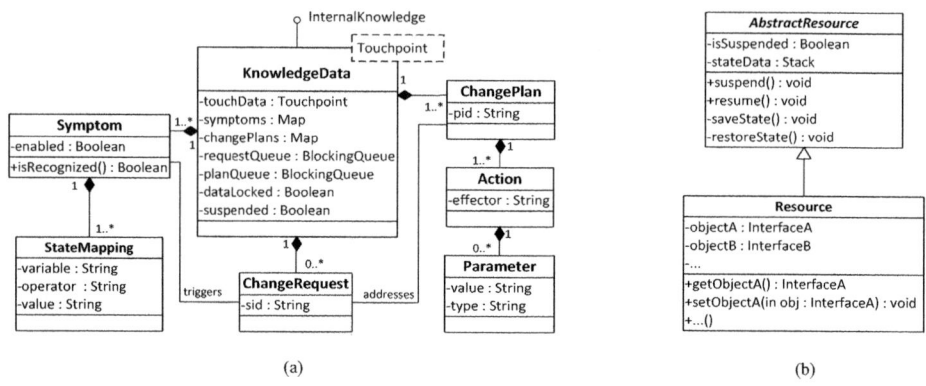

Fig. 6. (a) Design of Internal Knowledge, and (b) Managed Resources

StateMapping consists of: (1) attributes that hold information on a single state variable and an associated value, and (2) a relational operator. The method isRecognized() of the Symptom class computes the truth value of each State-Mapping, and returns the conjunction of the results to indicate whether or not the managed resource is in an undesired state.

Recognition of a symptom triggers the generation of a ChangeRequest object. Change requests contain a symptom identifier sid that is used to lookup a ChangePlan to address the problem. Each ChangePlan is composed of one or more Action objects, which provides the name of the effector method and an optional Parameter list. Two queues, requestQueue and planQueue, have been incorporated into the KnowledgeData class to hold change requests and change plans respectively. These blocking queues use producer-consumer relationships to facilitate safe communication among the MAPE functions.

4.3   Resource

Our detailed design of the resource R considers two scenarios: (1) developers are required to build R from scratch and/or have full access to modify its source code; and (2) a commercial off-the-shelf (COTS) component, whose source code is unavailable, is to be used as the primary basis for developing R.

Developing R with Code Access. Figure 6b provides a detailed class design for R when there are no limitations with respect to source code accessibility. Each managed resource derives from the class labeled AbstractResource in Figure 6b. This abstract class provides access control mechanisms at the resource-level to address our safety goal. These include the operations: suspend, resume, saveState, and restoreState.

State visibility and controllability are addressed by requiring that *getters* and *setters* be provided for all of R's private and protected variables. These include variables of both primitive and non-primitive data types. Although intrusive, this requirement ensures that test case pre- and post- conditions associated with object state can be setup and verified. To further improve the testability of R, our design emphasizes the use of dependency injection [22]. This mandates that all non-primitive data within R be declared as references to interfaces, rather than implementation classes (e.g., objects A and B in Figure 6b). Following such a design heuristic decouples the interface of each object in R from its source code, thereby allowing mock object implementations (stubs) to be easily swapped in and out of R during runtime testing.

Developing R without Code Access. In the scenario where R is a COTS component, the adapter design pattern can be used to facilitate the implementation of the safety mechanisms specified in Figure 6b. This would involve building a wrapper class that adds suspend and resume operations to the component's existing functionality. Care should be taken when developing the wrapper so that new errors are not introduced into R during this activity.

Using COTS can impede both the manageability and testability of R since there is usually no way to break encapsulation, and gain access to the component's private or protected members. However, the complementary strategy presented by Rocha and Martins [17] can be used to improve testability of components when source code is not available. Their approach injects built-in test mechanisms directly into intermediate code of the COT. Other approaches for improving the runtime testability of COTS exist in the literature, and may be applicable to R in this scenario.

4.4   Test Interface

A class diagram of the self-test support design is shown in Figure 7. Three categories of automated testing tools have been modeled for use in STACs, represented by the interfaces: ExecutionCollector – applies test cases to the resource to produce item pass/fail results; (2) CoverageCollector – instruments the source code and calculates line and branch coverage during test execution; and (3) PerformanceCollector – computes the total elapsed time taken to perform test runs.

The class SelfTestSupport realizes the collector interfaces, and is used to store the results of testing via the attribute testResults. After testing completes, this data structure can be queried by TMs to gather information such as the number of test failures; total elapsed time for testing; and the percentage of line and branch coverage. TMs can then store this information in their internal knowledge as test logs, and evaluate them against the predefined test policies. The SourceMap class is used to configure the self-test implementation by providing information on managed resources, including the location of related source code modules and automated test scripts.

5   Prototype

To investigate the feasibility of the ideas presented in this paper, we have applied system-wide AST to a self-configuring and self-healing *Communication Virtual*

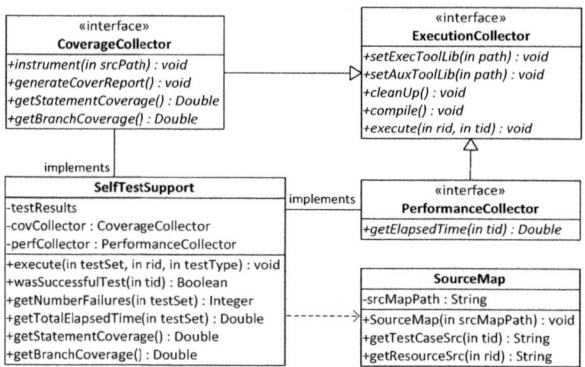

Fig. 7. Test Interface and Implementation

Machine (CVM) [4]. CVM is a model-driven platform for realizing user-centric communication services, and is the result of a collaboration between FIU SCIS and Miami Children's Hospital in the domain of healthcare.

5.1   Application Description

Allen et al. [1] leverage autonomic computing, and open-platform communication APIs, in the provision of a comprehensive set of communication services for CVM. Figure 8 shows the *Network Communication Broker* (NCB) layer of CVM. Through a series of dynamic adaptations, NCB self-configures to use multiple communication frameworks such as Skype, Smack, and Native NCB [8,19,23] (bottom-right). An NCB management layer exposes the communication services to its clients via a network independent API (top of Figure 8).

A layer of Touchpoint AMs directly manages these communication services and is responsible for dynamically adapting these components in the network configuration. An Orchestrating AM, labeled `OAMCommunication`, coordinates the Touchpoint AMs, and analyzes user requests stored in a call queue to determine if self-management is required. Requests for self-management can have two general forms: (1) a user's explicit request for communication that is not supported by the current configuration, thereby requiring self-configuration; and (2) the occurrence of other erroneous events such as failure of a communication service, thereby requiring self-healing.

5.2   Setup and Experimentation

Using the approach and supporting designs described in Sections 3 and 4, we incorporated self-testing into the NCB layer of CVM. A test manager (TM) was implemented at the orchestrating-level to monitor change requests generated by `OAMCommunication`. Change requests requiring dynamic adaptation were validated in-place by a Touchpoint TM, after disabling caller functions in the Communication Services Manager and Touchpoint AMs to ensure safety. The automated tools JUnit and Cobertura were used to support the testing process

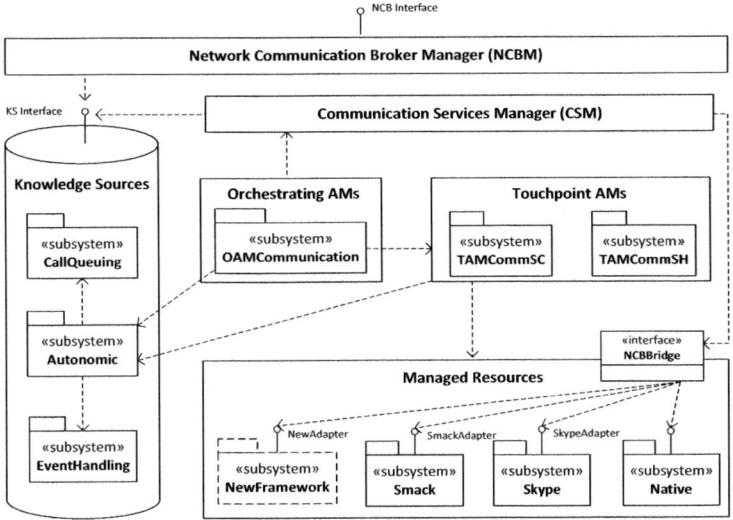

Fig. 8. Network Communication Broker (NCB) Layer of CVM

[5,6]. A total of 41 JUnit tests were developed to validate self-adaptations in the NCB, along with the necessary test drivers and stubs. Cobertura was set up to instrument the NCB implementation for statement and branch coverage.

Experiments were conducted using the CVM platform in order to gain insights into the benefits and challenges associated with the proposed approach. The experiments were designed to facilitate the observation and measurement of the: (1) effectiveness of self-tests in detecting faults and exercising the CVM implementation, and (2) impact of runtime testing on the processing and timing characteristics of the application. The Eclipse Test and Performance Tools Platform (TPTP) was used for timing test executions and measuring thread utilization during self-testing [21].

A mutation analysis technique was incorporated into the experimental design. This involved generating 39 faulty delta components by planting artificial defects into the interface and/or implementation of: (1) Skype, representing a proprietary closed-source component, and (2) Smack, representing an open-source component. 15 of the mutants were created manually, while the remaining 24 were generated automatically using MuJava [13]. A driver was written to simulate the environmental conditions necessary to induce self-configuration and self-healing of CVM using the mutant components, at which point self-testing would occur to produce the results.

5.3 Results

For the fault detection experiments 35 out of the 39 mutants were detected, producing a mutation score of 89.7%. Self-testing achieved 63% statement coverage and 57% branch coverage of the NCB's implementation. In addition, there

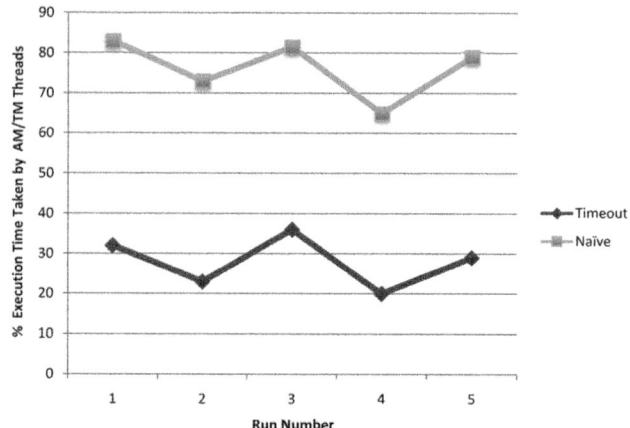

Fig. 9. Thread Utilization of Test Managers in CVM

was 100% method coverage of the communication service interfaces. Figure 9 provides the manager thread performance results of five experimental runs using two variants of the NCB. One variant uses a *naive* monitoring scheme that polls resources continuously, and the other applies a *timeout* based monitoring scheme that polls resource intermittently every 250ms. The data for the experimental runs were collected during a 2-way Skype AV to a 3-way Smack AV self-configuration.

5.4   Discussion

The findings of our prototype experimentation suggest that both system-wide AST and SAV are feasible. In particular, mutation analysis revealed highly favorable scores, with multiple test failures being produced at the integration and system-levels. Self-testing in the NCB successfully detected a cross section of bad mutants, and exercised a significant portion of the program structure.

As indicated by Figure 9, the initial runtime interleaving of the CVM and its self-testing process was highly biased in favor of testing. This led to observable degradation of the core CVM services, especially during the establishment of communication connections. However, introducing a small timeout into the TM threads of the NCB significantly improved the performance of the core CVM services. The timeout reduced the biased interleaving from a range of 85-65% to 35-20%, which was acceptable to CVM users.

Using safety mechanisms to debug the self-testing CVM was instrumental to the success of the project. Debugging and off-line testing of the NCB layer relied heavily on the use of suspend and resume operations within AMs and TMs. Developing self-tests for the NCB was a significant challenge due to its large size and complexity. Some tests required making asynchronous calls to the underlying communication frameworks. However, most open-source testing tools do not support asynchronous testing, which meant that we had to implement additional programs for this purpose.

Selecting and tailoring open-source testing tools for use in autonomic software presented additional difficulties, including: (1) locating trustworthy information on tool features and configuration procedures; (2) filtering tools that would not be suitable for the problem being tackled due to their reliance on external dependencies, e.g., Apache ANT, and (3) determining which report formats would be most appropriate for automatically extracting results in a uniform manner, e.g., CSV, XML, HTML. Threats to the validity of the investigation include performance error due to the instrumentation overhead, and the lack of similar studies for verifying experimental results.

6   Conclusion

Dynamically adaptive behavior in autonomic software requires rigorous offline and on-line testing. To narrow the gap between on-line testing and other advances in autonomic computing, we presented a system-wide approach for validating behavioral adaptations in autonomic software at runtime. Emphasis was placed on enabling on-line testing at different levels of the autonomic system, as well as maintaining operational integrity at runtime via built-in safety mechanisms. A prototype of a self-testing autonomic communication virtual machine was presented, and used to discuss the feasibility, challenges and benefits of the proposed approach. Future work calls for controlled experimentation of the self-testing CVM, and investigating runtime testing of structural adaptations.

Acknowledgments. The authors would like to thank Alain E. Ramirez for his contribution to this research. This work was supported in part by the NSF under grant IIS-0552555.

References

1. Allen, A.A., Wu, Y., Clarke, P.J., King, T.M., Deng, Y.: An autonomic framework for user-centric communication services. In: CASCON 2009, pp. 203–215. ACM Press, New York (2009)
2. Briand, L.C., Labiche, Y., Wang, Y.: An investigation of graph-based class integration test order strategies. IEEE Trans. Software Eng. 29(7), 594–607 (2003)
3. Da Costa, A.D., Nunes, C., Da Silva, V.T., Fonseca, B., De Lucena, C.J.P.: JAAF+T: a framework to implement self-adaptive agents that apply self-test. In: SAC 2010, pp. 928–935. ACM, New York (2010)
4. Deng, Y., Sadjadi, S.M., Clarke, P.J., Hristidis, V., Rangaswami, R., Wang, Y.: CVM-a communication virtual machine. J. Syst. Softw. 81(10), 1640–1662 (2008)
5. Doliner, M., Lukasik, G., Thomerson, J.: Cobertura 1.9 (2002), http://cobertura.sourceforge.net/ (June 2011)
6. Gamma, E., Beck, K.: JUnit 3.8.1 (2005), http://www.junit.org/ (June 2011)
7. IBM Autonomic Computing Architecture Team: An architectural blueprint for autonomic computing. Tech. rep., IBM, Hawthorne, NY (June 2006)
8. Jive Software: Smack API (November 2008), http://www.igniterealtime.org/projects/smack/ (June 2011)

9. Kephart, J., Chess, D.: The vision of autonomic computing. Computer 36(1), 41–52 (2003)

10. King, T.M., Babich, D., Alava, J., Stevens, R., Clarke, P.J.: Towards self-testing in autonomic computing systems. In: ISADS 2007, pp. 51–58. IEEE Computer Society Press, Washington, DC, USA (2007)

11. King, T.M., Ramirez, A., Clarke, P.J., Quinones-Morales, B.: A reusable object-oriented design to support self-testable autonomic software. In: SAC 2008, pp. 1664–1669. ACM, New York (2008)

12. Liu, H., Parashar, M., Hariri, S.: A component-based programming model for autonomic applications. In: ICAC 2004, pp. 10–17. IEEE, Los Alamitos (2004)

13. Ma, Y.S., Kwon, Y.R., Offutt, J.: Mu Java 3 (November 2008), http://cs.gmu.edu/~offutt/mujava/ (June 2011)

14. Patouni, E., Alonistioti, N.: A framework for the deployment of self-managing and self-configuring components in autonomic environments. In: WOWMOM 2006, pp. 480–484. IEEE Computer Society, Washington, DC, USA (2006)

15. Ramirez, A., Morales, B., King, T.M.: A self-testing autonomic job scheduler. In: ACM-SE 46, pp. 304–309. ACM Press, New York (2008)

16. van Renesse, R., Birman, K.P.: Autonomic Computing – A System-Wide Perspective. In: Parashar, M., Hariri, S. (eds.), Taylor & Francis, Inc., Bristol (2007)

17. Rocha, C.R., Martins, E.: A strategy to improve component testability without source code. In: SOQUA/TECOS, pp. 47–62 (2004)

18. Salehie, M., Tahvildari, L.: Self-adaptive software: Landscape and research challenges. ACM Trans. Auton. Adapt. Syst. 4(2), 1–42 (2009)

19. Skype Limited: Skype API (February 2007), https://developer.skype.com/ (June 2011)

20. Stevens, R., Parsons, B., King, T.M.: A self-testing autonomic container. In: ACM-SE 45, pp. 1–6. ACM Press, New York (2007)

21. The Eclipse Foundation: Test and Performance Tools Platform (November 2001), http://www.eclipse.org/tptp/ (June 2011)

22. Walls, C., Breidenbach, R.: Spring in Action. Manning Publications Co., Greenwich (2005)

23. Zhang, C., Sadjadi, S.M., Sun, W., Rangaswami, R., Deng, Y.: A user-centric network communication broker for multimedia collaborative computing, pp. 1–5 (November 2006)

24. Zhang, J., Cheng, B.H.C., Yang, Z., McKinley, P.K.: Enabling safe dynamic component-based software adaptation. In: WADS, pp. 194–211 (2004)

25. Zhang, J., Goldsby, H.J., Cheng, B.H.: Modular verification of dynamically adaptive systems. In: AOSD 2009, pp. 161–172. ACM, New York (2009)

26. Zhao, Y., Kardos, M., Oberthür, S., Rammig, F.J.: Comprehensive verification framework for dependability of self-optimizing systems. In: Peled, D.A., Tsay, Y.-K. (eds.) ATVA 2005. LNCS, vol. 3707, pp. 39–53. Springer, Heidelberg (2005)

A Configurable Environment Simulation Tool for Embedded Software

Yuying Wang, Xingshe Zhou, Yunwei Dong, and Sha Liu

College of Computer Science, Northwestern Polytechnical University,
Xi'an 710072, P.R. China
wangyy@nwpu.edu.cn

Abstract. Simulation platform is one of the most important tools for embedded software. For the diversity of embedded environment, it happens that one simulation model developed under a specific platform need to be transplant to another platform when the environment changes. This paper aims to make a brief study of the design and realization method of a configurable environment simulation tool for embedded software. Some kinds of interactive environment models are realized by S-function, which could be integrated into embedded software model for simulation. A configurable simulation monitor interface are designed so that needed monitor interface could be build easily for different user requirement. To improve the effect of simulation data acquisition, a new simulation monitor method is presented. The simulation result shows that this method is feasible and effective. By integrated the modeling function of Matlab/Simulink, This tool could support the whole stage of modeling, simulation and monitoring for embedded software.

Keywords: Simulation tool, Embedded system, Environment simulation, Configurable monitor software.

1   Introduction

Recent years, embedded system becomes one of the most important synthetic technical which has great impact on the evolution of people and the whole society. With the increasingly system size and complexity, the cost on embedded system verification raised sharply. The issues of how to guarantee the quality of embedded software within tight time and low cost in the procedure of system development becomes a major problem need to be faced.

Computer simulation can be used to reduce the expense and length of the design cycle of embedded software before prototype construction begins. The simulation method has been successfully applied into some practical industrial processing control systems to make good profit both economically and socially. At the early age of model driven embedded software development stage, the real target environment has not coming to be use or hardly be able to use, a similar simulation environment need to be offered so as the model based software could be valid as early as possible. Especially for the embedded system which usually

J.M. Alcaraz Calero et al. (Eds.): ATC 2011, LNCS 6906, pp. 47–59, 2011.

has strong interaction with outside environment for monitor and control, and will be used in difference fields. It will be hard to build multi-simulation environments for them to ensure the functionality and performance. An environment simulation tool is such necessary to support the simulation of embedded software. Environment models could simulate different embedded software environment by model building and integration.

The major functions should be supported by a simulation tool are [1]: specification for model description and their processing; execution and control of simulation application; analyzing, display and documentation for simulation results; and saving, searching and management for models, testing programs and data. An integrative simulation tool takes many advantages in the whole embedded software simulation process. It is not only the modeling and simulation of various projects can be operated by means of the developed simulation platform, but visualizing, monitoring and analysis can also be supported friendly.

This paper aims to make a brief study of the design and realization method of an integrative simulation platform MDES (Model Driven Embedded software Simulation tool), especially the environment simulation model and configurable interface development. We extend the Matlab/Simulink model lib with a set of environment model. To enhance the flexibility of monitor, we use the configuration technical to customize the simulation monitor interface. The communication configure, interface configure, simulation running, monitoring and result analysis are integrated into MDES under the support of modeling function of Simulink. The problem existed in traditional data acquisition method was analyzed and a new method of improving the data missing and repeating problems are presented and realized.

The rest of this paper is structured as follows. In Section 2 we summarized the related work of embedded system simulation platform design. Section 3 describes the approach taken for simulation tool, including the function design, architecture design and description of simulation process. A new simulation monitor method is presented in detail in Section 4. Finally conclusions are drawn and our future work is discussed in Section 5.

2   Related Works

There have been significant focus on this area recently and previous work includes several kinds of platform. A framework for modeling, simulation and automatic code generation of sensor network applications was presented in [2], which based on MathWorks tools and the application developer can configure the connectivity of the sensor network nodes and can perform behavioral simulation and functional verification of the application. After modeling and simulation, this framework can generate the complete application code for several target operating systems from the simulated model. Hugh H. T. Liu [3] presented an interactive design and simulation platform for flight vehicle systems development which adopts the co-simulation integration concept and enables the component design "plug-and-play" in a systems simulation environment. The smooth interactive design and simulation is achieved by an adaptive "connect-and-play" capability. The EODiSP [4] is a generic platform to support the development and operation of distributed simulations and implements the subset of HLA services required to support data-driven simulations by allow the simulation packages to interact together over a possibly distributed network. A real-time simulation approach with rapid prototyping for digital electronic engine control is proposed in [5] and an ECU-in-the-loop real-time simulation platform with this approach is developed.

While model based simulation platform gives people a quite feasible approach for the design, reusability and composition of models, [6,7,8] gives the examples of how simulation can be integrated in a MDA-based approach in order to allow quick development and simulation. Some methods of coupling UML model and Simulink model for consistent simulation are on researching in [9,10].

3   Our Approach

The environment simulation tool MDES is specifically aimed at supporting the development of UAV flight control simulation missions but is more generally suitable for simulators that are built by integrating simulation packages which interact by sending data to, and receiving data from each other or from sensors/actors etc.

3.1   Function Design

It's a two-step process in embedded system simulation. First, you create a graphical model of the system to be simulated, using the model editor. The model depicts the time-dependent mathematical relationships among the system's inputs, states, and outputs. Then, you use the model simulation function to simulate the behavior of the system over a specified time span. The MDES are designed as such a two stages supported simulator. The architecture of the simulation tool showed as Fig. 1.

The visual modeling, code generation and platform specific compile and link presented in Fig. 1 are established by the support of Matlab/Simulink. Although this paper focuses on environment simulation, model description is still an important function should be supported by simulation tool. So we use the method of imparting the graphical user interface-based modeling capabilities of Simulink. There are two kinds of model included in the model library, algorithm models and plant models. The algorithm models are encapsulation control algorithms offered by Simulink. The plant models are data communication and hardware platform related model supplied by MDES used to integrated with algorithm model for environment simulation. The major functions designed in MDES are:

– Simulation Engine
  The simulation engine is responsible for communication methods configuration and simulation control. MDES could support RS-232 COM port communication and UDP network connection for data collection. To enhance the

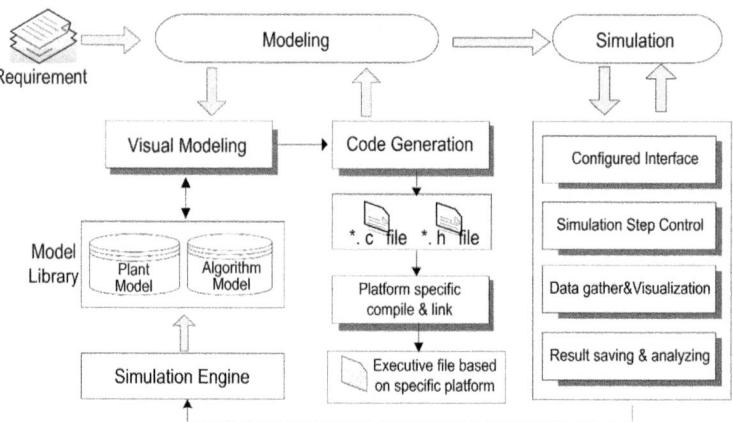

Fig. 1. Simulation platform architecture

real-time ability and degree of accuracy, simulation model download and simulation process control use network connection and simulation data acquisition use serial port communication by default. Simulation control progresses the simulation time, tracks of the entire simulation state and provides the front end to users. The controls in the configurable monitor interface could be bond conveniently with specified data channel of I/O card in model (*.mld) by parameters configure for simulation results perceiving directly.

– Interactive Environment Models
  Generally embedded software runs in complex physical environment. The simulation platform needs to offer the ability of building reusable models that can be composed into other simulation environment. So the requirements for modeling of outside environment should also be described in the model. The plant models aims at building the I/O board driver models and signal source models, are implemented as C based S-Function [11] and imported in Simulink as block diagram. When simulation function is changed or environment is altered, instead of rebuilding a new simulation model, we just need to rebuild the changed parts and reuse the rests. Another advantage is that the plant models can be distributed as stand-alone files or be used as Simulink files.

– Simulation Monitor Interface Configuration
  Usually the simulation tools used in different environment, different data type and data channel number need to be monitored and showed by appropriate display method for easily understand. A configurable monitored interface is an effectual method for such application. MDES provides the function for users to configure the simulation monitor interface flexibly by dragging, position and parameters setting. The interface customized by configuration function could be saved as a formatted file. When loading a configured file,

the corresponding interface will display and specified parameters will be set as saved.

- Simulation Step Control
  Simulation could be executed by simulation step control. The simulation process is based on xPC and the implementation of step control such as simulation model loading, download, simulation begin, pause and stop are based on Matlab API engine lib.
- Data Acquisition and Visualization
  The simulation results produced by running a simulation instance should be send back to the monitor computer from simulation machine. By bonding display controllers with specified data channel, different data could be showed visualization as instrument board, curve graph and so on.
- Simulation Result Saving and Analyzing
  The simulation results should be saved as data file for later analyzing. Besides results saving, MDES also could alert when the simulation result showed crossed the line for warning.

By supporting the environment models for graphics simulation modeling, configurable simulation interface building and process control, MDES gives a integrate simulation modeling and control environment. The strength of this solution lies in the scope and capability of the development process and a high degree flexibility.

3.2   Architecture Design

The simulation platform could be divided into three hierarchy use the view of function implementation showed as Fig. 2. The bottom layer is simulation machine with simulation module instance and communication module instance running on. Which could be seems as running support layout. The top layer facing to users provide simulation configuration interface application service. The functions provided by middle layer, simulation control and monitors could be called on the application service layer by simulation interface configured by users themselves according to specified simulation application. Each layer account for relatively independent function, so as to its implementation.

Simulation machine in bottom layer running the user defined module instances and communication module instance. Under the support of the control module, Matlab engine assemble the module and generate C code by RTW to get user define module instance. The needed module lib by modeling are provided by Simulink model lib and I/O driver model lib of MDES, we call it integrated environment models, included the source data models and I/O card models.

The configuration interface of simulation tool is an independent subsystem in charge of user interaction. There are two step when embedded software simulate, first, configure a monitor interface, second, running the simulation. The first part supported by the configuration interface of the simulation tool. Different monitor controllers are provided as NI Labview controllers and could be used directly by dragging and parameters setting to get a specific monitor interface. We aim at applying the idea of configuration programmable skill to generate the monitor interface according to the requirement of a specific simulation task, which takes the advantages of flexible of display controller, easily to change and available for further development.

The middle layer showed in Fig 2 implement function of control and monitor. Control module integrates the interface of Matlab for modeling. User defined modules are further development *.mdl module defined by user from Simulink. Communication modules are generate from I/O board module implement as S-function charge for data transform, which provided by MDES. The monitor module take charge of receiving data from simulation computer and send the data to bonded display controller which set by configuration interface for monitoring and analyzing. Multi-thread programming was used here for high performance. There are four sub-modules in this part: data acquisition module, data buffer module, data display module and channel configuration. The communication module instances created from located in the bottom layer are used to cooperate with data acquisition module for I/O transform.

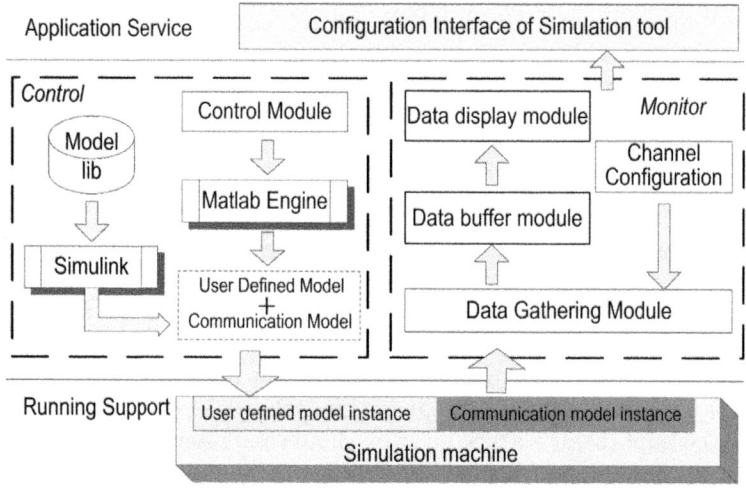

Fig. 2. Simulation platform architecture

- Data acquisition module: reading data from serial port and send to data buffering module.
- Data buffering module: Data buffering and decoding are treated here. In decoding function first transform the character and data, then sort out a group of data from serial port for different display controller.
- Data display module: Display the data as graphic visualization, like figure and curve to user. The controller API provided by NI company are used in function of display thread.

- Channel configuration module: The channel configuration is related with the configuring of monitor interface. It used to set a source data of a communication module for a display controller according to specific correspondence principle.
- Communication module instance: A communication module is a model after compiling, and a communication module instance is a executive target file after compiling. It implemented as S-function in Simulink, used for the communication of host machine and simulate machine. In the stage of modeling the communication module are composted into the environment model to connect with output data. When simulation running, it take concerted action with other modules in monitor part to improved the inefficient problem of usual method. The communication module will send the data come from simulator to data acquisition module by serial port initiatively. By adjust some parameters in Send Block of xPC Target Library for RS232 to get this improvement.

3.3 Simulation Process

A complete process of model driven embedded software simulation are:

- Simulation model developing: Building the embedded software/environment model according to the requirement. The embedded software runs on target machine to execute the control task. To building a model for it, the models in Simulink model lib need to be used. The environment models are used to simulate the outside environment when embedded software running, in hardware in loop simulation, these data may be provided by sensors and get by AD card. So the integrated environment model are added into the model lib for easily environment model building.
- Model compile and download: The simulation model, *.mdl will be convert to .c file and .h file by auto code generation. After C/C++ compiler the executive file of xPC target will be get. By calling the simulation engine, the executive file will be down loaded to xPC target to run the simulation. The down load could be fulfils by Simulink outside mode as well as simulation control in MDES. Simulation could also be pause or stop on the progress for further observation.
- Simulation monitor: The configuration monitor interface in MDES is very flexible in application. A new monitor interface could be generate easily on demand, or a previous monitor interface could be used if satisfy the needs The source data could be set here by bonding a display controller with a specific data channel of the simulation model. The simulation data transfer to the display controller will be showed graphically. Interim result also could be saved for further analyze. A monitor interface generated by MDES is show in Fig. 3.

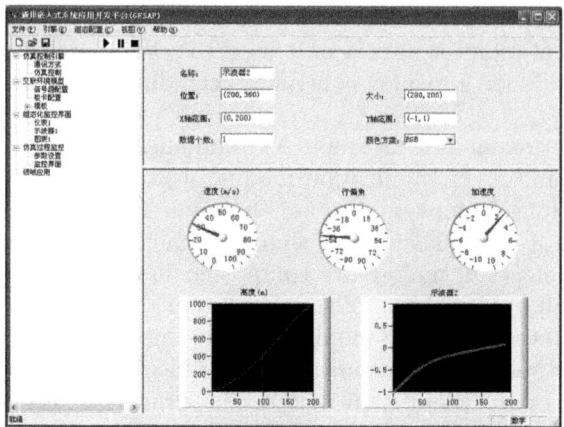

Fig. 3. A monitor interface generated by MDES

4   Simulation Monitor Method Design

xPC Target is essentially an real time operating system for the execution of control loop running on a second computer, allows a perfect real-time execution of the compiled model for rapid control prototyping, hardware-in-the-loop (HIL) simulation. To satisfy the requirement of simulation test bed, the monitor system should support some basic function such as parameter configure, simulation control, data saving and real time display. For the target machine could not save the interim result when simulation running, to save the simulation data real time dynamically become a major task of monitor system and responsible for getting precise simulation result and offer correct data for simulation analyzer.

There are three methods usually used for data transfer in xPC based monitor system: use Matlab API, use Matlab command line or use Simulink interact object. A common ground among these methods is they all adopt the C/S mode in implementation. The monitor computer served as a client, send request to server by Matlab API, command line or Simulink interact object. The simulation computer, xPC target, served as server handle the received request for parameter configure, simulation control, data acquisition, saving and display, showed as Fig. 4. About these tasks server handled, the simulation computer could response the request from monitor computer in time for parameter configure and simulation control for they have no much data need to transfer, so C/S mode have the ability to support these function. But for data acquisition, there are problem exit when using C/S mode.

4.1   Problem Description

The problem exit in data real time dynamic display when using C/S mode, showed as Fig. 5. In the coordinate, X-axis represents time, Y-axis represents the simple value. $t_1 \cdots t_6$ is the time the client (monitor computer) send the simple

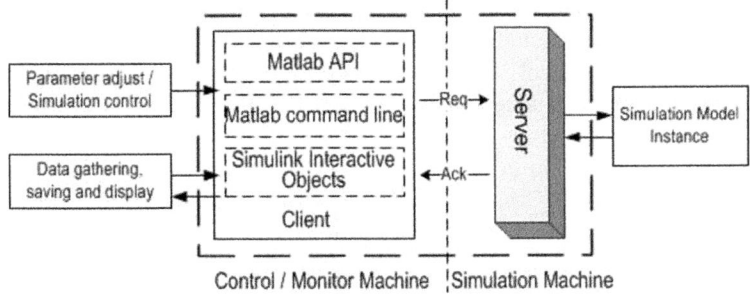

Fig. 4. Data transfer in xPC based simulation system

request to server (simulation computer). For the monitor usually build based on a normal system without real time ability, it could not give the guarantee to send the simple request with fix simple period. So the reality time of $t_1 \cdots t_6$ will be some of random. The result of this random is that the sampled data send back to the client also shows uneven distribution, which takes disadvantages for data analyzing. For example, the simulation period $T < T_2$, the client send request to the server on time t_1 and t_2 separately, but the server produce three data (simulation result) during this period. So the second data will be missed. In case of the simulation period $T > T_2$, the twice requests on time t_1 and t_2 from client will get same simple data, named data repeat sample.

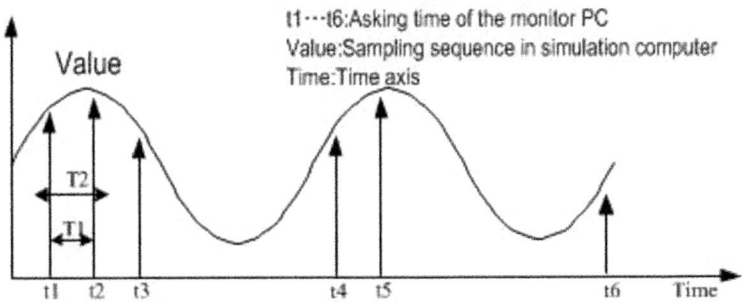

Fig. 5. Data collection in C/S method

Aim at the above problem, we put forward a new method and implement it in simulation monitor of MDES.

4.2   Solution of Simulation Monitor

The simulation monitor module could be divided into two part, monitor and simulation, connect with each other by Ethernet or by serial port. Logically the monitor module is composed by two level, Driver level and application level.

The driver lever take the charge of interact with simulation module, send control command to simulation machine, collect the simulation result from it and decode data. The application level offers monitor function to users, including simulation control, parameter adjusting, data display and saving. The simulation module is composed by server, user define models and communication module. Server is an interactive module supported by xPC environment used to accept the control parameter adjusting commands. User defined models are simulation models user defined according to the reality requirement. Communication models are Simulink models designed in MDES for data collection. The monitor module adopt the multi-thread programming methods and include a couple of threads: simulation control thread, parameter adjusting thread, result display thread, data saving thread, data decoding thread and data acquisition thread. The communication models are designed according to S-function standard of Simulink. Data display performance is improvement obviously in out method. The relative modules include:

- Communication Models
  Embedded software usually runs under special environment and need communication models to act as environment to support its simulation. By add the model into user defined simulation models and bond the needed signal with communication model, compile the whole model as an integrate model and generate the model instance. When running the simulation, the data connected with communication model will be acquainted and transferred to monitor computer. We use the code format "$A\#B\#C\#D\backslash r\backslash n$" in this paper, $ABCD$ represent the data need to transfer, "#" used to separate each data channel. By using it multiple data channels could be transfer in one data package. "$\backslash r\backslash n$" represents the end of a data package.
- Data Acquisition Thread
  The defect described above is caused by the time between the simulator and the monitor out of synchronism. So we use the method of sending data initiatively instead of C/S mode in data acquisition. In our improved method, the simulation computer sends sample data to monitor computer by communication model, showed as 6. So the sample period do not depend on the request period of the monitor computer, but depends on the period of the simulation. For the simulation computer build on the real time system with fixed simulation period, the distribution of the simple data could be uniformity with the period. As a result, the frequency of simulator and monitor do not need to match to achieve data consistency. The problem of repeat simple and data missing could be avoided. The procedure of data acquisition is: First, the thread check if there are data comes by function WaitForSingleObject(), if true, check the integrality of the data. Then, put the whole data package into data buffer (character "$\backslash r\backslash n$" means the end of a data package). Check if the user stop the monitor, if not, returns to check the serial port to inquire until the monitor stop, this thread exit. The data buffering used to save sample data for data acquisition thread. As a shared memory, the data decoding thread also use it to get data. To assure the synchronization

of data input and output, the data buffer is protected by critical section of Windows Compared with Mutex, Event and Semaphorewhich also support by windows for thread synchronization, Critical Section runs under running situation and has better efficiency.

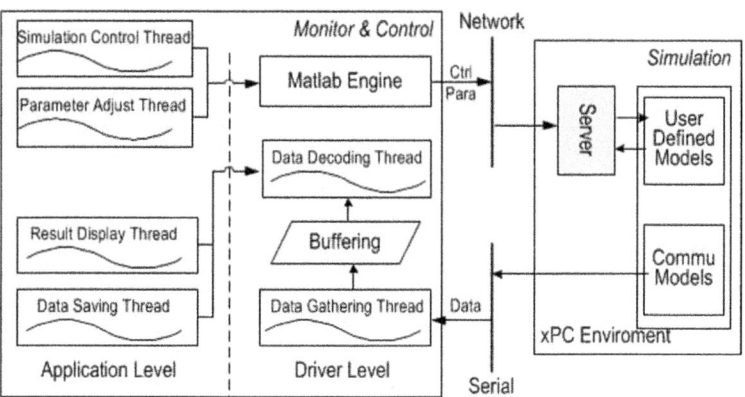

Fig. 6. Data collection in C/S method

- Data Decoding Thread
  The origin data will be get out by data decoding thread first, then decode according to the code rule used in communication model and send to display thread. So the task in this thread is buffer reading and data decoding. Buffer reading needs to assure the synchronization by Critical Section the same as data acquisition thread. Data decoding divide the data package into separate part by character "#" and save them as the same sequence as in data package.
- Result Display Thread
  The monitor data should be displayed by controllers. Virtual instrument is an important tool for data analyze. MDES integrate the NI virtual instrument by *Active X* to generated display interface. To show the data dynamically and timely, the data should be update from time to time. Each controller on monitor interface has a buffer; the data decoding thread separate the data package and send them to their corresponding controller buffer. Result display thread will check every buffer sequent for update and refresh the display interface.

4.3   Simulation Monitor Result

Here we use a simple example to show the effect of our simulation monitor method. We set simulation frequency as $100HZ$, simulation 1 sec. The simulation monitor result showed as Fig. 7. The line C_1 is draw according to data getting from C/S simulation mode, C_2 is the raw data of the simulation machine. The dotted line C_3 is the curve draw use the data in our improvement method. Compare these three curve we can see that C_2 and C_3 are well conformed, but C_1 missed some data and the wave form are distorted. The simulation monitor result shows that our method are pretty effect in simulation data acquisition.

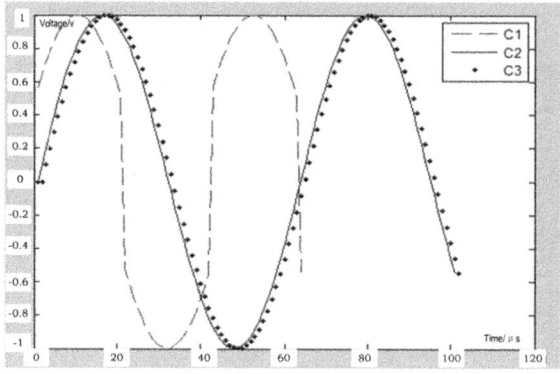

Fig. 7. Curve Comparation

5   Conclusions and Future Works

An integrated system modeling and simulation tool is present in this paper. The modeling function is achieved by the support of Matlab/Simulink and RTW. We build a lib of I/O driver models to support environment simulation. The I/O driver models includes A/D, D/A, DI, DO and CAN, all implemented as S-function added into model lib of Simulink. The I/O driver could be composed into the embedded software environment simulation model to act as data input/output of outside environment. The I/O driver could be reused in different simulation systems and so improve the convenience of hardware- in-loop simulation. The monitor function is offered by a configurable interface and data process modules under it. Usually a simulation tool is designed for a specific simulation application and hard to use in other area. In our design the monitor interface could be customized easily by configuration.

We analyze the problem exits in traditional simulation monitor method. Because the monitor do not based on real time system, simulation data is likely to be resend or be missed. In MDES C/S mode is not adopted as before, the simulator will send the result to monitor actively to make sure the correctness of the simulation result.

Further research work will be on the direction of Cyber Physical System (CPS) simulation method. The characteristic of CPS simulation should be studied and improvement method based on regularly simulation need to be put forward on. One promising area is the co-simulation of discrete model (such as UML, SysML) and continue model (such as Simulink). Simulation model transformation is also another way for efficient system modeling and simulation.

Acknowledgement. This paper is supported by the National Natural Science Foundation of China under Grant No.60736017 and the National High-Technology Research and Development Program of China under Grant No. 2011AA010101.

References

1. Liao, Y., Liang, J., Yao, X.: Real-time Simulation Theory and Supporting Technology. Press of National University of Defense Technology, China (2002)
2. Mozumdar, M., Gregoretti, F., Lavagno, L., Vanzago, L., Olivieri, S.: A framework for modeling, simulation and automatic code generation of sensor network application. In: 5th Annual IEEE Communications Society Conference on Sensor, Mesh and Ad Hoc Communications and Networks, pp. 515–522 (June 2008)
3. Liu, H.T., Berndt, H.: Interactive design and simulation platform for flight vehicle systems development. Journal of Aerospace Computing Information and Communication 3, 550–561 (2006)
4. Birrer, I., Carnicero-Dominguez, B., Egli, M., Fuchs, J., Pasetti, A.: Eodisp - an open and distributed simulation platform. In: Proceedings of the 9th Internation Workshop on Simulation for European Space Programmes (November 2006)
5. Lu, J., Qing Guo, Y., Quan Wang, H.: Rapid prototyping real-time simulation platform for digital electronic engine control. In: 2nd International Symposium on Systems and Control in Aerospace and Astronautics, pp. 1–5 (2008)
6. DeAntoni, J., Babau, J.P.: A mda-based approach for real time embedded systems simulation. In: 9th IEEE International Symposium on Distributed Simulation and Real-Time Applications, pp. 257–264. IEEE Computer Society, Los Alamitos (2005)
7. Monperrus, M., Long, B., Champeau, J., Hoeltzener, B., Marchalot, G., Jézéquel, J.-M.: Model-driven Architecture of a Maritime Surveillance System Simulator. Systems Engineering 13(3), 290–297 (2010)
8. Haouzi, H.E.: Models simulation and interoperability using mda and hla. Computing Research Repository abs/cs/060 (2006)
9. Farkas, T., Neumann, C., Hinnerichs, A.: An integrative approach for embedded software design with uml and simulink. In: 33rd Annual IEEE International Conference on Computer Software and Applications, vol. 2, pp. 516–521 (2009)
10. Sjöstedt, C.J., Shi, J., Törngren, M., Servat, D., Chen, D., Ahlsten, V., Lönn, H.: Mapping simulink to uml in the design of embedded systems: Investigating scenarios and transformations (2008)
11. Mathworks: S-functions. Website (2010), http://www.mathworks.com/help/toolbox/simulink/slref/sfunction.html

An Adaptive Management Mechanism for Resource Scheduling in Multiple Virtual Machine System

Jian Wan[1], Laurence T. Yang[2], Yunfa Li[1], Xianghua Xu[1],
and Naixue Xiong[3]

[1] Grid and Service Computing Lab, School of Computer Science and Technology,
Hangzhou Dianzi University, 310018, Hangzhou, China
{wanjian,yunfali,xhxu}@hdu.edu.cn
[2] Department of Computer Science
St. Francis Xavier University, Antigonish, NS, B2G 2W5, Canada
ltyang@stfx.ca
[3] Department of Computer Science, IS&T on Virtual Computing Lab
Georgia State University, Georgia, 30303, USA
xiongnaixue@gmail.com

Abstract. With the growth of hardware and software resources, the management of resource scheduling is becoming more and more difficult in multiple virtual machine system. It has become a very difficult problem that how to schedule the system resource and improve the service performance of resource. In order to solve this problem, we propose an adaptive management mechanism for resource scheduling. In the management mechanism, we first propose an adaptive management model for resource scheduling. Then, we present a genetic simulated annealing to resolve the management model. On the basis of the model and the algorithm, we design a management module. All these constitute an adaptive management mechanism for resource scheduling in multiple virtual machine system. In order to justify the feasibility and availability of the adaptive management mechanism for resource scheduling, a series of experiments have been done. The results show that it is feasible to adaptively manage and schedule the system resources and ensure the quality of service of resources in multiple virtual machine system.

1   Introduction

With the development of computer technology, the virtual machine has become a very important research topic. By using the virtualization technology, a computer system can aggregate a lot of data resources, software resources and hardware resources and make these resources to provide service for different tasks. Moreover, the virtualization technology can separate hardware and software management and provide a lot of useful features, which include performance isolation [1], server consolidation and live migration [2]. In addition, the virtualization technology can also provide secure and portable environment for some modern computing systems [3]. Therefore, the new computing theorem and model that the virtual technology embodies has been applied widely.

J.M. Alcaraz Calero et al. (Eds.): ATC 2011, LNCS 6906, pp. 60–74, 2011.

With the development of virtual machine technology, more and more hardware and software resources can be integrated into virtual machine. Thus, the existing virtualization technology can't be satisfied with the requirement of development of virtual machine system. In the case, people begin to explore a new system structure for various applications about virtual machine.

Because the virtualization technology can carve some individual physical machine into multiple virtual containers, people begin to build some multiple virtual machine systems for various applications [4] [5]. In these multiple machine systems, their architectures are same and divide into four levels, namely the multiple computers level, the multiple virtual machine monitors level, the single mapping management system level and the application system level. In general, the multiple computers level is made up of all kinds of hardware. They include: CPU, storage, network card and so on. In the multiple virtual machine monitors level, there is some virtual machine monitors. Each virtual machine monitor is managed and scheduled by the single image management system. The main function of each virtual machine monitor includes: managing its local physical machine safely, providing isolation between the virtual machine monitors and executing the commands that the single image management system sends to it. In the single image management system level, there is a single image management system. Its function includes: enabling each virtual machine to share the corresponding physical machine safely, providing isolation between the different virtual machines, providing some different strategies for virtual machine to access hardware resources, controlling all virtual machine monitors and managing the central datum. In the application system level, there are some different applications which can be run on the corresponding virtual machines.

Because there are a lot of advantages by using the multiple virtual machine system, the scale that people need the multiple virtual machine system is more and more large. However, with the rapid growth of virtual machine system, the management of all kinds of hardware and software resources is becoming more and more difficult. Moreover, the utilization ration and the service performance of resource scheduling will reduce with the growth of the scale of computer system. Thus, there are two inconsistent factors between how to expand the scale of the computer system and how to manage resource and improve the utilization ration of resource scheduling.

In order to solve this problem, we propose an adaptive management mechanism for resource scheduling in multiple virtual machine system. In the adaptive management mechanism, we first propose an adaptive management model for resource scheduling. Then, we present a genetic simulated annealing algorithm to resolve adaptive management model. On the basis of the model and the algorithm, we design a management module. All these constitute an adaptive management mechanism for resource scheduling.

The rest of this paper is organized as follows: we discuss the related works in section 2. In section 3, we propose an adaptive management mechanism for resource scheduling in multiple virtual machine system. In section 4, a series of experiments are done and the results are analyzed. Finally, the conclusions are drawn in section 5.

2   Related Works

In traditional virtual machine system, system resources are managed and controlled by a virtual machine monitor [6]. Each virtual machine schedules corresponding system resources for different tasks by using some resource scheduling algorithms, which are provided by a virtual machine monitor. With the development of virtual machine system, the service performance of resource begins to be widely concerned. In order to improve the service performance of resource, a lot of resource scheduling algorithms and performance analysis methods of service are presented and make a great progress in the aspect. These algorithms and methods can be simply shown as follows.

Lottery scheduling [7] provides a more disciplined proportional sharing approach than fair-share schedulers. Each client receives a number of tickets proportional to its share. A lottery scheduler then randomly picks a ticket and schedules the client that owns this ticket to receive a CPU slice.

In a deadline-based scheduling system, such as Atropos [8], the processes declare future CPU needs to the system: the process can express a required CPU reservation and CPU needs per time period. Thus, the scheduler uses real time-algorithms to ensure time guarantees. The problem of scheduling periodic tasks with hard deadlines is well researched in the literature for real-time applications.

The borrowed virtual time (BVT) scheduling algorithm is proposed by Duda et al [9]. The essential of this algorithm is fair-share scheduler based on the concept of virtual time, dispatching the runnable virtual machine (VM) with the smallest virtual time first. Moreover, the algorithm provides low-latency support for real-time and interactive applications by allowing latency sensitive clients to "warp" back in virtual time to gain scheduling priority. The client effectively "borrows" virtual time from its future CPU allocation.

The Simple Earliest Deadline First (SEDF) scheduling algorithm is presented by Govindan et al [10]. In this algorithm, each domain specifies its CPU requirements. After all runnable domains receive their CPU share, SEDF will distribute this slack time fairly manner. In fact, the time granularity in the definition of the period impacts scheduler fairness.

The Credit Scheduling algorithm is described in [11]. It is Xen's latest proportional share scheduler featuring automatic load balancing of virtual CPUs across physical CPUs on an SMP host. Before a CPU goes idle, it will consider other CPUs in order to find any runnable virtual CPU (VCPU). This approach guarantees that no CPU idles when there is runnable work in the system.

In [12], Menon et al present a diagnosing performance overhead method about resource scheduling in the xen virtual machine environment. In this method, a toolkit is used to analyze performance overheads incurred by networking applications running in Xen VMs. The toolkit enables coordinated profiling of multiple VMs in a system to obtain the distribution of hardware events such as clock cycles and cache and TLB misses.

In [13], the authors analyze and compare the CPU schedulers in the Xen virtual machine monitor (VMM) [14] in the context of traditional workload managers. They use the open source Xen virtual machine monitor to perform a comparative evaluation of three different CPU schedulers for virtual machines and analyze the impact of the CPU scheduler and resource allocation on application performance.

In [15], the authors present a novel virtual I/O scheduler (VIOS) that provides absolute performance virtualization by being fair in sharing I/O system resources among operating systems and their applications, and provides performance isolation in the face of variations in the characteristics of I/O streams. In the scheduler, the VIOS controls the coarse-grain allocation of disk time to the different operating system instances and the output scheduler may determine the fine-grain interleaving of requests from the corresponding operating systems to the storage system.

Though the above methods and management mechanisms are very powerful tools for correspondingly application in the traditional virtual machine system, they will still confront a lot of difficulties for resource scheduling in multiple virtual machine system because the resource scheduling mechanism of multiple virtual machine system is different with the virtual machine system. Moreover, the above methods and the management mechanisms don't consider the dynamic conditions of system resources. In addition, the above methods and mechanisms do not present any method to migrate a virtual machine resource for corresponding tasks. In order to overcome these disadvantages, we present an adaptive management mechanism for resource scheduling in multiple virtual machine system.

3   Adaptive Management Mechanism

In general, each virtual machine first submits tasks to the single image management system level in a multiple virtual machine system. Then, the single image management system begins to control and schedule corresponding virtual machine monitor and physical resources for these tasks. At last, these physical resources provide corresponding service for tasks in term of certain control mechanisms and management strategies.

Based on the service processes of multiple virtual machine system, we propose an adaptive management mechanism for resource scheduling. In the management mechanism, we first present an adaptive management model for resource scheduling and then propose a genetic simulated annealing algorithm to resolve adaptive management model. At last, we design a management module for resource scheduling in multiple virtual machine system.

3.1   Adaptive Management Model

In a multiple virtual machine system, the type and the total number of physical resources usually are steady. And the total number of physical resources that all virtual machines can schedule in any time is less than the total number of system resources. If we use R_i to denote the ith physical resource, m to denote the total number of physical resources and R to denote the set of physical resources, we can get $R=\{R_1, R_2, R_3, ..., R_m\}$. Similarly, if we use vm_i to denote the ith virtual machine, n to denote the total number virtual machine and *VM* to denote the set of virtual machine in the multiple virtual machine system, we can get $VM=\{vm_1, vm_2, vm_3, \ldots, vm_n\}$.

In a multiple virtual machine system, physical resources need to be managed by the single image management system level and the corresponding virtual machine monitor. When some tasks are submitted to different virtual machines, these virtual machines need to schedule corresponding physical resource for these different virtual machines. Moreover, when the tasks that a virtual machine is submitted are too much, the virtual machine may be migrated. Therefore, a management model is needed for these different tasks in the multiple virtual machine system.

In order to conveniently describe the adaptive management model in multiple virtual machine system, some notation and definitions are used in the rest of this paper and these notation and definitions are summarized here.

M the total number of physical machines in the multiple virtual machine system

R_i the physical resource of the ith physical machine

$v_i{\rightarrow}R_j$ the ith virtual machine schedule physical resource R_j

t_0 the beginning time that tasks are processed

t_i the ith time that tasks are processed

$q_i(t_0)$ the number that tasks begin to be processed in the ith virtual machine

$\lambda_i(t)$ the rate that the ith virtual machine submits tasks to the single image management system and the corresponding virtual machine monitor at the time t

$u_i(t)$ the rate that the ith virtual machine gets services, which is managed and controlled by the single image management system and the corresponding virtual machine monitor at the time t

$x+$ a non-negative, which is an abbreviation for max(x; 0).

In the multiple virtual machine system, we assume that each virtual machine can schedule the system resource in term of the corresponding request order. Using a combination of online measurement, prediction and adaptive management, we can dynamically determine the resource share that each virtual machine can schedule, which is based on the response time and the task number that each virtual machine submits.

Considering multiple virtual machines can submit tasks to the multiple virtual machine system and the multiple virtual machine system can provide service for the corresponding tasks, we can assume that the mode that different virtual machines submit tasks may be parallel and the service mode that different virtual machine may also be parallel. Moreover, the service mode that each virtual machine gets is the *First Input First Out* mode for the same type tasks.

In general, each task that a virtual machine submits is serviced by multiple hardware and software resources, such as the CPU, NIC, disk, etc. But there are the single image management system and multiple virtual machine monitors, all these resources may be regard as a coordinate entirety. The resources that each virtual machine schedule will be a part of the whole system resources.

In the multiple virtual machine system, if the tasks that a virtual machine system submits are heavy, the virtual machine may be migrated. Therefore, there are two main factors, which decides a virtual machine should be migrated or not. One is the rate that the virtual machine submits tasks and the other is the rate that the virtual machine gets services. If the values of $\lambda_i(t)$ and $u_i(t)$ are constant, the amount of tasks at time t is given by

$$q_i(t) = [q_i(t_0) + (\lambda_i(t) - u_i(t)) * (t - t_0)]^+ \qquad (1)$$

Intuitively, in each virtual machine, the amount of tasks at the time t is the sum of the initial number and the amount task arriving in this interval minus the amount of task serviced in this duration. Since the queue length is non-negative, we use $q_i(t)$ to denote the amount of tasks at any time t in the ith virtual machine.

Depending on the particular values of $q_i(t_0)$, the rate that the ith virtual machine submits tasks $\lambda_i(t)$ and the rate that the ith virtual machine gets services $u_i(t)$, the amount of tasks $q_i(t)$ may become overload or zero at the time t for the ith virtual machine. To understand the overload periods and the zero time of virtual machine, we consider the following scenarios, based on the assumption of constant $\lambda_i(t)$ and $u_i(t)$

(1). the amount of tasks growth: If $\lambda_i(t) < u_i(t)$, then the amount of tasks will increase with the growth of service time $t-t_0$. Thus, the tasks that the ith virtual machine need to process may be overload in a certain time.

(2). the amount of tasks depletion: if $\lambda_i(t) > u_i(t)$, then the amount of tasks will decrease with the growth of service time $t-t_0$. Thus, the tasks lied in the waiting queue may be zero in a certain time for the ith virtual machine.

(3). the amount of tasks stabilization: if $\lambda_i(t) = u_i(t)$, then the amount of tasks will remain fixed ($=q_i(t_0)$) during the service time phase. Hence, it is impossible that the load may be overload or zero for the ith virtual machine.

Since the type and the total number of physical resources usually are steady in the multiple machine system, we can use C to denote the total of physical resources. Thus, we can get the following equation

$$C=R_1+R_2+R_3, \ldots, +R_m \qquad (2)$$

If we use δ_i to denote the percent that the ith virtual machine can schedule the system resources, then we can get the following equation

$$C_i= \delta_i *C \qquad (3)$$

In the multiple virtual machine system, in order to ensure the quality of service of system, two conditions should be taken into account. One is that the loads of each physical machine keep balance as much as possible and the other is the total number of virtual machine migration keep the minimum as much as possible. Based on the two conditions, we use the optimal theory to present a theoretical model for the adaptive management of resource scheduling in the multiple virtual machine system. The theoretical model can be described as follows:

$$f(\delta) = \max(C - \sum_{i=1}^{n} \delta_i * C), st$$

$$q_i(t) \leq q_i(t_0) \tag{4}$$

$$0 \leq \delta_i \leq 1 \tag{5}$$

$$0 \leq \sum_{i=1}^{n} \delta_i \leq 1 \tag{6}$$

Here, Equation (4) denotes that the amount of tasks at time t is no more than that of tasks at the initiate state, which need to be processed by the ith virtual machine. This equation indicates that the ith virtual machine doesn't need to be migrated. Equation (5) denotes that the amount of physical resources that the ith virtual machine can schedule is no more than the total of the multiple virtual machine system. Equation (6) denotes that the total of physical resources that all virtual machines can schedule is no more than the total of the multiple virtual machine system.

In fact, the above theoretical model is an objective function. It is also a multi-objective optimization question. The aim that the objective function is presented here includes two factors. One is to keep the minimum of physical resources that all virtual machine can schedule and the other is to keep the minimum that virtual machine need to be migrated. Because the total of virtual machine and physical machine are limited, it is a NP-hard problem that how to resolve the optimal result.

3.2   Genetic Simulated Annealing Algorithm

At present, people usually use the genetic algorithm and the annealing algorithm to resolve the above similar optimal problem. In the genetic algorithm, the biology evolution theory is often adopted. And people usually use the selection strategy and the content strategy of nature to resolve the optimal problem. In the genetic algorithm, the search ability of algorithm is strong for the overall search process and is weak for the local search process. In the annealing algorithm, two circulation programs are used to resolve the optimal problem, which is based on some limited conditions. In the annealing algorithm, the search ability of algorithm is weak for the overall search process and is strong for the local search process. Therefore, the two algorithms have respective advantage and disadvantage.

Considering the states of resource scheduling in the multiple virtual machine and the characteristics of the above two algorithm, we present a genetic simulated annealing algorithm to resolve the above optimal problem. The basic principle of the genetic simulated annealing algorithm is: First, we randomly choose a group initial solution, namely a group initial value. Then, we begin to search the optimal solution in the global scope of domain. At last, we repeated execute the search process till the results are satisfied with the termination conditions. By using some selecting methods, we ensure the optimal result. The genetic simulated annealing algorithm can be described as follows:

Step 1: Make sure the virtual machine set $V=\{v_1, v_2, v_3, \ldots, v_n\}$ and the physical resources $R=\{R_1, R_2, R_3, \ldots, R_m\}$

Step 2: Make sure the initial value of tasks that each virtual machine submits $q_i(t_0)$, $(i=1,2,3,\ldots,n)$

Step 3: Make sure the rate $\lambda_i(t)$ that the ith virtual machine submits tasks to the single image management system and the corresponding virtual machine monitor at the time t $(i=1,2,3,\ldots,n)$

Step 4: Make sure the rate $u_i(t)$ that the rate that the ith virtual machine gets services, which is managed and controlled by the single image management system and the corresponding virtual machine monitor at the time t, $(i=1,2,3,\ldots,n)$

Step 5: randomly choose a group initial value $\delta = \{ \delta_1, \delta_2, \delta_3, \ldots \delta_n \}$

Step 6: Calculate $q_i(t)$ at the time t $(i=1,2,3,\ldots,n)$

Step 7: If $q_i(t) \leq q_i(t_0)$, then { go to Step 10} Else {go to Step 8}

Step 8: Randomly choose an initial value ρ_0, an infinitely small number ε, and $k=0$

Step 9: If $k \leq n$ Then { $\alpha \leftarrow 1 - k/n$;

$$\rho_{k+1} \leftarrow \rho_k * \alpha ;$$
$$\Delta\delta_k \leftarrow \delta_k - \rho_k ;$$

If $0 \leq \Delta\delta_k \leq 1$ Then { $\delta_k^* \leftarrow \Delta\delta_k$ } Else { $\delta_k^* \leftarrow \delta_k$ }

$$\delta^* \leftarrow \{\delta_1^*, \ldots \delta_k^*, \delta_{k+1}, \ldots \delta_n\}$$
$$\Delta f(\delta) \leftarrow f(\delta) - f(\delta^*)$$

If $\Delta f(\delta) > 0$ Then { $\delta \leftarrow \delta^*$

If $|\rho_{k+1} - \rho_k| < \varepsilon$ Then { go to Step 10 } Else { $k \leftarrow k+1$, go to Step 8}

}
}

Else { $\delta \leftarrow \delta^*$,go to Step 10 }

Step 10: Output $\delta = \{ \delta_1, \delta_2, \delta_3, \ldots \delta_n \}$

Step 11: End

3.3   Management Module

Based on the service processes of multiple virtual machine system and the above proposed adaptive management model, we build a management module for resource scheduling in multiple virtual machine system. The structure of the management module is shown as Fig. 1

In the management module, there are four submodules, namely monitor submodule, allocator submodule, scheduler submodule, manager submodule. The main function of monitor submodule includes: monitoring the running state of each virtual machine monitor, feedback the information that each virtual machine monitor monitors, monitoring the running state of each physical machine, feedback the information that each virtual machine schedules physical resources, transferring the monitoring information to the manager submodule, and receiving the monitoring command from the manager submodule. The main function of allocator submodule includes: receiving the allotting command about tasks from the manager submodule, transferring the allotting command to corresponding physical machines, and allotting tasks to corresponding physical machines. The main function of scheduler submodule includes: receiving the scheduling command about system resources from the manager sbumodule, transferring the scheduling command to corresponding physical machines, and scheduling corresponding physical machines for tasks. The main function of manager submodule includes: receiving the monitoring information that the monitor submodule transmits, transferring the monitoring command to the monitor submodule, transferring the allotting command to the allocator submodule, counting the allotting state of tasks about each physical machine, computing the scheduling state of system resources, transferring the scheduling command to the scheduler submodule.

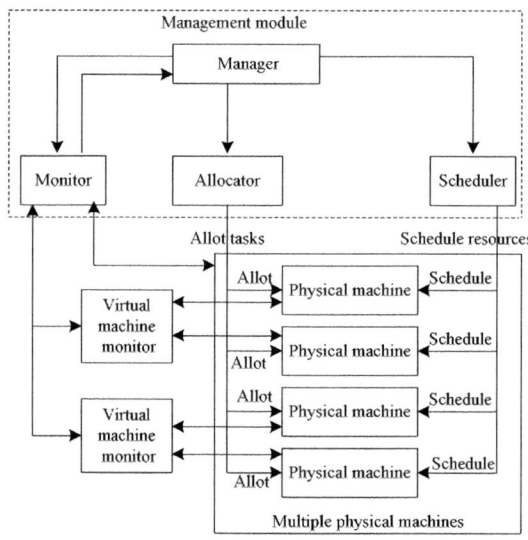

Fig. 1. The management module for resource scheduling

In the manager submodule, when the multiple virtual machine system begins to compute the scheduling state of system resources, our proposed adaptive management model and the genetic simulated annealing algorithm are used. By using the adaptive management model, the genetic simulated annealing algorithm and our built management module, the multiple virtual machine system can get the optimal results of resource scheduling and can schedule corresponding system resources for tasks.

4   Experiments and Results Analysis

In order to validate the efficiency of our proposed adaptive management mechanism for resource scheduling in multiple virtual machine system, we first do a series of experiments. In these experiments, we use the open source of Xen, the virtualization technology to construct a multiple virtual machine system. Then, we will analyze the results of experiments. The processes can be described as follows.

4.1   A Series of Experiments

In our constructed multiple virtual machine system, there are some management mechanisms and methods for resource scheduling. The management mechanisms and methods include our proposed adaptive management mechanism, the load balancing mechanism [16], the credit scheduling algorithm [11]. The image management system can respectively use these algorithms and mechanisms to schedule the physical machine and provide service for tasks.

In our experiments, there are six physical machines ($(R_1, R_2, R_3, R_4, R_5$ and $R_6)$ and each physical machine only has two same processors. Moreover, the hardware and the software configurations of each physical machine are same. And the operation system that each physical machine used is windows XP. In addition, we use the multiple virtual machine system to built eight virtual machines and three virtual machine monitors. Each physical machine is respectively managed by a virtual machine monitor and each virtual machine monitor can schedule the corresponding resources for one or more virtual machines. Moreover, all virtual machine monitors are managed or scheduled by the single image management system in our experiments. The eight virtual machines are named vm_1, vm_2, vm_3, vm_4, vm_5, vm_6, vm_7 and vm_8, respectively. Similarly, the three virtual machine monitors are respectively named VMM_1, VMM_2 and VMM_3.

In our experiments, the task that each virtual machine submits is to resolve the inverse matrix for an invertible matrix. The invertible matrix is a 5 order matrix. In the experiments, the rate that each virtual machine submits task to the single image management system may be different each other and the rate that each virtual machine submits task will be equality in different time phase. The rate that each virtual machine submits tasks to the single image management system is 24 times/second, 29 times/second, 19 times/second, 32 times/second, 30 times/second, 21 times/second, 19 times/second and 29 times/second, respectively. In addition, the percent that each virtual machine can schedule the physical resources of the multiple virtual machine system in the initiate state is 10%, 15%, 10%, 15%, 15%, 10%, 10% and 15%, respectively. Moreover, the process that each virtual machine submits task keep same in order to research the service state of physical machines in different resource scheduling algorithms and mechanisms.

By using the statistical method, we can get the rate that each physical machine provides service for the tasks in the three resource scheduling algorithms and mechanisms, respectively. The results are shown as Fig. 2, Fig. 3, Fig. 4, Fig. 5, Fig. 6, Fig.7, respectively.

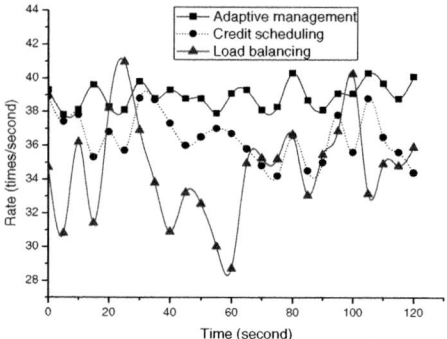

Fig. 2. The rate that the R_1 physical machine provide services in different scheduling algorithms and mechanisms

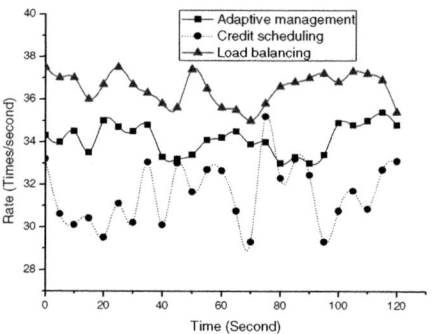

Fig. 3. The rate that the R_2 physical machine provide services in different scheduling algorithms and mechanisms

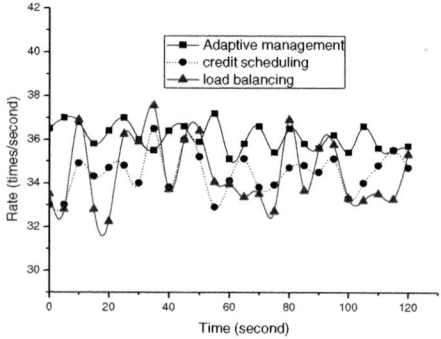

Fig. 4. The rate that the R_3 physical machine provide services in different scheduling algorithms and mechanisms

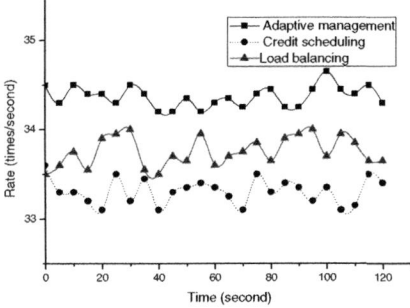

Fig. 5. The rate that the R_4 physical machine provide services in different scheduling algorithms and mechanisms

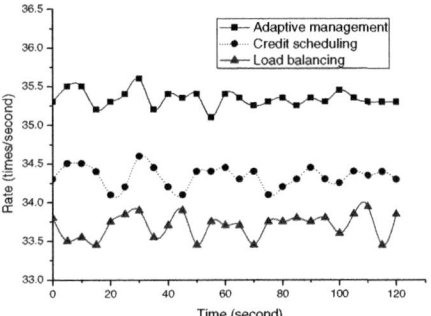

Fig. 6. The rate that the R_5 physical machine provide services in different scheduling algorithms and mechanisms

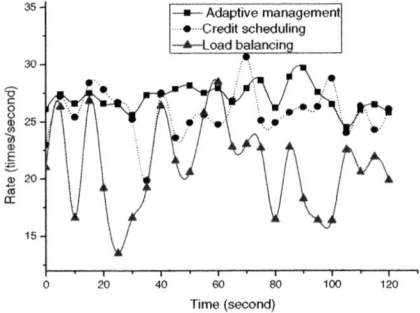

Fig. 7. The rate that the R_6 physical machine provide services in different scheduling algorithms and mechanisms

Based on the results of experiments, we can get the even rate that each physical machine provide service for tasks in the three resource scheduling algorithms and mechanisms. The results are shown as Table 1.

Table 1. The even rate that each physical machine provide services for tasks in the three resource scheduling algorithms and mechanisms

	Adaptive Management (Time/Second)	Credit scheduling (Time/Second)	Load balancing (Time/Second)
R_1	38.944	36.5	34.588
R_2	34.14	31.594	36.524
R_3	36.116	34.456	34.482
R_4	34.37	33.31	33.752
R_5	35.34	34.334	33.702
R_6	27.09	25.806	21.032

Similarly, we can also get the mean square deviation of rate that each physical machine provides service in the three resource scheduling algorithms and mechanisms. The result are shown as Table 2

Table 2. The mean square deviation of rate that each physical machine provides services in the three resource scheduling algorithms and mechanisms

	Adaptive Management	Credit Scheduling	Load Balancing
R_1	0.74782	1.43875	2.96803
R_2	0.71239	1.51776	0.73444
R_3	0.58643	0.90143	1.58212
R_4	0.11547	0.14216	0.16424
R_5	0.10607	0.13285	0.15777
R_6	1.14373	2.11494	3.87330

4.2   Results Analysis

In this section, we will analyze the results of our experiments. In order to describe the analyzing process conveniently, we use $T_{Adaptive}$, T_{Credit} and T_{Load} to denote the even rate that the multiple virtual machine system provides services for tasks in the three resource scheduling algorithms and mechanisms, respectively. Then, we can get:

$T_{Adaptive}$ =38.944+34.14+36.116+34.37+35.34+27.09=206 (times/second)
T_{Credit} =36.5+31.594+34.456+33.31+34.334+25.806=196 (times/second)
T_{Load} =34.588+36.524+34.482+33.752+33.702+21.032=194 (times/second)

Because $T_{Adaptive} > T_{Credit} > T_{Load}$, the even rate that the multiple virtual machine system provides services for tasks in our proposed control mechanism is faster than that in the other two scheduling algorithms. This indicates: the rate that the multiple virtual machine system provides services for tasks in our proposed control mechanism is faster than that in the other two scheduling algorithms.

If we use $D_{Adaptive}$, D_{Credit} and D_{Load} to denote the mean square deviation of the rate that the multiple virtual machine system provides service in the three resource scheduling algorithms and mechanisms, respectively. Then, we can get:

$D_{Adaptive}$=(0.74782+0.71239+0.58643+0.11547+0.10607+1.14373)/6= 0.56865
D_{Credit}=(1.43875+1.51776+0.90143+0.14216+0.13285+2.11494)/6 = 1.04132
D_{Load}=(2.96803+0.73444+1.58212+0.16424+0.15777+3.87330)/6 = 1.57998

Because $D_{Load} > D_{Credit} > D_{Adaptive}$, the mean square deviation of rate that the multiple virtual machine system provides service in our proposed adaptive management mechanism for resource scheduling is smaller than that in the other two scheduling algorithms. This indicates: the stability that the multiple virtual machine system provides services for tasks in our proposed adaptive management mechanism is better than that in the other two scheduling algorithms.

Based on the above analyses for our experiment results, we can find our proposed adaptive management mechanism is efficient and is better than that in the other two scheduling algorithms in multiple virtual machine system.

5   Conclusions

With the development of computer technology, the resource scheduling management has been become a very important research topic in multiple virtual machine system. In order to ensure the utilization ration and the service performance of resource scheduling, we first propose an adaptive management model for resource scheduling. Then, we present a genetic simulated annealing algorithm to resolve adaptive management model. On the basis of the model and the algorithm, we design a management module. All these constitute an adaptive management mechanism for resource scheduling in multiple virtual machine system. In order to justify the feasibility and availability of the adaptive management mechanism for resource scheduling, a series of experiments have been done. The results show that it is feasible to adaptively manage and schedule the system resources and ensure the quality of service of resources in multiple virtual machine system.

Acknowledgment. This paper is supported by National Basic 973 Research Program of China under grant No.2007CB310900, National Science Foundation of China under grant No. 60873023, 60973029, Zhejiang Provincial Natural Science Foundation of China under Grant No. Y1090297 and Y6090312, Startup Foundation of School Grant No. KYS055608103.

References

1. Creasy, R.J.: The Origin of the VM/370 Time-Sharing System. IBM Journal of Research and Development 25(5), 483–490 (1981)

2. Kallahalla, M., Uysal, M., Swaminathan, R., Lowell, D., Wray, M., Christian, T., Edwards, N., Dalton, C., Gittler, F.: SoftUDC: A Software-Based Data Center for Utility Computing. IEEE Computer 37(11), 46–54 (2004)

3. Sugerman, J., Venkitachalam, G., Lim, B.H.: Virtualizing I/O Devices on VMware Workstation's Hosted Virtual Machine Monitor. In: Proceeding of USENIX Annual Technical Conference, pp. 1–4. USENIX, Boston (2001)

4. Li, Y.F., Xu, X.H., Wan, J., Li, W.Q.: A Real-Time Scheduling Mechanism of Resource for Multiple Virtual Machine System. In: The 5rd ChinaGrid Annual Conference (ChinaGrid 2010), pp. 137–143. IEEE Computer Society, Zhongshan (2010)

5. Li, Y.F., Xu, X.H., Wan, J., Li, W.Q.: A Control Mechanism about Quality of Service for Resource Scheduling in Multiple Virtual Machine System. In: The First Workshop on Engineering and Numerical Computation (ENC 2010), pp. 1362–1368. IEEE Computer Society, Wuhan (2010)

6. Smith, J.E., Nair, R.: The Architecture of Virtual Machines. IEEE Computer 38(5), 32–38 (2005)

7. Waldspurger, C.A.: Lottery and Stride Scheduling: Flexible Proportional-share Resource Management. Technical report, Cambridge, MA, USA (1995)

8. Leslie, I.M., Mcauley, D., Black, R., Roscoe, T., Barham, P.T., Evers, D., Fairbairns, R., Hyden, E.: The Design and Implementation of an Operating System to Support Distributed Multimedia Applications. IEEE Journal of Selected Areas in Communications 14(7), 1280–1297 (1996)

9. Lin, B., Dinda, P.A.: Towards Scheduling Virtual Machines Based on Direct User Input. In: The first International Workshop on Virtualization Technology in Distributed Computing, p. 6. IEEE Press, USA (2006)

10. Korotaev, K.: Hierarchical CPU Schedulers for Multiprocessor Systems, Fair CPU Scheduling and Processes Isolation. In: IEEE International Conference on Cluster Computing, p. 1. IEEE Press, Los Alamitos (2005)

11. An, J.F., Fan, X.Y., Zhang, S.B., Wang, D.H.: An Efficient Verification Method for Microprocessors Based on the Virtual Machine. In: Yang, L.T., Zhou, X.-s., Zhao, W., Wu, Z., Zhu, Y., Lin, M. (eds.) ICESS 2005. LNCS, vol. 3820, pp. 514–521. Springer, Heidelberg (2005)

12. Menon, A., Santos, J.R., Turner, Y., Janakiraman, G.J., Zwaenepoel, W.: Diagnosing Performance Overheads in the Xen Virtual Machine Environment. In: Proceedings of the 1st International Conference on Virtual Execution Environments (VEE 2005), Chicago, IL, USA, pp. 13–23 (2005)

13. Cherkasova, L., Gupta, D., Vahdat, A.: Comparison of the Three CPU Schedulers in Xen. SIGMETRICS Performance Evaluation Review 25(2), 42–51 (2007)

14. Willmann, P., Shafer, J., Carr, D., Menon, A., Rixner, S., Cox, A.L., Zwaenepoel, W.: pConcurrent Direct Network Access for Virtual Machine Monitors. In: Proceedings of the IEEE 13th International Symposium on High Performance Computer Architecture, pp. 306–317. IEEE Press, Washington, DC, USA (2007)

15. Seelam, S.R., Teller, P.J.: Virtual I/O Scheduler: A Scheduler of Schedulers for Performance Virtualization. In: Proceedings of the 3rd International Conference on Virtual Execution Environments (VEE 2007), pp. 105–115. ACM Press, San Diego (2007)

16. Zhao, M., Zhang, J., Figueiredo, R.J.: Distributed File System Virtualization Techniques Supporting On-Demand Virtual Machine Environments for Grid Computing. Cluster Computing 9(1), 45–56 (2006)

Virtualization with Automated Services Catalog for Providing Integrated Information Technology Infrastructure

Robson de Oliveira Albuquerque[1,2], Luis Javier García Villalba[1],
Osmar Ribeiro Torres[2], and Flavio Elias Gomes de Deus[2]

[1] Group of Analysis, Security and Systems (GASS)
Department of Software Engineering and Artificial Intelligence (DISIA)
School of Computer Science, Office 431
Universidad Complutense de Madrid (UCM)
Calle Profesor José García Santesmases s/n
Ciudad Universitaria, 28040 Madrid, Spain
{robson,javiergv}@fdi.ucm.es
[2] Department of Electrical Engineering (ENE)
Universidade de Brasília (UnB)
Asa Norte – Brasilia, D. F., Brazil
robson@redes.unb.br, osmar@oi.net.br, flavio@nmi.unb.br

Abstract. This paper proposes a service catalog service integrated with virtualized systems aiming at the possibility of raising and automating the availability in an IT (Information Technology) infrastructure. This paper demonstrates that aligning the server virtualization concepts and infrastructure management tools is possible to have gains in time and costs when compared to systems without automated service catalog. The main results presented illustrates that the use of a virtualized environment, with a standard services catalog and specific tools for infrastructure management, provides a time saving, reducing the request interval to a new server from several days to a few hours.

1 Introduction

Organizations considered leaders in its industries are no longer purely focused on costs, but they have also become companies focused in value.The present panorama forces them to aspire, at the same time, in one hand for the gain of productivity and efficiency, and on the other hand, for an increase in the area of capacity of Information Technology (IT) in meeting the new demands of business strategy [1].

The agile, reliable and precise obtaining of technological resources might meet the demands of the two challenges proposed. It is evident that the servers infrastructure (hardware, software and IT services) used need to evolve in order to sustain the technological innovations by leveraging IT resources (for IT resources, it is considered the servers infrastructure, involving hardware and software).

It is taken into account the need of integration amongst the various concepts and technologies involved to support an IT service. For this paper, the definition of "IT service" used is presented by Galup *et al* [1], where it is related to one or more IT

J.M. Alcaraz Calero et al. (Eds.): ATC 2011, LNCS 6906, pp. 75–91, 2011.
© Springer-Verlag Berlin Heidelberg 2011

systems that enable a business process, taking into account that an IT system is a combination of hardware, software, facilities, processes and people. This article proposes the development of an automated catalog of services, integrating it with an infrastructure management tool and servers virtualization platforms.

The integration of servers virtualization tools with an infrastructure management tooland the services catalog aim at some objectives. First, standardizing the requests for new operational resources, such as servers, basic software and applications. Second, automating the availability of the requested resources as soon as they are approved. Third, reducing the time of availability of a new server, and at last, minimizing operational costs with specialized labor.

Currently, the time required to deliver an IT service depends directly on the stages of request, approval, acquisition, and installation of hardware/software exclusive to serve only one set of applications or systems.

Infrastructure management tools and an adequate control of the entire IT infrastructure can help reduce costs. Companies may losemoney without a services catalog, since its users do not know which IT services are supported by the IT department in terms of virtualization. Besides that, without a well-defined configuration management process, there is also an underutilization of IT resources.

Many companies utilize services from the IT area that cannot be interrupted. Thus, servers are required to remain connected full time and to be responsible for supporting a given service, for instance, a financial transaction server.

Therefore, in the same company there might have various computers with underutilized resources. An alternative solution to this problem is the use of virtualization [2] to group diverse services and other applications that need to be available in parallel.

With virtualization it is possible to consolidate and isolate different virtual machines, multiple operating systems (O.S.), thus uniting various logical servers on a single physical device [3], as illustrated in Figure 1.

The major contribution of this article isthe development of the System of Requests Registration of IT Infrastructure (SRRITI),which was created in order to integrate the concepts of three technologies: servers virtualization tools, infrastructure management tool and the services catalog. As an additional contribution, we can highlight the presentation of some results on simulation tests, proving the gains of this work.

In order to present the System of Requests Registration of IT Infrastructure (SRRITI), its contribution, its functionalities and concepts involved, this paper is organized as follows: in section II the concepts analyzed in the proposed work are presented. In section III the proposal of a service catalog for virtual servers is displayed and the environment is described. In section IV, the tests and results are introduced, and in section V the conclusions and future work are presented.

2   Bibliographic Review

Up to the present moment, proposals for servers virtualization [4], with an infrastructure management tool [5], and a services catalog [1], have been treated as independent concepts and do not serve the purpose of integration and cost reduction sought in this work.

According to [7] the major software is licensed for one single CPU, that is, the user has the right to use the software in one single system. When the discussion comes to large enterprise the situation is much worse because the need is to use software in more CPU at the same time but the demand for hardware varies.

When it is considered the time and cost of hardware and software, virtualization became an alternative for companies interested in providing system infrastructure without having to add more physical devices.

The System of Requests Registration of IT Infrastructure (SRRITI) proposes the integration between the previous concepts to serve its purposes.

A more detailed description of these concepts can be found in the following sections.

2.1 Virtual Machines

A virtual machine (VM) can be defined as an efficient and isolated duplicate of a real machine. In other words, it is an isolated copy of a physical system and this copy is fully protected.The term virtual machine has been described in the 1960s from one term of operating system, or a software abstraction that sees a physical system (real machine) [2].

The heart of the system, known as virtual machine monitor (VMM), runs directly on hardware. It implements the multiprogramming, thus providing not one, but multiple virtual machines to the next layer located above, as it is shown in Figure 1. Indeed, they are exact copies of the hardware [7].

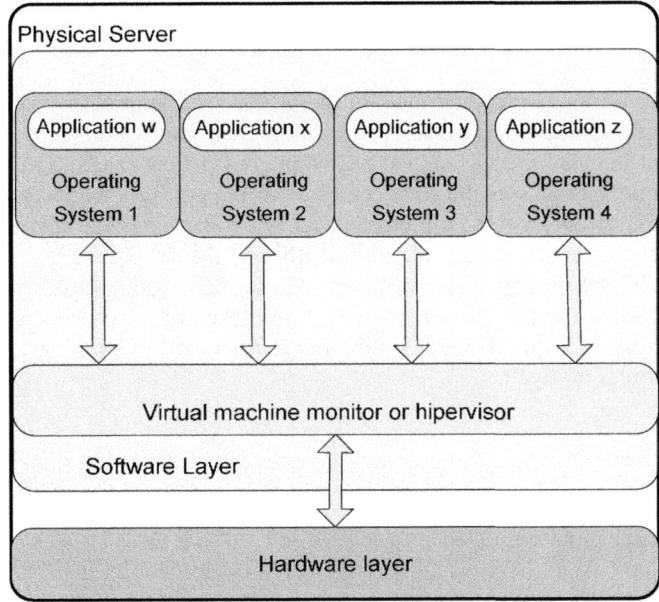

Fig. 1. A Physical Machine with 4 Virtual Machines

By running multiple instances of virtual machines on the same hardware, an efficient use of its processing power is also provided. In data centers, the reduction of physical machines means reduced costs for physical infrastructure such as space, power, cabling, cooling, support and maintenance of various systems [4].

There are four main architectures for virtualization in modern computing that allow the illusion of isolated systems: emulators, full virtualization, paravirtualization and virtualization in operating system level [8].

For this article, the full virtualization was chosen in virtue of the support for implementation given by nearly all virtualization software suppliers which were researched and cited.

2.2   Tools for Virtualization

Any person who currently uses a computer knows that there is something called operating system, which somehow controls the diverse devices composing it. The classical definition for operating system is a software layer inserted between the hardware and the applications that perform tasks for the users, and whose goal is to make the use of computers at the same time, more efficient and convenient [6].

There are commercial solutions, free software, integrated to operating systems, etc. It would be impossible and outside the scope of this article, to comment on all of them, therefore, we chose to present only the ones which are currently market leaders: VMware[9], Xen [8], QEMU[10] and Virtual Box[11]. Besides them, there is Microsoft's answer to the worldwide movement of virtualization [12].

2.3   Data Center Environment Management Tools

If a company wants to make the most of the process of computerization, organizational innovations are needed to sustain the technological innovations [13].

Tools that manage the virtualized environment (virtual machine motors), and also enable the management of the data center environment as a whole, are being developed. These machines can be either physical or virtual, amongst these initiatives, the ones researched were: Cobber[14], Puppet [15] and BladeLogic [5].

The tool BladeLogic was integrated into the service catalog developed in this work in order to enable the automation of availability tasks of a new server. This tool was chosen because of its differentiated amount of resources in relation to the other two competing tools surveyed.

2.4   Services Catalog

The IT services catalog is a menu offered by the information technology department to users of this corporation [16].

The catalog has all the services offered, software and corporate systems that can be installed and supported, avoiding users to request something that is not supported by the IT department.

With the increasing dependency of organizations in relation to Information Technology (IT), the importance of IT Service Management becomes larger every day. It is an excellent opportunity for IT to demonstrate its value and ability to leverage and bring innovation to business processes. But this is not a simple task.It demands clarity of focus and attention of the IT area [1].

2.5   Related Work

In [18] there is a discussion that agrees with the importance of a service catalog. When the infrastructure comes to a cloud environment it becomes important to formally represent knowledge in a services catalog. The focus is to enable automatic answering of user requests and sharing of building blocks across service offerings. In their work is proposed an ontology-driven methodology for formal modeling of the service offerings and associated processes.

[19] presents a model to support decision making for investments in IT services and affirms that it contributes to IT service portfolio management. Their work analyzes business impacts and investment options considering a Service Level Agreement (SLA) policy.

Discussion about the integration of multiple virtualized management tools for enterprise is discussed in [20]. It points that enterprise systems are in direction of the cloud and thus presents a strategy for accomplishing the migration process. It also considers the importance of integrated system management in user environment perspective.

When automation comes to the point of view regarding technology, [21] presents a large discussion of the subject. It presents reviews, benefits, domains and levels of application. One of the main contributions of the work presented is that automation inspires creative work and develops newer solutions. Than concludes the work with several emerging trends in collaborative control and automation, and risks to anticipate and eliminate situations where automation cannot be forget.

3   Proposal of the System of Requests Registration of IT Infrastructure

This section is divided in small parts to describe the main characteristics and functionalities of SRRITI.

3.1   System Persistent Layer

In order to collect users' information in a standardized way, the SRRITI was developed. The System provides its users with the hardware and software settings supported by the IT department. The whole system was developed using HTML and PHP pages and the support of a database as persistence layer.Table 1resumes the main tables and its characteristics.

Table 1. Resume of System Persistence Layer

NAME	DESCRIPTION
1.tb_usuarios	Storage system users' information such as profile and user identification.
2.tb_servidor_fisico	Table for the physical server pool that may support virtualized environment
3.tb_servidor_logico	Its main function is to standardize the names of the systems and main OS available for virtualization.
4.tb_requisicoes	Main system tableandstoresinformationaboutuser requests and status.
5.tb_hardware_processad or	Stores information about physical infrastructure total number of available processors.
6.tb_hardware_capacidad e_disco	Disk size related to physical available capacity.
7.tb_hardware_memoria	Memory size related to physical available capacity
8.tb_hardware_placa_red e	Stores the network interfaces speed to the virtualized hardware.
9.tb_software_sistema_op eracional	This table stores the OS that has been previously prepared for installationusing a data center management tool.
10.tb_software_backup	Maintains the backup software that has been previously prepared to be installed for backing up a virtualized system.
11.tb_software_monitorac ao	Maintains the monitoring software that has been previously prepared to be installed for the virtualized system.
12.tb_software_automaca o	Stores the automation software for the selected virtualized system.
13.tb_software_servidor_ http	This table stores software for HTTP servers that are available for installation in a virtualized environment.
14.tb_software_transferen cia_arquivos	It maintains software for file transfer servers that are available for installation in a virtualized environment.
15.tb_software_banco_de _dados	Stores software for Database servers that are available for installation in a virtualized environment.

3.2   System Logics

The project was designed segmenting administration functions, registration of requests, and approval of registered requests. According to the user's credentials, he or she is redirected to the screen functionalities, in agreement with his/her previously registered profile.

Once the request is registered in the system, there must be an approval of the solicitation before it can be provided. The consultation to a request and its subsequent approval is accessed by users who have the approver profile or administrator.

At the moment of approval of a new server request, the files, which will interface with the virtualization tool in order to create the new server, are generated in disk. The files of interface with the infrastructure management tool are also created in order to install the operating system, and the previously registered applications. At this point it is chosen the physical machine where the virtual machine will be created. Figure 2 demonstrates the flow of a new request. Moreover, it is also possible to provision a physical machine without any virtualization feature within the developed system.

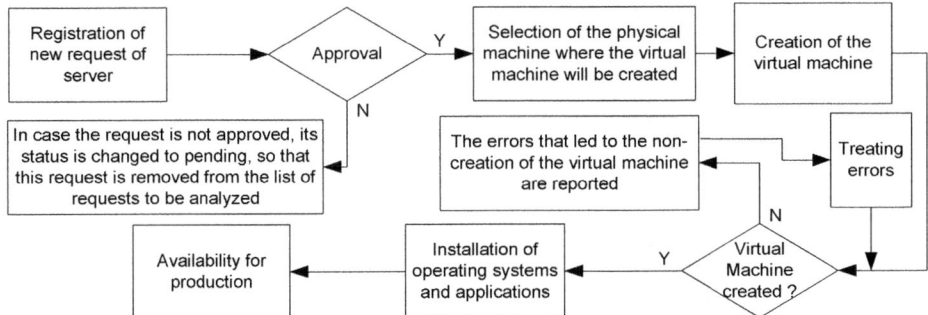

Fig. 2. Flowchart of a New Request

All the files created have the request number to which they are associated; therefore, it is possible to run more than one provisioning at the same time.

3.3   System Basic Caractheristics and Functions

SRRITI was developed using PHP with Apache HTTP Web Server and MySQL as database server. The system divides the user profile based in three main modules: 1) user requests, where users perform its system requests; 2) system approval, where system requests are approved following enterprise process policy by IT department; 3) the SRRITI administration, which is conducted by IT specialists in virtualization and system data center management.

The developed system has a lot of input screens where users can perform its actions based on its profile. As an example, Figure 3 shows one of the screens of SRRITI. There it is presented the registration of a new request from a server. On this screen, certain items are available: processor, disk capacity, memory size, speed of network card, operating system, monitoring software, backup software, automation software, software for transferring files and database software.

The main advantage of SRRITI is that in concentrates the user requests in one point of control and thus reduces de process complexity of requesting a new virtualized system.

It is important to consider that the automation of IT infrastructure is recommended for large enterprises with a heterogeneous and complex computing park. There are no well-known reports regarding the minimum number of servers or database, or even operating systems that suggest the minimum amount of the related items cited above should be automated.

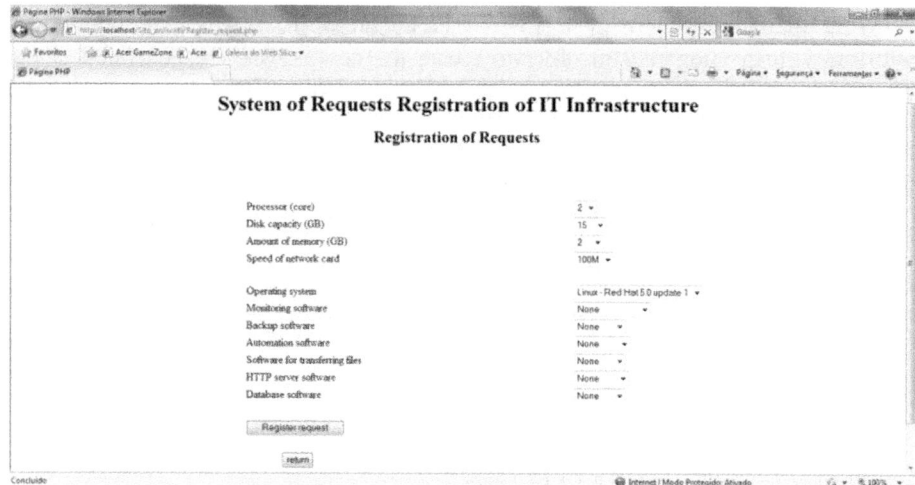

Fig. 3. Screen of Registration of Requests of the System SRRITI

3.4   System Main Outputs

Once the user completes a request for a virtualized service and has the IT department approval, SRRITIautomatically generates scripts to be directly executed in the data center management tool. SRRITIsystem files outputs are based in well-known standards as XML and BAT files, which are easily interpreted and may be imported and integrated in most systems and tools using common programing language. Figure 4 shows a XML output example.

```xml
<?xml version="1.0"?>
<Virtual-Machines>
    <Virtual-Machine>
        <Name>SVLL00001</Name>
        <Host>localhost.brasiltelecom.com.br</Host>
        <Datacenter>ha-datacenter</Datacenter>
        <Guest-Id>winXPProGuest</Guest-Id>
        <Datastore>datastore1</Datastore>
        <Disksize>15728640</Disksize>
        <Memory>4096</Memory>
        <Number-of-Processor>1</Number-of-Processor>
        <Nic-Network>Virtual Machine Network</Nic-Network>
        <Nic-Poweron>0</Nic-Poweron>
    </Virtual-Machine>
</Virtual-Machines>
```

Fig. 4. XML Output of an User System Request

Also there are other XMLs inputs to the system, for instance, system name, system mac-address, system profile, system OS, etc. Each of them depends of the user request and availability of the IT infrastructure. Once the creation of a new virtualized environment is allowed by IT personal, SRRITI reads the XMLs files as data input than connects to the data center management tool and pass the new virtualized system parameters to be created. The whole process is automated using specific commands depending on the data center management tools. Figure 5 shows one type of command that can be executed.

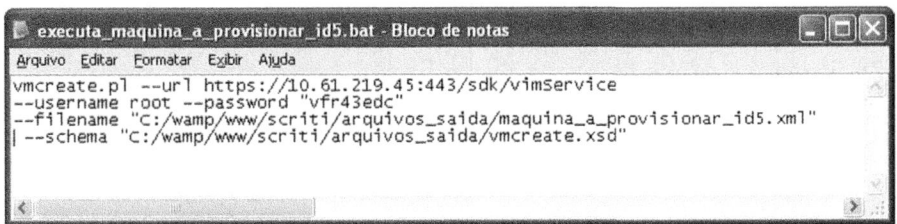

Fig. 5. System Command for Creating a Virtualized System

4   Tests and Results

The testing environment was built seeking to clarify the following questions:

a) Is it viable to automate the availability of a new server from a service request?

b) Is it possible to develop and integrate a services catalog with hypervisors and IT infrastructure management tools, enabling a reduction in the time availability of a new server and also reducing the operating system installation time?

c) How much can the operating cost be reduced by using the integration of concepts and tools presented?

SRRITI was tested as a response to the questions presented.

4.1   Testing Environment

For this article the VMware ESX Server 4, which is the base software for creating virtual data center, was used. The ESX server is a virtual machine monitor that virtualizes hardware resources like processor, memory, storage and networking. Thus, the ESX Server allows a physical server to be partitioned into several isolated and secure virtual machines and, each one is seen as a physical machine in a conventional network infrastructure.

Tests for the creation of virtual machines were performed. Following this, the installation of the operating systems RedHat Enterprise Linux 5.0 update 1 and Windows Server 2003, with various configurations of central processing unit (CPU) and variation of Random Access Memory (RAM), took place.

All the tests were performed by booting only a VM at a time in order to avoid any kind of interference in the tests due to the amount of memory allocated in some other virtual machine.

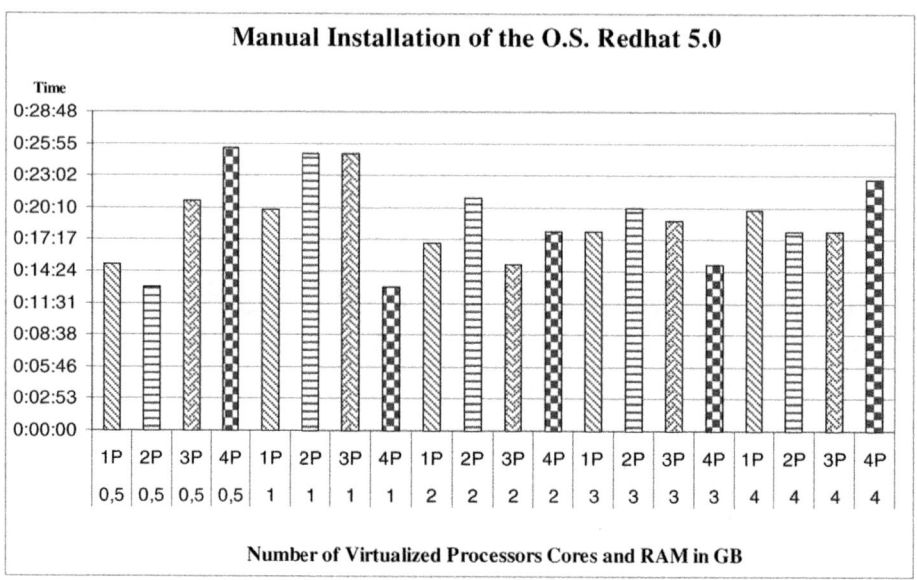

Fig. 6. Manual Installation of RedHat Enterprise Linux 5.0 update 1

The graphs of this paper are organized as follows: on the left side, it is shown the time spent for installation in the format hours: minutes: seconds (h:m:s). At the bottom of each graph, the number of processors (cores: from 1P to 4P) of the virtual machine created, and the amount of RAM in GB (from 0,5 to 4) allocated to each machine, respectively, are presented.

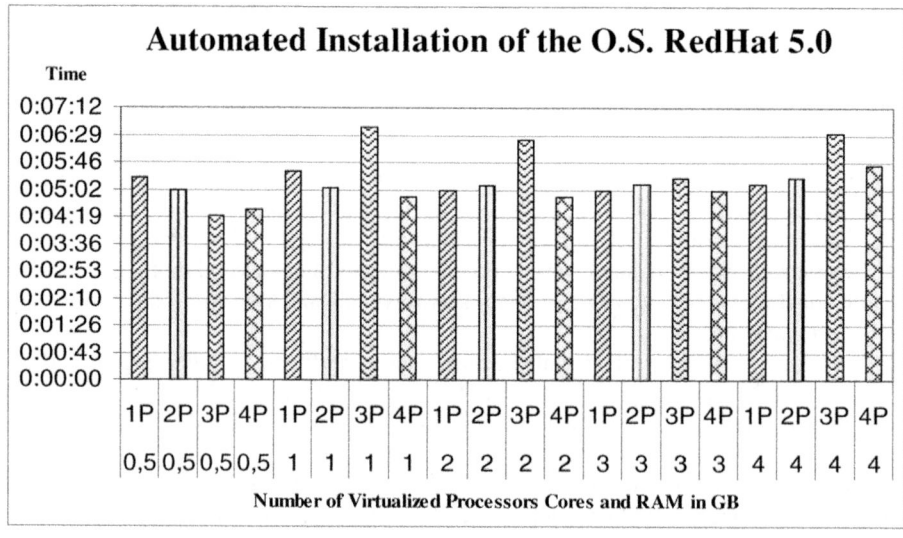

Fig. 7. Automated Installation of RedHat Enterprise Linux 5.0 update 1

Figure 6 illustrates the results obtained in the tests of the manual installation of the operating system, RedHat Enterprise Linux 5.0 update 1. Figure 7 presents the results obtained in the automated installation tests of the operating system RedHat Enterprise Linux 5.0 update 1 utilizing SRRITI.

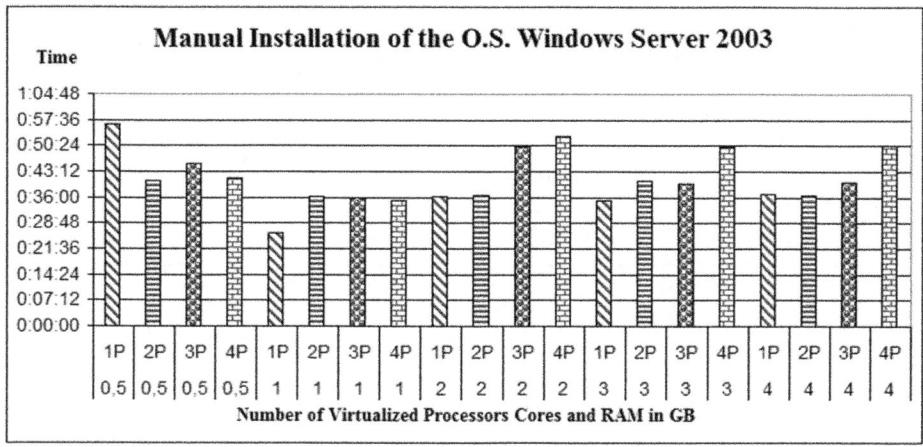

Fig. 8. Manual Installation of the O.S. Windows Server 2003

Figure 8 shows the results obtained in the manual testing of installation of Windows Server 2003 operating system. Figure 9 illustrates the results obtained in the automated test of installation of Windows Server 2003 operating system.

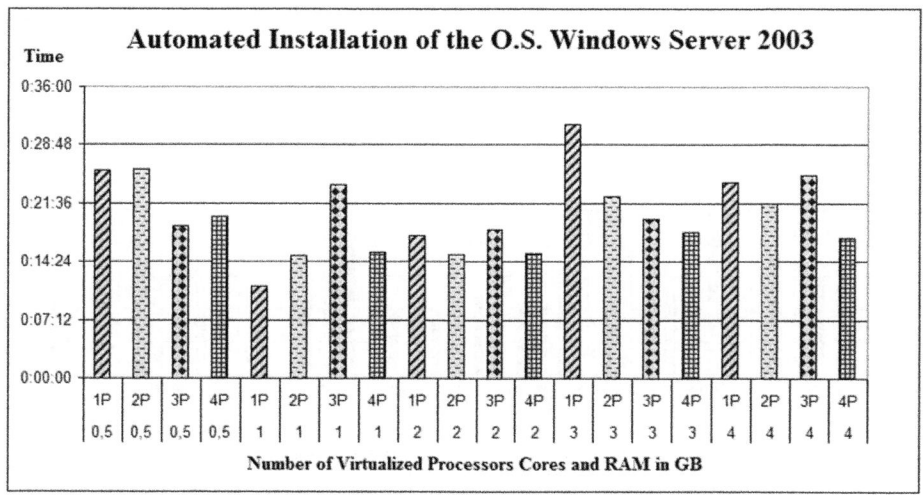

Fig. 9. Automated Installation of the O.S. Windows Server 2003

As shown in Figures 6 through 9 the numbers of processors are not changed because the objective of these tests was to compare the time that the same machine with the same characteristics would take to perform the process of installation of the virtualized environment in a manual fashion compared to an automated fashion provided by SRRITI.

4.2   Comparison of Results

Technology can be used for automating operations. The objective is to replace the effort and provide the human qualification via technologies that allow the same processes to be executed at a lower cost, under control and continuity.

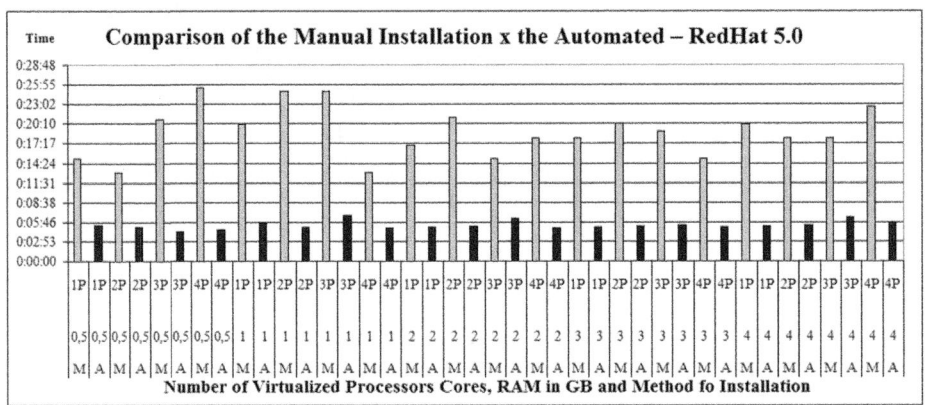

Fig. 10. Comparison of the Manual Installation x the Automated - O.S. Redhat Enterprise Linux 5.0 update 1

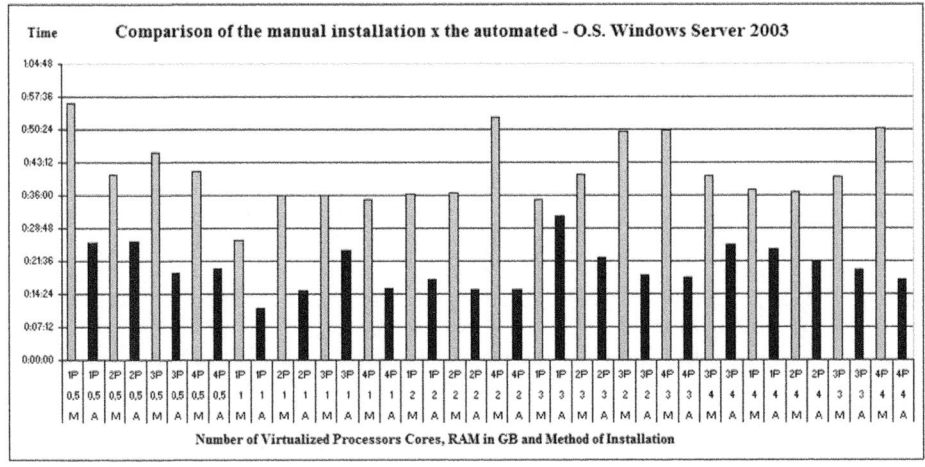

Fig. 11. Comparison of the Manual Installation x the Automated - O.S. Windows Server 2003

Automating a process, which is executed manually, initially, aims at reducing the possibility of human error and, in the background, increasing the productivity by making available a good or service. This can be verified comparing graphs of results in Figures 10 and 11. They show that an automated process has better time results that a manual installation process.

In addition, information concerning time spent with installation; number of processors (cores) of the virtual machine created; amount of RAM in GB; and the method used for installation manual (M) versus automated (A) are also described.

The system SRRITI proposed in this paper, confirms these concepts.The productivity gain ranged from 57.56% for the scenario of two processors and 2 GB of RAM in the worst case, to 82.30% for the installation of the operating system RedHat Enterprise Linux, including three processors and 0.5 GB RAM, as it is presented in Figure 10.

In relation to the operating system Windows Server 2003, the productivity gain ranged from 10.38% for the scenario of one processor and 3 GB RAM, representing the worst case, to 70.91% in a scenario of four processors and 2 GB RAM, which was the best case as illustrated in Figure 11.

4.3   Comparative Analysis of Costs Estimate

In the case of a large telecommunications enterprise studied in this paper, after analyzing the whole process that is used to make an virtualized system available (Figure 12), it was observed that the process takes 46 days from the user request up to the deploy of the user request. Considering an 8-hour workday, it is possible to conclude that from the request to its proper availability, 368 working hours are required in order to provide a new server. These are reference values, which were obtained through the analysis of the studied process which are also listed in Table 2.

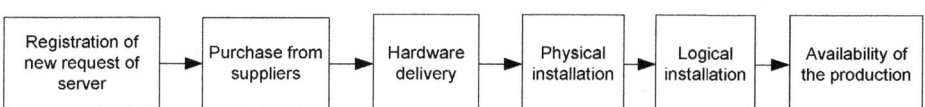

Fig. 12. The Process of a Large Telecommunications Company in Order to Make a Server Available

Based on a salary survey [17], in Table 2, the average salary of a support analyst is presented (expressed in Brazilian currency, reals). The final amount was divided by the total working days within a month, and then this value was divided by the total of working hours. These calculations are needed to reach the analyst's value of one hour of work.

Table 2. Amount of Time Demanded for the Availability of a New Server without Virtualization

Reference Value	Description
46	Workdays in order to make a new server available
8	Daily work hours
368	Total of hours needed for creating a new server

In Table 3 the value of an analyst's hour of work is presented. This value is multiplied by the total of hours needed for creating a new server. The final amount represents how much it costs for a company to create a new server using only specialized labor.

Table 3. Cost of one Hour of Work of a Support Analyst

Reference Value	Description
R$4616,48	Average salary of a senior Linux support analyst.
22	Total of workdays in a commercial month.
R$209,84	Valueof a workday.
R$ 26,23	Value of one hour of work of a Linux support analyst.

Table 4 presents a financial analysis utilizing non-automated virtualization infrastructure.

Table 4. Cost for a Company with Specialized Labor to Create a New Server without Virtualization

Reference Value	Description
368	Total of hours needed to make a new server available
R$26,23	Value of a support analyst's hour of work
RS 9.652,64	Total cost of an analyst working for 46 days

In Table 5 a financial analysis using virtualization and the automated process integrated with the services catalog are shown, also the amount of time needed in order to make a new server available through the system SRRITI, which was developed and presented in this paper.

Table 5. Financial Analysis of the Cost utilizing Virtualization

Reference Value	Description
48	Total of hours needed in order to make a new server available with virtualization
RS 26,23	Value of a support analyst's hour of work
RS 1259,04	Total cost in order to make a new server available

The approval of request may be responsible for the time increase in making a new server available, and for this reason, it was considered the worst case: two workdays or 16 hours were necessary for the new server to become available. This analysis is resumed in Table 6.

In order to solve this matter, a set of physical servers with available resources to enable the creation of virtual machines is demanded.

Table 6. Financial Analysis of the Cost of the Automated Process Integrated with the Services Catalog

Reference value	Description
16	Total of hours needed to make a new server available
RS 26,23	Value of a support analyst's hour of work
RS 419,68	Total cost in order to make a new server available

5   Conclusions

Automating a process for a few executions can be more financially costly and onerous in amount of time than executing the proceeding manually. However, after a defined number of repetitions in each specific environment, the time invested, and, consequently, the capital allocated, are to compensate the time spent on automating the task.

The automated process reduced the amount of time demanded for the availability of a new server in virtue of the standardization of requests. With the standardization of the requests, it was possible to automate the delivery of required resources as soon as they were approved. This fact reduced the costs with specialized labor.

Table 7 presents data on the reduction of time and operating costs achieved through the utilization of the System of Requests Registration of IT Infrastructure (SRRITI). Comparing the time to deliver a new server with virtualization to SRRITI, there was a time reduction of 66.67% with the use of the system SRRITI.

Table 7. Comparative analysis of time and cost

Scenario	Time (in work hours)	Cost (in Reais R$)	Percentagegain (*)
WithoutVirtualization	368	9,652.64	--
WithVirtualization	48	1,259.04	66.67
Via the system SRRITI	16	419.68	95.65

(*) The percentage gain considers the time column in relation to the system SRRITI.

With the integration of concepts presented in this paper (virtualization, infrastructure management and services catalog), and through SRRITI it was possible to observe the gains offered and their true contribution to the standardization and automation of IT services. The reduction of time and costs also adds essential value to the System of Requests Registration of IT Infrastructure.

5.1   Future Work

As future work, new studies regarding trust, virtualization, cloud and service catalog may be necessary in order to provide more availability do users in mixed environments.

Trust and security [22], [23] [24] have become crucial to guarantee the healthy development of cloud platforms. Most studies tries to provide solutions for concerns such as the lack of privacy and protection. These characteristics are important to guarantee security and author rights.

When trust comes to discussion, it is also important to consider that there is no common trust and reputation consensus in distributed environment, for example, to guarantee that a pool of servers are trustworthy in the same service catalog. That makes trust and reputation analysis fully dependent of specific variables and the definitions of the environment that it is attached to.

In the cloud the situation gets more complicated because it is necessary to employ trusts model in cloud environments to guarantee users security and privacy.

Acknowledgements. This work was supported by the Ministerio de Ciencia e Innovación (MICINN, Spain) through Project TEC2010-18894/TCM and the Ministerio de Industria, Turismo y Comercio (MITyC, Spain) through Project AVANZA COMPETITIVIDAD I+D+I TSI-020100-2010-482.

References

1. Galup, S.D., Dattero, R., Quan, J.J., Conger, S.: An overview of IT service management. Communications of the ACM - Security in the Browser CACM Homepage table of contents archive 52(5), 124–127 (2009); ISSN: 0001-0782 EISSN: 1557-7317
2. Poniatowski, M.: Foundations of Green IT: Consolidation, Virtualization, Efficiency, and ROI in the Data Center. Prentice Hall, Englewood Cliffs (2009); ISBN: 0-13-704375-9
3. Benevenuto, F., Fernandes, C., Santos, M., Almeida, V.A.F., Almeida, J.M., Janakiraman, G.J., Santos, J.R.: Performance Models for Virtualized Applications. In: ISPA Workshops Conference Proceedings, pp. 427–439 (2006)
4. Carlsson, N., Arlitt, M.: Towards more effective utilization of computer systems. In: Proceeding of the Second Joint WOSP/SIPEW International Conference on Performance Engineering. ACM, New York (2011); ISBN: 978-1-4503-0519-8
5. BMC. BMC Service Automation The next step in the evolution of Business Service Management. BMC Software (2009),
   http://documents.bmc.com/products/documents/10/45/91045/9104
   5.pdf (accessed on January 05, 2010)
6. Stallings, W.: Operating Systems: Internals and Design Principles, 5th edn. Prentice Hall, Englewood Cliffs (2005); ISBN-10: 0131479547
7. Tanenbaum, A.S.: Modern Operating Systems, 3/E. Prentice Hall, Englewood Cliffs (2008); ISBN-10: 0136006639. ISBN-13: 9780136006633
8. Govindan, S., Choi, J., Nath, A.R., Das, A., Urgaonkar, B., Sivasubramaniam, A.: Xen and Co.: Communication-Aware CPU Management in Consolidated Xen-Based Hosting Platforms. IEEE Transactions on Computers, 1111–1125 (August 2009)
9. VMWARE. VMware ESX e VMware ESXi. VmWare (2010),
   http://www.vmware.com/files/br/pdf/products/VMW_09Q1_BRO_ESX
   _ESXi_BR_A4_P6_R2.pdf (access January 20, 2010)
10. Becker, M.: Qemu/systemc cosimulation at differet abstraction levels.University of Paderborn/C-LAB. Fuerstenallee 11, 33102 Paderborn,
    http://adt.cs.upb.de/quf/quf2011_proceedings.pdf#page=13
    (access January 25, 2010)

11. Virtualbox. VirtualBox. VirtualBox (2010),
    http://www.virtualbox.org/wiki/VirtualBox_architecture
    (access January 22, 2010)
12. Microsoft. Microsoft Virtual Server. Microsoft (2010),
    http://www.microsoft.com/windowsserversystem/virtualserver/
    (access January 25, 2010)
13. Lundvall, B.-Å.: National Systems of Innovation: Toward a Theory of Innovation and In-
    teractive Learning. The Anthem Other Canon Series. Paperback (January 1, 2010)
14. COBBLER. Cobbler. cobbler (2010),
    https://fedorahosted.org/cobbler/ (access March 05, 2010)
15. PUPPETLABS. Introducing Puppet. Puppetlabs (2009),
    http://www.puppetlabs.com/puppet/introduction/
    (access September 01, 2010)
16. Curtis, D., Brittain, K:. Document the IT Service Portfolio Before Creating the IT Service
    Catalog. Gartner Research. ID Number: G00163200 (January 2009),
    http://confluence.arizona.edu/confluence/download/attachment
    s/2459667/document_the_it_service_port_163200+%282%29.pdf
17. Info Magazine. Brazilian Salary Resarch. RH Info Human Resource Consulting (2010),
    http://www.rhinfo.com.br/sal-ti.htm (access November 05, 2010)
18. Deng, Y., Head, M., Kochut, A., Munson, J., Sailer, A., Shaikh, H.: An ontology based
    approach for cloud services catalog management. In: Maglio, P.P., Weske, M., Yang, J.,
    Fantinato, M. (eds.) ICSOC 2010. LNCS, vol. 6470, pp. 680–681. Springer, Heidelberg
    (2010)
19. Queiroz, M., Moura, A., Sauvé, J., Bartolini, C., Hickey, M.: A model for decision support
    in business-driven IT service portfolio management using SLA-dependent criteria and un-
    der uncertainty. In: Proceedings of the International Conference on Management of Emer-
    gent Digital EcoSystems. ACM, New York (2009)
20. Ezaki, Y., Hitoshi, M.: Integrated Management of Virtualized Infrastructure That Supports
    Cloud Computing: ServerView Resource Orchestrator. Fujitsu Science Technology Jour-
    nal (2011),
    http://www.fujitsu.com/downloads/MAG/vol47-2/paper18.pdf
21. Nof, S.Y.: Automation: What It Means to Us Around the World. Springer Handbook of
    Automation, pp. 13–52. Springer, Heidelberg (2009)
22. Wang, H.-z., Huang, L.-s.: An improved trusted cloud computing platform model based on
    DAA and Privacy CA scheme. In: IEEE International Conference on Computer Applica-
    tion and System Modeling, ICCASM 2010 (2010); ISBN: 978-1-4244-7235-2
23. Shen, Z., Li, L., Yan, F., Wu, X.: Cloud Computing System Based on Trusted Computing
    Platform. In: IEEE International Conference on Intelligent Computation Technology and
    Automation (ICICTA), China, vol. 1, pp. 942–945 (2010)
24. Li, X.-Y., Zhou, L.-T., Shi, Y., Guo, Y.: A Trusted Computing Environment Model in
    Cloud Architecture. In: Proceedings of the Ninth International Conference on Machine
    Learning and Cybernetics, Qingdao, China, pp. 11–14 (July 2010); ISBN: 978-1-4244-
    6526-2

Research on Modeling and Analysis of CPS*

Zhang Yu, Dong Yunwei, Zhang Fan, and Zhang Yunfeng

School of Computer Science and Technology, Northwestern Polytechnical University,
710072 Xi'an, China
yuzhang.nwpu@gmail.com, {yunweidong,zhangfan}@nwpu.edu.cn,
yfzhang_nwpu@163.com

Abstract. Cyber-Physical Systems (CPS) are physical and engineered systems whose operations are integrated, monitored, and controlled by embedded computational cores that are often distributed and reconfigurable online. Due to the criticality of CPS, high-confidence CPS are critical to the infrastructure of our society. We research on modeling and analysis of CPS. We propose a hierarchical and compositional modeling approach based on AADL to solve the tight coupling between physical and cyber world. We extend AADL by annex and separate the component abstraction of CPS model into three categories. And we propose basic transformation rules to translate the CPS model into the networks of timed automata. Then we use model checker UPPAAL to analysis system qualities. We present a case study about analysis of automatic collision avoidance system derived from vehicle in the end.

Keywords: CPS, AADL, networks of timed automata.

1 Introduction

As computers become ever-faster and communication bandwidth ever-cheaper, computing and communication capabilities will be embedded in all types of objects and structures in the physical environment. Such systems that bridge the cyber-world of computing and communications with the physical world are called CPS [1].

CPS is integrations of computation with physical processes. Embedded computers and networks monitor and control the physical processes, usually with feedback loops where physical processes affect computations and vice versa [2]. The cyber and physical components of CPS cooperatively deliver system functionalities and jointly contribute to properties such as temporal correctness, real-time response, and energy conservation. CPS engineering must account for the interacting and interdependent behaviors of both types of components to provide system-level property guarantees. CPS is a new research direction in recent years, but as its scientific and technological importance as well as its potential impact on grand challenges in a number of critical, CPS have received increasing attention from industry to academia.

With the increasing non-function attributes (security, safety and reliability) requirements of embedded system, MDA (Model Driven Architecture) which allow

---

* This paper is supported by the National Science Foundation of China (No.60736017) and National High-Tech Research and Development Plan of China (No. 2011AA010101).

J.M. Alcaraz Calero et al. (Eds.): ATC 2011, LNCS 6906, pp. 92–105, 2011.

detecting problems with these non-functional properties early on are becoming more and more popular. Karsai [3] proposes a model-integrated development approach that addresses the development needs of such CPS through the pervasive use of models. A complete model-based view is proposed that covers all aspects of the hardware and software components, as well as their interactions. Jensen [4] decomposes MBD into ten fundamental steps and introduces an iterative design process. Both of the modeling approaches in their report are only a preview. Various formal languages have been proposed for specifying embedded systems, e.g., LOTOS [5], Co-design Finite State Machines (CFSMs) [6], and Petri-net based languages such as PRES [7]. Models in these languages are verified directly or indirectly (via translation). AADL [8] (Architecture Analysis and Design Language) is a modeling language which supports MDA to analysis architecture of systems with respect to the non-functional properties. But AADL is a modeling language for embedded software system and lack of capacity to specify physical process.

Well-known tools for analysis hybrid systems include UPPAAL [9], HyTech [10], Kronos [11], etc. The performance of UPPAAL is much better than other tools like HyTech, and Kronos in time and space [12]. UPPAAL is a model checker for real-time systems, based on constraint-solving and on-the-fly techniques, developed jointly by Uppsala University and Aalborg University. It is appropriate for systems that can be modeled as a collection of non-deterministic processes with finite control structure and real-valued clocks, communicating through channels or shared variables.

The next section provides an overview of AADL and timed automata. Section 3 gives a detailed modeling technology to define a component-based architectural for CPS. Section 4 presents research on analysis of CPS. Section 5 presents a case study to the analysis of automatic collision avoidance system derived from vehicle. Section 6 summarizes our work and prospect.

2   AADL and Timed Automata

2.1   Overview of AADL

In November 2004, the Society of Automotive Engineers (SAE) released the aerospace standard AS5506, named AADL. The AADL is a modeling language that supports early and repeated analyses of a system's architecture with respect to performance-critical properties through an extendable notation, a tool framework, and precisely defined semantics [13].

The language employs formal modeling concepts for the description and analysis of application system architectures in terms of distinct components and their interactions. It includes abstractions of software, computational hardware, and system components for (a) specifying and analyzing real-time embedded and high dependability systems, complex systems, and specialized performance capability systems and (b) mapping of software onto computational hardware elements.

The AADL is especially effective for model-based analysis and specification of complex real-time embedded systems. The component abstractions of AADL are shown in Fig.1.

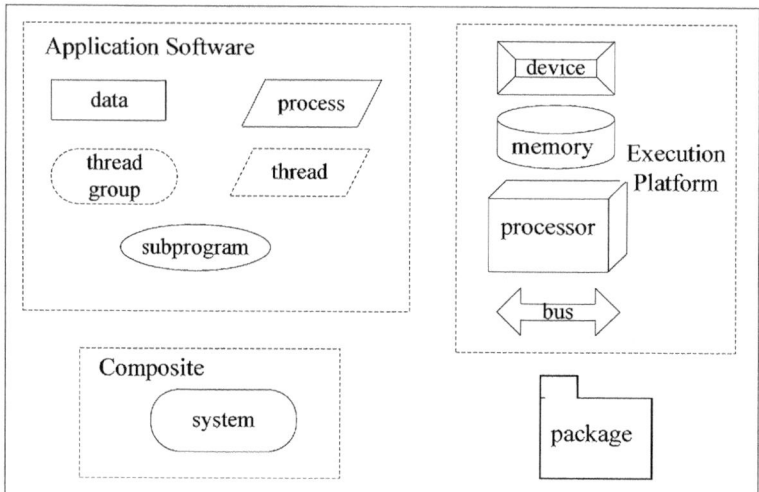

Fig. 1. Component Abstraction of the AADL

AADL annex enables a user to extend the AADL, allowing the incorporation of specialized notations within a standard AADL model. For example, a formal language that enables an analysis of a critical aspect of a system (e.g., reliability analysis, security, or behavior) can be included within an AADL specification. In addition, AADL mode represents an operational mode state, which manifests itself as a configuration of contained components, connections, and mode-specific property value associations. When multiple modes are declared for a component, a mode transition behavior specifies possible runtime passage which events cause a mode switch and the new mode.

2.2   Overview of Timed Automata

Timed automata [14] were introduced as a formal notation to model the behavior of real-time systems. Its definition provides a simple, and yet general, way to annotate state-transition graphs with timing constraints using finitely many real-valued clock variables. Automated analysis of timed automata relies on the construction of a finite quotient of the infinite space of clock valuations.

Clock Constraints & Clock Interpretations
An atomic constraint compares a clock value with a time constant, and a clock constraint is a conjunction of atomic constraint. Any value from Q, the set of nonnegative rational, can be used as a time constant. Formally, for a set X of clock variables, the set $\Phi(x)$ of clock constraints ϕ is defined by the grammar

$$\phi := x \leq c \mid c \leq x \mid x < c \mid c < x \mid \phi_1 \wedge \phi_2, \tag{1}$$

where x is a clock in X and c is a constant in Q.

A clock interpretation v for a set X of clocks assigns a real value to each clock: that is, it is a mapping from X to the set R of nonnegative real. We say that a clock interpretation v for X satisfies a clock constraint Φ over X if Φ evaluates to true according to the values given by v.

Timed automata
Timed automata T is six tuples <S, S^0, A, X, I, E>, where

S is a finite set of locations,
$S^0 \subseteq S$ is a set of initial locations,
A is a finite set of labels,
X is a finite set of clocks,

I is a mapping that labels each locations in S with some clock constraint in $\Phi(x)$, and $E \subseteq S \times A \times 2X \times \Phi(x) \times S$ is the set of switches. A switch <s, a, Φ, λ, s'> represents a transition from location s to location s' on symbol a. Φ is a clock constraint over X that specifies when the switch is enabled, and the set $\lambda \subseteq X$ gives the clocks to be reset with this switch.

The semantics of a timed automation A is defined by associating a transition system S_A with it. A state of S_A is a pair (s, v) such that s is a location of A and v is a clock interpretation for X such that v satisfies the invariant I(s). There are two types of transitions in S_A: State can change due to elapse of time; State can change due to a location switch.

3   Modeling

Due to the inherent and ever-growing complexities of CPS, modeling technologies must be scalable. And the modeling technology must specify the intellectual heart of CPS: tight coupling between physical and cyber process. We adopt a hierarchical and compositional approach to model CPS. The core of this approach is based on AADL.

We extend AADL by annex. The component abstraction of CPS is shown in Fig.2. The component abstraction of the CPS model is separated into three categories: cyber component, physical component and interactive component. Below we will detail the three components.

3.1   Cyber Component

The cyber component are represented by AADL. AADL is used to model and analyze the software and hardware architecture of embedded systems. The main modeling notion of AADL is component.

Within the AADL, a component is characterized by its identity (a unique name and runtime essence), possible interfaces with other components, distinguishing properties (critical characteristics of a component within its architectural context), and subcomponents and their interactions. Components can be a software application or an execution platform. The cyber components include: thread, thread group, process, data, subprogram, processor, memory, bus and system [8].

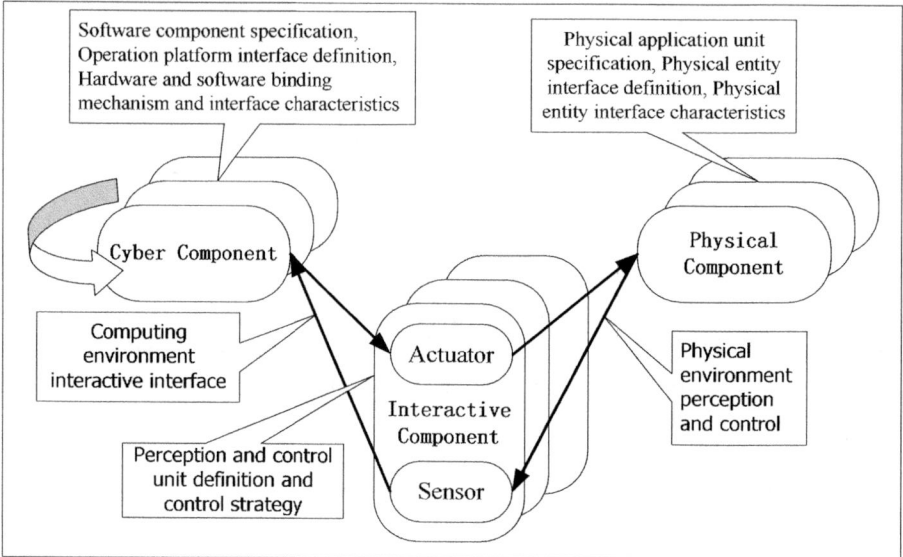

Fig. 2. Component Abstraction of CPS

3.2   Physical Component

Physical process is mainly represented by differential equation. The most important problem in the research of modeling and analysis of CPS is not the union of cyber and physical problems, but rather their tight coupling between physical and cyber world. We use agent-based technique to model the physical process [15, 16].

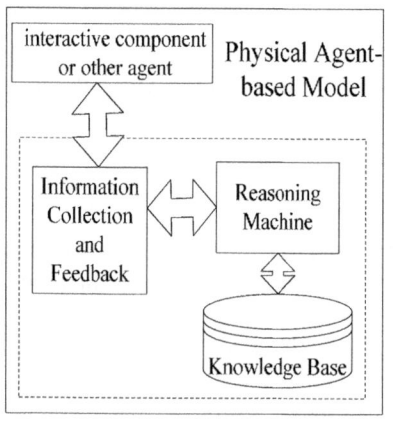

Function Physical_Agent (percept) return action
{
   Static:
   state,   /*current state desperation of agent*/
   rules,   /*reaction rules*/
/* Perception reaction*/
   state <--> interpret <--> Input/Output (percept);
   /*match based on rules*/
   rule <-- Rule_Match(state, rules) ;
/*generate action based on rules */
   action <-- Rule_Action(rule);
   return action;
}

(a) Composition of Physical Agent-Based   (b) Mechanism of Physical Agent-Based

Fig. 3. Physical Agent-Based model

A Physical Component P is five tuples <S, R, I, C, A>, where S is a finite set of states, R is a finite set of rules, I is a finite set of reasoning functions, C is a finite set of communication and control, A is a set of actions. The physical agent-based model is shown in Fig.3.

The autonomy and adaptivity of agents enables them to capture the cyber abstractions and interfaces [17]. According to the "stimulate - response" model, the work process of Physical_Agent is from sensory information to output action, namely "judge condition - generate action". According to the information from outside and reaction rules, it selects the best action, and then performs the action and updates the content of knowledge base according to the action of environmental impact.

For example, we model vehicle. We focus on velocity and position for a vehicle. Changes in position or velocity are governed by Newton's laws which are reaction rules. The position of a vehicle in space, therefore, is represented by function of the form f: R → R. Functions of this form are known as continuous signals. Velocity and position are the integral of acceleration, given by

$$\begin{cases} \forall t > 0, \dot{x}(t) = \dot{x}(0) + \int_0^t \ddot{x}(\tau)d\tau \\ \\ \forall t > 0, x(t) = x(0) + \int_0^t \dot{x}(\tau)d\tau \end{cases} \tag{2}$$

where x represents position, $\dot{x}$ represents velocity, $\ddot{x}$ is the second derivative of x with respect to time (the acceleration).

By utilizing the extension capabilities of AADL, we build CPS annex. The CPS annex can be used to define physical agent-based model and properties of components facilitating analysis of the architecture.

3.3   Interactive Component

The interactive components are represented by the AADL component device. The device component can be viewed as a unit in the environment that is accessed or controlled by the cyber and physical component.

Device abstractions represent entities that interface with the external environment of an application system. The interactive components include sensor and actuator. Sensor gathers information from physical process. And the actuators according to computing result to affect the physical process. Through the interactive component, we can represent the closed-loop interactions between physical and cyber process.

Therefore, Our CPS model include three types of component: cyber component, physical component and interactive component. Components interact exclusively through defined interfaces. A component interface consists of directional flow through: data ports, event data ports, event ports for asynchronous events, synchronous subprogram calls and explicit access to data components. Within the architectural for CPS, property sets can be declared that include new properties for components and other modeling elements. So the CPS model can define the interaction of distributed software components, the networks that bind them together, and the interaction via sensors and actuators with physical dynamics.

4   Analysis with Timed Automata Network

Based on the component-based architectural for CPS, we research on analysis of CPS. We propose an approach based on networks of timed automata. According to transformation rules, we translate the CPS model to the networks of timed automata. And then use model checker UPPAAL to analysis system qualities. The analysis process is shown in Fig.4.

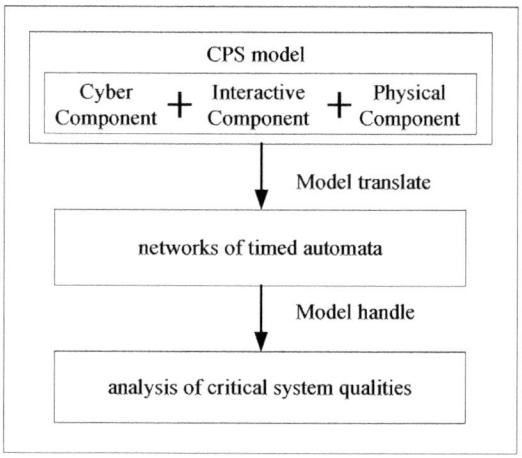

Fig. 4. Analysis Process of CPS

We mainly focus on the early prediction and analysis of critical system qualities—such as safety, security, and reliability. The analysis is based on component and at the architectural design level. Timed automata network is a set of timed automata $\{T_1 \| \ldots \| T_n\}$. Several timed automata are run in parallel and synchronised with one another. Those timed automata are interacted each other via channel or shared variables as a whole.

Suppose that as in section 2, state machines T_1 and T_2 are given by the six tuples,

$$T_1 = <S_{T1}, \ S^0_{T1}, \ A_{T1}, \ X, \ I_{T1}, \ E_{T1}> , \tag{3}$$

$$T_2 = <S_{T2}, \ S^0_{T2}, \ A_{T2}, \ X, \ I_{T2}, \ E_{T2}> , \tag{4}$$

Then the networks of timed automata T is given by

$$T = T_1 \| T_2 = <S_T, \ S^0_T, \ A_T, \ X, \ I_T, \ E_T> , \tag{5}$$

where $S_T = S_{T1} \times S_{T2}$,
$$S^0{}_T = (S^0{}_{T1}, S^0{}_{T2}),$$
$$A_T = (A_{T1}, A_{T2}),$$
$$I_T = (I_{T1}, I_{T2}),$$

E_T:
$$\frac{T_1 \xrightarrow{A_{T1}, x, \phi(x_{T1})} T_1'}{T_1 \parallel T_2 \xrightarrow{A_{T1}, x, \phi(x_{T1})} T_1' \parallel T_2},$$

$$\frac{T_2 \xrightarrow{A_{T2}, x, \phi(x_{T2})} T_2'}{T_1 \parallel T_2 \xrightarrow{A_{T2}, x, \phi(x_{T2})} T_1 \parallel T_2'},$$

$$\frac{T_1 \xrightarrow{A_{T1}} T_1', T_2 \xrightarrow{A_{T2}} T_2'}{T_1 \parallel T_2 \xrightarrow{A_{T1} \cup A_{T2}} T_1' \parallel T_2'},$$

$$\frac{T_1 \xrightarrow{x} T_1', T_2 \xrightarrow{x} T_2'}{T_1 \parallel T_2 \xrightarrow{x} T_1' \parallel T_2'}.$$

4.1 Transformation Rules

We translate the CPS model into the timed automata to analysis non-functional properties of CPS systems. There are three types of component: cyber component, physical component and interactive component. Components interact exclusively through defined interfaces. And Interactions among components are specified explicitly. Two complementary approaches are identified [2]: cyberizing the physical (CtP) means to endow physical subsystems with cyber-like abstractions and interfaces; and physicalizing the cyber (PtC) means to endow software and network components with abstractions and interfaces that represent their dynamics in time. And we take the cyberizing the physical approach. So we analyze connection relationship between components by the following transformation rules.

Rule 1: Map the cyber component to the timed automata based on AADL mode.

Rule 2: Map the physical component to the timed automata based on physical reaction rules.

Rule 3: Map the interactive component to channel or shared variable.

Rule 4: The two categories (cyber component and interactive component) with physical component must be alternative in a timed automaton. Map them to different timed automata in timed automata network.

Rule 5: Map constraint (timing requirements such as period, worst-case execution time, arrival rates and deadlines) between ports in cyber component and interactive component to jump guard in timed automata.

4.2 Analysis with UPPAAL

Based on transformation rules, we can build timed automata network. And then we can analyze the networks of timed automata instead of CPS model. The networks of timed automata can capture discrete continuous changes with differential equations.

So we can use UPPAAL to analyze networks of timed automata. By the tool, we analyze all possible executions which include all states and state transitions. Now we can take two basic analysis algorithms: reachability analysis and loop detection.

Reachability analysis checks safety property. It checks whether something (bad) happen or not. Loop detection checks liveness property. Liveness property means something (good) must happen/should be repeated.

We can use requirement specification language of UPPAAL (shown in Table 1) to check system qualities [9]. Below is Requirement Specification BNF-grammar.

$$\text{Prop::= 'A[]' Expression | 'E<>' Expression | 'E[]' Expression | A<> Expression | Expression --> Expression .} \tag{6}$$

Table 1. Requirement Specification Language of UPPAAL

Name	Property	Equivalent Property
Possibly	E<> P	
Invariantly	A[]P	not E<> not P
Potentially always	E[]P	
Eventually	A<>P	not E[] not P
Leads to	P-->Q	A[] (P imply A<>Q)

UPPAAL supports powerful checking functions. Through the tool, we can find the early prediction and analysis of critical system qualities efficiently.

5   Case Study

In this paper we present a case study in the application of our approach to the analysis of ACAS (Automatic Collision Avoidance System) derived from vehicle.

ACAS is aimed at prevent collisions and improve vehicle safety. In ACAS, vehicle measures distance of roadblock over range radar to allow itself to track vehicle and predict possible collisions. Here we simplified the scene. Vehicle is driven in a one-way street. And we only consider dangerous ahead. VSC compares the distance between safe braking and roadblock to make samrt instructions, such as emergency brake for safety precaution. The Architecture of ACAS is shown in Fig.5.

The Architecture of ACAS contains three subsystems: Vehicle_System, Vehicle_Speed_Control_System and Warning_System.

Vehicle_System represents physical vehicle. As we focus on velocity and position for a vehicle, Vehicle_System describe changes in position or velocity which is based on Newton's laws (see equation 2).

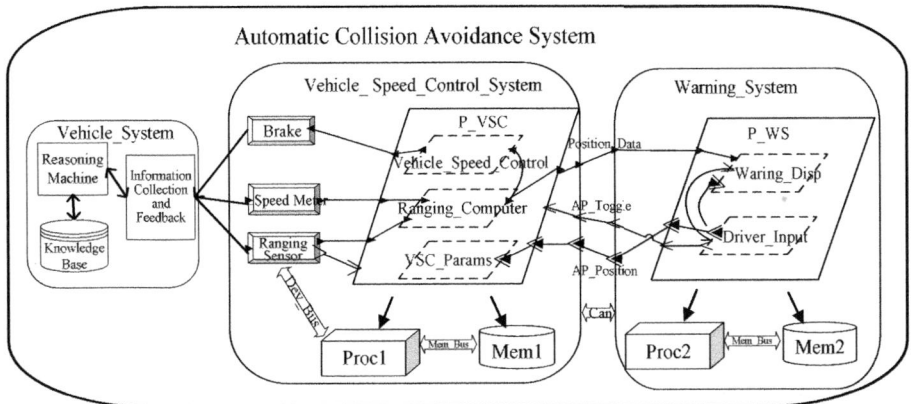

Fig. 5. The Architecture of ACAS

Vehicle_Speed_Control_System implements core function. It collects the physical information from sensor (Ranging Sensor and Speed Meter), compute this information, and then generate feedback control to affect vehicle through actuator (Brake). The process P_VSC contains three threads: Ranging_Computer, Vehicle_Speed_Control and VSC_Params. Ranging_Computer calculates and analyzes current situation based on physical information. Vehicle_Speed_Control controls Brake according to instruction from Ranging_Computer. VSC_Params receives the driver input parameters from Warning_System and updates the internal data structures of this process accordingly.

The Warning_System implements the interactivity between driver and ACAS. It considers the driver factor. The driver can shutdown ACAS manually.

Based on our basic transformation rules, we build timed automata network. There are five timed automata in the network: DS, PV, VSC, PVSC and WS. DS and PV represent physical process. And the other three automata represent cyber process. DS, which is shown in Fig.6, specifies distance of roadblock and uses shared variable L to trace the distance. PV, which is shown in Fig.7, specifies velocity of vehicle and uses shared variable V to trace the velocity. WS, which is shown in Fig.8, represents Warning_System and uses shared variable ip to trace driver input. VSC, which is shown in Fig.9, represents result status of Vehicle_Speed_Control. PVSC, which is shown in Fig.10, represents P_VSC. Each related timed automata are connected by channel or shared variable. PV uses channel ac, dc and done to indicate the vehicle is accelerating, slow or halt. PVSC uses shared variables emer and channel ec to inform whether take emergency brake or not.

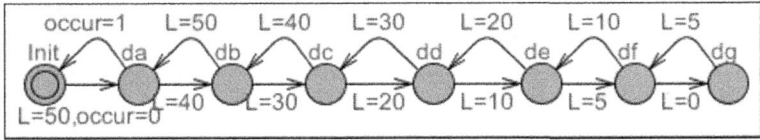

Fig. 6. Modeling the Distance between Safe Braking and Roadblock(DS). The location in this timed automaton represents distance state, such as da representation of 50 meters. It uses shared variable L to record the distance.

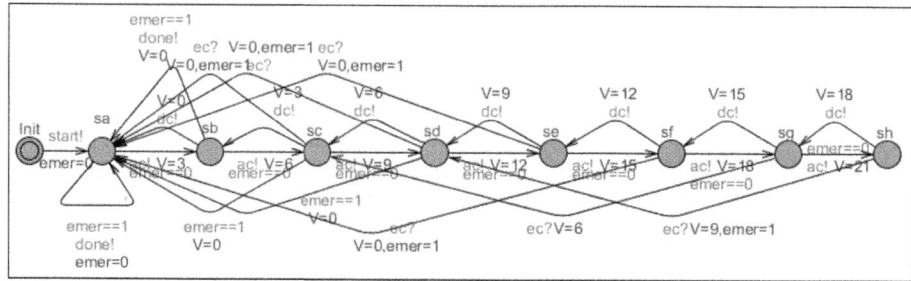

Fig. 7. Modeling the Physical Vehicle (PV). The location in this timed automaton represents velocity of vehicle, such as sh representation of 21 meters per second. It uses shared variable V to record the velocity.

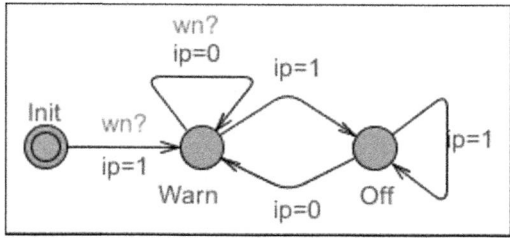

Fig. 8. Modeling the Warning_System(WS). The location in this timed automaton represents the Warning_System's on/off state. It uses shared variable ip to record driver input.

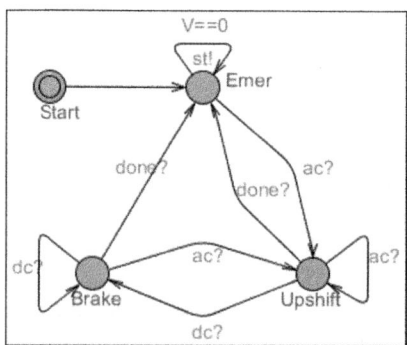

Fig. 9. Modeling the Vehicle_Speed_Control(VSC). The location in this timed automaton represents the result status of Vehicle_Speed_Control. There are three states: Brake state, Upshift state and Emer state. The transition between locations is mainly based on timed automaton PV through channel.

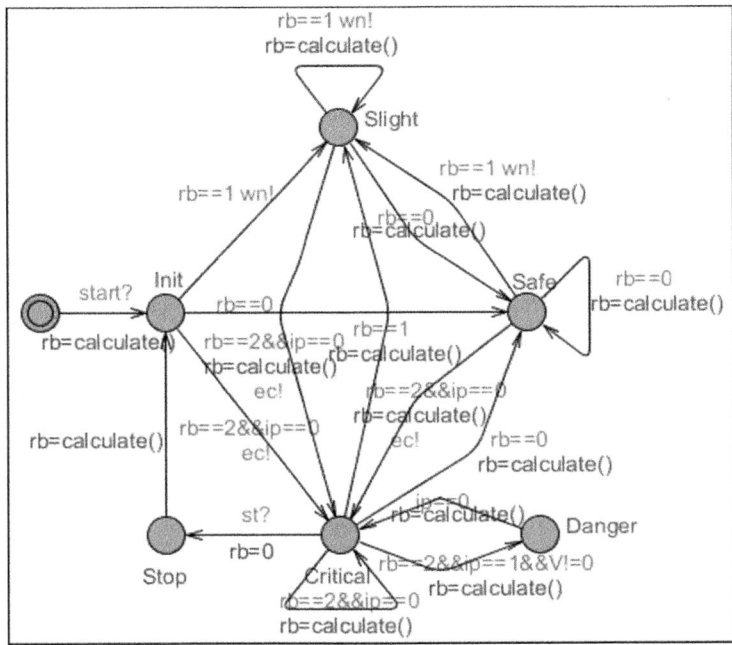

Fig. 10. Modeling the P_VSC (PVSC). The location in this timed automaton represents the state of vehicle speed control. There are five major states: Critical state, Danger state, Slight state, Safe state and Stop state. The function, calculate(), is used to estimate the vehicle safety conditions. The timed automaton controls vehicle by channel ec. It collects the distance of roadblock and velocity of vehicle by shared variable L and V.

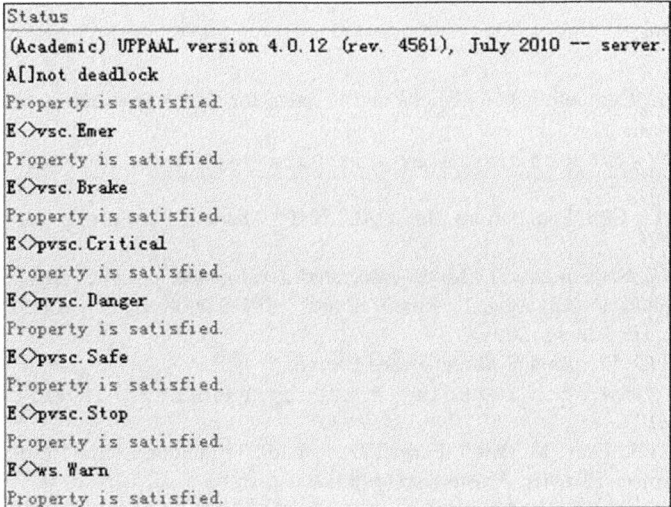

Fig. 11. Result of Analysis with UPPAAL. This shows that the ACAS doesn't deadlock and the location in the timed automata network is reachable.

And then we analyze the reachability and the deadlock of the ACAS. The analysis result is shown in Fig.11. From the analysis results, it is clear that the ACAS doesn't deadlock. States contained in each of them can be reachable. So the properties which we concern are satisfied. We assure the ACAS is trustworthy according our analysis.

6   Conclusion and Future Work

The paper proposed a modeling and analysis approach to assure the high-confidence CPS. We adopt a hierarchical and compositional modeling approach based on AADL to solve the inherent multi-semantics nature between physical and cyber process. We research on analysis approach based on networks of timed automata. According to our basic transformation rules, we translate the CPS model to the networks of timed automata. And then use model checker UPPAAL to analysis system qualities. We present a case study to prove the feasibility of the approach.

The combination of AADL, timed automata, and UPPAAL is a natural, realistic approach to analysis CSP for some non-functional properties. Our experiment verifies our approach how well the combination worked for CPS. Due to the inherent and ever-growing complexities of CPS, modeling and analysis technologies must be scalable. Major challenges that must be addressed in order to achieve scalable CPS analysis include: (1) how to design for effective analysis; (2) how to cope with the inherent multi-semantics nature of the cyber and physical components. Therefore, we plan to research compositional verification to effectively reduce the verification complexities and reuse the verification efforts when possible. We will further perform more experiments with more subtle situations. Moreover, we will enhance the ability of specification definition of CPS and consider the timing semantics of CPS.

References

1. Lee, E.A.: Computing Foundations and Practice for Cyber-Physical Systems: A Preliminary Report,
   http://www.eecs.berkeley.edu/Pubs/TechRpts/2007/EECS-2007-72.html
2. Lee, E.A.: CPS Foundations. In: DAC 2010, Anaheim, California, USA, June 13-18 (2010)
3. Karsai, G., Sztipanovits, J.: Model-integrated development of cyber-physical systems. In: Brinkschulte, U., Givargis, T., Russo, S. (eds.) SEUS 2008. LNCS, vol. 5287, pp. 46–54. Springer, Heidelberg (2008)
4. Jensen, J.C.: Elements of Model-Based Design,
   http://www.eecs.berkeley.edu/Pubs/TechRpts/2010/EECS-2010-19.html
5. Van Eijk, P., Diaz, M. (eds.): Formal Description Technique Lotos: Results of the Esprit Sedos Project. Elsevier, Amsterdam (1989)
6. Balarin, F., Hsieh, H., Jurecska, A., Lavagno, L., Sangiovanni-Vincentelli, A.L.: Formal verification of embedded systems based on CFSM networks. In: DAC (1996)

7. Cortes, L.A., Eles, P., Peng, Z.: Formal coverification of embedded systems using model checking. In: EUROMICRO (2000)
8. SAE Aerospace. SAE AS5506: Architecture Analysis and Design Language (AADL), Version 1.0 (2004)
9. Larsen, K.G., Pettersson, P., Yi, W.: Uppaal in a nutshell. International Journal on Software Tools for Technology Transfer 1(1-2), 134–152 (1997)
10. Henzinger, T.A., Ho, P.-H., Howard, W.-T.: Hytech: A model checker for hybrid systems. International Journal on Software Tools for Technology Transfer 1(1-2) (1997)
11. Yovine, S.: Kronos: A verification tool for real-time systems. International Journal on Software Tools for Technology Transfer 1(1-2), 123–133 (1997)
12. Hua, G., Lei, Z., Xiyong, Z.: UPRAAL-a Tool Suit for Automatic Verification of Real-time Systems. Control and Automation Publication Group 22(5-3), 52–54 (2006)
13. Feiler, P.H., Gluch, D.P., Hudak, J.J.: The Architecture Analysis & Design Language (AADL): An Introduction. International Society of Automotive Engineers, USA (2006)
14. Alur, R., Dill, D.L.: A theory of Timed Automata. Theoretieal Computer Science 126, 183–235 (1994)
15. Rinaldi, S.M.: Modeling and simulating critical infrastructures and their interdependencies. In: Proceeding of the 37th Annual Hawaii International Conference on System Sciences (2004)
16. Lin, J., Sedigh, S., Miller, A.: A General Framework for Quantitative Modeling of Dependability in Cyber-Physical Systems: A Proposal for Doctoral Research. In: The 33rd Annual IEEE International Computer Software and Applications Conference (2009)
17. Macal, C.M., North, M.J.: Tutorial on agent-based modeling and simulation. In: Proceeding of the 37th Winter Simulation Conference, WSC 2005 (2005)

Towards a Protocol for Autonomic Covert Communication

Wanqi Li and Guanglei He

Computer Science and Engineering Department, Sichuan University Jinjiang College,
620860 Penshan, China
vanchi.lee.7@gmail.com, guanglei@gmail.com

Abstract. The complexity of covert communication management is the main barrier towards the massive application of covert communication. In this paper, a protocol for autonomic covert communication is proposed to deal with the management complexity of covert communication system, and the environmental changes in the course of covert communication. Simulation results are provided to illustrate the self-star properties of the proposed scheme.

Keywords: Covert communication, autonomic computing, evolution, batch steganography, protocol.

1 Introduction

Encrypted communication focuses on keeping the content of communication meaningless to unauthorized parties, while covert communication aims to conceal the very existence of communication using steganographic or watermarking schemes, so that the adversary can't find an evident target to attack. In the course of covert communication, the message is sent through the host channel by hiding it within the cover signal, and extracted by the target recipient with a shared key. Since covert communication won't change the throughput of the host communication channel, and the alteration on the cover signal is of small amount, the secret information is expected to be invisible both spatially and statistically.

In covert communication, message is embedded in the redundancy of cover signal. Despite the fact that almost all digital media are suitable for covert communication, digital image is the standard choice because of its ubiquitous presence and abundant redundancy. However, information hiding would inevitably disturb the statistical features of the cover image because of the Markov type property of the image pixels, and the experience has told us that the statistical distortion caused by the embedding process will eventually leak the presence of the hidden information [1-12]. The main concerns of steganography are undetectability and capacity, while watermarking pays more attention to removal resistance. These two classes of information hiding schemes can be selected accordingly to handle different types of communication circumstances.

J.M. Alcaraz Calero et al. (Eds.): ATC 2011, LNCS 6906, pp. 106–117, 2011.

Cover and stego objects are frequently represented by feature vectors in the process of steganography and steganalysis, where the feature values are supposed to be connected with detectability [1-3, 11-19]. The embedding impact (or distortion) is defined in regard to the distance between the stego object (a point in the feature space) and the cloud of cover objects. The game of modern steganography is for the hider to minimize the embedding impact and for the warden (the adversary aiming at destroying the hidden data) to try her or his best to distinguish stego objects from the innocent [20]. Though there're remarkable attempts to give quantitative definitions of stego security [21-22], a steganographic scheme is considered secure if the warden can detect the stego object no better than random guessing. Since the distributions of cover and stego objects in the feature space are highly dependent on the cover source, the stego scheme applied, the setting of the stego scheme and the embedding rate (the ratio of bits embedded and bits sent), it is essential for the hider to choose appropriate parameters considering the current circumstance, in order to achieve the desired degree of robustness of the covert communication system. A system is called robust if it can resist against the uncertainties of environmental changes.

However, figuring out the appropriate parameters for a covert communication system under different circumstances is a very sophisticated task even for an expert with related background, not to mention when it comes to an ordinary user. And it is the complexity of covert communication management that blocks the way towards massive application of covert communication. The complexity of covert communication management is mainly caused by the subtle dependences between different components of the system, rather than the scale of the software. In fact, the software of steganography or watermarking is usually quite uncomplicated. There're simply too many choices to make for the system given too little information. Furthermore, most parameters can't be determined until the run time because of their dependencies on the actual communication environment, and many parameters need to be adjusted constantly in regard to the environmental changes.

In this paper, an autonomic covert communication system is introduced to deal with the complexity of covert communication management. Self-management property is essential for the system to adapt to the environmental changes of covert communication. The management of communication system is described as an evolutionary process on the way of improving the survivability of the system in AORTA (AutonOmic network control and mAnagement system) introduced in [23]. The proposed covet communication system in this paper also adopts the basic idea of "natural select" on the way to "survive" in regard to the environmental changes.

The problem of designing practical covert communication system is evidently related to batch steganography and pooled steganalysis [9-11], because communication is usually expected to be mutual and constant rather than one-way and one-off. But since its first introduction in [9] 2003, very inadequate attention has been paid to this subject with regard to its importance for massive application. The author believes that the main reason for this inaction is that designing robust autonomic covert communication system is a mission that could only be achieved with participants from both the fields of autonomic computing and information hiding.

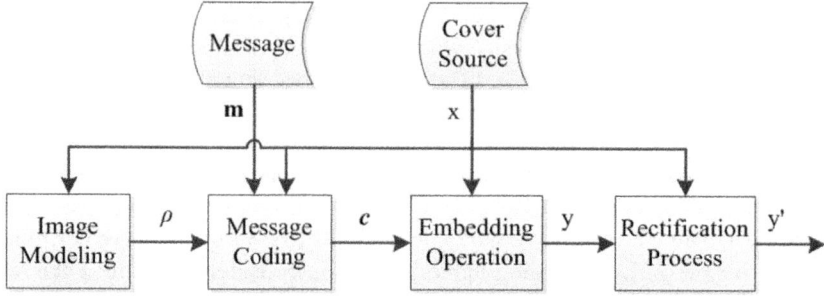

Fig. 1. High-level diagram of a steganography algorithm

The aim of this paper is to give a tentative discussion of the problem of designing efficient, reliable and application-friendly covert communication system of self-* properties [24] and the result is a basic protocol for autonomic covert communication. In the next section, the problem of autonomic covert communication is formally described. A basic protocol for autonomic covert communication is introduced in Section 3. Simulation results are provided in Section 4. Conclusions and an outline for future work are given in Section 5.

2   Problem Formulation

In this paper, a cover object refers to an object originally generated by the cover source, whether or not there's embedded message in it. A packet refers to a stego object with certain amount of hidden information. Since discussions in this paper are not confined to any specific stego scheme, a packet is considered as the basic unit of communication, rather than stego elements like pixels. For readers unfamiliar with steganography and steganalysis, introductions and reviews of the related topics can be found in [1, 4, 12, 25-26].

2.1   Covert Communication

In order to avoid causing abnormal throughput of the host channel, at least one cover source is required for the sender to conduct covert communication. The sender is supposed to be able to hide information in the "innocent" cover objects generated by the source, i.e. for each source, the sender occupies at least one applicable stego or watermarking scheme.

Denote a cover object as x and the ith cover source as X_i. Then x is an instance of the random variable X_i. Let $\pi_\theta(x)$ be the feature vector of object x in the feature space, which is dependent on the stego setting θ. Since we don't have any assumption about the involved stego schemes, we'll simply say that $\theta = \theta_0$ if there's no hidden message in the object, and $\theta = \theta_1$ otherwise, where θ_0 is the null stego setting and θ_1 is the stego setting for a specific stego scheme. The null stego setting θ_0 corresponds to the original cover object, while θ_1 describes the stego scheme, penalty function, coding algorithm, embedding operation, embedding rectification method and all the related parameters used to embed the message [1-3, 9, 13-19, 32]. A high-level diagram of a steganography algorithm is shown in fig. 1. Detailed discussion of each component in fig. 1 is beyond the scope of this paper. The basic object considered in this work, as mentioned above, is the output of the stego algorithm, which we call a packet. In this paper, the only thing we need to know about the embedding process is that the stego setting θ_1 contains all the necessary specifications of a steganographic algorithm, which dictates the statistical features of the generated stego object.

With the above notations, the problem of steganalysis can be formulated in the form of statistical hypothesis testing with a feature vector $\pi_\theta(x)$:

$$H_0 : \theta = \theta_0 \text{ (no embedded message)}$$
$$H_1 : \theta = \theta_1 , r > 0 \text{ (there is embedded message)} \tag{1}$$

A warden is said to be active if she or he is always trying to remove the hidden message in the suspected objects. In the later part of this paper, an active warden is assumed to have full access to all packets through the host channel.

Since the embedded message might be removed or destroyed by the warden, the information channel (IC) of covert communication is not reliable. To implement reliable communication over unreliable channel, certain kind of feedback mechanism is required. Define the rate of successful transmission (RST) as $p = c_{ACK}/c_{sent}$, where c_{ACK} is the number of acknowledged packets and c_{sent} is the number of packets sent. The RST p is expected to have inverse ratio with the embedding rate r, which is defined as $r =$ bits embedded $/$ bits sent , because the more bits embedded, the more likely the warden would notice the statistical distortion of the stego object [9-10, 12, 22]. In addition to embedding rate, RST is also affected by the stego setting θ_1 , characteristics of the corresponding source X_i, and the warden's ability of detection. The bandwidth of the covert communication channel is defined as $B = rpN$, where N is the number of bits sent through the host channel per unit time. A sender's task is to choose appropriate stego setting θ_1 from the set Θ of all candidate stego settings and control the embedding rate r for available sources with the aim of improving the bandwidth B.

Note that the content of the embedded message is supposed to be protected by mechanisms under Kerckhoffs's principle, so that the warden is incapable of extracting the embedded information without the secret key, which makes her or him a passive attacker [10-11, 21-22].

2.2   Communication Environment and Uncertainties

The external communication environment consists of two parts: the set of all available sources $X_i \subset \mathcal{X}$ and the unknown warden. Unfortunately, both of them are uncertain (stochastic) entities and their statistical features might change instantly without a warning. The available sources are dictated by the host channel and its traffics are very hard to predict. The warden's behavior is largely unknown. We address the warden's problem [10], which is described by (1), in three different cases:

- θ_0 and θ_1 are completely known. This means that the stego scheme in consideration is public. Examples fit situation can be found in [4-8, 12].
- θ_0 and θ_1 are partially known. This means that a large training set is available to be used to estimate the stego settings. Steganalysis schemes under this category can be found in [2-3, 9, 12].
- θ_0 and θ_1 are completely unknown. Clustering techniques are used to attack this problem in [11].

There are two options for the warden to remove the hidden message in a suspect packet. One is to remove the hidden message by altering the packet. The first option is enough to most steganographic schemes. But when it comes to the message embedded by watermarking scheme, which is of strong removal resistance, the warden might have to destroy the hidden message along with the cover object. In either case, the recipient is not supposed to receive the secret message.

By collecting available stego schemes and cover-stego object pairs, the warden can adjust the feature set and train the classifier accordingly towards better detection accuracy. Thus if the sender is using fixed sources and stego settings, sooner or later, the warden will find a leak. An archetypal illustration of this situation can be found in Fridrich's report of last year's BOSS competition [2-3, 13, 27]. So for the sake of robustness, we also expect the interior environment, i.e. the set Θ of all candidate stego settings, is unpredictable for the warden, which means the process of stego setting selection should observe stochastic from the outside.

2.3   Evolution and Optimization

The distribution of cover objects in the feature space is determined by the cover source and the feature set applied. It is the stego setting and embedding rate that dictate the distance from the stego object to the cloud of cover objects in the feature space, which is directly related to the detection rate (chance that a stego object is detected). The only way for the sender to improve the bandwidth is to find the optimal stego settings and rates for different sources and cover objects.

As described above, if the secret message is successfully extracted by the recipient, the sender is supposed to receive some kind of feedback. Based on the feedback information, the system will update the corresponding RST and other records describing the external environment. All these records are used to evaluate the "survivability" of different stego settings under the current circumstance. To improve the expected bandwidth, survivable stego settings with higher embedding rate will be selected by the system. So in effect, the bandwidth will be gradually optimized as the system is adapting to the environment. The set Θ of all applicable candidate stego settings shall be maintained continually so that when a stego setting is found invalid against the warden's detection, it can be removed from the candidate list. Sometimes an updated version of a scheme or a new scheme is needed. The embedding rates for different sources and stego settings also need to be constantly adjusted in regard to the environment. The result of the constant optimization of the system is the continual evolution towards the adaptation to the changing environment.

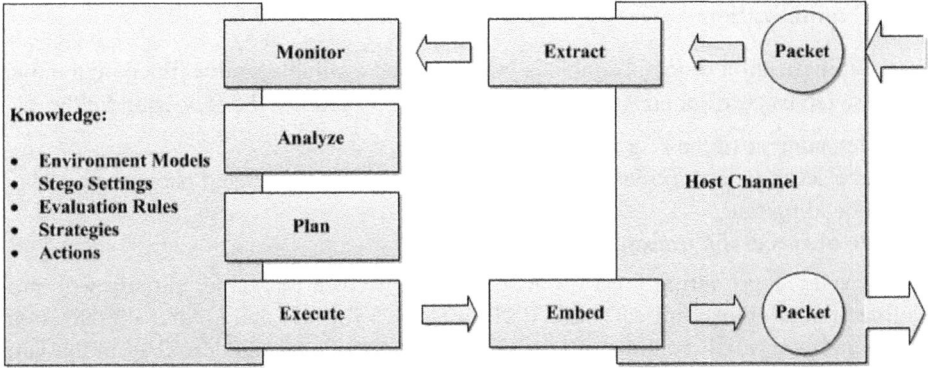

Fig. 2. Structure of an autonomic element

2.4   Autonomic Covert Communication System

The evolutionary process described above is very similar to the process of natural selection. Each candidate stego setting is assigned a survival value w.r.t. the knowledge acquired from the environment. Only the stego settings with acceptable survival value will be selected. Because the actual evaluation rule and evolution strategy might be distinct for different applications, we avoid giving any specific description about them for the reason of generality.

IBM's "Autonomic Computing" framework [24] is used as a reference model to sketch our basic idea. As shown in fig. 2, the managed element parasites on the host channel. The autonomic manager is responsible to control the embedding and extraction process, and optimize the system according to the environment information acquired from the feedbacks. The warden is not presented in this diagram, because it's not what the autonomic manager can observe directly. Environmental model describes the way the autonomic manager perceives the environment, and it could be extremely simple when the IC is assumed to be secure and reliable; or extremely sophisticated when the IC is unreliable and the topology of the autonomic communication network is very complicated and dynamic [28-29]. Evaluation rule is used to assign survival values to all stego settings in Θ. Different evaluation rule shall be selected for different goals like maximizing the bandwidth and minimizing the packet losses. Strategies of the autonomic manager describe the system's different specifications in response to user's high-level instructions. Finally, actions are all the operations that can be performed by the autonomic element to achieve different goals.

In the next section, a basic protocol for autonomic covert communication based on this framework is introduced.

3   Autonomic Covert Communication Protocol

Write $X_i \subset \mathcal{X}$ the ith source of the sender, where $i \in S$ and S is the index set of all available sources. Write θ_{ij} the jth stego setting for source X_i, where $j \in \Theta_i$ and Θ_i is the index set of all valid stego settings for source X_i.

3.1   Initialization

In the initialization process, a table is built for each available source. Each item in one of these tables corresponds to a valid stego setting θ_{ij} and has the following fields:

- Index number of the stego setting.
- Stego setting: description about the stego scheme and the related parameters.
- Embedding rate.
- Rate of successful transmission (RST).

All valid stego setting for a given source are listed in this table, initially with pre-defined initial embedding rates and RSTs $p(i, j) = 1$ for all i and j. After initialization, $r(i, j)$ and $p(i, j)$ will be constantly updated by the mechanisms described in the later part of this section.

A connection is established before any meaningful message is sent. The main purpose of connection establishment is to make sure that the recipient side is capable of extracting the message embedded by the sender.

3.2   Packet Transfer and Feedback

To achieve reliable covert communication, there're three requirements that must be guaranteed by the packet transfer process: 1) no transferred data bits are corrupted; 2) no data bits are lost; 3) all data bits are delivered in the order which they are sent. Note that all the data bits in discussion are the bits representing the secret message. Even if the cover object is corrupted during the transmission process, the extracted message still might be correct for robust stego schemes. The following mechanisms are needed to implement reliable covert communication over unreliable channel:

- Error detection: checksum or error-correcting code is used to detect and possibly correct the bit errors of the data extracted by the recipient.
- Feedback: the recipient is responsible to notify the sender if the message is successfully extracted.
- Loss detection: a packet is considered lost if the sender has been waiting long enough for the acknowledgement message.
- Retransmission: a packet that is received in error or lost will be retransmitted by the sender.
- Ordered buffering: the received packets are ordered according to their sequence number before delivered to the user.

The problem of reliable data transfer is a well-studied subject. Introductions of the related algorithms can be found in [30]. To implement the above mechanisms, the following information is required to be contained in a packet:

- Stego setting that can be used to extract the hidden message.
- Number of bits embedded.
- Sequence number.
- Checksum for the embedded message.
- Content of the message (might be encrypted).

Note that all the above fields are supposed to be protected under Kerckhoffs's principle, which means that the warden shall be incapable of extracting any useful information unless she or he has the key.

We won't provide any specification of the feedback message in this paper because of the lack of a model for covert communication environment. A further discussion about the warden's behavior is needed in the future.

3.3   Evaluation and Optimization

The algorithm of lottery scheduling [31] is used to perform stego setting selection and provide the unpredictability described in Section 2. An example of the ticket function generating the ticket value for the jth stego setting of source i is:

$$t(i, j) = \frac{r(i, j)p(i, j)}{Z(i)}, \tag{2}$$

where $Z(i) = \sum_j r(i, j)p(i, j)$ is the normalizing factor. This definition of ticket function allows the stego settings with higher rate and RST to have better chance to be selected, which will result in a better expected bandwidth. However, under different circumstances, we might want to weight the rate and RST differently. In that case, a more sophisticated ticket function is required. Note that the ticket value here is equivalent to the survival value described in Section 2 and the ticket function corresponds to the evaluation rule.

Every time a packet is sent or acknowledged, the corresponding RST will be updated. In order to optimize the bandwidth, the rates of different stego settings shall be adjusted accordingly. But again, we won't provide any specification of the rate control algorithm here for the exactly same reason mentioned earlier. Nonetheless, we believe that a properly modified version of the ubiquitous additive-increase, multiplicative-decrease (AIMD) algorithm from the TCP congestion control will suffice for most situations.

3.4   Knowledge Acquisition and Environmental Adaptation

With the increase of knowledge about the communication environment, steganalysis schemes can be applied to find the leakage of the system so that defensive mechanisms can be used to protect the system. In this subsection, we briefly introduce three possible ways for the system take advantage of the accumulated knowledge about the warden in order to adapt to the changing environment.

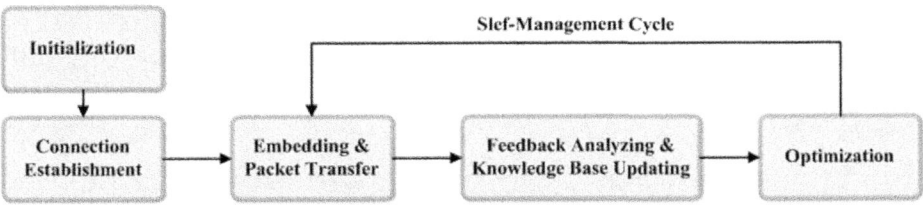

Fig. 3. Diagram of the proposed protocol

The feature set used by the warden is usually of high dimension, but the importance of different features can be measured by methods like Fisher's Linear Discriminant [13]. Thus the most distinguishable features between the lost packets and successfully transferred packets can be extracted from the previous records. This process is called feature selection in [13]. The selected features represent our knowledge about the characteristics of the warden. These features provide a guideline for the system to improve the undetectability by performing embedding impact minimization [13-19].

Another approach to take advantage of the accumulated information about the warden is clustering analysis. Maximum Mean Discrepancy (MMD) is used in [11] along with clustering algorithms to distinguish the guilty sources from the innocent. With the result provided by this method, we can avoid hiding information in cover object that falls into the guilty region (area where most packet losses happen), and improve the RSTs.

Distinct from the above evasive defending strategies, there is a more aggressive measure that can be taken. Once the characteristics of the warden are learned, inverse additive noise [33] can be introduced to the stego object for fake features, which will break the premises of the warden about the information channel and eventually invalidate the warden's steganalysis detector.

In order to improve the survivability of the system, all these three adaptation strategies take advantage of the accumulated information about the warden by either preserving the critical features of the stego object or faking them.

The diagram of the proposed protocol is shown in fig. 3.

3.5   Topics Unspecified

The problem of addressing is not mentioned in this paper, because the way the data propagate via the covert communication channel is application-dependent and the covert communication system is, but a parasite system over the host channel. The situation is the same when it comes to routing. There're just simply too many factors so dependent on the host channel that any specification about them might badly restrict the generality of the proposed scheme. However, we believe that, in the future, the uncertainties and diversities of the communication environment can be properly handled with ideas from the fields related to autonomic networking [23-24, 28].

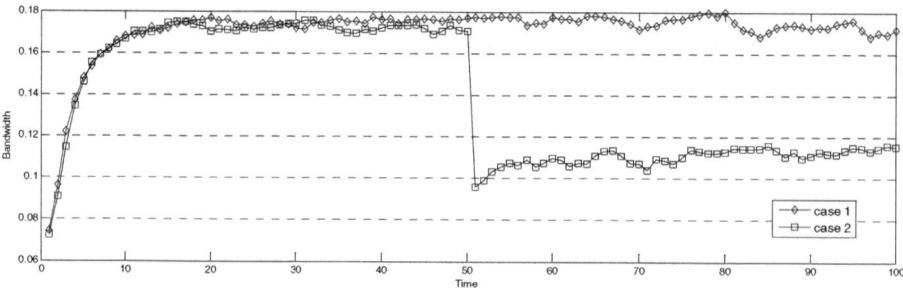

Fig. 4. Bandwidth of the covert channel measured at different time

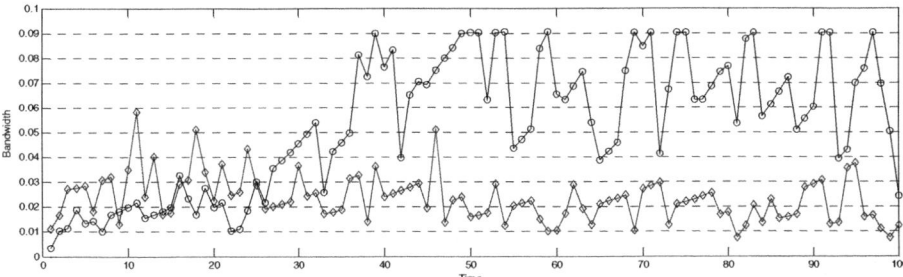

Fig. 5. Bandwidth when there's only one stego setting available

4   Simulation Results

The proposed protocol is experimented by unicasting under simulated environments in three different cases. The stego settings and the corresponding steganalysis detector used in the experiment are decided with references to [1-8, 12, 32-33]. The simulation results are shown in fig. 4 and fig. 5.

In the first case (shown by the blue line in fig. 4), the sender is assumed to have initially 10 valid stego settings for each of the 10 available sources. This experiment aims to illustrate the adaptability of the system by the gradually optimized bandwidth over time.

The initial condition of the second case (shown by the green line in fig. 4) is the same with case one. But later in this case, the steganalysis detector is updated in regard to the previous stego traffics collected by the warden, which means the most selected stego settings before the update would now become the most vulnerable. This explains the sudden shrinkage of bandwidth in the point where the update happens. The later recovered bandwidth is not as good as the previous, because the stego settings used after the update are among the secondary choices before the update. This case tells us that the system has to keep up with the warden's improvement, or else the bandwidth will get worth as a result of the warden's growing experience.

In the last case, the sender has only one source and one valid stego setting. Based on the accumulated knowledge about the warden, inverse additive noise is introduced to provide fake features, in order to invalidate the warden's detector. In fig. 5, the blue line represents the bandwidth when the system doesn't have any environmental adaptation behavior, while the green line represents the bandwidth where inverse additive noise is introduced to defend the system against the warden's detection. Obviously, the undetectability of the packet is effectively improved after the fake features are introduced.

5   Conclusions and Future Work

Covert communication aims to conceal the very existence of the communication, so that the adversary wouldn't have any evident target to attack. Since invisibility is vital to the covert communication system, the system is expected to be self-manageable without any human intervention. In this paper, a protocol for autonomic covert communication is proposed in order to deal with the complexity of covert communication management. The proposed covet communication system adopts the basic idea of "natural select" on the way to "survive" against different environmental changes. The simulation results given in Section 4 illustrate some of the self-* properties of the proposed system. Nonetheless, as an early step towards the goal of building autonomic covert communication system, many important issues are unspecified.

The author believes that the goal of building robust covert communication system can only be achieved with participants from both the fields of information hiding and autonomic computing. A pragmatic model of the warden's behavior would be crucial for the autonomic element to make the right decisions in the future. Stronger learning algorithms are also needed to improve the adaptability of the system.

Reference

1. Fridrich, J., Pevný, T., Kodovský, J.: Statistically undetectable jpeg steganography: dead ends challenges, and opportunities. In: MM&Sec, pp. 3–14 (2007)
2. Fridrich, J., Kodovsk, J., Goljan, M., Holub, V.: Breaking HUGO: the Process Discovery. In: Information Hiding (to appear, 2011)
3. Fridrich, J., Kodovsk, V., Holub, M.: Steganalysis of content-adaptive steganography in spatial domain. In: 13th Information Hiding Conference, Prague, Czech Republic, May 18-20 (2011)
4. Provos, N., Honeyman, P.: Hide and Seek: An Introduction to Steganography. IEEE Security & Privacy, 32–44 (2003)
5. Ker, A.D.: Steganalysis of LSB Matching in Grayscale Images. IEEE Signal Processing Letters 12(6), 441–444 (2005)
6. Ker, A.D.: Resampling and the Detection of LSB Matching in Color Bitmaps. In: Security, Steganography, and Watermarking of Multimedia Contents, pp. 1–15 (2005)
7. Harmsen, J.J., Bowers, K.D., Pearlman, W.A.: Fast Additive Noise Steganalysis. In: Security, Steganography, and Watermarking of Multimedia Contents, pp. 489–495 (2004)
8. Fridrich, J., Goljan, M., Hogea, D.: Steganalysis of JPEG images: Breaking the F5 algorithm. In: Petitcolas, F.A.P. (ed.) IH 2002. LNCS, vol. 2578, pp. 310–323. Springer, Heidelberg (2003)
9. Ker, A.D.: Batch steganography and pooled steganalysis. In: Camenisch, J.L., Collberg, C.S., Johnson, N.F., Sallee, P. (eds.) IH 2006. LNCS, vol. 4437, pp. 265–281. Springer, Heidelberg (2007)
10. Trivedi, S., Chandramouli, R.: Active steganalysis of sequential steganography. In: Delp III, E.J., Wong, P.W. (eds.) Proc. of SPIE Security and Watermarking of Multimedia Contents, vol. 5020, pp. 123–130 (2003)
11. Ker, A.D., Pevný, T.: A new paradigm for steganalysis via clustering. In: Proc. SPIE Media Watermarking, Security, and Forensics XIII, vol. 7880, pp. 0U01-0U13. SPIE, CA (2011)
12. Wu, S.-Z., Zhang, X.P., Wei-Ming, Z.: Recent Advances in Image-Based Steganalysis Research. Chinese Journal of Computers 32(7), 1247–1263 (2009)

13. Pevný, T., Filler, T., Bas, P.: Using high-dimensional image models to perform highly undetectable steganography. In: Böhme, R., Fong, P.W.L., Safavi-Naini, R. (eds.) IH 2010. LNCS, vol. 6387, pp. 161–177. Springer, Heidelberg (2010)
14. Fridrich, J., Filler, T.: Practical Methods for Minimizing Embedding Impact Steganography. In: Security, Steganography, and Watermarking of Multimedia Contents IX, San Jose, CA, vol. 6505, pp. 2–3 (2007)
15. Fridrich, J., Goljan, M., Soukal, D.: Wet paper codes with improved embedding efficiency. IEEE Transactions on Information Forensics and Security, 102–110 (2006)
16. Fridrich, J., Goljan, M., Lisonek, P., Soukal, D.: Writing on wet paper. In: Security, Steganography, and Watermarking of Multimedia Contents, pp. 328–340 (2005)
17. Filler, T., Judas, J., Fridrich, J.: Minimizing embedding impact in steganography using trellis-coded quantization. In: Media Forensics and Security (2010)
18. Filler, T., Fridrich, J.: Gibbs Construction in Steganography. IEEE Trans. on Info. Forensics and Security 5(4), 705–720 (2010)
19. Filler, T., Judas, J., Fridrich, J.: Minimizing Additive Distortion in Steganography Using Syndrome-Trellis Codes. In: Media Forensics and Security (to appear, 2011)
20. Simmons, G.J.: The Prisoners' Problem and the Subliminal Channel. In: CRYPTO 1983, pp. 51–67 (1983)
21. Cachin, C.: An information-theoretic model for steganography. In: Aucsmith, D. (ed.) IH 1998. LNCS, vol. 1525, pp. 306–318. Springer, Heidelberg (1998)
22. Chandramouli, R., Memon, N.: Steganography Capacity: A Steganalysis Perspective. In: Proc. SPIE, Security and Watermarking of Multimedia Contents, Santa Clara, CA, USA, vol. 5020, pp. 173–177 (2003)
23. Tizghadam, A., Leon-Garcia, A.: AORTA: Autonomic Network Control and Management System. In: IEEE Conference on Computer Communications Workshops, INFOCOM, pp. 1–4 (2008)
24. Kephart, J.O., Chess, D.M.: The Vision of Autonomic Computing. IEEE Computer, 41–50 (2003)
25. Morkel, T., Eloff, J., Olivier, M.: An Overview of Image Steganography. In: Proceedings of the Fifth Annual Information Security South Africa Conference (ISSA 2005), Sandton, South Africa (2005)
26. Westfeld, A.: F5-A steganographic algorithm. In: Moskowitz, I.S. (ed.) IH 2001. LNCS, vol. 2137, pp. 289–302. Springer, Heidelberg (2001)
27. Filler, T.: Pevný, T, Bas, P.: BOSS (July 2010),
    http://boss.gipsa-lab.grenobleinp.fr/BOSSRank/
28. Jelger, C., Tschudin, C.F., Schmid, S., Leduc, G.: Basic Abstractions for an Autonomic Network Architecture. In: WOWMOM, pp. 1–6 (2007)
29. Mortier, R., Kiciman, E.: Autonomic network management: some pragmatic considerations. In: Proceedings of the 2006 SIGCOMM Workshop on internet Network Management, INM 2006, Pisa, Italy, September 11 - 15, pp. 89–93. ACM Press, New York (2006)
30. Kurose, J., Ross, K.: Computer Networking: A top-down approach 4e. Addison-Wesley, Reading (2007)
31. Waldspurger, C.A., Weihl, W.E.: Lottery Scheduling: Flexible Proportional-Share Resource Management. In: Proc. OSDI, pp. 1–11 (1994)
32. Wanqi, L.: A Network-Flow-Based Method for Embedding Rectification (to appear)
33. Wanqi, L.: Defensive Steganography: A Novel Way against Steganalysis (to appear)

Autonomous Online Expansion Technology for Wireless Sensor Network Based Manufacturing System

Md. Emdadul Haque, Fan Wei, Takehiro Gouda, Xiaodong Lu, and Kinji Mori

Department of Computer Science
Tokyo Institute of Technology
2-12-1 Oookayama, Meguro-Ku, Tokyo, Japan
{haque,wei,gouda,lu}@mori.cs.titech.ac.jp,
mori@cs.titech.ac.jp.com

Abstract. Wireless sensor networks (WSNs) is an attractive data collection paradigm for indoor and outdoor monitoring environment. In WSN based manufacturing system environment sensor addition, relocation and reorganization are necessary with the addition or modification of production lines. This sensor addition or relocation sometime increases the sensor density in some areas of the network. In high sensor density area new sensors cannot connect the network due to the capacity constraints of the network. For the environment this paper proposes a two layers autonomous decentralized heterogeneous wireless sensor network architecture. The first layer consists of sensors and the second layer consists of routers. Each sensor is connected with a router and each router is connected with sensors and routers. This paper proposes a technology to make a group of local routers (which is called as community) for switching connected sensors by the routers of the high density areas of the network. A router of a high sensor density area initiates the community construction for switching a connected sensor to another router in the community, if new sensor wants to join the router. The switching is possible if the connected sensor is under the communication range of the other router of low density area. Sometime the community is necessary to expand or shrink based on situation. This paper introduces the community technology to achieve online expansion of the network. The simulation results show the effectiveness of the proposed technology.

Keywords: Autonomous decentralized system, sensor switching, online expansion, wireless sensor networks.

1   Introduction

The recently advances in wireless communication and the embedded system have made economically feasible to produce low-cost, low power sensor nodes to deploy in the environment for collecting data about the physical phenomena. These sensor nodes are massively deployed in indoor or outdoor environment to collect data about the physical phenomena. There are many potential applications of wireless sensor networks: target tracking [1], traffic management [2], emergency navigation [3], surveillance [4], factory monitoring [5], and so on.

J.M. Alcaraz Calero et al. (Eds.): ATC 2011, LNCS 6906, pp. 118–131, 2011.

In order to assure quality production of different kinds of products the factory system needs efficient monitoring and controlling of the environment. In order to satisfy these system requirements a large number of sensors are necessary to install in the environment. Since the user requirements change over time, the system needs to reorganize the production lines and sensors as well. These sensors addition, relocation or reorganization sometime increases the sensor density in some areas of the network. For resource constraints network some sensors of the high density areas cannot connect the network. As a result online expansion is one of the main problems for the system.

Since the homogenous ad hoc sensor networks have poor fundamental performance limits and scalability [6], [7] and the target environment is an indoor manufacturing plant, a heterogeneous architecture is suitable for the system. A two layer Autonomous Decentralized Wireless Sensor Network (ADWSN) architecture is proposed based on autonomous decentralized system [9] for the environment. The first layer consists of sensors and the second layer consists of routers. Each sensor is connected with router and each router is connected with sensors and routers. The routers have high capacity and can maintain connectivity with a number of sensors. Although routers have high capacity they can maintain connectivity with fixed number of sensors due to processing, memory etc. constraints. The routers make group which is called as a community [9], [10] (considering similar organization of a human community) for switching a connected sensor by sharing information in the community.

In this paper we assume a decentralized system where each router has a lot of functions, for example, data aggregation, data forwarding, controlling some processes of the system etc. Only some aggregated data are sent to gateway and the rest are used by the router to control that part of the manufacturing system. To control the system the router needs timely information from sensors. So, we assume each router has a capacity to maintain connectivity with a fixed number of sensors.

If a router connects the maximum possible number of sensors (which we call the capacity of the router) that router cannot allow any new sensor to connect with it. In that case we call the router as a full router. A full router initiates a community with local routers to switch a connected sensor to a free router (if a router is not full then it is a free router) in the community, when a new sensor wants to join the router. All routers in the community cooperate by sharing information to help the full router for the sensor switching. A sensor connected with a router can be switched to another free router, if the sensor (which we call as common sensor) is under the communication of the router. Community has no head or leader node (as like human community) and the community members cooperate with each other for sharing free spaces of free routers.

One of the assumptions in this paper is that the topology of the network changes dynamically. So, the number of connected sensors of the routers changes over time. Sometime in a community it might happen that there is no free router to switch a sensor for a full router. In that situation the community expansion is necessary for the online expansion. Note that in some cases the expansion is not possible due to lack of common sensors. Similarly community shrinking is also necessary for a big community or unused part of a community. As a result this paper proposes a community reconstruction technology to resize the community. The reconstruction technology consists of community expansion and shrinking technologies. The contributions of this paper are to introduce the community technologies in wireless sensor networks for online expansion.

The rest of this paper is organized as follows. In the next section we describe some related works. Section 3 describes the proposed system architecture. Section 4 describes the community construction and the coordination technologies. Section 5 presents the community reconstruction technology that includes community expansion and shrinking technologies. Section 6 presents simulation results. We conclude this paper in Section 7.

2   Related Works

There have been some research efforts found in the manufacturing industry to improve the quality of products for example [5], [11], [12], [13], [14] considering quality, design issues etc.

Heterogeneous architectures have been proposed by many researchers [15], [16], [17], [18], [19], [20] using mostly clustering concept. Most of existing works on clustering technique select a head based on degree of connectivity [19], [20] randomization [17], cluster ID [18] etc. However, most of existing works do not consider the load balancing among the clusters.

A load balanced clustering technique is found in [21]. In the paper the authors proposed a algorithm to increase the lifetime of the network. In the algorithm the authors distributed the sensor nodes among several gateways as a centralized manner during network initialization time. The paper shows with simulation that the algorithm can balance the sensor load among the gateways efficiently for a static network.

In [22] another algorithm is discussed on load balanced clustering issue that also described load balancing during network initialization time. The algorithm is proposed to enhance the scalability of the network with multiple gateways. In the algorithm the authors assume that each gateway knows the overall topology of the static network. In the paper they show that the load balancing problem is optimally solvable in polynomial time if all sensors have uniform traffic load.

However, most of the published papers discuss the load balancing issue from static network point of view. Most of them consider the election of a cluster head and some of then considers the sensor load balancing issue. The papers that consider the sensor load switching are mostly centralized algorithm for static network. All the algorithms are applicable for network initialization time load balancing. In the network the gateway or powerful nodes and only dedicated to data aggression, data forwarding etc. but not for partial control of the system. As a result we proposed a new technology for online expansion of a dynamic network (considering the capacity limits of router nodes for timeliness).

3   The Architecture

The proposed architecture is shown in Fig. 1. The architecture consists of two physically different types of nodes: a large number of sensors and less number of routers. Routers are generally placed under the ceiling of the roof of the manufacturing plant and formed a mesh network among each other. Sensors are arranged as a one-hop star topology around the routers. The routers in the architecture form the community to share free spaces for online expansion in production manufacturing system. To control the production process actuators are connected with routers. The routers control the actuators based on local information. Sometime clients also connect to the routers with PDA to monitor the plant.

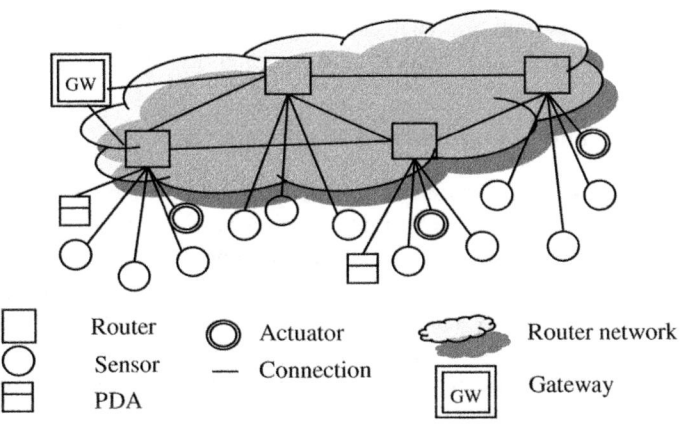

Fig. 1. The proposed architecture

The network consists of different kinds of sensors to measure various physical phenomena such as temperature, humidity, pressure, light, presence or absence of certain kinds of chemical or objects etc. It wakes up asynchronously due to limited battery power and can not directly access to other sensors. We assume some sensors are mobile and most of the others are fixed.

Routers are always wake up because of AC power. The main functions of router are data aggregation, forwarding message, maintaining connectivity with sensors, information sharing in the community, controlling the processes etc. For quality of monitoring or controlling the manufacturing plant each router needs timely information from sensors. As a result we assume each router can maintain connectivity with limited number of sensors due to the constraints of processing, memory capacity etc. The number of sensors connected to a router at a particular time is called the sensor load of the router. The maximum number of sensors a router can maintain connectivity is called the capacity of the router.

The capacity also includes processing loads for actuators, clients, message forwarding etc. For simplicity, in this paper we consider only sensor processing load.

The main assumption of this paper is that each router knows its capacity. If a router is connected with maximum possible number of sensors, we call the router as a fully loaded router or full router. On the other hand a router not fully loaded is called free capacity router or free router or resource available router.

4   Community Technology

This paper proposes a group of autonomous routers as a community to achieve the online expansion of the network. There are several ways to make the community for example; a router can make a community with all routers within h hop. The problem of this method is defining the value of h. If h is very small then the community may not satisfy the sensor switching, as a result it needs to increase h and proceed again (i.e., successive construction). That causes a lot of messages and time consuming as well. In this paper we propose a contentious community construction technology.

4.1   The Community Construction Technology

A full router starts the community construction based on the space request message from an unconnected sensor. Note that at first a new sensor sends a joining request message to join the network. All routers in its communication range reply with connected sensors list, list of sensors under the communication range etc. If all routers in the range are full, the sensor sends a spaces request message to the routers one by one until it gets the connectivity. A full router that receives a space request message starts the community construction. The router constructs the community to make free space for the unconnected sensor.

A full router starts the community construction by sending a community formation request message to all of its neighbor routers. Suppose, at a specific time m new sensors want to join with a router R_i. The router R_i sends a community formation request message as $Request$ $(R_i, N_{Ri}, S_{Ri}, SC_{Ri}, ComID, m)$ after setting a timeout. That means R_i needs to switch m sensors (generally $m = 1$, but in some case $m > 1$ is also possible) to other routers to allow the joining of the m new sensors. Where N_{Ri} is the neighbor routers list, S_{Ri} is the connected sensors list, SC_{Ri} is the list of sensors under the communication range and $ComID$ is the id of the community. Note that assigning a unique community id is out of the scope of this paper. A neighbor router R_j introduces some delay and forwards the message, if it has no free capacity and at least a common sensor that is connected with the request sender. Before forwarding the message each router introduces some delay so that the message could not flood the whole network.

Suppose R_j has f $(f < m)$ free capacity and r sensors in its communication range that are connected with R_i. R_j joins the community and forwards the message after inserting its neighbor routers list, connected sensors list, list of sensors under the communication range as $Request$ $(R_j, N_{Ri} \cup N_{Rj}, S_{Ri} \cup S_{Rj}, SC_{Ri} \cup SC_{Rj}, r - f, m)$, if $r > f$. R_j also sends a reply message to R_i as $Reply$ (R_j, LS_j, X_j), where LS_j is the list of sensors under its communication range that can receive from R_i, X_j is the list of neighbor routers, list of connected sensors, list of sensors under the communication range of all routers as received in the request message including that of R_j. If $m \leq r \leq f$ then R_j does not forward the request message. If R_j has at least a sensor in its communication range that is connected with request sender R_i then R_j joins the community, otherwise it does not join the community.

If router R_j has common sensors i.e., $r > 0$ but no free capacity i.e., $f = 0$, then the router forwards the message as $Request$ (R_j, $N_{Ri} \cup N_{Rj}$, $S_{Ri} \cup S_{Rj}$, $SC_{Ri} \cup SC_{Rj}$, r, m). If the router R_j has enough free capacity to satisfy the complete request i.e., $f \geq r \geq m$, then the router sends a suppression message to stop the community expansion. Since we propose the continuous community construction technology, a step is necessary to stop the community expansion. The suppression message is used to stop the community expansion. All routers which forward the request message also forward the suppression message without delay. At the same time the router sends a reply message as $Reply$ (R_j, LS_j, X_j). Table I summarizes the actions of routers based on different values of the parameters r, f and m. Fig. 2 shows a community which is constructed by R_3, where the shaded circular node indicates the unconnected sensor and capacity of each router is 3. In the community construction R_3 first sends the community construction request message. R_4, R_7, R_8 join the community since they have common sensor. R_8 sends a community suppression message since it has free space. But suppose before receiving the suppression message R_4 forwards the community construction request message. So finally the community consists of routers R_1, R_3, R_4, R_5, R_7, R_8.

Table 1. Router Action Table

Values of parameters	Action
$f = 0$, $r > 0$	Forward
$f \geq 0$, $r = 0$	No action
$f > 0$, $r > 0$, $f < m$, $r > f$	Reply and forward
$f > 0$, $r > 0$, $f < m$, $r < f$	Reply
$f \geq r \geq m$	Reply and suppress

The reply messages traverse only through the path to the initiator router. When the initiator router receives sufficient reply messages from routers or timeout expires then it sends a suppression message to stop the community expansion. A router that receives the suppression message forwards the message without delay. If a router has sufficient free capacity and common sensors that router can also send the suppression message (as discuss in previous paragraph). Since the request message forwards with delay and the suppression message forwards without delay, the suppression message catches the request message after certain time. That means when a router receives a suppression message before forwarding the request message it stops forwarding the request message. In this way the community is confined in a limited area of the network. After the community construction the community initiator router switches sensors to free routers that will discuss in next subsection.

In some case the community construction automatically stop or partially stop in some directions due to unavailable of common sensors. For the following condition the community construction request message of the initiator router R_i can not be forwarded for expansion.

$$S_{Ri} \cap (\bigcup_j SC_{Rj}) = \phi \tag{1}$$

That means one router is in one community which is an extreme case of the community construction and that is unlikely for high density sensor network. In that case the router cannot connect the new sensor.

Since in the community construction process each router introduces some delay, the construction takes some time. For every similar case it is not suitable for a router to construct the community and after sensor switching vanish the community. As a result after the community construction we want to preserve the community for future use by the routers of the community. If a full router of an existing community needs to switch some sensors it initiates community coordination in the existing community.

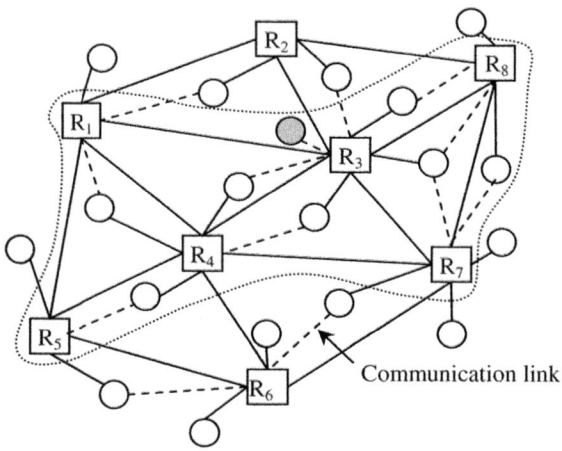

Fig. 2. A community constructed by router R_3

If a router receives more than one community construction request message then the router joins the first message received router's community. That means if two routers start the community construction at the same time in an area, then there will be two separate communities.

4.2   Community Coordination Technology

A router can switch a connected sensor to another neighbor router if the sensor is under the communication of the neighbor router. More specifically, a router R_i can switch a sensor to a neighbor router R_j with at least one free space if:

$$R_j \in N_{Ri} \quad \text{and} \quad S_{Ri} \cap SC_{Rj} \neq \phi \tag{2}$$

To switch a sensor each router use sequence of operations. The router first sends a request message to the neighbor router providing the sensor id. The receiver router sends a positive acknowledgement if that router has at least a free space. After receiving the acknowledgement the sender router disconnects the connected sensor and informs the sensor to reconnect the neighbor router that id is also given to the sensor.

Similarly multi-hop sensor switching is also possible. Suppose a router R_i wants to switch a sensor to a n-hop neighbor router R_k through the path $R_i, \ldots R_k$. For multi-hope sensor switching the receiver router should have at least a free space and on the path all adjacent ordered pair routers have to satisfy the following condition:

$$\{R_m \in N_{Rl} \ and \ S_{Rl} \bigcap SC_{Rm} \neq \phi\}$$
$$for \ all \ l \geq i \ and \ m \leq k \tag{3}$$

To switch a sensor R_i sends a sequence of instruction for a sequence of reconnection to all the routers on the path. If all routers on the path send positive acknowledgement, R_i disconnects its sensor, connects new sensor and informs R_{i-1} to connect the disconnected sensor. Similarly all routers on the path do the same operation. Fig. 3 shows an example where router R_3 switches its sensors to router R_8 and after that it connects the new sensor.

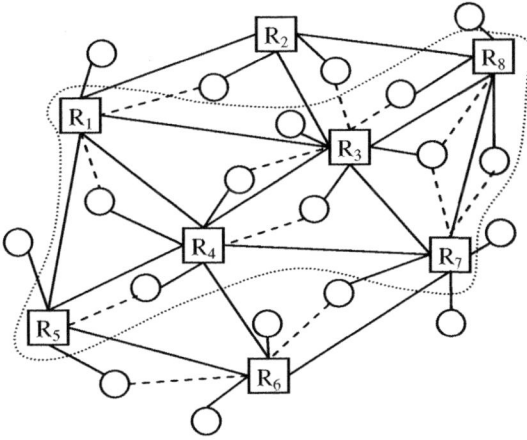

Fig. 3. The community after sensor switching

After the community construction the full router find the sensor switching path by exploring a breadth first search tree. To explore the tree the router uses the reply messages received during the community construction phase. In the tree each node indicates the router and edge indicates that parent node has a connected sensor under the communication range of child node. A community initiator router expands the tree based on received message during the community construction time.

An existing community member (in any time after the community construction) use coordination to switch a sensor within the community. If a full router of a community wants to switch a sensor, it initiates the community coordination in the community by sending a coordination request message as $Coord \ (R_i, N_{Ri}, S_{Ri}, SC_{Ri}, 1, 1)$. In this case the neighbor routers in the same community act same as shown in Table 1. The exception is that for forwarding the coordination request message routers do not introduce any delay or send the suppression message. That means the coordination request message flooded over only within community without delay. Note that a full router of a community starts the coordination for sensor switching when it receives a space request message from an unconnected sensor. The coordination initiator router also finds a free router for sensor switching using a breadth first search tree exploration after receiving the reply messages.

If a community can not satisfy the sensor load switching request of a full router and the community has a boundary community then the router initiate community to community sensor switching. If a boundary router of the community has a common sensor with the coordination initiator route then the router sends a request message to switch a sensor to the boundary community. Note that the boundary router has the information about the boundary community. The boundary router of the first community sends a request message to switch a sensor to the boundary router of the second community. The boundary router of the second community initiates (if that is a full router) the community coordination for receiving a sensor from the router. If the boundary router of second community router can switch a sensor then it replies to the boundary router of the first community. The boundary router of the first community sends a reply message to the coordination initiator router and switches sensor accordingly.

5   Community Reconstruction Technology

If a community has no free space or load switching path, then the community needs to expand. A full router first initiates community coordination to switch a sensor. If the coordination fails, it starts the expansion process. It generally takes more time if we expand the community in separate phase. In this paper we propose coordination and expansion in same phase.

5.1   Community Expansion Technology

If a boundary router receives a coordination request message and can not satisfy the sensor switching that router starts the expansion process. A boundary full router starts the expansion by sending an expansion request message. A router which receives the request message introduces some delay (similar to community construction) and forwards the message if the router has no free space but the common sensor. The coordination message forwards in the community without delay but the expansion request message forwards with delay. The router that starts the community expansion sends the suppression message, if the router receives sufficient reply messages. The router that has enough free capacity and common sensors can also send the suppression message similarly to community construction. Note that the suppression message forwards over only the expanded part of the community.

In some cases it is also possible that the present community can satisfy the request but some routers expand the community during the coordination time. Fig. 4 shows the situation, where router R_4, R_7, R_8 starts the community expansion. In the mean time suppose router R_3 finishes the sensor switching with R_1. After the community expansion R_4, R_7 send reply messages to the initiator router. The initiator then sends a reply message to inform that the sensor switching is already finished. The boundary router then dissolves the expanded part of the community because the new part is not necessary. Note that R_5, R_6 leaves the community when R_4, R_7 initiate the shrinking of the expanded part. If we do the coordination and expansion in separate phases, the coordination initiator needs more time for sensor switching when sensor switching is not possible in the community.

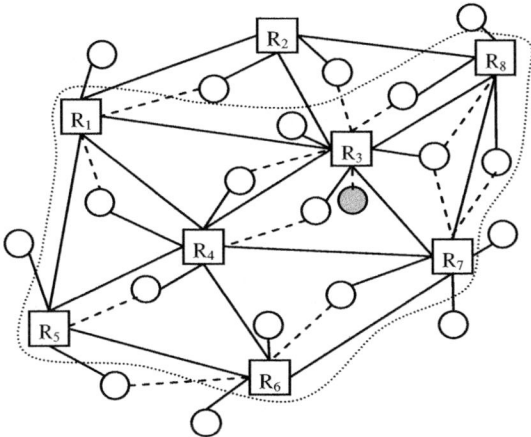

Fig. 4. A community that expand by router R_4 and R_7

5.2   Community Shrinking Technology

We propose the community shrinking technology to shrink the unnecessary part of the community. The shrinking decreases the number of messages in the community. The community expansion process includes a part of community shrinking process. But sometime more shrinking is necessary. Suppose the initial community is big and some boundary free routers do not receive any coordination request message for a long time. The similarly situation may happen in expanded part of the community. In this paper we propose the community shrinking in two situations. The first shrinking during the community expansion time that we have already discussed in the previous subsection and second shrinking is based on common sensor or others quantity.

If all the common sensors of a boundary router leave the network then the boundary router leaves the community. For another kind of community shrinking each router stores historical data about last coordination request message receiving time (t). If t is greater than certain threshold then a boundary free router leaves the community.

The route leaves the community by assigning a null community id and informs all the neighbor routers. After receiving the message the neighbor routers may leave the community based on the same statistics. Note that the routers that receive the community leaving message become the boundary router.

6   Simulation Result

We have implemented our proposed technology with 30 routers and different number of sensors distributed in a 50m×50m×3m area. Routers are randomly distributed under the ceiling of the manufacturing system and sensors are distributed in lower half of the plant area. We simulate different setups with number of sensors 200, 250 and 260. We set sensor communication range = 10m, router communication range = 25m and capacity of each router is 10. Community construction request message forwarding delay is 30ms. Each sensor generates 1 packet/sec, each packet length is 200bytes and radio bandwidth is 100kbps. We assume 10% of sensors are mobile in the plant area in a straight line of 5m/min speed. Fig. 5 shows the number of connected sensors with and without the community technology. The figure shows that the number of connected sensors with the community is always much higher than without the community.

To simulate a dynamic network we consider during the network operation time, sensor joining and leaving rate (from the first simulation setup of 200 sensors) are 15 and 5 per min respectively. The simulation time = 5 min. Fig. 6 shows the number of connected sensors in the network with the community construction and reconstruction technologies for $t = 1$ min and without the community. The figure shows that community technology also increases the number of connected sensors significantly for a dynamic network.

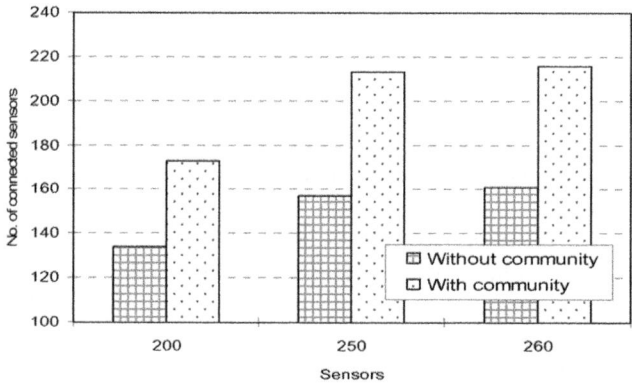

Fig. 5. No. of connected sensor for different network setups

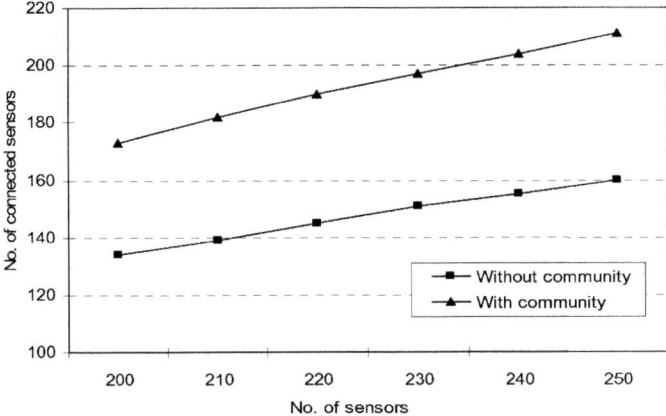

Fig. 6. Comparison of connected sensor for a dynamic network

We also find the effect of community reconstruction technology for the dynamic network. Fig. 7 shows the numbers of connected sensors with and without the community reconstruction technology. Note that without reconstruction when a full router fails to switch a sensor in the community, it can not connect any new sensor.

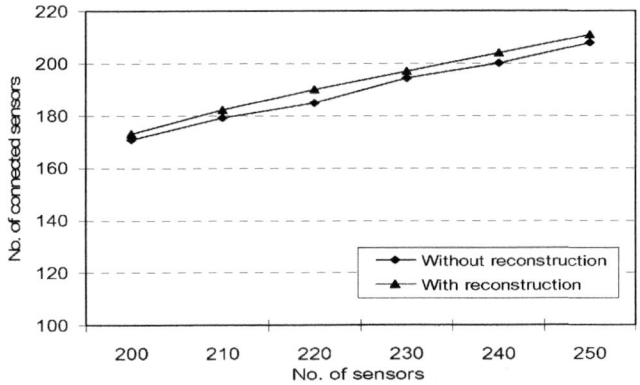

Fig. 7. Comparison of connected sensor for dynamic network

We also find the average sensor connection time with preserving the community for future coordination and without preserving the community. In this case we use the same simulation setup that varies the topology over time. The result shows that the average sensor connection time little bit improve by preserving the community for future coordination as shown in Fig. 8.

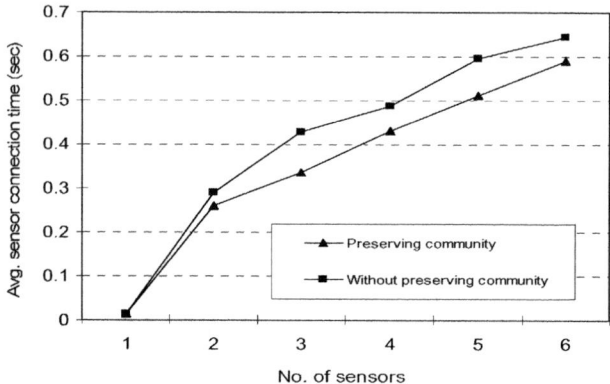

Fig. 8. No. of connected sensors with and without the reconstruction technology

7   Conclusions

This paper discusses about the community construction and reconstruction technologies in wireless sensor networks for online expansion. The community is constructed by a full router which needs to switch its connected sensors. The community helps to connect more sensors by utilizing the free spaces or free routers in community. To utilize the free spaces of a community, the community routers share information. After sharing information a full router finds free routers and the paths to switch one or more sensors to other routers. If the community has lack of free routers in the community then the community routers expand the community.

With the proposed community construction and reconstruction technologies the number of sensors can be increased in the network; as a result online expansion can be achieved for the system. Without such kinds of community technology the free spaces of router can not be utilized to expand the network.

References

1. The 29 Palms Experiment: Tracking Vehicles with a UAV-Delivered Sensor Network, http://www.eecs.berkeley.edu/pister/29PalmsOI03
2. Hsieh, T.T.: Using Sensor Networks for Highway and Traffic Applications. IEEE Potentials 23(2), 13–16 (2004)
3. Tseng, Y.C., Pan, M.S., Tsai, Y.Y.: Wireless Sensor Networks for Emergency Navigation. Computer 39(7), 55–62 (2006)
4. Kahn, J.M., Katz, R.H., Pister, K.S.J.: Mobile networking for 'smart dust'. In: Proc. 5th IEEE/ACM MOBICOM, pp. 271–278 (August 1999)
5. Connolly, M., O'Reilly, F.: Sensor networks and food Industry. In: Workshop on Real-World Wireless Sensor Networks, Stockholm, Sweden (2005)
6. Lee, J.J., Krishnamachari, B., Kuo, C.C.J.: Impact of Heterogeneous Deployment on Lifetime Sensing Coverage in Sensor Networks. In: IEEE SECON (2004)

7. Du, X., Guizani, M., Xiao, Y., Chen, H.H.: Two Tier Secure Routing Protocol for Heterogeneous Sensor Networks. IEEE Transactions on Wireless Communications 6(9), 3395–3401 (2007)
8. Mori, K., Shiibashi, A.: Trend of autonomous decentralized system technologies and their application in IC card ticket system. IEICE Trans. on Comm. E92-B(2), 445–460 (2009)
9. Ragab, K., Kaji, N., Mori, K.: ACIS: A Large-scale autonomous decentralized community communication infrastructure. IEICE Trans. on Info. and Sys. E87-D(4), 937–946 (2004)
10. Mahmood, K., Lu, X., Horikoshi, Y., Mori, K.: Autonomous pull-push community construction technology for high-assurance. IEICE Trans. on Info. and Sys. E92-D(10), 1836–1846 (2009)
11. Wentworth, S.M.: Microbial sensor tags. IFT (The Institute of Food Engineering) Annual Meeting Book of Abstracts, Chicago, Illinois, USA (July 2003)
12. Ong, K.G., Puckett, L.G., Sharma, Loiselle, B.V., Grimes, M., Bachas, C.A., Leonidas, G.: Wireless passive resonant-circuit sensors for monitoring food quality. In: Proceeding of SPIE–The International Society for Optical Engineering, Boston, MA, USA, vol. 4575, pp. 150–159 (October 2001)
13. MEMS come to Oz wine industry. Electronic News (June 2004)
14. Anastasi, G., Farruggia, O., Re, G.L., Ortolani, M.: Monitoring high-quality wine production using wireless sensor networks. In: Proceeding of the 42nd Hawaii International Conference on System Sciences, Hawaii, pp. 1–7 (January 2009)
15. Akyildiz, I.F., Su, W., Sankarasubramaniam, Y.: Wireless Sensor Networks: A Survey. Computer Networks 38, 393–422 (2002)
16. Cerpa, A., Estrin, D.: ASCENT: Adaptive Self-Configuring Sensor Networks Topologies. In: Proc. INFOCOM 2002, New York (June 2002)
17. Rabiner Heinzelman, W., Chandrakasan, A., Balakrishnan, H.: Energy-Efficient Communication Protocols for Wireless Microsensor Networks. In: Proc. Hawaii Intl Conf. on System Sciences (HICSS 2000) (January 2000)
18. Baker, D.J., Emphemides, A.: A Distributed Algorithm for Organizing Mobile Radio Telecommunication Networks. In: Proc. Intl. Conf. in Distributed Computer Systems (April 1981)
19. Gerla, M., Tsai, J.T.C.: Multicluster, Mobile, Multimedia Radio Network. ACM/Baltzer Journal of Wireless Networks 1, 255–265 (1995)
20. Parekh, A.K.: Selecting Routers in Ad-Hoc Wireless Networks. In: Proc. SBT/IEEE Intl. Telecommunications Symposium (August 1994)
21. Gupta, G., Younis, M.: Load-Balanced Clustering of Wireless Sensor Networks. In: ICC 2003 (2003)
22. Low, C.P., Fang, C., Ng, J.M., Ang, Y.H.: Load-Balanced Clustering Algorithms for Wireless Sensor Networks. In: ICC 2007 (2007)

Self-organized Message Scheduling for Asynchronous Distributed Embedded Systems

Tobias Ziermann[1,*], Zoran Salcic[2], and Jürgen Teich[1]

[1] University of Erlangen-Nuremberg, Germany
{tobias.ziermann,teich}@informatik.uni-erlangen.de
[2] The University of Auckland, New Zealand

Abstract. A growing number of control systems are distributed and based on the use of a communication bus. The distributed nodes execute periodic tasks, which access the bus by releasing the messages using a priority-based mechanism with the goal of minimal message response times. Instead of randomly accessing the bus, a dynamic scheduling of messages technique based on adaptation of time offsets between message releases is used. The presented algorithm, called DynOAA, is executing on each node of the distributed system. It takes into account the current traffic on the bus and tries to avoid simultaneous release of messages by different nodes, hence reduces the likelihood of conflicts and need for repeated release. In this paper, we first address single bus (segment) systems and then extend the model and the offset adaptation algorithm to systems that use multiple buses (segments) connected by a communication gateway. A rating function based on the average of maximum response times is used to analyze DynOAA for the case of CAN-bus systems based on bit-accurate simulations. Experiments show the robustness of the algorithm (1) in case of fully asynchronous systems, (2) ability to deal with systems that change their configuration (add or remove message release nodes) dynamically and (3) model systems containing multiple bus segments connected by a gateway. The approach is also applicable to other priority-based bus systems.

1 Introduction

In this paper, we target distributed control embedded systems based on the use of multiple computing nodes connected by a communication bus. Typical applications include automotive systems, industrial automation, home automation, healthcare systems and robotics. The common characteristic of such applications is that the communication over the bus is triggered periodically and the amount of data exchanged is relatively small. However, the time between sending data from the source node to receiving it on the destination node, called

* This work was supported in part by the German Research Foundation (DFG) under contract TE 163/15-1.

J.M. Alcaraz Calero et al. (Eds.): ATC 2011, LNCS 6906, pp. 132–148, 2011.
© Springer-Verlag Berlin Heidelberg 2011

message response time, is crucial and subject to real-time constraints. An example of communication bus and protocol perfectly suited for this task is the Controller Area Network (CAN) [1]. In this paper, we will focus on CAN, but the methods introduced are in principle suited for any priority-based communication protocol.

The design of the communication system in distributed control systems is a very complex task, which is very often performed using hand-based procedures, which is error prone, and time consuming when needed to repeat because of the change of system configuration and requirements. The use of automated methods and tools is a better option, but fails if the design is faced with large design space, which increases the computational complexity of the task, hence making design tools effectively unusable. Also, the use of design tools is based on the assumption that all design parameters and inputs are known in advance, which most often is not the case. For example, message release offsets [7], an efficient technique to reduce response times of the communication bus, can be calculated in advance, but the assumption that their statically calculated values will be the best throughout system operation results in a pessimistic solution, with non-optimal use of the system bus. We want to avoid these disadvantages of offline methods by considering the current traffic situation and adapt online.

We recently proposed [12] a solution of dynamically adapting the message release offsets by individual nodes (and software tasks) of the distributed system, which resulted in the reduced message response times for CAN-based systems. Compared to our initial work, this paper presents several new contributions: (1) The formal model is refined and extended to systems with multiple bus segments. (2) The rating function of the schedule is further improved to allow a better comparison between schedules of different approaches and scenarios. (3) We loosen the assumption that the monitoring period of DynOAA is synchronized and demonstrate that it has only little influence on the performance of the method. (4) We conducted experiments which incorporate dynamic changes of the system configuration during run-time and show the robustness of DynOAA. (5) The behavior of the system is experimentally analyzed for the case that only a fraction of all nodes apply DynOAA. Finally, (6) first preliminary results for using DynOAA on systems with multiple bus segments are obtained and reported.

The rest of the paper is organized as follows. In Section 2, we define the problem and position our work in the context of related work. Section 3 gives the details of the proposed dynamic adaptation method, the dynamic offset adaptation algorithm (DynOAA), and illustrates its operation for single-segment systems. Section 4 further extends DynOAA to allow the use in multi-segment systems and evaluates it by the developed simulator. Conclusions and future work are given in Section 5.

2   Problem Definition and Related Work

In this section, we outline the assumptions for the modeling of CAN-based systems and position our work to the existing related work. The measure of performance in the form of a rating function is also introduced.

2.1   Context

The CAN specification [1] defines the data link layer and roughly describes the physical layer of the ISO/OSI-Model. At the data link layer, a message-oriented approach is chosen. Four different types of frames are used to transfer messages: Data frames, Remote Transmit Request frames, Overload frames and Error frames. The most important is the data frame that is used for data exchange. Each data frame has its unique identifier. This 11 bit long identifier defines the message priority by which the bus access is granted. Bus arbitration is done by Carrier Sense Multiple Access with Bitwise Arbitration (CSMA/BA). The method of bitwise arbitration can be described as follows: Each node that would like to have access to the bus, starts sending its message as soon as the bus is idle for the time of 3 bits. Every sent bit is also watched. When the sent bit differs from the watched one, then a message with higher priority is also sending and transmission is stopped. After sending the identifier, only the message with the highest priority is left and has exclusive bus access.

The major advantage of using CAN is that its huge popularity, particularly in the automotive sector, which allows mass production of the CAN controllers and their integration with the microprocessors used in the computation nodes, resulting in very cheap solutions. Another advantage is availability of software built for the CAN infrastructure [9], which is the result of many years of use of CAN. On the other hand, a big disadvantage is the limited maximal data rate of 1 Mbit/s, which is the relic of the early conception of the bus, and significantly limits its application domain. From this reason, other communication buses such as Flexray [6] and real-time Ethernet [5], have been proposed. However, the introduction of new buses is related to a significantly increased cost to design and manufacturing of new computation nodes, which includes both hardware and software which already exist for CAN-based systems. Our work therefore goes in the other direction, where we are trying to breathe new life into CAN-based systems by allowing better use of the available data rate and increasing the performance of systems built on the CAN bus without changes of the system infrastructure.

The main problem caused by the limited bandwidth is the increase in response times, defined as the time between attempts to release the message to the time when actual message transfer begins, especially when the workload of the system increases (typically above 50%). This increase is caused by simultaneous attempts of multiple tasks to access the bus and release a message. Several approaches try to optimize the scheduling of messages on CAN by adjusting the priority of the messages. One way is to divide the message streams into different categories and schedule them with known scheduling techniques such as earliest deadline first [13,4]. Another way is to use fuzzy logic to select the priority [2]. The different priorities are established by using several bits from the identifier. This has the disadvantage that the number of available identifiers is reduced from 2048 to 32 and 128, respectively. Already in current automotive applications more than 128 identifiers are needed, which makes this suggestion infeasible.

Therefore, we are using a different, less interfering, approach: If tasks send messages periodically, which is most often the case in distributed control systems, simultaneous access can be avoided by adding an appropriate offset to a message release time. An approach that assigns statically calculated fixed offsets of messages that are assumed to be synchronous by using off-line heuristics is proposed in [8]. Although the approach results in better response times, it does not take into account the dynamics of the system operation and resulting traffic. Instead, the approach is based on a-priori given, static assumptions. Additionally, it doesn't consider the asynchronous nature of the nodes (and tasks) that communicate over CAN bus, which is caused by each node running on its own clock. Because of different clocks and clock drifts, the optimal offsets ideally should change dynamically and adapt to the changing conditions on the bus. This is further supported by the fact that the start of the tasks is not synchronized, resulting in additional randomization of initial offsets. In order to solve this, the dynamic offset adaptation algorithm (DynOAA) has been proposed [12] recently as the solution to the changes of the recent bus traffic, resulting in better response times and also in an increased level of scheduling fairness.

2.2   System Model

The system we are targeting can be described by a set of nodes communicating over the bus as shown in Fig. 1. One or more tasks on each node may initiate a communication, i.e. release messages.

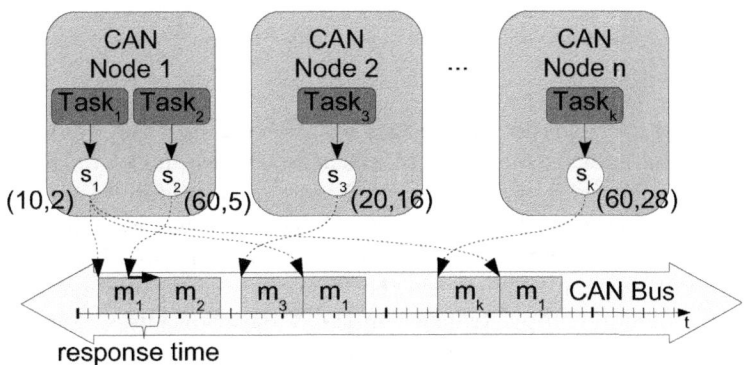

Fig. 1. CAN-Bus based system model

In our model, we abstract the tasks by considering only the mechanism used to release *messages* called a *stream*. A stream s_i can be characterized by a tuple (T_i, O_i) with $0 \leq O_i \leq T_i$, that is, by a period T_i (time between any two consecutive messages generated by stream s_i) and an offset O_i. The offset is relative to a global time reference. It can therefore drift over time, because the local time reference can differ from the global one. The *hyper-period* P is the least common multiple of all periods $lcm\{T_1, T_2, ..., T_k\}$. Assuming a synchronous system, the schedule is finally periodic with the hyper-period. A *scenario* consists of k streams. We assume the priorities are set by the designer, typically according to the stream period so that a rate monotonic scheduling is achieved.

A *message* m_i is a single release or CAN frame of the stream. The time between a message release and the start of its uninterrupted transfer over the bus is the *response time* of the message. We don't add the constant non-preemptive time to transfer the message to the response time, because then a response time of zero is always the best possible case for every message independent of its length. This will simplify later comparisons between different schedules. In Fig. 1, for example, the response time of message m_2 is three time slots, because it is delayed by the running message m_1. The *worst case response time* $WCRT_i(b, e)$ of a stream i during a certain time interval starting at time b and ending at time e is the largest response time of all messages of the stream recorded during that time interval. For example, an analytical approach would calculate $WCRT_i(0, \infty)$.

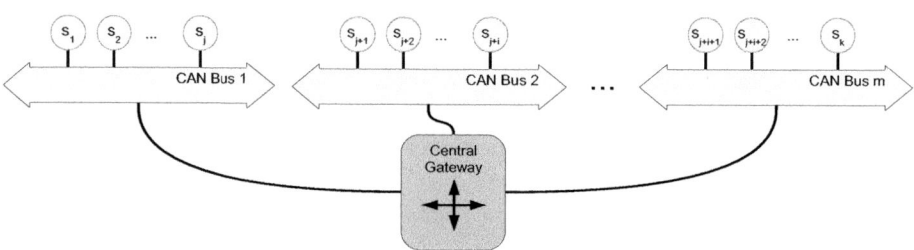

Fig. 2. System model for a multi-segment Controller Area Network

In this paper, we extend this model by allowing m buses connected by a gateway. Each stream is connected to exactly one bus and can send messages to one or multiple buses, as depicted in Figure 2. Therefore, a multi-segment stream s_i' is characterized by a tuple (T_i, O_i, B_i, D_i), that is additionally by a source bus B_i, it is connected to and a set of destination buses D_i. The response times of a multi-segment stream are the times between a message release and the start of its uninterrupted transfer on the destination buses. The worst case response time is, analog to the single-segment case, the largest of these response times. A message that is transmitted on a different bus then the source bus will be called a *routed message*. For the gateway, we make the following assumptions:

- The gateway is central, so it is connected to every bus. It has to be ensured that all connection requirements of the streams are fulfilled. Delays caused by computational load on the gateway are neglected. This is a reasonable assumption, because the operation speed of the gateway is multiples of the communication protocol.
- The gateway uses priority-based transmission with unlimited buffers. This means, in contrast to a first-in-first-out strategy, when several routed messages are pending for transmission, the message with the highest priority will get transmitted.
- A routed message will be pending as soon as the complete message on the source bus has been transmitted.

In our model, we assume discrete time with a minimal system time resolution defined a priori. All stream characteristic times are multiples of this minimal time resolution.

2.3   Rating Approach

In [12] a new metric for comparison of schedules in the form of a rating function is introduced and used to show the advantage of an online approach. We will use this as a basis for comparison. In this paper, we extend the definition by dividing the rating function by the number k of streams that release messages, thus enabling comparisons of schedules for different number of streams. It is defined as follows:

$$r(t) = \frac{\sum_{i=1}^{k} \frac{WCRT_i(t-P,t)}{T_i}}{k} \tag{1}$$

In words, the rating represents the average of all streams maximum response time during the last hyper-period relative to the stream's period. In the case of multi-segment CAN systems, we distinguish between two cases: (1) if the whole system is rated, the WCRTs as described in Section 2.2 are considered and (2) for comparison of a single segment in a multi-segment system, the modification of the rating is explained in Section 4.

3   Single-Segment Scheduling

In our approach, we exploit the dynamic adaptation of message release offsets over time as the traffic on the CAN bus changes. Because it cannot be assumed that there is a single global observer that knows the complete system status and operation, the decisions to change offsets are based on traffic monitoring carried by the individual streams. The algorithm, as well as examples of its operation, are presented in Section 3.1. The robustness to an asynchronous and a changing system are shown in Section 3.3 and 3.4, respectively.

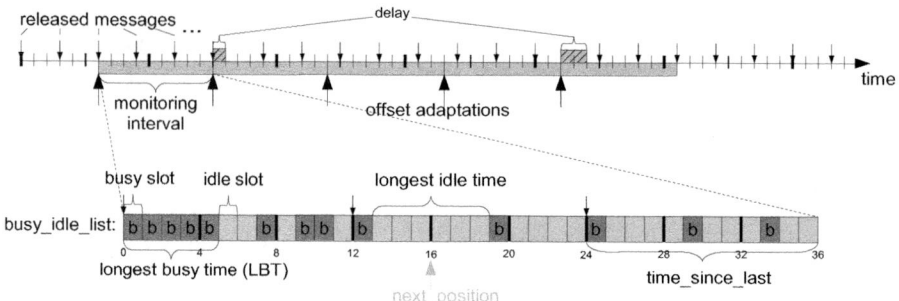

Fig. 3. DynOAA illustration - timing diagram and busy_idle_list on a single node

3.1 DynOAA

The dynamic offset adaptation algorithm (DynOAA) [12] is run on each node independently and periodically. For the sake of completeness, we will illustrate the operation of DynOAA in short as shown in Figure 3. In the upper part of the figure, on the top of the time line, the periodically released messages of the stream are indicated by small arrows. The larger arrows on the bottom of the time line indicate the instances when the adaptations start or when DynOAA is run.

Before the adaptation takes place, the bus is monitored by each stream for a time interval being equal to the maximum period of all streams. A list, from now on called *busy_idle_list*, is created. An example of it is shown in the lower part of Figure 3. It contains for each time slot during the *monitoring interval* an idle element if the bus is idle and a busy element if the bus is busy. The length of a time slot is the transmission time of one bit. From the busy_idle_list, we can find the *longest idle time* and *longest busy time* (LBT), which are the maximum continuous intervals when the bus was idle or busy, respectively. The variable *time_since_last* denotes the amount of time passed between the current time and the time the last message was released for this particular stream. This value is needed to calculate when the next message would be released. The *next_position* is the time that indicates when in the next cycle a message should be scheduled. It is chosen in the middle of the longest idle time interval. The next message of the stream is then delayed, i.e., the offset is adjusted, so that a message is released at the time specified by next_position.

In distributed systems, all streams are considered independent from each other. If more than one stream starts to execute the adaptation simultaneously, there is a high probability that the value of *next_position* at more than one stream will be identical. Instead of spreading, the message release times would in that case be clustered around the same time instance. Therefore, we need to ensure only one stream is adapting its offsets at the same time. Ensuring that only one node is adapting is achieved if all nodes make the decision whether to adapt or not based on a unique criterion based on the same information, the traffic on the bus in this case. The criterion we use is to select the stream belonging to the first busy slot of the LBT. The idea is that this stream causes the biggest delay, because it potentially could have delayed all subsequent messages in the busy period and therefore should be moved first. If there are more than one LBT of equal length, the first one is chosen. If the monitoring phases of all nodes are synchronized, this mechanism ensures that all nodes elect the same stream for adaptation.

The algorithm is best explained on the example from Figure 3. A stream with a period of 12 time slots (ts) is considered. The transmission of one message is assumed to take one ts. The algorithm passes through two phases. In the first phase, monitoring, the busy-idle list in the lower part of Figure 3 is created. The first message of the LBT belongs to the stream under consideration. Therefore, in the second phase, it will adapt, i.e., the next release will be delayed. In order to calculate the needed delay, the next position is determined first by choosing the middle of the longest idle time, which is in this case 16 ts. The delay is then calculated as:

$$
\begin{aligned}
delay &= (next\_position + time\_since\_last) \bmod period \\
&= (16\,ts + 12\,ts) \bmod 12\,ts \\
&= 4\,ts
\end{aligned}
$$

The delay causes the move of the releases of this stream in the next hyper period by additional 4 ts. For the messages at positions 1 to 4 this means, if they were delayed, then their response time is reduced.

3.2   Evaluation

In order to evaluate the quality of our approach, we developed and used our own CAN bus simulator. The reason for this was that no available simulator can describe scenarios we needed and extract the required properties. Our simulator is event-driven with the simulation step size being equal to the transmission time of one CAN bit. The full CAN protocol is reproduced by assuming worst-case bit-stuffing. We can only simulate the synchronous case, where all nodes have the same time base. This means if the offsets are fixed, the schedule repeats after time equal to the hyper-period. The asynchronous case is simulated by using different random initial offsets. The simulation assumes the error-free case. Our simulation engine is comparable to RTaW-Sim[11]. Although RTaW-Sim offers more functionality, such as error insertion and clock drift, and runs much faster, it does not provide provisions to change offsets at run-time that is needed to test DynOAA.

The scenarios used for our experiments consist of synthetic scenarios automatically generated by Netcarbench [3] and are typical for the automotive domain with a bus load that can be freely adjusted. A bus speed of 125 kbit/s is assumed. Typical for practical implementations is that there are not to many different periods (e.g., 5 - 10) that are mostly multiples of each other. This results in a small hyper period. In the example scenarios, it is always 2 seconds, which is also the largest period.

Figure 6 shows the rating function of Eq. 1 over time for different scenarios. The experiments were always run for 10 different random offset initializations. The continuous lines in the plots represent the average of these 10 runs, while the vertical error bars indicate the maximum and minimum value of the rating function at that instance of time. We can see that it converges very fast to a stable value. The plot also shows that we are always improving significantly compared to the non-adaptive case which is represented by the rating values at time zero.

3.3   Asynchronous Monitoring

In Section 3.2, we assumed the monitoring intervals were synchronized. However, in an distributed system, the monitoring intervals of the streams are asynchronous, so choosing the adapting stream gets more difficult. We cannot guarantee anymore that exactly one stream is adapting, as is shown in the example in Figure 4. In the example, the monitoring phase of the two streams overlap in such a way that the longest idle time is the same, but the longest busy period is different. Therefore, streams 1 and 2 would schedule their messages simultaneously. Nevertheless, given the monitoring phases have the same length, the maximal number of streams scheduled to the same idle time is two. This means the effect is not severe as the experiments in the following text will show.

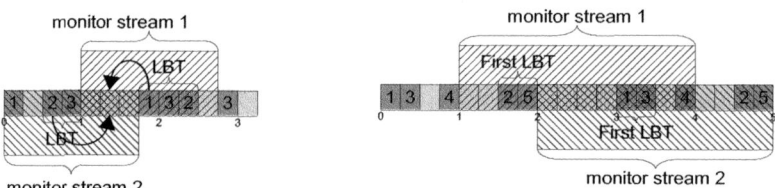

Fig. 4. Example where asynchronous adaptation leads to scheduling of two stream to the same position

Fig. 5. Example where the adaptation stops because no stream is first of the first longest busy period

Another problem with asynchronous monitoring occurs when there are several longest busy periods with the same length. If the streams always choose the first LBT, it can lead to a stop of adaptation, because no stream will adapt. How this can happen is shown in the example in Figure 5. On the one hand, this problem can be simply avoided by choosing randomly the LBT that is considered. On the other hand, if the monitoring periods are synchronous, the random selection can cause that several streams adapt simultaneously to the same position.

In Figure 7, the rating over time for a scenario with 50% load is depicted. The meaning of the error bars is similar to the one described for Figure 6. Table 1 shows the average rating values for cases from Figure 7. The results for

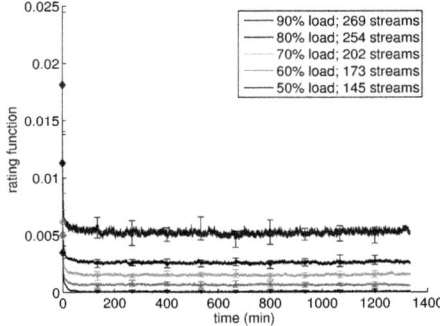
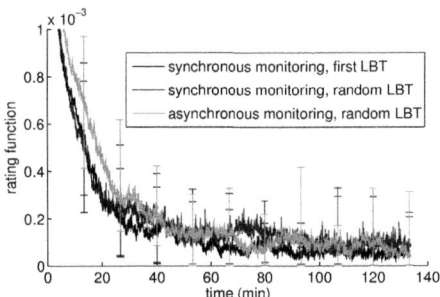

Fig. 6. Rating function as a function of time for different application and load scenarios

Fig. 7. Rating function as a function of time, comparing synchronous to asynchronous monitoring and choosing the first LBT to choosing a random LBT for deciding which stream adapts

asynchronous monitoring, and choosing which stream to adapt based on a random LBT are not displayed, because, as described above, the adaptation in the simulation gets stuck. As expected, the setup with synchronous monitoring and choosing which stream to adapt based on the first LBT performs best. However, the difference in performance is negligible considering the variation within the results. Results with other scenarios, not shown here, reveal a similar behavior, leading to the conclusion that DynOAA also works well for asynchronous monitoring, which would be the case in a real distributed system. The experiments in the rest of the paper are always run with asynchronous monitoring and random LBT.

Table 1. Average rating value over the whole simulation time for the scenario in Figure 7

synchronous monitoring, first LBT	$2.0011 \cdot 10^{-4}$
synchronous monitoring, random LBT	$2.3788 \cdot 10^{-4}$
asynchronous monitoring, random LBT	$2.5792 \cdot 10^{-4}$

3.4 Adaptation in Dynamically Changing Systems

In this work, we model the first time the dynamic changes of the system configuration by allowing addition and removal of streams during system operation. At this stage, only preliminary simulation runs are performed which indicate behavior of the system when the configuration of the system changes. We start

with the system operation with a fixed number of streams. When a stream
is removed from the system, the response times of the remaining streams will
either decrease or stay the same, depending on whether the removed stream
delayed the transmission of another stream or not. Similarly, when a stream
is added, the response times of the other streams increases or stays the same
depending on whether the added stream delays another stream or not. The goal
of the adaptation, keeping the response times as short as possible, is achieved
by adapting the offsets dynamically and finding a new set of offsets for the
current scenario that does not depend on the set of offsets for the case before
the change of system configuration. We demonstrate this behavior by running
DynOAA for different initial offset assignments and comparing the rating value
after the system has converged. The results of experiments in Figure 6 (see
Section 3.2) show exactly that, because the system converges to a certain rating
value depending on the used scenario and not on the initial offset assignment.

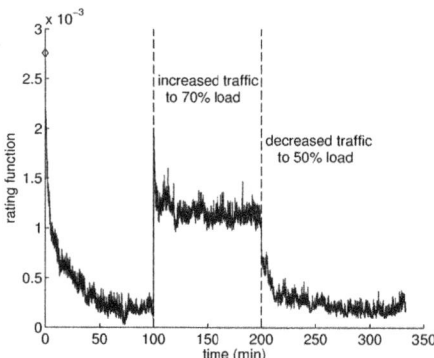 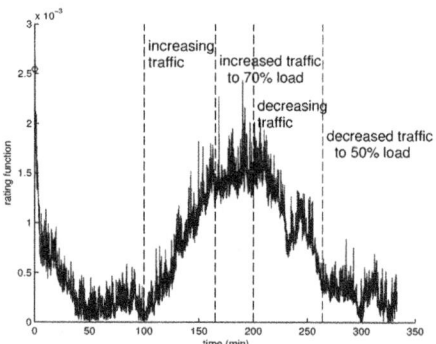

Fig. 8. Rating function as a function of
time for a scenario in which at time 100
min, 64 streams are added such that the
load increased from 50% to 70%. At time
200 min, these streams are removed again.

Fig. 9. Rating function as a function of
time for a scenario in which at time 100
min, 64 streams are added one every
minute such that at time 164 min, the
load is increased from 50% to 70%. At
time 200 min, these streams are removed
again one every minute.

Because the adaptation is constantly performed, the rating value fluctuates
even when the system is not changing configuration. Therefore, the reaction on
adding or removing one stream will not be obvious. However, we can show the
system reaction when several streams are added or removed. In Figure 8, we show
the scenario in which 64 streams are abruptly added to the system at time 100
min, and then removed at time 200 min. Corresponding system load increased
from 50% to 70% and back to 50%, respectively. Figure 9 illustrates the system
behavior when the change was not abrupt, but rather gradual. From time 100
min, 64 streams are added to the system at the rate of one stream per minute,

and then after time 200 min the streams are removed from the system, one stream per minute. It is obvious that the DynOAA adapts offsets and stabilizes the value of the rating function in each case for each new configuration. Further analysis of dynamic system configuration changes is part of our future work.

4   Multi-segment Scheduling

Data rate limitations of CAN can be overcome in some applications by using multi-segment systems. In this paper, we present the case of the system where the segments are connected through a single gateway. Firstly, multiple segments can help to increase the capacity of priority-based communicating embedded systems. Secondly, even though DynOAA reduces the message response times to a minimum for a given load, the multi-segment approach can potentially reduce the load of the individual segments and thus reduce the message response times further. We consider a simple case where a single segment is split into up to five segments. Gains can be expected if the inter-segment communication is not too intensive. Finally, the reason for a multi-segment approach can be purely practical. For example, in the development of large distributed systems, which consist of multiple application domains, the systems are designed by multiple teams whose efforts cluster around individual domains implemented on single-segment system. The integration of the overall system becomes easier if it only requires connection of multiple segments via a gateway.

4.1   Partial Adaptation

An obstacle for applying DynOAA to multi-segment systems is that the current traffic information for the whole system is no longer available to each node, because a certain fraction of messages is routed by the gateway. This means that the nodes change their offsets based only on information on local traffic of the segment they are connected to. Section 4.2 will demonstrate the influence of this on the system performance.

Another problem in multi-segment case is that it is not possible to influence the release of all messages on a segment directly. For example, messages received from the streams of the other bus segments are not aware of the traffic situation on the receiving bus segment and cannot perform correct adaptation. The knowledge of the full traffic situation would be possible by using the gateway to collect the traffic information and transmit (broadcast) it to all nodes on all segments, but it would result in additional overhead and require additional bandwidth. Therefore, this option is left out in our work.

Based on the above analysis, our decision was to first analyze the case in which only a part of the streams, belonging to the messages on one segment, perform DynOAA and adapt their offsets, while the others are not doing that, and we call this partial adaptation. This type of behavior can then be extrapolated to the multi-segment systems directly. The problem with the partial adaptation is that the DynOAA can select a stream that does not adapt as one that should adapt, and the intended goals would not be achieved. In the case of our synchronous simulation, it even can lead to complete stop of the adaptation. However, a slight modification of the DynOAA corrects the algorithm operation and makes it suitable for the partial adaptation case. The solution is outlined in the following paragraphs.

During traffic monitoring, in addition to the information whether a slot is busy or idle, we record the information whether the busy slot is allocated by an adapting or non-adapting stream in the *annotated busy_idle_list*. This information can be provided by using an indicator (flag) associated with the current message with two possible values, adapting or non-adapting. This indicator could be statically assigned to each message stream at design time, but the flexibility of dynamic adaptation and self-organization would be lost in that case. Therefore, we propose to use the last (least significant) bit of the CAN identifier to assign a priority to the stream to indicate whether it is adapting or not. This has the additional advantage that there is no need to keep the list of all streams and at the same time allows flexible insertion and removal of nodes from the system. The penalty for the adopted approach is that the number of available identifiers is halved. In our opinion, this is not a big disadvantage because the number of still available identifiers is large enough to cover the needs of real distributed systems. The number of available identifiers becomes $2032/2 = 1016$, which is large enough to represent real-life systems. For example, in the current VW Golf VI (2010 model), 49 nodes with an average of 140 streams are used [10]. In addition, due to the limited capacity of the CAN bus, the number of needed identifiers will most probably not grow.

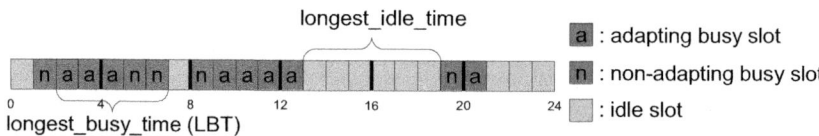

Fig. 10. Example of an annotated busy_idle_list, storing for each time slot during monitoring whether it is idle or busy by an adapting or non-adapting stream

From the annotated busy_idle_list, each node again calculates the longest idle time and longest busy time (LBT). The longest idle time is determined similar to the description given in Section 3.1. As for the LBT, we choose the maximum continuous interval in which the bus was busy starting with an adapting busy slot. This way we ensure that the first slot of the LBT belongs to an adapting stream and, therefore, the adaptation is done. This stream also represents the adapting stream that potentially delays most other streams. In the example in Figure 10, even though the second busy time has four adapting busy slots, the first slot of the first busy time, i.e., here LBT, potentially delays four time slots, while the first one of the second busy time only delays three slots. Therefore, it is better to adapt the first, as it is chosen by the algorithm. In

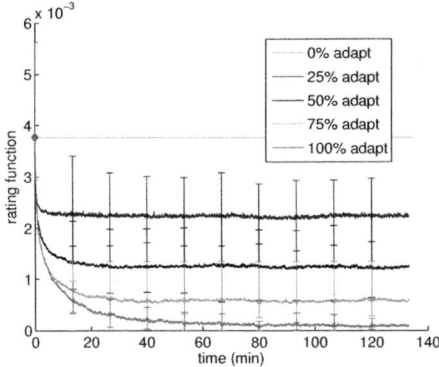 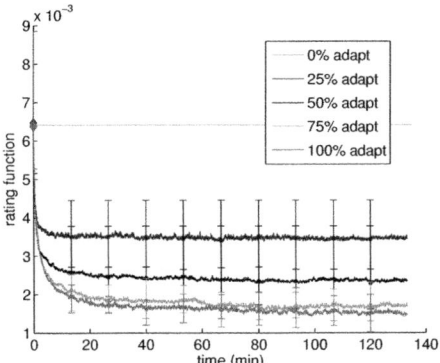

Fig. 11. Rating function as a function of time for different fractions of streams adapting for a scenario with 50% load

Fig. 12. Rating function as a function of time for different fractions of streams adapting for a scenario with 70% load

Figure 11 and 12, it is shown how the enhanced DynOAA performs for different numbers of adapting streams (and nodes) expressed as a fraction of total number of streams. The experiments carried out for this case are similar to the experiments from Figure 4. For the 50% load scenario, if none of the streams are adapting, the rating value in average is constant at 0.00376. If 50% of the streams are adapting, the rating value converges to an average of 0.00124. This is less than a half of the value of for the non-adapting ones:

$$0.00124 < \frac{0.00376}{2} = 0.00188.$$

For the 70% load scenario, this observation is strengthened further. The performance difference between all (100%) adapting and 75% adapting streams is very small. In addition, the experiments show that the time needed to converge to a stable state depends on the number of streams that are adapting. The converged state is reached faster if fewer streams are adapting.

4.2   Multi-segment Systems

The conditions to run DynOAA on multi-segment systems, by allowing some messages no to adapt, have been outlined and established in Section 4.1. In the multi-segment system case, the routed messages are simply considered as non-adapting messages. In order to evaluate the performance of DynOAA for multi-segment networks, we first generated single-segment scenarios by Netcarbench [2] and then provided additional information on the source and destination segments for each message stream, given a number of segments in the system.

We performed a number of experiments to analyze the performance of multi-segment systems using our rating function in Eq. 1. All the results should be considered as preliminary and a work in progress. These experiments were performed under certain conditions and assumptions which are outlined below. We first assumed that the source segment of each stream is assigned by uniformly distributing all the streams to the available segments. The destination segment is characterized by two parameters, *percentage of routed* and *percentage of received segments*. The first parameter specifies the percentage of streams that are routed at all, i.e., whether the destination bus is different than the source bus. The second parameter specifies the percentage of segments, from all available segments, which are included in the destination segment set. Which stream is routed and which segment is chosen as the destination is determined randomly, excluding the case when the source and destination segment are the same. For example, for the case of eight streams in the system with four segments with 50% routed and 25% received messages, two streams are assigned to each segment. One of these two streams has one other segment as its destination.

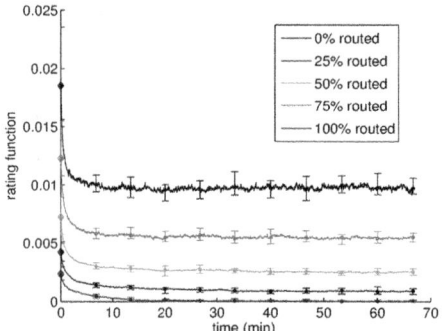 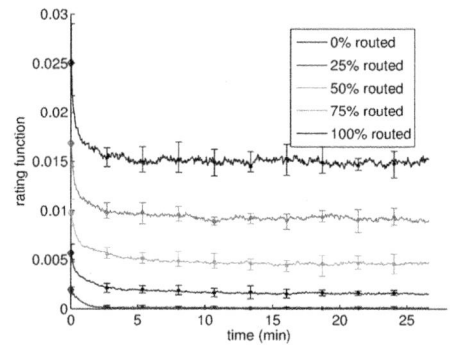

Fig. 13. Rating function as a function of time for a scenario with two segments with different fractions of streams routed to the other segments

Fig. 14. Rating function as a function of time for a scenario with 4 segments with different fractions of streams routed to the other segments

For the experiments presented in this section, the streams of the scenario with 80% load from Section 3.2 are used. The received parameter is set to 50%. In Figure 13 and 14, it is shown how the enhanced DynOAA performs for different multi-segment scenarios. The experiments carried out for this case are similar to the experiments presented in Figure 4. These experiments show that when using DynOAA for the multi-segment systems, the rating value decreases,i.e., performance improves compared to random chosen values, as denoted by the value at time zero.

The experiments shown in Figure 15 are done under assumption of the same workload on each segment, because all streams from the initial set at every segment are either directly scheduled or are routed streams. First, it has to be noted that the rating value is increasing with the number of segments for DynOAA at the converged state, as well as for randomly set offsets at time zero. Also, it can be noted that the decrease of the rating value is most likely due to the increased routing and not the result of degradation of performance of

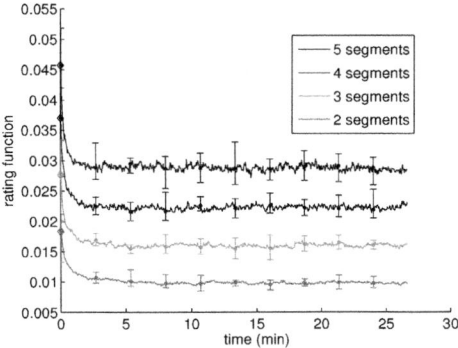

Fig. 15. Rating function as a function of time for scenarios with 2 to 5 segments with 100% routed and 100% received

DynOAA, which uses information local to the segment on which it performs. However, more experiments are needed in future to validate these assumptions.

5   Conclusions and Future Work

Self-organization through dynamic adaptation of message scheduling is a promising way of giving a new life to the existing communication buses used for distributed embedded systems in applications such as automotive or industrial control. We specifically target communication buses, which use priority-based scheduling schemes. The main idea of adapting message offsets in bus-based systems and avoidance of conflicts by simultaneous release of multiple messages has been refined into the algorithm for dynamic offset adaptation, DynOAA. The algorithm is first developed and analyzed for single-bus systems in which all streams adapt the offsets dynamically, and then further enhanced for the case when only certain nodes are adapting. It is shown that by allowing partial adaptation it is possible to use DynOAA also for multi-segment systems in which all segments, consisting of one bus, are homogeneous (the same bus type) and use a single central gateway for their interconnection. The results of experiments run by using a newly developed bit-accurate simulator that incorporates DynOAA and its variations show significant improvement of performance over existing, static scheduling approaches. In particular, the proposed approach results in significantly shorter response times of messages and allows therefore in consequence a much higher utilization of the bus (in our case CAN bus), thus extending applicability of the existing bus technology. The price paid for adaptation is relatively small additional work that has to be performed on the side of system nodes. Our future work includes a closer analysis of the stability of the adaptation process, implementation and its analysis of DynOAA on real microprocessor platforms and further extension of the multi-segment approach with a more realistic model of the gateway.

References

1. CAN Specification 2.0 B. Robert Bosch GmbH, Stuttgart, Germany (1991)
2. Bai, T., Hu, L., Wu, Z., Yang, G.: Flexible fuzzy priority scheduling of the CAN bus. Asian Journal of Control 7(4), 401–413 (2005)
3. Braun, C., Havet, L., Navet, N.: NETCARBENCH: A benchmark for techniques and tools used in the design of automotive communication systems. In: 7th IFAC International Conference on Fieldbuses and Networks in Industrial and Embedded Systems. Citeseer (2007)
4. Di Natale, M.: Scheduling the can bus with earliest deadline techniques. In: Proceedings of the 21st IEEE Real-Time Systems Symposium, pp. 259–268 (2000)
5. Felser, M.: Real-time ethernet - industry prospective. Proceedings of the IEEE 93(6), 1118–1129 (2005)
6. FlexRay Consortium. FlexRay Communications Systems - Protocol Specification v3.0 (2009), http://www.flexray.com
7. Goossens, J.: Scheduling of offset free systems. Real-Time Systems 24(2), 239–258 (2003)
8. Grenier, M., Havet, L., Navet, N.: Pushing the limits of CAN-scheduling frames with offsets provides a major performance boost. In: Proc. of the 4th European Congress Embedded Real Time Software (ERTS 2008). Citeseer, Toulouse (2008)
9. Pfeiffer, O., Ayre, A., Keydel, C.: Embedded networking with CAN and CANopen. Copperhill Media (2008)
10. Racu, R.: The role of timing analysis in automotive network design. In: Talk, 4th Symtavision News Conference on Timing Analysis, Braunschweig, Germany (2010)
11. RTaW-Sim. Real-time at Work CAN Simulator, http://www.realtimeatwork.com/
12. Ziermann, T., Salcic, Z., Teich, J.: DynOAA - Dynamic Offset Adaptation Algorithm for Improving Response Times of CAN Systems. In: Proceedings of Design, Automation and Test in Europe (DATE 2011), March 14-18. IEEE Computer Society, Grenoble (2011)
13. Zuberi, K.M., Shin, K.G.: Non-preemptive scheduling of messages on controller area network for real-time control applications. In: Rtas, p. 240. IEEE Computer Society, Los Alamitos (1995)

Hierarchical-CPK-Based Trusted Computing Cryptography Scheme[*]

Fajiang Yu[1,2], Tong Li[2], Yang Lin[2], and Huanguo Zhang[1,2]

[1] School of Computer, Wuhan University, Wuhan, Hubei, 430072, P.R. China
fjyu@whu.edu.cn
[2] Key Laboratory of Aerospace Information Security and Trusted Computing,
Ministry of Education in China

Abstract. PKI-based trusted computing platform (TCP) requires platform users to apply for multiple Platform Identity Key (PIK) certificates to provide remote attestation, users must pay the fee of digital certificates, which increases users' economic burdens and leads there is hardly any TCP has really performed the core function of trusted computing, platform remote attestation, so the application of TCP is not very wide. This paper presents a trusted computing cryptography scheme based on Hierarchical Combined Public Key (HCPK), which can reduce the risk of single Private Key Generator (PKG), and let the verifier authenticate TCP directly without third party, so platform users do not need to apply additional digital certificates. This scheme can reduce users' cost of using TCP, and encourage the development of TCP application.

Keywords: Trusted Computing, Combined Public Key (CPK), Hierarchical Combined Public Key (HCPK), Trusted Cryptography Module (TCM).

1 Introduction

Platform remote attestation is one of core functions of trusted computing [1,2]. Before platform providing remote attestation to a verifier, platform users must apply for Attestation Identity Key (AIK) certificate from privacy CA based on Endorsement Key (EK) in Trusted Platform Module (TPM). Because of high cost of PKI CA construction and operation, users should pay some administration fees of AIK certificates. For protecting the privacy of platform identity, users need apply for multiple AIK certificates for different applications, which further increases users' economic burdens. So there is hardly any TCP has really performed the core function of trusted computing, platform remote attestation, and the application of TCP is not very wide.

---

[*] This work is supported by the National Natural Science Foundation of China, Grant No: 60673071, 60970115, 91018008, and the Fundamental Research Funds for the Central Universities in China, Grant No: 3101044.

J.M. Alcaraz Calero et al. (Eds.): ATC 2011, LNCS 6906, pp. 149–163, 2011.

For reducing the dependence on privacy CA, Trusted Computing Group (TCG) added one method named Direct Anonymous Attestation (DAA) in TPM 1.2 specifications. DAA employs the methods including Camenisch Lysyanskaya (CL) signature, zero knowledge proof based on discrete logarithm, Fiat Shamir heuristics, group signature and etc. When using DAA, a verifier can affirm that one requesting platform is a host of one real TPM, the verifier can not obtain real identity information about TPM. DAA needs to provide zero knowledge proof at least for three times during one process of identity authentication, which leads low efficiency and implementation complexity. There is few practical applications of DAA.

Being aware of the importance of trusted computing which is a basic security solution for computing platform, as early as in 2006, China Cryptography Administration began to collect correlative institutions for writing *Trusted Computing Platform Cryptography Scheme* and *Technology Specification of Cryptographic Support Platform for Trusted Computing*. China Cryptography Administration released *Functionality and Interface Specification of Cryptographic Support Platform for Trusted Computing* in 2007, which requires Trusted Cryptography Module (TCM, corresponding to TPM) to use *state public key cryptographic algorithm SM2 based on elliptic curves (ECC)* of China. There is also some difference between the subscription process of Platform Identity Key (PIK, corresponding to AIK) certificate and normal certificate, so users can not apply for PIK certificate from current CAs which has supported SM2, and we never see that one privacy CA for TCM is in operation.

In 2003, Identity-Based Combined Public Key (IBCPK, CPK called for short) is presented by one famous cryptography expert of China, Nan Xianghao, in *a profile to network security techniques* [3] for the first time. CPK suffered conspiracy attack and private key collision [4,5], some solutions has been given out [6,7], and CPK also has been developed from version 1.0 to 5.0 [8,9,10,11]. In CPK, Entity's identity name just is public key, there is no need of online database for managing public keys. CPK can form very large key space based on small scale of key seed matrix, directly distribute public key seed matrix to entities, and the entity can be authenticated directly without third party. Comparing with Identity-Based Encryption (IBE) [12,13] based on bilinear map, CPK has high efficiency performance.

This paper presents a trusted computing cryptography scheme based on CPK, which can let the verifier authenticate TCP directly without third party, platform users do not need to apply additional digital certificates. This scheme can reduce users' cost of using TCP, and encourage the development of TCP application. ECC has been implemented in TCM, and CPK is presented by Chinese expert for the first time, which have created good conditions for our research.

2   PKI-Based Trusted Computing Cryptography Scheme

PKI-based TCM key architecture is shown as Figure 1. The manufacture generates an EK during manufacturing stage of TCM. EK is an asymmetric key pair which is stored in the non-volatile protected storage area in the TCM. EK also can be regenerated by the user before obtaining platform ownership. One TCM only have just one EK during its life cycle. Before using TCP, users must take ownership of the platform at first. When taking ownership, TCM generates a Storage Root Key (SRK), which is used to protect users' storage key, sign key, seal key and etc.

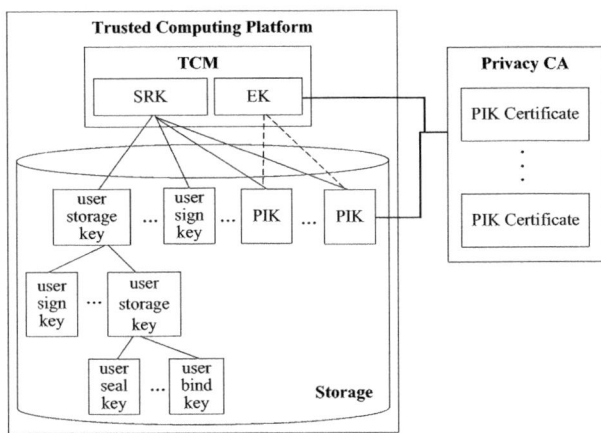

Fig. 1. PKI-based TCM key architecture

Platform remote attestation is one of core functions of trusted computing, at first the platform should prove its identity is trusted. In order to protect privacy, the platform doesn't directly use EK to sign for identity authentication. Users have to request TCM to generate PIK, and apply for PIK certificate from private CA based on EK. The privacy of corresponding relationship between EK and PIK is protected by privacy CA. PIK private key is also protected by SRK. Users should ask TCM to generate different PIKs and apply for different PIK certificates for different applications. Then one TCM and its host platform may have multiple PIKs. Thus, users can use different PIK for identity authentication in different situations, in order to protect the privacy of platform identity.

The procedures of generating of PIK, applying for, signing and activating PIK certificate are shown as Figure 2.

1. Platform user sends a command `MakeIdentity` to TCM via TCM Service Module (TSM). TCM generates a PIK and encrypt private part of PIK with SRK. Then TCM use private key of PIK to sign the digest value of public key of private CA and public part of PIK, the signature is $\mathsf{PIKSign} = \mathrm{Sign}(\mathsf{PIK_{Pri}}, H(\mathsf{CAK_{Pub}} \parallel \mathsf{PIK_{Pub}}))$. TCM returns public part of PIK $\mathsf{PIK_{Pub}}$ and $\mathsf{PIKSign}$.

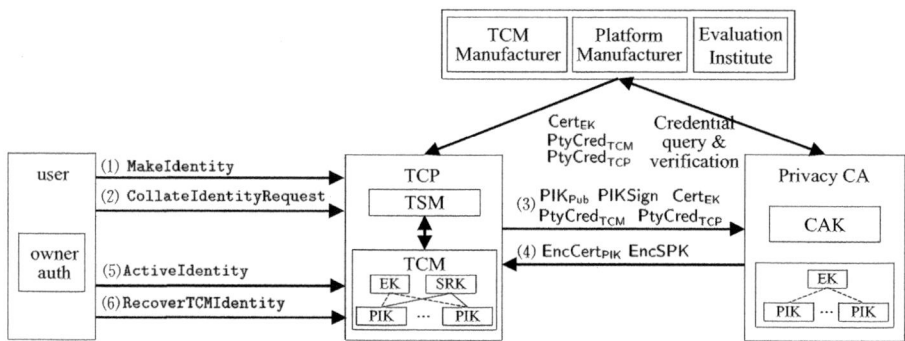

Fig. 2. Procedures of generating of PIK, applying for, signing and activating PIK certificate

2. Platform user sends a request `CollateIdentityRequest` to TSM for getting EK certificate $Cert_{EK}$ and property certificate for TCM and its host platform from evaluation institute and manufacturer $PtyCred_{TCM}$, $PtyCred_{TCP}$.

3. Platform user sends the message including PIK_{Pub}, PIKSign, $Cert_{EK}$, $PtyCred_{TCM}$, $PtyCred_{TCP}$ to private CA and applies for PIK certificate.

4. Privacy CA verifies $PtyCred_{TCP}PtyCred_{TCM}Cert_{EK}$, then it will use PIK_{Pub} to verify PIKSign. After these two verifications, privacy CA generates and signs PIK certificate $Cert_{PIK}$, then randomly generates a symmetric key sessionKey and use it to encrypt $Cert_{PIK}$ to get $EncCert_{PIK}$ = AEnc(sessionKey, $Cert_{PIK}$). Finally, it use the public key of EK to encrypt the digest of sessionKey and public part of PIK to get EncSPK = SEnc(EK_{Pub}, sessionKey $\|$ H(PIK_{Pub})). Private CA sends $EncCert_{PIK}$, EncSPK to TCP.

5. Platform user sends a request `ActiveIdentity` to TCM via TSM. TCM use the private key of EK to decrypt EncSPK, sessionKey $\|$ H(PIK_{Pub}) = SDec(EK_{Pri}, EncSPK). We can determine whether sessionKey decrypted is right by judging the correctness of H(PIK_{Pub}), while only the valid TCP can get the correct sessionKey. TCM returns sessionKey.

6. Platform user sends a request `RecoverTCMIdentity` to TSM, TSM uses sessionKey to decrypt $EncCred_{PIK}$, and gets PIK certificate $Cert_{PIK}$ = ADec(sessionKey, $EncCert_{PIK}$).

3   CPK Introduction

The mathematical base of CPK is the following ECC combination theorem [4]:

Theorem 1 (ECC Combination Theorem). *ECC parameters are* $\langle p, a, b, G, n \rangle$, *that is given one elliptic curve E based on the selected finite field* F_p: $y^2 \equiv (x^3 + ax + b)(\bmod\ p)$. *G is the generator of one additive cyclic sub-group of points on E. n is the order of this group. If there are* $h(h \in \mathbb{Z}, 1 < h < n)$ *ECC key pairs:* $(d_1, Q_1), (d_2, Q_2), \ldots, (d_h, Q_h)$, *the summary of these h private* keys is denoted as d, the summary of these h public keys is denoted as Q, that is $d = \left(\Sigma_{i=1,2,\ldots,h}d_i\right) \bmod n, Q = \Sigma_{i=1,2,\ldots,h}Q_i$, then (d,Q) also is one ECC key pair.

Proof (of ECC Combination Theorem).
　　Because $(d_1,Q_1),(d_2,Q_2),\ldots,(d_h,Q_h)$ are ECC key pairs, then

$$Q_1 = d_1G, Q_2 = d_2G, \ldots, Q_h = d_hG$$
$$Q = d_1G + d_2G + \ldots + d_hG$$
$$Q = \left((d_1 + d_2 + \ldots + d_h)(\bmod n)\right)G = dG$$

So (d,Q) is a ECC key pair.

The basic components of CPK include private key seed matrix $(d_{ij})_{m\times h}$, public key seed matrix $(Q_{ij})_{m\times h}$, the mapping function set F, and the algorithm of combining public and private key Alg_{KG} [8]:

1. **Private Key Seed Matrix** $(d_{ij})_{m\times h}$

$$(d_{ij})_{m\times h} = \begin{pmatrix} d_{11} & d_{12} & \ldots & d_{1h} \\ d_{21} & d_{22} & \ldots & d_{2h} \\ \vdots & \vdots & \vdots & \vdots \\ d_{m1} & d_{m2} & \ldots & d_{mh} \end{pmatrix}$$

　　where $h, d_{ij}, d_{i'j'} \in \mathbb{Z}, 1 < h, d_{ij}, d_{i'j'} < n, i, i' \in \mathbb{Z}_m, j, j' \in \mathbb{Z}_h$. Only under the condition $i = i'$ and $j = j'$, $d_{ij} = d_{i'j'}$, otherwise $d_{ij} \neq d_{i'j'}$. $(d_{ij})_{m\times h}$ is just stored in Private Key Generator (PKG) as a secret.
2. **Public Key Seed Matrix** $(Q_{ij})_{m\times h}$

$$(Q_{ij})_{m\times h} = \begin{pmatrix} Q_{11} & Q_{12} & \ldots & Q_{1h} \\ Q_{21} & Q_{22} & \ldots & Q_{2h} \\ \vdots & \vdots & \vdots & \vdots \\ Q_{m1} & Q_{m2} & \ldots & Q_{mh} \end{pmatrix}$$

　　where $Q_{ij} = d_{ij}G, i \in \mathbb{Z}_m, j \in \mathbb{Z}_h$. $(Q_{ij})_{m\times h}$ is public to all entities.
3. **Mapping Function Set** $F = \{f_1, f_2, \ldots, f_h\}$

$$f_i : \{0,1\}^l \mapsto \{1, 2, \ldots, m\}, in \in \mathbb{Z}_h$$

　　where l is the length of entity identity defined by the system. F is public.
4. **Algorithm of Combining Public and Private Key** Alg_{KG}
　　CPK directly uses entity identity $\text{ID}_{\mathbb{E}}$ as public key, the combined public or private key pair $(d_{\mathbb{E}}, Q_{\mathbb{E}})$ is:

$$d_{\mathbb{E}} = \left(\Sigma_{i=1,2,\ldots,h}d_{r_ii}\right) \bmod n, Q_{\mathbb{E}} = \Sigma_{i=1,2,\ldots,h}Q_{r_ii}, r_i = f_i(\text{ID}_{\mathbb{E}})$$

　　Alg_{KG} is public.

The CPK component mentioned above is the basic component defined by CPK1.0. In CPK1.0, one entity's private key $d_{\mathbb{E}}$ is a linear combination of elements in private key seed matrix. Because the mapping function set F is public, $\mathbb{E}$ can write a linear equation $d_{\mathbb{E}} = (d_{r_1 1} + d_{r_2 2} + \ldots + d_{r_h h}) \bmod n$ based on its identity. If there are $m \times h$ entities launching a conspiracy attack, then $m \times h$ linear equations can be wrote. If these $m \times h$ equations are linearly independent, then $m \times h$ unknown variants can be worked out, that is the all elements in private key seed matrix $(d_{ij})_{m \times h}$.

The conspiracy attack on CPK1.0 need not work out all seed private key. Suppose there are two entities $\mathbb{E}_1$ and $\mathbb{E}_2$, their private keys are $d_{\mathbb{E}_1}$ and $d_{\mathbb{E}_2}$, their public keys are $Q_{\mathbb{E}_1}$ and $Q_{\mathbb{E}_2}$ respectively. $d_{\mathbb{E}_1}$ conspires with $d_{\mathbb{E}_2}$, that is $d_{\mathbb{E}_1}$ is combined with $d_{\mathbb{E}_2}$ linearly: $d_{\text{Atk}} = (a_{\text{Atk}} d_{\mathbb{E}_1} + b_{\text{Atk}} d_{\mathbb{E}_2}) \bmod n$, $Q_{\mathbb{E}_1}$ is combined with $Q_{\mathbb{E}_2}$ linearly: $Q_{\text{Atk}} = a_{\text{Atk}} Q_{\mathbb{E}_1} + b_{\text{Atk}} Q_{\mathbb{E}_2}$. Try to select $\text{ID}_{\text{Try}} \in \{0,1\}^l$, and compute $Q_{\text{Try}} = \Sigma_{i=1,2,\ldots,h} Q_{r_i i}, r_i = f_i(\text{ID}_{\text{Try}})$. If $Q_{\text{Try}} = Q_{\text{Atk}}$, then this is a successful conspiracy attack. $(d_{\text{Atk}}, Q_{\text{Atk}})$ is a valid key pair, and it can pretend to be a valid entity, but d_{Atk} is not generated by PKG.

In order to resist the conspiracy attack and keep the character of CPK, CPK5.0 [11] adds separation private key sequence $(Sd_i)_k$ and separation public key sequence $(SQ_i)_k$, $i \in \{1, 2, \ldots, k\}$, k is the number of separation keys, $SQ_i = Sd_i G$. $(Sd_i)_k$ is stored in PKG as a secret. $(SQ_i)_k$ is public. Some functions also are added into the mapping function set: $F = \{f_1, f_2, \ldots, f_h\} + \{f_{S_1}, f_{S_2}, \ldots, f_{S_t}\}, t \in \mathbb{Z}, 1 < t < k$:

$$f_{Si} : \{0,1\}^l \mapsto \{1, 2, \ldots, k\}, i \in \{1, 2, \ldots, t\}$$

The combined private and public key in CPK5.0 are:

$$\text{CPriK}_{\mathbb{E}} = \left(d_{\mathbb{E}} + \Sigma_{i=c_1, c_2, \ldots, c_t} Sd_i\right) \bmod n$$
$$\text{CPubK}_{\mathbb{E}} = Q_{\mathbb{E}} + \Sigma_{i=c_1, c_2, \ldots, c_t} SQ_i, c_i = f_{S_i}(\text{ID}_{\mathbb{E}})$$

By using the separation key sequence, CPK5.0 multiplies the difficulty of conspiracy attack.

CPK also has the possibility of key collision. Document [6,7] have presented an optimized scheme of CPK seed matrix to avoid key collision.

4   HCPK-Based Trusted Computing Cryptography Scheme

4.1   Motivation for HCPK

In the CPK cryptosystemall private keys can be generated by PKG. If PKG is attacked, all private keys will be leaked out, PKG is at a high risk. CPK can form very large key space based on small scale of key seed matrix, so in theory the flatting management of CPK keys can be implemented, that is all the private keys can be generated by one PKG. But in practice, PKG should verify the identity of every entity, then generates and distributes private key, when PKG is in a large network application system, the single PKG might became a bottle neck. If there are too many entities, it is hard for PKG to distribute private key into each entity in a security controlled environment.

In order to disperse security risk and work load of single PKG, this paper presents a Hierarchical CPK architecture (HCPK) by referring HIBE [14]. In HCPK, every PKG of each layer has its own private key seed matrix. If some PKG at some level is attacked, its private key seed is leaked out, only the entities belonged to this PKG will be affected, the security of other entities are still guaranteed. Even root PKG is attacked, the entities' private keys won't be leaked out. PKG at every level only needs to verify the identities of the entities belong to the PKG and its next level PKG, generate and distribute the corresponding private keys. In HCPK, the work load of root PKG is distributed to other low level PKGs, the private key distribution can be done locally under a security environment.

4.2   Hierarchical Combined Public Key (HCPK)

To have a clear understanding, we describe HCPK based on CPK1.0, the construction of HCPK based on CPK5.0 can use the method similarly.

1. **Setup**
   (a) Given one elliptic curve E based on the selected finite field F_p: $y^2 \equiv (x^3 + ax + b)(\mod p)$, G is the generator of one additive cyclic subgroup of points on E, n is the order of this group. ECC parameters are $\langle p, a, b, G, n \rangle$, which are public.
   (b) Building mapping function set: $F = \{f_1, f_2, \ldots, f_{h_{\max}}\}$, $f_i : \{0,1\}^l \mapsto \mathbb{Z}_m, i \in \mathbb{Z}_{h_{\max}}$, where $h_{\max}$ is the maximum number of columns in all PKG public and private key seed matrixes, $1 < h_{\max} < n$, l is the length of entity identity $\text{ID}_\mathbb{E}$. F is public.
   (c) Choosing one HASH function: $H : \{0,1\}^* \mapsto \mathbb{Z}_p$. H is public.
   (d) PKG_k builds private key seed matrix. PKG_k represents the PKG at level k, $k \geqslant 0$, PKG_0 represents root PKG. There is only one root PKG in every HCPK system. PKG_k builds private key seed matrix $(d_{ij}^k)_{m \times h_k}$, where $h_k \in \mathbb{Z}, 1 < h_k < h_{\max}, d_{ij}^k, d_{i'j'}^k \in \mathbb{Z}, 1 < d_{ij}^k, d_{i'j'}^k < n, i, i' \in \{1, 2, \ldots, m\}, j, j' \in \{1, 2, \ldots, h_k\}$. Only under the condition $i = i'$ and $j = j'$, $d_{ij}^k = d_{i'j'}^k$, otherwise $d_{ij}^k \neq d_{i'j'}^k$. $(d_{ij}^k)_{m \times h_k}$ is just stored in PKG_k as a secret.
   (e) PKG_k builds public key seed matrix $(Q_{ij}^k)_{m \times h_k}$, where $Q_{ij}^k = d_{ij}^k G, i \in \{1, 2, \ldots, m\}, j \in \{1, 2, \ldots, h_k\}$. $(Q_{ij}^k)_{m \times h_k}$ is public.

2. **Extract**
   $\mathbb{E}_t$ represents a entity at level t, $t \geqslant 1$, $\mathbb{E}_t$ may be the PKG at level t. The identity tuple of $\mathbb{E}_t$ is: $(\text{ID}_1, \text{ID}_2, \ldots, \text{ID}_t)$, where $\text{ID}_1, \text{ID}_2, , \text{ID}_{t-1}$ are the identities of $\mathbb{E}_t$'s ancestor PKGs at level 1, 2, , $t - 1$ respectively. ID_t is the identity of $\mathbb{E}_t$. $(\text{ID}_1, \text{ID}_2, \ldots, \text{ID}_t)$ is public. The parent PKG of $\mathbb{E}_t$ PKG_{t-1} compute:

$$d_{\mathbb{E}_t} = \left(d_{t-1} + \Sigma_{i=1,2,\ldots,h_{t-1}} d_{r_i i}^{t-1}\right) \mod n, r_i = f_i(\text{ID}_t)$$

where d_{t-1} is the private key of PKG_{t-1}. If $t = 1$, then PKG_{t-1} is PKG_0 and $d_{t-1} = 0$. $d_{\mathbb{E}_t}$ is stored in $\mathbb{E}_t$ as a secret.

3. **Sign**

   Signature and verification schemes are based on the algorithms in document[15].

   Entity $\mathbb{E}_t$ signs message m with the private key $d_{\mathbb{E}_t}$:

   (a) Compute $h = H(m)$;

   (b) Choose a random $r \in [1, n - 1]$;

   (c) Compute $(x_r, y_r) = rG$;

   (d) Compute $u = (h + x_r) \bmod n$, if $u = 0$ or $u + r = 0$, then goto (b);

   (e) Compute $v = ((1 + d_{\mathbb{E}_t})^{-1} \cdot (r - u \cdot d_{\mathbb{E}_t})) \bmod n$, if $v = 0$ then goto (b);

   (f) The signature is $\sigma = (u, v)$.

4. **Verify**

   Verify the signature $\sigma = (u, v)$ of m signed by $\mathbb{E}_t$, the identity tuple of $\mathbb{E}_t$ is $(\mathrm{ID}_1, \mathrm{ID}_2, \ldots, \mathrm{ID}_t)$:

   (a) Compute $Q_{\mathbb{E}_t} = \Sigma_{k=1,2,\ldots,t}\left(\Sigma_{i=1,2,\ldots,h_{k-1}} Q_{r_i^k}^{k-1}\right), r_i^k = f_i(\mathrm{ID}_k)$;

   (b) Compute $h = H(m)$;

   (c) Compute $t = (u + v) \bmod n$;

   (d) Compute $(x_r, y_r) = vG + tQ_{\mathbb{E}_t}$;

   (e) Compute $u' = (h + x_r) \bmod n$;

   (f) If $u = u'$, then the signature is right.

4.3 Application of HCPK in Trusted Computing

According to TCM production, evaluation and application, a four levels HCPK can be used in trusted computing, as is shown in Figure 3. Under the root PKG authenticated by China Cryptography Administration, every TCM manufacturer and enterprise user build their own PKGs, and individual users can use manufacturer PKG directly.

The scale of public and private key seed matrix in root PKG, manufacturer PKG and enterprise PKG is determined by the amount of their subaltern PKGs and TCMs respectively. Root PKG only needs to generate and distribute private keys for manufacturer PKGs, the security of private keys distribution can be

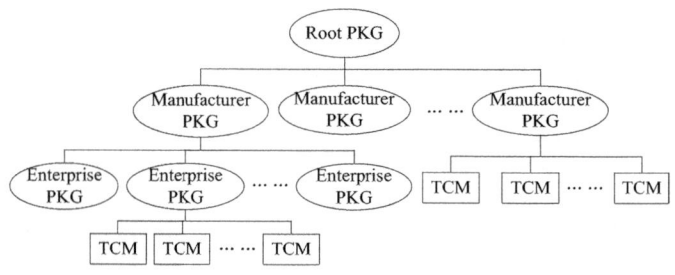

Fig. 3. Trusted Computing HCPK

guaranteed more easily, and the work load also are reduced. Similarly, manufacturer PKG generates and distributes private keys for enterprise PKGs or TCMs, enterprise PKG generates and distributes private keys for TCMs, which also can be done in a local controlled security environment. During identity verification of TCM host platform, identity tuple $(ID_{Man}, ID_{Ent}, ID_{TCM})$ or (ID_{Man}, ID_{TCM}) should be used, where ID_{Man}, ID_{Ent}, ID_{TCM} are the identity of manufacturer PKG, enterprise PKG and TCM respectively.

If one enterprise PKG is attacked and its private key seed matrix is leaked out, only the TCMs belonged to the enterprise are affected, since other manufacturer PKGs have their own private key seed matrixes. Even if the root PKG has been attacked, it will not completely expose all TCMs' private keys, because manufacturer PKGs, enterprise PKGs have their own private key seed matrixes.

During platform identification, the TCM on Access Request Platform (ARP) uses its own PIK private key to sign given PCR values. The verifier receives the signature, according to identification tuple $(ID_{Man1}, ID_{Ent1}, ID_{TCM})$, it is able to compute the corresponding ECC public key of PIK private key, and complete identity verification consequently.

4.4   TCM Key Architecture Based on HCPK

Within the architecture of HCPK, PIK private key is directly generated by manufacturer PKG or enterprise PKG based on TCM identity ID_{TCM}. Platform users need not apply for PIK public key certificate based on EK. There is no need for a privacy CA to maintain the database of PIK certificate, because the identity tuple $(ID_{Man}, ID_{Ent}, ID_{TCM})$ or (ID_{Man}, ID_{TCM}) just is the PIK public key.

PKI-based platform can have multiple PIKs and the corresponding certificates, in order to protect the privacy of platform identity. To ensure the security of private key distribution and using, CPK-based PIK private key are usually directly loaded into TCM by PKG in one controlled and security environment. With the limited memory capacity, TCM fails to save multiple PIK private keys. It also is unable to generate PIK dynamically for CPK-based platform, because the security of CPK private key online distribution can not be guaranteed easily. So there is only one PIK on CPK-based platform. Compared with PKI-based platform, CPK-based platform has a more simplified TCM key architecture, which is shown in Figure 4. The anonymity of platform identity can be ensured by TCM ring signature.

In order to authenticate TCP directly without third party, there also are CPK parameters including public key seed matrix stored in TCM.

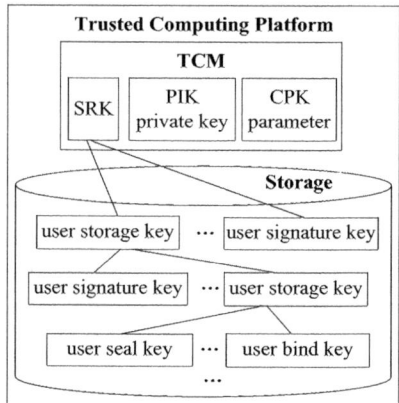

Fig. 4. HCPK-based TCM key architecture

4.5   Cross-Domain Platform Identity Authentication Based on HCPK

CPK usually loads CPK parameters into all entities in one security domain, for authenticate TCP directly without third party and online database. Because PKG is at high security risk, different institutes or organizations will establish their own PKGs. However in some application scenarios, ARP and the verifier may belong to different security domains, which needs cross-domain remote authentication and resource access. Since each security domain has its own PKG, different PKG usually has different CPK parameters, so it is unable to do cross-domain authentication directly.

Within the architecture of HCPK, considering the most typical situation of cross-domain attestation, ARP and verifier belong to different enterprise PKGs, and this two enterprise PKGs belong to different manufacturer PKGs. Even ARP and verifier belong to different security domains, but they belong to a same root PKG, sharing same CPK parameters, which is shown in Figure 5, it is able to do cross-domain attestation directly.

5   Security Analysis

Security analysis of CPK resistance against conspiracy attack and private key collision caused by mapping function are out of the scope of this paper, we just analyse the security of HCPK-based trusted computing cryptography scheme, that is the security of platform identity authentication with PIK private key based on HCPK. This paper also does not care the security problems caused by specific implementations, and just analyses the security of HCPK signature scheme based on Computation Diffie-Hellman Problem (CDHP) in random oracle model.

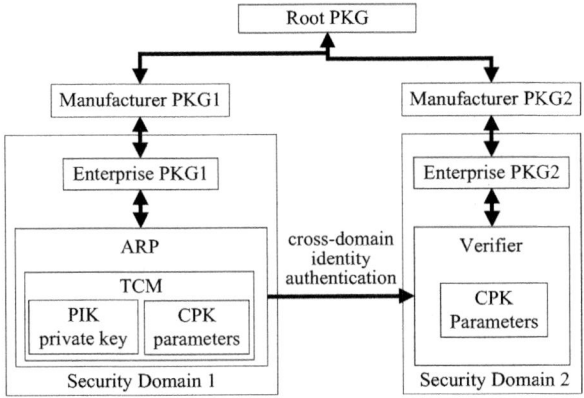

Fig. 5. Cross-domain platform identity authentication based on HCPK

Computation Diffie-Hellman Problem (CDHP): There is an additive cyclic sub-group of points on one elliptic curve in a finite field F_P, G is the generator of the group, n is the order of the group. Given $(G, aG, bG), a, b \in \mathbb{Z}_n$, compute abG.

5.1   Attack Model and Security Definition

The most general known notion of security of an ID-based signature scheme is Existential Forgery on Adaptively Chosen Message and ID Attacks (EF-ACM-IA) presented in document [16]. CPK is a ID-based cryptography scheme, the model of EF-ACM-IA on HCPK is (the adversary algorithm is denoted as $\mathcal{A}$, the challenger playing the following game against $\mathcal{A}$ is denoted as $\mathcal{C}$):

1. $\mathcal{C}$ runs **Setup** of HCPK system, and gives returned system parameters to $\mathcal{A}$;
2. $\mathcal{A}$ issues the following queries as he wants:
   (a) Mapping function query. $\mathcal{A}$ gives an identity name ID, $\mathcal{C}$ computes $f_i(\text{ID}), i = 1, 2, \ldots,$
       $h_{\max}$, and returns the result to $\mathcal{A}$;
   (b) HASH function query. $\mathcal{A}$ gives a message m, $\mathcal{C}$ computes $H(m)$, and returns the result to $\mathcal{A}$;
   (c) **Extract** query. $\mathcal{A}$ gives an identity tuple $(\text{ID}_1, \text{ID}_2, \ldots, \text{ID}_t)$, $\mathcal{C}$ runs **Extract**, and returns the result, a private key d_t, to $\mathcal{A}$;
   (d) **Sign** query. $\mathcal{A}$ gives a private key d_t and a message m, $\mathcal{C}$ runs **Sign**, and returns the result, a signature σ , to $\mathcal{A}$;
3. $\mathcal{A}$ outputs $\big((\text{ID}_1, \text{ID}_2, \ldots, \text{ID}_t), m, \sigma\big)$, where $(\text{ID}_1, \text{ID}_2, \ldots, \text{ID}_t)$ and m are not equal to the inputs of any query to **Extract** and **Sign**, respectively. $\mathcal{A}$ wins the game if σ is a valid signature of m for $(\text{ID}_1, \text{ID}_2, \ldots, \text{ID}_t)$.

Definition 1. *If no polynomial time algorithm $\mathcal{A}$ has non-negligible probability advantage of winning above game, then HCPK signature scheme is secure under EF-ACM-IA.*

5.2 Security Proof

First we modify the above game of EF-ACM-IA on HCPK as Existential Forgery on Adaptively Chosen Message and Given ID Attacks (EF-ACM-GIA): Given an identity tuple $(\mathrm{ID}_1, \mathrm{ID}_2, \ldots, \mathrm{ID}_t)$ in step (1), $\mathcal{C}$ returns system parameters to $\mathcal{A}$ together with $(\mathrm{ID}_1, \mathrm{ID}_2, \ldots, \mathrm{ID}_t)$. In step (3), $\mathcal{A}$ must output the given $(\mathrm{ID}_1, \mathrm{ID}_2, \ldots, \mathrm{ID}_t)$ together with corresponding message m and signature σ as its final result.

Referring Lemma 1 in document [16], the following Lemma 1 can be obtained:

Lemma 1. *If there is an algorithm $\mathcal{A}_0$ which can win the game of EF-ACM-IA to HCPK signature scheme with polynomial running time t_0 and probability advantage ϵ_0, then there is an algorithm $\mathcal{A}_1$ which can win the game of EF-ACM-GIA with polynomial running time $t_1 \leqslant t_0$ and probability advantage $\epsilon_1 \geqslant \epsilon_0 \cdot (1 - 1/n)/q_F$, where q_F is the maximum number of queries to mapping function asked by $\mathcal{A}_0$. The numbers of queries to mapping function, HASH function, **Extract** and **Sign** asked by $\mathcal{A}_1$ are the same as those of $\mathcal{A}_0$.*

Lemma 2. *If there is an algorithm $\mathcal{A}_1$ which can win the game of EF-ACM-GIA with polynomial running time t_1 and probability advantage $\epsilon_1 \geqslant 10(q_S + 1)(q_S + q_H)/n$, then CDHP can be solved by an algorithm $\mathcal{A}_2$ with polynomial running time $t_2 \leqslant 23q_H t_1/\epsilon_1$ and probability advantage $\epsilon_2 \geqslant 1/9$, where q_H, q_S are the maximum number of queries to HASH function and **Sign** asked by $\mathcal{A}_1$ respectively.*

Proof (Lemma 2).

The algorithm $\mathcal{A}_1$ can be viewed as an adversary with adaptively chosen message attack to the non-ID-based scheme obtained by fixing an ID in HCPK-based signature scheme. So we can refer correlative lemma or theorem in document [17].

> **Lemma 4 in document [17].** Let $\mathcal{A}$ be a Probabilistic Polynomial Time (PPT) Turing machine whose input only consists of public data. The number of queries that $\mathcal{A}$ can ask to the random oracle and the number of queries that $\mathcal{A}$ can ask to the signer are denoted as q_R and q_S respectively. Assume that, within a time bound t, $\mathcal{A}$ produce, with probability $\epsilon \geqslant 10(q_S + 1)(q_S + q_R)/n$, a valid signature (m, r, h, σ). If the triples (r, h, σ) can be simulated without knowing the secret key, with an indistinguishable distribution probability, then, a replay of the attacker $\mathcal{A}$, where interactions with the singer are simulated, outputs two valid signatures (m, r, h, σ) and (m, r, h', σ'), such that $h \neq h'$, within time $t' \leqslant 23q_R t/\epsilon$ and with probability $\epsilon' \geqslant 1/9$.

The signature value of HCPK signature scheme $\sigma = (u, v)$, so the two valid signatures are $(m, r, h, (u, v))$ and $(m, r, h', (u', v'))$.

Since $u = (h + x_r) \bmod n$ and $v = ((1 + d_{\mathbb{E}_t})^{-1} \cdot (r - u \cdot d_{\mathbb{E}_t})) \bmod n$, so

$$u - h \equiv x_r (\bmod\ n), \quad vG + (u + v)Q_{\mathbb{E}_t} = rG$$

Similarly, $u' - h' \equiv x_r(\text{mod } n), v'G + (u' + v')Q_{\mathbb{E}_t} = rG$, then

$$\begin{cases} u - h \equiv u' - h'(\text{mod n}) \Leftrightarrow (u - h)Q_{\mathbb{E}_t} = (u' - h')Q_{\mathbb{E}_t} & (1) \\ vG + (u + v)Q_{\mathbb{E}_t} = v'G + (u' + v')Q_{\mathbb{E}_t} & (2) \end{cases}$$

Compute $(2) - (1)$: $(v - v' + h - h') \cdot d_{\mathbb{E}_t}G = (v' - v)G$

Suppose $a = v - v' + h - h', b = d_{\mathbb{E}_t}$, then $abG = (v' - v)G$. That is we have known G, $aG = (v - v' + h - h')G$ and $bG = Q_{\mathbb{E}_t}$, we can compute abG, and CDHP can be solved, so Lemma 2 has been proved.

Combining Lemma 1 and 2, we can get Theorem 2.

Theorem 2. *If there is an algorithm $\mathcal{A}_0$ which can win the game of EF-ACM-IA to HCPK signature scheme with polynomial running time t_0 and probability advantage $\epsilon_0 \geqslant 10(q_s + 1)(q_s + q_H)q_F)/(n - 1)$, then CDHP can be solved by an algorithm $\mathcal{A}_2$ with polynomial running time $t_2 \leqslant 23q_H q_F t_0/(\epsilon_0(1 - 1/n))$ and probability advantage $\epsilon_2 \geqslant 1/9$, where q_F, q_H, q_s are the maximum number of queries to mapping function, HASH function and **Sign** asked by $\mathcal{A}_0$ respectively.*

Because there is no probabilistic polynomial time algorithm which can solve CDHP up to now, there is no algorithm $\mathcal{A}_0$ which can win the game of EF-ACM-IA to HCPK signature scheme with polynomial running time and non-negligible probability advantage, and HCPK signature scheme satisfies the requirements in Definition 1.

6   Performance Analysis

This paper analyses the performance of HCPK-based TCM cryptography scheme compared with PKI-based scheme. Because of limited resources, TCM has high performance requirement of cryptography scheme. This paper mainly analyses the calculation performance on TCM of the two cryptography schemes, and does not analyse the performance of PKI-based TPM cryptography scheme, because TPM uses RSA algorithm, TCM uses ECC algorithm, it is uneasy about comparing the performance of RSA with ECC directly.

The differences between HCPK and PKI-based cryptography scheme mainly are in PIK generation and signature signing. Because signature verification can be done on the host, this paper does not analyze the performance difference in PIK signature verification.

HCPK-based PIK private key is generated by parent PKG of TCM, and is distributed and loaded into TCM directly, there is no need for TCM to do any calculation.

PKI-based PIK creation includes generating of PIK, applying for, signing and activating PIK certificate. PIK is generated by TCM, the time spent is denoted as T_{KeyGen}. TCM uses PIK private key to sign the digest of privacy CA public key and PIK public key, the time spent is denoted as $T_{\text{Hash}} + T_{\text{Sign}}$. TCM also needs to use EK private key for decrypting to get the session key for encrypting

PKI certificate, the time spent is denoted as T_{SDec}. PKI-based TCM may crate multiple PIKs, so it will multiply the time spent.

The time spent by HCPK-based TCM for signing PCR value with PIK private key is the same as PKI-based TCM, denoted as T_{Sign}. For using PIK in PKI-based TCM, PIK must be loaded into TCM by using command TCM_LoadKey firstly, the time spent is denoted as T_{LdKey}.

The comparison of TCM performance between HCPK-based cryptography scheme and PKI-based scheme is shown in Table 1.

Table 1. Comparison of TCM perforamnce between HCPK-based scheme and PKI-based scheme

	time spent on PIK creation	time spent on PIK signing
HCPK-based scheme	0	T_{Sign}
PKI-based scheme	$x(T_{KeyGen} + T_{Hash} + T_{Sign} + T_{SDec})$	$T_{LdKey} + T_{Sign}$

We can see from Table 1 that HCPK-based cryptography scheme has a great advantage of TCM performance compared with PKI-based scheme.

In addition, some TCM commands about EK and PIK can be reduced in HCPK-based TCM, such as TCM_CreateEndorsementKeyPair, TCM_CreateRevocableEK, TCM_RevokeTrust, TCM_ReadPubEK, TCM_MakeIdentity, TCM_ActivateIdentity and etc, which also can save TCM storage space, simplify TCM implementation, and improve the performance of TCM.

7   Conclusion and Future Work

PKI-based TCP requires platform users to apply for multi PIK certificates, the annual fee of one certificate is about 8 $, so users of PKI-based TCP must pay $8x$ $ one year. HCPK-based TCP can reduce the risk of single PKG, and let the verifier authenticate TCP directly without third party, platform users do not need pay any fee for applying additional digital certificates. HCPK-based trusted computing cryptography scheme also can be implemented without any modification of current TCM hardware. So HCPK-based TCP can reduce users' cost of using TCP. HCPK-based trusted computing cryptography scheme can simplify TCM key architecture, and authenticate cross-domain platform identity. This paper has proved that HCPK signature scheme is secure under EF-ACM-IA in random oracle model. Comparing with PKI-based scheme, HCPK-based cryptography scheme has obvious advantage in the performance of TCM. HCPK and PKI-based platforms can authenticate each other, and HCPK-based cryptography scheme also can be implemented on TPM.Next.

In future, we will consider how to protect the anonymity of PIK private key and platform identity based on HCPK, and design a platform remote attestation protocol based HCPK, which can directly authenticate cross-domain platform without third party, and protect the privacy of platform component information.

References

1. Shen, C., Zhang, H., Wang, H., et al.: Research and development of trusted computing. Science China: Information Science 40(2), 139–166 (2010) (in chinese)
2. Shen, C., Zhang, H., Feng, D., et al.: Survey of information security. Science China: Information Science 37(2), 1–22 (2007) (in chinese)
3. Nan, X., Chen, Z.: A profile to network security techniques. National Defense Industry Press, Beijing (2003) (in chinese)
4. Chen, H., Guan, Z.: Explanation of some questions about CPK. China Information Security 9, 47–49 (2007) (in chinese)
5. Wang, G., Wang, M., Wu, D., et al.: Analysis of the CPK random collision probability. China Information Security 11, 87–88 (2008) (in chinese)
6. Rong, K., Li, Y.: A optimized scheme of the CPK seed matrix. Journal of Computer Engineering and Applications 42(24), 120–121 (2006) (in chinese)
7. Xing, H.: Research and applications of the key technologies of combined public key. Engineering master dissertation of National University of Defense Technology (2009) (in Chinese)
8. Nan, X.: Identity authentication based on CPK. National Defense Industry Press, Beijing (2006) (in Chinese)
9. Nan, X.: CPK-crypotosystem and cyber security. National Defense Industry Press, Beiing (2008) (in Chinese)
10. Nan, X.: Cyber security technical framework — Trusting system based on identity authentication. Electronic Industry Press, Beijing (2010)
11. Nan, X.: Combined Public Key (CPK) Cryptosystem Standard (v5.0). Network & computer security (2010) (in Chinese)
12. Shamir, A.: Identity-based cryptosystems and signature schemes. In: Blakely, G.R., Chaum, D. (eds.) CRYPTO 1984. LNCS, vol. 196, pp. 47–53. Springer, Heidelberg (1985)
13. Boneh, D., Franklin, M.: Identity-based encryption from the weil pairing. In: Kilian, J. (ed.) CRYPTO 2001. LNCS, vol. 2139, pp. 213–229. Springer, Heidelberg (2001)
14. Gentry, C., Silverberg, A.: Hierarchical ID-based cryptography. In: Zheng, Y. (ed.) ASIACRYPT 2002. LNCS, vol. 2501, pp. 548–566. Springer, Heidelberg (2002)
15. China Cryptography Administration. State Public Key Cryptographic Algorithm SM2 Based on Elliptic Curves (December 2010) (in Chinese), http://www.oscca.gov.cn/UpFile/2010122214822692.pdf (March 2011)
16. Cha, J.C., Cheon, J.H.: An identity-based signature from gap diffie-hellman groups. In: Desmedt, Y.G. (ed.) PKC 2003. LNCS, vol. 2567, pp. 18–30. Springer, Heidelberg (2002)
17. Pointcheval, D., Stern, J.: Security Arguments for Digital Signatures and Blind Signatures. Journal of Cryptology 13(3), 361–396 (2000)

Facilitating the Use of TPM Technologies Using the Serenity Framework

Antonio Muñoz and Antonio Maña

Computer Science Department
University of Málaga
{amunoz,amg}@lcc.uma.es

Abstract. Trusted platform modules (TPMs) specification is highly complex and therefore the deployment of TPM –based security solutions is equally complicated and difficult; although they can provide a wide range of security functionalities. In order to make TPM technology available to system engineers without their needing to have in-depth knowledge of trusted computing specifications we propose, in this paper, to develop an approach using security patterns to specify TPM-based security solutions. Ideally suited to producing precise specifications of TPM –based solutions for certain security goals are the refined notions of security patterns developed in the SERENITY research project.

1 Introduction

Security patterns, described informally using either plain text or semi formal languages with graphical visualisations, have successfully been used to describe security solutions in such a way as to make them available to system engineers who are not necessarily experts in security engineering [1,2,5,6,7,8,10]. In the SERENITY research project [9] the notion of security patterns has been extended to concrete specifications of re-usable security mechanisms for AmI (ambient intellligence) systems. Also included is information on the properties satisfied and context conditions. The Trusted Computing Group [3] specifies the trusted computing platform (TPM) and so these types of security solutions have proven to be particularly useful for describing security solutions reliant on TPMs. Usually because of the complexity of their standard, only experts on trusted computing are able to develop TPM-based solutions for non trivial requirements. One way to make TPM-based solutions available for wide-scale use in software development is to describe re-usable solutions in terms of security patterns. As most of the complexity is in the selection of TPM commands and the details of the calls to a particular security service this makes high-level patterns using plain text less suitable. So in this paper we use a fairly simple example of a TPM-based security solution to demonstrate and motivate the refined notion of security patterns developed in SERENITY. Also developed in SERENITY are more complex security patterns are studied for example certified migration keys to control the migration of data between a set of platforms.

J.M. Alcaraz Calero et al. (Eds.): ATC 2011, LNCS 6906, pp. 164–174, 2011.

One area where the need for confidentiality and mechanisms to protect data confidentiality is amply demonstrated is in the field of medicine as the following scenario shows. A patient continues their treatment at home whilst still being monitored by their medical centre. Let us imagine that following a doctor's visit the patient requires a prescription to be filled but cannot go to the pharmacy and therefore the doctor issues an electronic prescription which he sends to the medical centre. Once it reaches the centre it is dealt with by a social worker who is responsible for getting it filled and delivering it to the patient. The prescription is therefore stored in the social worker's PDA (personal digital assistant used to denote any portable device able to perform this task) and sent from there to the pharmacy's PC. Obviously the patient's details are confidential with only those authorised able to access the prescription; in this case the doctor, relevant staff at the medical centre, the social worker and naturally the pharmacist. Imagine a case where the social worker loses their PDA, there are mechanisms in place to protect confidentiality; as there are for data transfer via the Internet. Possible solutions are;

- Access control provided by the device's operating system
- Software encryption
- A device protected by a TPM (Trusted Platform Module) to encrypt data and bind it to the TPM.

At first glance the first two mechanisms would be suitable for preventing attacks "from outside" but imagine the attacker actually has the device in their possession, they could gain access to the whole device and therefore study the encryption application to find out the decryption key or password and then apply it to all manner of attacks. We therefore find the third solution, relying as it does on a TPM to be the most effective, as the owner of the device does not provide an advantage to a possible attacker. They find themselves powerless to attack a TPM as we will go on to show.

2 Introduction to TPM Technology

A TPM is usually implemented as a chip integrated into the hardware of a platform (such as a PC, a laptop, a PDA, a mobile phone). A TPM owns shielded locations (i.e. no other instance but the TPM itself can access the storage inside the TPM) and protected functionality (the functions computed inside the TPM can not be tampered with). The TPM can be accessed directly via TPM commands or via higher layer application interfaces (the Trusted Software Stack, TSS). The TPM offers two main basic mechanisms: it can be used to prove the configuration of the platform it is integrated in and applications that are running on the platform, and it can protect data on the platform (such as cryptographic keys). For realizing these mechanisms, the TPM contains a crypto co-processor, a hash and an HMAC algorithm, a key generator, etc. In order to prove a certain platform configuration, all parts that are engaged in the boot process of the platform (BIOS, master boot record, etc) are measured (i.e. some integrity measurement hash value is computed), and the final result of the accumulated hash values is stored inside the TPM in a so-called Platform Configuration Register (PCR).

An entity that wants to verify that the platform is in a certain configuration requires the TPM to sign the content of the PCR using a so-called Attestation Identity Key (AIK), a key particularly generated for this purpose. The verifier checks the signature and compares the PCR values to some reference values. Equality of the values proves that the platform is in the desired state. Finally, in order to verify the trustworthiness of an AIK's signature, the AIK has to be accompanied by a certificate issued by a trusted Certification Authority, a so-called Privacy CA (P-CA). Note that an AIK does not prove the identity of the TPM owner.

Keys generated and used by the TPM have different properties, some (so-called non-migratable keys) can not be used outside the TPM that generated them, some (like AIKs) can only be used for specific functions. Particularly interesting is that keys can be tied to PCR values (by specifying PCR number and value in the key's public data). This has the effect that such a key will only be used by the TPM if the platform (or an application) configuration is in a certain state (i.e. if the PCR the key is tied to, contains a specific value). In order to prove the properties of a particular key, for example to prove that a certain key is tied to specific PCR values, the TPM can be used to generate a certificate for this key by signing the key properties using an AIK.

To request a TPM to use a key (e.g. for decryption), the key's authorisation value has to be presented to the TPM. This together with the fact that the TPM specification requires a TPM to prevent dictionary attacks provides the property that only entities knowing the key's authorisation value can use the key.

Non-migratable keys are especially useful for preventing unauthorised access to some data stored on the platform. Binding such a key to specific PCR values and using it to encrypt the data to be protected achieves two properties: the data can not be decrypted on any other platform (because the key is non-migratable), and the data can only be decrypted when the specified PCR contains the specified value (i.e. when the platform is in a specific secure configuration and is not manipulated).

3   An Introduction to the Serenity Framework

This section gives an overview of the Project Framework. The main objective of Serenity is to provide a framework for the automated treatment of security and dependability issues in AmI scenarios. For this purpose the project is two-folded: (i) capturing the specific expertise of the security engineers in order to make it available for automated processing, and (ii) providing run-time support for the use and the monitoring of these security and dependability mechanisms. These two cornerstones have been deployed by means of:

- A set of S\D modeling artefacts (S\D artifacts, for short), used to model security and dependability solutions (S&D solutions) at different levels of abstraction. S&D solutions are isolated components that provide security and/or dependability services to applications. The use of different levels of abstraction responds to the need of different phases of the software development process. These artefacts are supported by an infrastructure created for

the development and the validation of S&D solutions. This infrastructure includes concepts, processes and tools used by security experts for the creation
of new S&D solutions ready for automatic processing.

- A development framework. Under the name of Serenity Development-time
Framework (SDF) there is an infrastructure that supports the development of
secure applications. These secure applications, called Serenity-aware applications, are supported by S&D solutions, consequently, they include references to the aforementioned S&D artefacts.
- A run-time framework, called Serenity Run-time Framework (SRF). The
SRF provides support to applications at run-time, by managing S&D solutions and by monitoring the systems' context. A further description of the
SRF can be found at [4].

Once infrastructural pieces have been described, the rest of this section explains how
to use S&D modelling artefacts to bridge the gap between abstract S&D solutions and
actual implementations of these S&D solutions. Interested readers could refer to Section 3 in order to find information on how the SRF supports applications at run-time.

Back to the abstractions, five main artefacts are provided to achieve a logical
way to represent S&D solutions in the Serenity project: S&DClasses, S&DPatterns,
IntegrationSchemes, S&DImplementations and ExecutableComponents. These artefacts,
depicted in figure 1, represent S&DSolutions using semantic descriptions at different
levels of abstraction. The main reason for using different artefacts, each one addressing an abstraction level, is that, by doing this, it is possible to cover the complete life
cycle of secure applications, especially at development and run-time phases.

- S&DClasses represent abstractions of a set of S&DPatterns, characterized for
providing the same S&D Properties and complying with a common interface.
This is one of the most interesting artefacts to be used at development time by
system developers. The main purpose of this artefact is to facilitate the dynamic substitution of S&D solutions at run-time, while facilitating the development
process. Applications request S&D Solutions to the SRF to fulfill a set of S&D
requirements. Usually, these requirements are hard coded by means of calls to
S&DClasses or S&DPatterns interfaces. At run-time all S&DPatterns (and
their respective S&DImplementations, described below) belonging to the same
S&DClass, will be selectable by the SRF automatically.
- S&DPatterns are precise descriptions of abstract S&D solutions. These descriptions contain all the information necessary for the selection, instantiation,
adaptation, and dynamic application of the solution represented by the
S&DPattern. S&DPatterns describe the security pattern's functionalities and
how to use them in a structured way. The most interesting elements of the
S&DPattern structure are: (i) The pattern interface, describing the functionalities provided and how to use them; (ii) references to the S&DClasses the
S&DPattern belongs to; and (iii) the ClassAdaptor, describing how to adapt
the S&DPattern interface to the S&DClass interface. S&DPatterns represents
monolithic isolated S&D solutions, but a special type of S&D artefact called
\textit{Integration Scheme (IS)} also exists, which consists on an S&D solution at the same level than S&DPatterns. They represent S&D solutions

that are built by means of combining other S&DPatterns. At Serenity-aware application development time, Integration Schemes are used similarly as S&DPatterns are. However, they differ in their development process, presented in \cite{Antonio2006}. All along this paper we use the notion of S&DPatterns to refer to S&DPatterns and Integration Schemes indistinctly.

- S&DImplementations are specification of the components that realize the S&D solutions. S&DImplementations are not real implementations but their representation/description. An S&DImplementation describes an implementation of an S&DPattern and, thus, a S&DPattern may have more than one S&DImplementation.

- Finally, ExecutableComponents are real implementations of the S&DImplementations. These elements are not used at development time, but they are the realization of the selected S&D solution at run-time. An ExecutableComponent works as a stand-alone executable S&D solution ready to provide its services to applications. They are software, and sometimes hardware, components.

Every S&D solution provides at least one security property. Every S&DPattern (and every Integration Scheme) refer to an S&D solution. On the contrary, every S&D solution can be represented by one or more S&DPatterns and/or Integration Scheme. Each S&DPattern is implemented by means of at least one S&DImplementation. Finally, there is an ExecutableComponent entity for each S&DImplementation. While, S&DClasses are the most abstract level entities to represent S&D solutions, ExecutableComponents, being software components, are the lowest abstraction level way to represent an S&D solution. For the representation of S&D solutions, following the Serenity approach, developers need to count on, at least, one artefact for every level of the hierarchy.

To sum up, S&DClasses, S&DPatterns and S&DImplementations are development-time oriented artefacts, while ExecutableComponents are especially suitable for run-time. Serenity-aware applications include references to development-time artefacts. Depending on the artefact level of abstraction, at run-time, the SRF has more/less flexibility to select S&D S&D S&D S&D solutions. In other words, this approach enables the creation of open architectures where, at run-time, the SRF completes by applying the ExecutableComponents that implements the S&D solutions fixed at development-time. The main purpose of introducing this approach is to facilitate the dynamic substitution of S&D solutions at run-time while facilitating the development process.

4   Using TPM Functionalities to Prevent Unauthorized Access to Data

Returning to our previous example of the electronic prescription. Assuming that the PDA is protected by TPM, our solution uses TPM functionality to prevent unauthorised access to the patient's details (in this case their prescription). This is carried out in three stages. Firstly a public key, with given properties, is requested from the social worker (or rather their TPM) by the medical centre. Among these properties is that the key shall be non-migratable, bound to the TPM of the social worker's PDA, and should have certain PCR values (ensuring it hasn't been tampered with). A TPM generated certificate proves the key's properties. Then the medical centre encrypts the patient's prescription using that key and the resulting ciphertext is sent to the social worker's PDA, where finally the prescription is decrypted and sent to the pharmacy using the key's authorisation data. In the following paragraphs we explain in more detail how the key's properties ensure none other than the social worker can carry out the decryption.

4.1 Phases 1 and 2 – Setup and Encryption

First, the medical centre requires a key from the social worker's PDA that is non-migratable and bound to specific PCR values. The following message sequence chart (msc) shows the subsequent communication between their PDA and the PDA's TPM for generating this key. The actions are as follows:

1. The PDA starts an object specific authorisation session OSAP.

2. With TPM CreateWrapKey the social worker's PDA requires the TPM to generate a command contains the key's usage authorisation data (we do not discuss here where the key's authorisation data comes from, it can for example be presented them or by their PDA).

3. The TPM generates keyA and returns the key blob.

4. The PDA then requests its TPM to generate a certificate for keyA:
   - It starts an object independent authorization protocol with TPM OIAP.
   - Then it loads keyA into the TPM.
   - It starts another OIAP session.
   - It loads an AIK into the TPM.
   - With TPM CertifyKey it then lets the TPM generate a certificate for keyA using the AIK. (Again we do not discuss where the AIK's authorization data comes from.)
   - The TPM returns the certificate.

The social worker's PDA now sends this certificate and the AIK certificate issued by the P-CA to the medical centre which in turn verifies the certificates and checks in particular that the requested key has the required properties (non-migratable,bound to specific PCR values). The medical centre then uses the public part of the key to encrypt the patient's prescription and sends the ciphertext to the social worker's PDA. This ensures confidentiality of the patient's data during communication between the centre and the PDA.

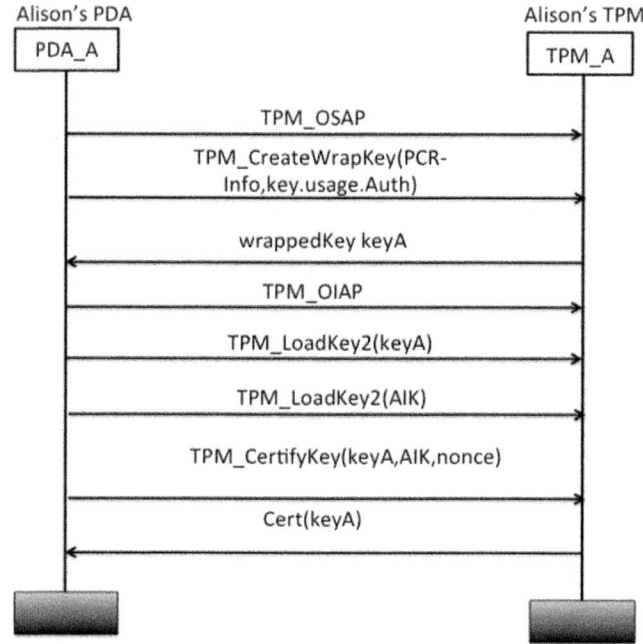

Fig. 1. Phases 1 and 2 setup and encryption

4.2   Phase 3 – Data Retrieval

The encrypted description is stored on the PDA. When the social worker wants to transfer the prescription to the pharmacy it needs to be decrypted which has to be done by the TPM. The following figure describes the necessary commands exchanged between the PDA and the PDA's TPM. Again, we do not discuss which entity provides key authorisation data necessary for the process.

1. Social worker's PDA starts an OIAP session.
2. The PDA then loads keyA into the TPM.
3. With TPM UnBind the PDA lets the TPM decrypt the prescription using the private part of keyA.
4. TPM A checks that the PCR values for PDA A correspond to those that the key is tied to and then uses the key to decrypt the prescription blob.
5. TPM A returns the prescription, which can then be forwarded by the PDA to the pharmacy.

The key's properties prevent unauthorised access to the patient's data during storage on the PDA: Since the key is non-migratable, only the PDA's TPM can decrypt the data. Binding the key to specific PCR values ensures that the TPM only decrypts the data while the PDA is not being manipulated. Finally, assuming that the social worker does not reveal the key authorisation data to anybody, the key will only be used by the TPM after authorisation is given by the social worker.

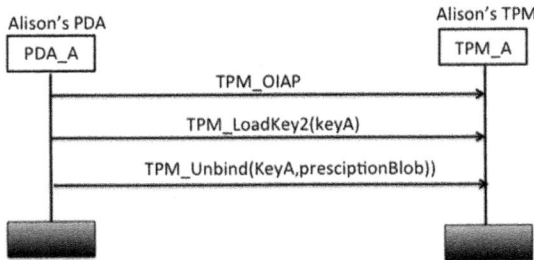

Fig. 2. Phase 3 decryption

5   Capturing the TPM Solution

Security patterns represent a suitable means to make TPM functionality available to application developers. However, in order for patterns to serve our purposes, we need them to contain at least the following information:

1. the security requirement it addresses (in our case to prevent unauthorised access to data sent to and then stored on a TPM protected device);
2. the assumptions on the environment that need to hold, both before and during the operation (for example, the TPM has to be active);
3. the roles of the entities involved (in our case these are the medical centre and the PDA);
4. the precise services offered by the pattern for each of the roles;
5. the parameters that must be instantiated;
6. any additional information that may help in the selection and application of the pattern; and
7. information regarding the pattern itself (source, version, certificates, etc).

With this information, application developers can decide whether the security requirements fulfilled by the pattern match the ones needed by the application and whether the environment the application shall run in meets the assumptions specified in the pattern.

5.1   SERENITY Patterns

In the project SERENITY, security and dependability (S&D) patterns are described using a specification language that meets the requirements listed above. These patterns especially support applications that run in unpredictable and dynamic contexts. To this end, SERENITY patterns are described using three modelling artefacts:

- The first SERENITY artefact is called S&D Class. S&D Classes provide homogeneous mechanisms to access S&D services and allow developers to delay the decision about the most appropriate solution until runtime, when the information required to make a sound decision (about the context, type and capabilities of other parties, etc.) is available. In our case, developers can use the S&D Class ("SimpleConfidentialStorage.cen.eu") that represents confidentiality services and includes a high-level interface (with function calls such as SetupConfidentialStorage, AcceptConfidentialStorage, StoreConfidential, etc) which hides the complexity of the TPM technology.

- The second of the SERENITY artefacts, called S&D Pattern, is used to represent abstract solutions such as authentication protocols, encryption algorithms, or TPM functionality. The main purpose of this artefact is to guarantee the interoperability of different implementations of a solution. S&D patterns achieving the same requirement can refer to the same S&D Class. All patterns belonging to one S&D Class provide compatible interfaces which enables their dynamical selection and use. Patterns contain all the information necessary to select solutions appropriately addressing certain security requirements. The pattern specifying our example solution contains, among other details, an interface section with all function calls that the solution uses (in particular it contains all TPM command calls). Furthermore a so-called "Interface Adaptor" specifies how each of the Class function calls is translated to a sequence of pattern function calls. In our case, the Interface Adaptor contains for example the following:

$$RetrieveConfidential(d,c) ::= \{TPM\_OIAP, TPM\text{-}LoadKey2(kA),$$
$$TPM\_UnBind(kA,Ciphertext,d)\}$$

- The third artefact provided by SERENITY is the S&D Implementation, which represents specific realisations of an S&D Solution. All S&D Implementations of an S&D Pattern must conform directly to the interface, monitoring capabilities, and any other aspect described in the S&D Pattern. However, they also have differences, such as the specific context conditions that are required, performance, target platform, programming language or any other feature not fixed by the pattern. Implementations that realise the TPM pattern can for example defer in the platform they shall run on and in the platform's operating system. These three artefacts provide a precise description of S&D Solutions that supports both development time and runtime processes. All SERENITY artefacts are stored in a SERENITY library and thus made available to application developers. Selection of the artefacts and their integration into applications is supported by the SERENITY Runtime Framework (SRF), a suite of tools to support the automated management of S&D Solutions based on our modelling artefacts [4].

5.2 SERENITY Operation

One interesting aspect to remark on is the use of the previously described artefacts. Let us illustrate it using our scenario. The developers of the healthcare system identify the requirement that patient data needs to be confidential not only during transmissions but also when stored in the social worker's PDA. After searching some available SERENITY online libraries, they identify the S&D Class SimpleConfidentialStorage.cen.eu as fulfilling this requirement adequately. Hence the class's function calls are integrated into the application. Now the application developers have two choices: to select an appropriate pattern and implementation of the class and integrate it into the application during development time, or to leave this decision open. They decide to delegate the pattern and implementation selection to the SERENITY Runtime Framework (SRF) of the PDA. At runtime, in order to realise the services of the S&D Class, the SRF identifies the best available S&D Implementation and its corresponding S&D Pattern, according to the current context and the preconditions included in both artefacts. In our case, the best option is an implementation of the "TPMConfidentialStorage.serenity-project.org" S&D Pattern, which uses the TPM-based solution described in section 4.

The SRF activates the solution (which may require initialization steps as described in the artefacts) and provides a reference to it to the healthcare application. The SRF uses the Interface Adaptor provided by the S&D Pattern to translate the calls made by the application to the calls provided by the selected solution. In this way the healthcare applications can transparently access the S&D services it needs without knowing in advance which specific solution is use to provide them.

6   Conclusions and Future Work

In this paper we have aimed to show how complex technologies such as TPM can be used at both runtime and development and how security patterns, especially SERENITY, can facilitate the use of these technologies and devices. Currently we are focusing on three main lines of research: the development of the SERENITY Runtime Framework, the universality and flexibility of modelling artefacts' structure and contents, and finally, for producing the information contained in the pattern the necessary mechanisms and tools.

Acknowledgment. The work in this paper was partly co-sponsored by the EC Framework Programme as part of the ICT PASSIVE project (http://ict-passive.eu/) and the "Advanced Security Service cERTificate for SOA " ASSERT4SOA project (http://www.assert4soa.eu/).

References

1. Fernandez, E.: Security patterns. In: Procs. of the Eigth International Symposium on System and Information Security, SSI 2006, Keynote talk, Sao Jose dos Campos, Brazil (November 2006)
2. Fernandez, E., Rouyi, P.: A pattern language for security models. In: Pattern Languages of Program Design, PLoP 2001 (2001)
3. T. C. Group. TCG TPM Specification 1.2 (2006),
   http://www.trustedcomputing.org
4. Gallego, B., Serrano, D., Muñoz, A., Maña, A.: Security Patterns, towards a further level. In: The International Conference of Security and Cryptography, SECRYPT 2009, pp. 349–356 (2009)
5. Romanosky, S.: Security design patterns part 1, v1.4 (2001)

6. Armenteros, A., Muñoz, A., Maña, A., Serrano, D.: Security and Dependability in Ambient Intelligence scenarios: The communication prototype. In: International Conference on Enterprise Information Systems (2009)
7. Schumacher, M., Fernandez, E., Hybertson, D., Buschmann, F., Sommerlad, P.: Security Patterns - Integrating Security and Systems Engineering. John Wiley Sons, Chichester (2005)
8. Schumacher, M., Roedig, U.: Security engineering with patterns. Springer, Heidelberg (2001)
9. SERENITY. System engineering for security and dependability. IST project, funded by the EC (2006), http://www.serenityproject.org/
10. Wassermann, R., Cheng, B.: Security patterns. Technical Report MSU-CSE-03-23, Department of Computer Science, Michigan State University (August 2003)

Spam Detection on Twitter Using Traditional Classifiers

M. McCord and M. Chuah

Computer Science & Engineering Department,
Lehigh University,
Bethlehem, PA 18015, USA
{mpm308,chuah@cse}@lehigh.edu

Abstract. Social networking sites have become very popular in recent years. Users use them to find new friends, updates their existing friends with their latest thoughts and activities. Among these sites, Twitter is the fastest growing site. Its popularity also attracts many spammers to infiltrate legitimate users' accounts with a large amount of spam messages. In this paper, we discuss some user-based and content-based features that are different between spammers and legitimate users. Then, we use these features to facilitate spam detection. Using the API methods provided by Twitter, we crawled active Twitter users, their followers/following information and their most recent 100 tweets. Then, we evaluated our detection scheme based on the suggested user and content-based features. Our results show that among the four classifiers we evaluated, the Random Forest classifier produces the best results. Our spam detector can achieve 95.7% precision and 95.7% F-measure using the Random Forest classifier.

Keywords: Social network security, spam detection, machine learning.

1   Introduction

Online social networking sites such as Facebook, LinkedIn and Twitter allow millions of users to meet new people, stay in touch with friends, establish professional connections and more. According to the report in [9], Twitter is the fastest growing social networking site among all the social networking sites. Twitter provides a micro-blogging service to users where users can post their messages, called tweets. Each tweet is limited to 140 characters and only text and HTTP links can be included in the tweets. Such tweet exchanges allow friends/colleagues to communicate and stay connected.

Twitter users have different levels of awareness with respect to security threats hidden in social networking sites. For example, a previous study has showed that 45% of users on a social networking site readily click on links posted by any friend in their friendlists' accounts, even though they may not know that person in real life [11]. Thus, spammers are attracted to use Twitter as a tool to send unsolicited messages to legitimate users, post malicious links, and hijack trending topics. Spam is becoming an increasing problem on Twitter as well as on other online social networking sites. A study shows that more than 3% of the messages are spam on Twitter [1,2,15]. Even the trending topics, which are the most tweeted-about-topics on Twitter, were

J.M. Alcaraz Calero et al. (Eds.): ATC 2011, LNCS 6906, pp. 175–186, 2011.

attacked by spammers. A trending-topic attack reported in [3] forced Twitter to temporarily disable the trending topics so as to remove the offensive terms.

To deal with increasing threats from spammers, Twitter provides several ways for users to report spam. A user can report a spam by clicking on the "report as spam" link in their home page on Twitter. The reports are investigated by Twitter and the accounts being reported will be suspended if they are found to be spam. Another publicly available method is to post a tweet in the "@spam @username" format where @username mentions a spam account. However, even this service is also abused by spammers. Some Twitter applications also allow users to flag possible spammers. Additional methods and applications to reduce Twitter spam are described in [4]. Twitter also puts efforts into closing suspicious accounts, and filtering out malicious tweets. However, some legitimate Twitter users complain that their accounts were mistakenly suspended by Twitter's cleaning efforts [5]. All these ad hoc methods depend on users to identify spam manually based on their own experience. We need some tools that can automatically identify spammers. In addition, we need more accurate but efficient spam detection methods to avoid causing inconvenience to legitimate users.

In this paper, we first study the differences between the tweets published by spammers and legitimate users. Our goal is to identify useful features that can be used in traditional machine learning schemes to automatically distinguish between spamming and legitimate accounts. The major contributions of this paper are as follows:

- We propose using user-based features and content-based features to facilitate spam detection
- We compare the performance of four traditional classifiers, namely Random Forest, Support Vector Machine, Naïve Bayesian and K-Nearest Neighbor classifiers, in their abilities to distinguish suspicious users from normal ones.
- We developed a prototype to evaluate the detection scheme based on our suggested features. The results show that our spam detection system has a 95.7% precision and 95.7% F-measure using the Random Forest Classifier.

The rest of the paper is organized as follows. In Section 2, we give some background about the Twitter site, and discuss related work. In Section 3, we discuss the various user-based and content-based features we proposed. In Section 4, we describe the characteristics of these user-based and content-based features based on the dataset we have collected. In Section 5, we first describe how our spam detection method works. Then, we report our evaluation results. We conclude in Section 6.

2   Background and Related Work

2.1   The Twitter Social Network

Twitter is a social networking site just like Facebook and MySpace except that it only provides a microblogging service where users can send short messages (referred to as tweets) that appear on their friends' pages. A Twitter user is only identified by a username and optionally by a real name. A Twitter user can start "following" another user X. Consequently, that user receives user X's tweets on her own page. User X who is "followed" can follow back if she so desires. Tweets can be grouped using hashtags which are popular words, beginning with a "#" character. Hashtags allow users to efficiently search tweets based on topics of interest. When a user likes some-one's tweet, she can "retweet" that message. As a result, that message is shown to all her followers. A user can decide to protect her profile. By doing so, any user who wants to follow that private user needs her permission. Twitter is the fastest growing social networking site with a reported growth rate of 660% in 2009 [9].

2.2   Related Work

Since social networks are strongly based on the notion of a network of trust, the ex-ploitation of this trust might lead to significant consequences. In 2008, an experiment showed that 41% of the Facebook users who were contacted acknowledged a friend request from a random person [10]. L. Bilge et al [11] show that after an attacker has entered the network of trust of a victim, the victim will likely click on any link con-tained in the messages posted, irrespective of whether she knows the attacker in real life or not. Another interesting finding by researchers [12] is that phishing attempts are more likely to succeed if the attacker uses stolen information from victims' friends in social networks to craft their phishing emails. For example, phishing emails from shoppybag were often sent from a user's friendlist and hence a user is often tricked into believing that such emails come from trusted friends and hence willingly pro-vides login information of his/her personal email account. In [13], the authors created a popular hashtag on Twitter and observed how spammers started to use it in their messages. They discuss some features that might distinguish spammers from legiti-mate users e.g. node degree and frequency of messages. However, merely using sim-ple features like node degree and frequency of messages may not be enough since there are some young Twitter users or TV anchors that post many messages.

A larger spam study was reported in [14]. The authors in [14] generate honey pro-files to lure spammers into interacting with them. They create 300 profiles each on popular social networking sites like Facebook, Twitter and MySpace. Their 900 ho-ney profiles attract 4250 friends request (mostly on Facebook) but 361 out of 397 friend requests on Twitter were from spammers. They later suggested using features like the percentage of tweets with URLs, message similarity, total messages sent, number of friends for spam detection. Their detection scheme based on the Random Forest classifier can produce a false positive rate of 2.5% and a false negative rate of 3% on their Twitter dataset.

In [15], the authors propose using graph-based and content-based features to detect spammers. The graph-based features they use include the number of followers, the number of friends (the number of people you are following) and a reputation score which is defined as the ratio between the number of followers over the total sum of the number of followers and the number of people a user is following. The conjecture is that if the number of followers is small compared to the amount of people you are following, the reputation is small and hence the probability is high that the associated account is spam. The content-based features they use include (a) content similarity,

(b) number of tweets that contain HTTP links in the most recent 20 tweets, (c) the number of tweets that contain the "@" symbols in a user's 20 most recent tweets, (d) the number of tweets that contain the "#" hashtag symbol. Using a Bayesian classifier, the author found that out of the 392 users that are classified as spammers, 348 are really spam accounts and 44 users are false positives so the precision of his spam detection scheme is 89%.

3   User-Based and Content-Based Features

In this section, we discuss the features we extract from each Twitter user account for the purpose of spam detection. The features extracted can be categorized into (i) user-based features and content-based features. User-based features are based on a user's relationships e.g. those whom a user follow (referred to as friends), and those who follow a user (referred to as followers) or user behaviors e.g. the time periods and the frequencies when a user tweets.

3.1   User-Based Features

In Twitter, you can build your own social network by following friends and allowing others to follow you. Spam accounts try to follow large amount of users to gain their attention. The Twitter's spam and abuse policy [6] says that, "if you have a small number of followers compared to the amount of people you are following", then it may be considered as a spam account. Three user-based features, namely the number of friends, the number of followers, and the reputation of a user are computed for spam detection in [15]. The reputation of a user is defined in [15] as

$$R(j) = \frac{n_i(j)}{n_i(j) + n_O(j)} \tag{1}$$

where $n_i(j)$ represents the number of followers user j has and $n_o(j)$ represents the number of friends ("following") user j has. However, in our work, we only use the number of followers and the number of "following" as part of our user-based features.

3.1.1   Distribution of Tweets over 24-Hour Period
In addition, we define statistics that are based on the percentage distribution of tweets in each of the 8 3-hour periods within a day (e.g. 1st time slot is from 0-3hr, 2nd is from 3-6 hr, etc) posted by a user. Our conjecture is that spammers tend to be most active during the early morning hours while regular users will tweet much less during typical sleeping hours. We compute these 8 statistics based on the local time associated with the location reported in a user's profile.

3.2   Content-Based Features

For content-based features, we use some obvious features e.g. the average length of a tweet. Additional content-based features are described in subsequent subsections.

3.2.1   Number of URLs

Since Twitter only allows a message with a maximum length of 140 characters, many URLs included in tweets are shortened URLS. Spammers often include shortened URLs in their tweets to entice legitimate users to access them. Twitter filters out the URLs linked to known malicious sites. However, shortened URLs can hide the source URLs and obscure the malicious sites behind them. While Twitter does not check these shorten URLs for malware, any user's updates that consist mainly of links are considered spam according to Twitter's policy. In [15], the authors use the percentage of tweets containing HTTP links in the user's 20 most recent tweets. If a tweet contains the sequence of characters "http;// or www., this tweet is considered containing a HTTP link. In our work, we use the number of HTTP links that are contained in a user's 100 most recent tweets.

3.2.2   Replies/Mentions

A user is identified by a unique username and can be referred to using the @username format in tweets on Twitter. Each user can send a reply message to another user using the @username+message format where @username is the message receiver. Each user can reply to anyone on Twitter whether they are his friends/followers or not. He can also mention another @username anywhere in his tweet, rather than just at the beginning. Twitter automatically collects all tweets containing a username in the @username format in his replies tab. The reply and mention features are designed to help users track conversation and discover each other on Twitter.

However, spammers often abuse this feature by including many @usernames as unsolicited replies or mentions in their tweets. If a user includes too many replies/mentions in his tweets, Twitter will consider that account as suspicious. The number of replies and mentions in a user account is measured by the number of tweets containing the @symbol in the user's 20 most recent tweets in [15]. However, we used a feature that measures the total number of replies/mentions in the most 100 recent tweets for each user.

3.2.3   Keywords/Wordweight

Since we observe that the contents in spammers' tweets contain similar words, we define two metrics to help identify spammers. First, we created a list of spam words that are often found in spammers' tweets and the associated probabilities of these words, and a list of popular words in legitimate tweets and the associated probabilities of these words. Our two defined metrics using this information are: (a) the keywords metric which counts the average number of spam words found in the 100 most recent tweets. For example, if we find a total of 50 spam words in the 100 most recent tweets, the keyword metric of that user will be 50/100, (b) the word weight metric which is defined as the difference between the sum of weighted probabilities of spam words and the sum of weighted probabilities of legitimate words found in a user's tweets. Assume that the word "hello" appears in a user's tweet and the weight of the word "hello" in the spamword list is 0.2 while the weight of that same word "hello" in the regular word list is 0.1, then the wordweight based on this word "hello" will be 0.2-0.1=0.1. The final wordweight is the sum of the weights for all words from the spamword and regular word lists that can be found in a user's tweets.

3.2.4   Retweets/Tweetlen

Twitter allows users to retweet tweets generated by other users. All retweets start with the symbol @RT. The number of retweets in the 20-100 most recent tweets of a user is also used as one of the content-based features in our spam detection system. The average tweet length is also used as a content feature.

3.2.5   Hashtags

Trending topics are the most-mentioned terms on Twitter at that moment, this week or this month. Users can use the hashtag, which is the #symbol followed by a term describing or naming the topics, to a tweet. If there are many tweets containing the same term, the term will become a trending topic. Spammers often post many unrelated tweets that contain the trending topics to lure legitimate users to read their tweets. Twitter considers an account as spam "if a user posts multiple unrelated updates to a topic using the # symbol". The number of tweets which contains the symbol "#" in a user's 100 most recent tweets is used as one of the content-based features in [15]. However, in our work, we count the total number of hashtags in the 100 most recent tweets of each user.

4   Analysis of Collected Data

To evaluate the detection method, we randomly pick about 1000 Twitter user accounts and manually label them to two classes: spam and non-spam. Each user account is manually evaluated by reading the 20, 50, 100 most recent tweets posted by the user and checking the number of followers and following in his/her user profile page. Then, we extracted all the relevant user-based and content-based features that we have described in Section 3. Since we observe that we get better classification results with the most 100 tweets, we only report the results we get with the most 100 tweets. Fig 1(a) to (1d) show the characteristics of the user-based features, namely (a) the number of followers, (b) the number of "following" (or friends as defined in [15]), (c) the reputation, and (d) average posting percentage over a 24-hour period. Feature (c) is not used in our detection scheme. We merely include it so that we can compare the characteristics of our dataset with those used by the author in [15]. As we can see form Fig 1(a) the number of followers for legitimate users can be very large but the number of followers for each spammer is typically smaller than that of an average legitimate user. Specifically, the average number of followers for spammers is 4435.7 while that for legitimate users is 7293.1 for our dataset.

From Fig 1(b), we see that the number of "following" for spammers is higher than that for legitimate users. The average number of "following" for spammers is 3535.2 while it is only 1107.7 for legitimate users. Fig 1(c) shows that unlike the plot of reputation (defined in Eqn (1) in Section 3.1) shown in [15], our plots show that the reputation of spammers span a similar range to what is observed for legitimate users and hence reputation metric may not be useful in helping us identify spammers in our dataset. Fig 1(d) shows the average posting percentage over the eight 3-hour interval within a day. The plot clearly shows that normal users tend to tweet during late afternoon while spammers tend to tweet mostly during the early hours.

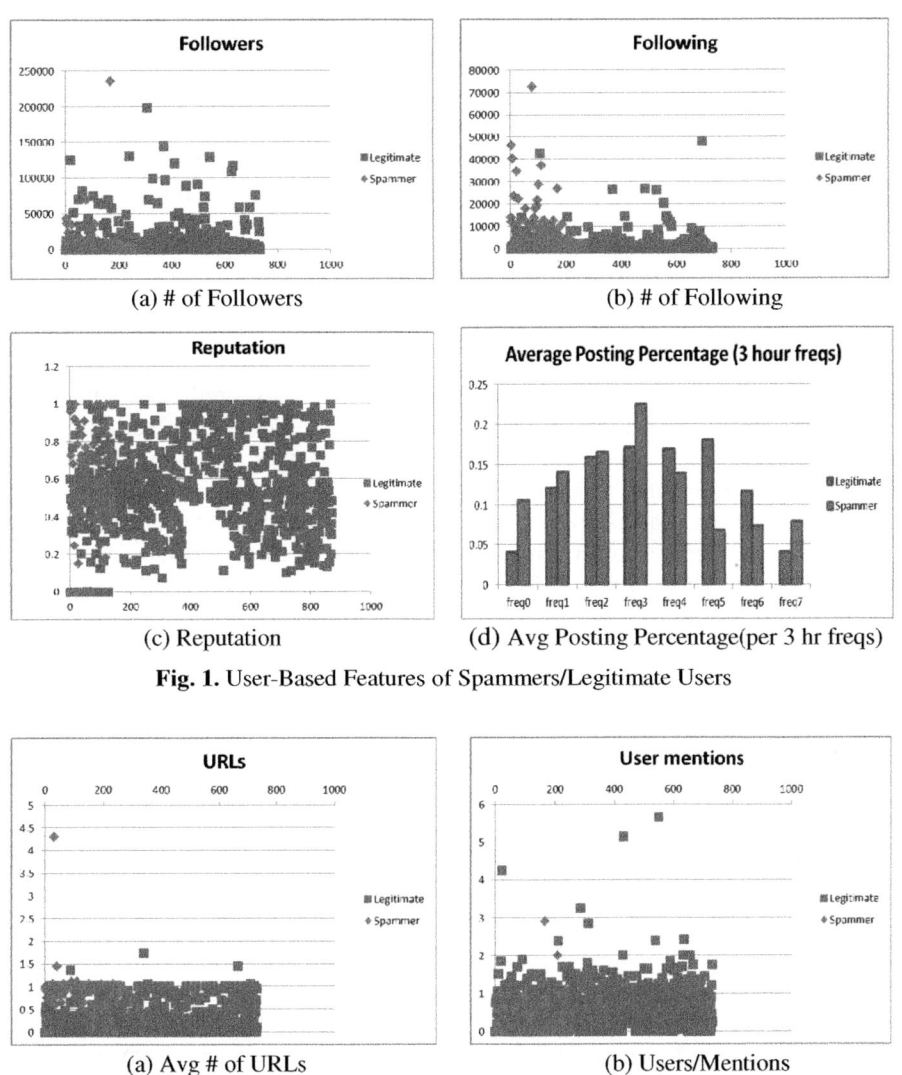

(a) # of Followers

(b) # of Following

(c) Reputation

(d) Avg Posting Percentage(per 3 hr freqs)

Fig. 1. User-Based Features of Spammers/Legitimate Users

(a) Avg # of URLs

(b) Users/Mentions

(c) # of Hashtags

(d) Wordweight

Fig. 2. Characteristics of Content-Based Features of Spammers/Legitimate Users

Figs 2(a)-2(d) show the differences between the content-based features of spammers/legitimate users. In Fig 2(a), we see that spammers tend to have an average of 1 link in each of their tweets. As for user mentions shown in Fig 2(b), there are some normal users that carry more user mentions in their tweets. From Fig 2(c), we see that spammers use much more hashtags than normal users. The plot in Fig 2(d) shows that the wordweight for a spammer is usually higher than that of a regular user.

5   Spam Detection and Evaluations

5.1   Spam Detection

Based on the above identified features, we proceed to use traditional classifiers to help detect spammers. In this work, several classic classification algorithms such as Random Forest, Naïve Bayesian, Support Vector Machines, and K-nearest neighbors are compared. The Random Forest classifier [19] is known to be effective in giving estimates of what variables are important in the classification. This classifier also has methods for balancing error in class population unbalanced data sets.

The naïve Bayesian classifier is based on the well-known Bayes theorem. The big assumption of the naïve Bayesian classifier is that the features are conditionally independent, although research shows that it is surprisingly effective in practice without the unrealistic independence assumption [7]. To classify a data record, the posterior probability is computed for each class [15]:

$$P(Y \mid X) = \frac{P(Y) \prod_{i=1}^{d} P(X_i \mid Y)}{P(X)} \tag{2}$$

Since P(X) is a normalized factor which is equal for all classes, only the numerator needs to be maximized in order to do the classification for the Naïve Bayesian classifier.

The Support Vector Machine method we used is the SMO scheme implemented in the WEKA tool. This SMO scheme, designed by J.C. Platt [16], uses a sequential minimal optimization algorithm to train a support vector classifier using polynomial or RBF kernels. The SMO classifier has been shown to outperform Naives Bayesian classifier in email categorization in [17] when the number of features increases. The K-Nearest Neighbor method implemented in the WEKA tool is the IBK classifier [18].

5.2   Evaluations

We used the standard metrics for measuring the usefulness of our detection scheme that uses our chosen user and content-based features. The typical confusion matrix for our spam detection system is shown below

		Prediction	
		Spam	Not Spam
True	Spam	a	b
	Not Spam	c	d

where a represents the number of spams that were correctly classified, b represents the number of spams that were falsely classified as non-spam, c represents the number of non-spam messages that were falsely classified as spam, and d represents the number of non-spam users that were correctly classified. The following measures are used: precision, recall, and F-measure where the precision is $P=a/(a+c)$, the recall is $R=a/(a+b)$, and the F-measure is defined as $F=2PR/(P+R)$. We have results based on the most recent 20,50 and 100 tweets. Here, we only report the results for the most recent 100 tweets. Our results using the most recent 100 tweets are tabulated in Table 1.

Table 1. Classification Results Using User-Based & Content-Based features (most recent 100 tweets)

Classifier	Precision	Recall	F-measure
RandForest	0.957	0.957	0.957
SMO	0.935	0.931	0.932
NaiveBayes	0.916	0.914	0.915
Ibk(KNN equivalent)	0.928	0.928	0.928

Unlike the results reported in [15], we see that the Random Forest classifier produces the best results, followed by the SMO, Naïve Bayesian and K-NN neighbor classifiers. The good performance of the Random Forest Classifier is not surprising since this classifier can deal with imbalanced data sets (we have data for more regular users than spammers). SMO also has relatively good performance. Naïve Bayesian classifier performs poorer may be because the 100 tweets/user statistics may be noisier than the dataset in [15]. Comparing our results with those reported in [15], we believe that even though we did not use the content similarity feature, our wordweight feature and the percentages of tweet distribution over the 3-hour intervals help our detector to achieve good results.

In Fig 3, we plot the classification results using only user-based features. In Fig 4, we plot the classification results using both user-based and content-based features

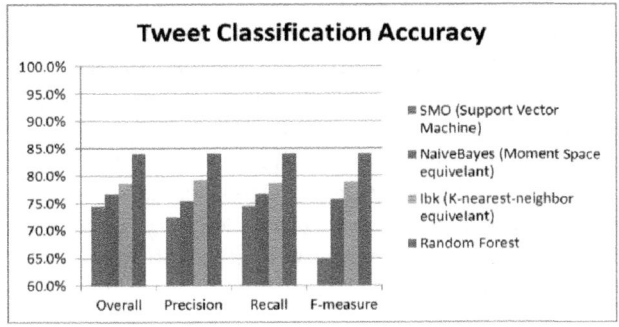

Fig. 3. Classification Resutls Using Only User-Based Features with Traditional Classifiers

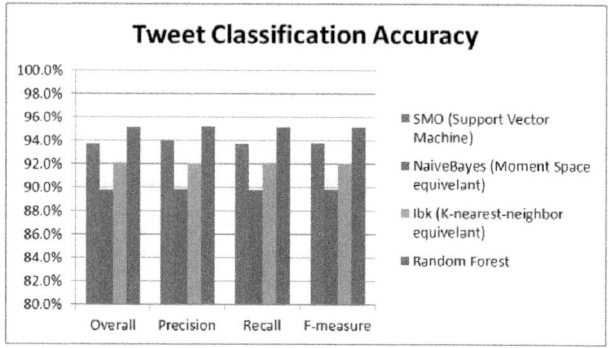

Fig. 4. Classification Results Using Both User & Content-Based Features with Traditional Classifiers

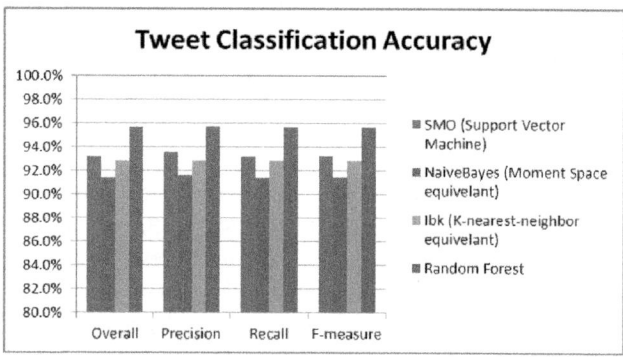

Fig. 5. Classification Results Using Both User-Based & Content-Based Features but without the 3-hour interval statistic with Traditional Classifiers

while in Fig 5, we plot the classification results using all features in Fig 4 except the 8 3-hour interval related tweet distribution features. Comparing Fig 3 with Figs 4 & 5, one can clearly see the benefits of adding the content-based features.

Fig 6 shows the classification results using the features that the researchers describe in [15] with our dataset while Fig 7 shows the classification results using the features that the researchers describe in [14]. Recall that we use wordweight to replace the pairwise content similarity metric. Our results reported in Fig 5 are slightly better than those in Figs 6 & 7. For example, the overall accuracy is only 93.5% with the features suggested in [15], 94.4% with the features suggested in [14] while with our features, we get 95.7% (all with the Random Forest Classifier). Out of the 258 spammers, our detector can correctly classify 240 spammers. Thus, our recall is 93%. Using the features suggested in [14], we can only identify 229 spammers while using the features suggested in [15], we can only identify 230 spammers (89% similar to what they report in their paper).

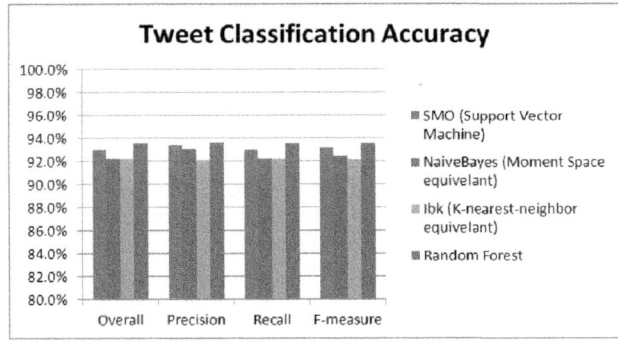

Fig. 6. Classification Results using features suggested in [15]

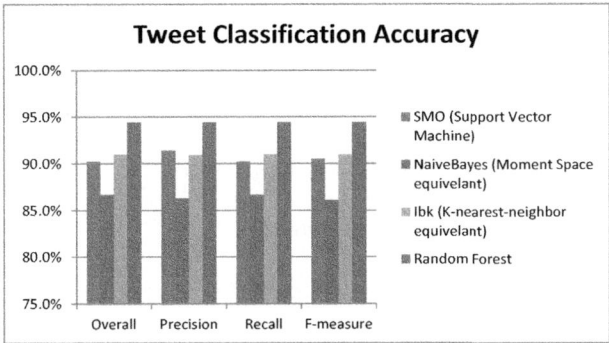

Fig. 7. Classification Results using features suggested in [14]

6   Conclusion

In this paper, we have suggested some user-based and content-based features that can be used to distinguish between spammers and legitimate users on Twitter, a popular online social networking site. These suggested features are influenced by Twitter spam policies and our observations of spammers' behaviors. Then, we use these features to help identify spammers. We evaluate the usefulness of these features in spammer detection using traditional classifiers like Random Forest, Naïve Bayesian, Support Vector Machine, K-NN neighbor schemes using the Twitter dataset we have collected. Our results show that the Random Forest classifier gives the best performance. Using this classifier, our suggested features can achieve 95.7% precision and 95.7% F-measure. Based on our dataset, our features provide slightly better classification results when compared to those suggested in [14] or [15]. Our next step is to evaluate our detection scheme using larger Twitter dataset as well as possibly wallpost datasets from other online networking sites like Facebook. We also hope to include the content similarity metric in our near future work.

References

1. Mowbray, M.: The Twittering Machine. In: Proceedings of the 6th International Conference on Web Information and Technologies (April 2010)
2. Analytics, P.: Twitter study (August 2009),
   http://www.peranalytics.com/blog/wp-content/uploads/2010/05/Twitter-Study-August-2009.pdf
3. CNET. 4 chan may be behind attack on twitter (2009),
   http://news.cnet.com/8301-13515_3-10279618-26.html
4. How to; 5 Top methods & applications to reduce Twitter Spam,
   http://blog.thoughtpick.com/2009/07/how-to-5-top-methods-applications-to-reduce-twitter-spam.html
5. Twitter, Restoring accidentally suspended accounts (2009a),
   http://status.twitter.com/post/136164828/restoring-accidentally-suspended-accounts
6. Twitter. The twitter rules (2009b),
   http://status.twitter.com/post/136164828/restoring-accidentally-suspended-accounts
7. Rish, I.: An empirical study of the naïve bayes classifier. In: Proeedings of IJCAI Workshop on Empirical Methods in Artificial Intelligence (2005)
8. Forman, G.: An extensive empirical study of feature selection metrics for text classification. J. Mach. Learn. Res. 3, 1289–1305 (2003)
9. Compete site comparison,
   http://siteanalytics.compete.com/facebookcom+myspace.com+twitter.com/
10. Sophos facebook id probe (2008),
    http://www.sophos.com/pressoffice/news/articles/2007/08/facebook.html
11. Bilge, L., et al.: All your contacts are belong to us: automated identifty theft attacks on social networks. In: Proceedings of ACM World Wide Web Conference (2009)
12. Jagatic, T.N., et al.: Social Phishing. Communications of ACM 50(10), 94–100 (2007)
13. Yardi, S., et al.: Detecting Spam in a Twitter Network. First Monday 15(1) (2010)
14. Stringhini, G., Kruegel, C., Vigna, G.: Detecting Spammers on Social Networks. In: Proceedings of ACM ACSAS 2010 (December 2010)
15. Wang, A.H.: Don't Follow me: Twitter Spam Detection. In: Proceedings of 5th International Conference on Security and Cryptography (July 2010)
16. Platt, J.: Sequential Minimal Optimization: A fast algorithm for training support vector machines. In: Schoelkopf, B., et al. (eds.) Advanced in Kernel Methods – Support Vector Learning. MIT Press, Cambridge
17. Berger, H., Kohle, M., Merkl, D.: On the impact of document representation on classifier performance in email categorization. In: Proceedings of the 4th International Conference on Information Systems Technology and IST Applications (May 2005)
18. Aha, D., Kibler, D.: Instance-based Learning Algorithms. Machine Learning 6, 37–66
19. Breiman, L.: Random Forests. Machine Learning 45(1) (October 2001)

True Trustworthy Elections: Remote Electronic Voting Using Trusted Computing

Matt Smart and Eike Ritter

School of Computer Science
University of Birmingham
{m.j.smart,e.ritter}@cs.bham.ac.uk

Abstract. We present a new remote, coercion-resistant electronic voting protocol which satisfies a number of properties previously considered contradictory. We introduce trusted computing as a method of ensuring the trustworthiness of remote voters, and provide an extension to our protocol allowing revocable anonymity, on the grounds of it being a legal requirement in the United Kingdom.

1 Introduction

One of the driving factors for electronic elections is *remote voting*—the notion that a voter can vote from any location. Achieving this whilst also achieving coercion resistance (i.e., allowing the voter to vote in the presence of a coercer, without being able to prove how they are voting, or whether their vote is valid) is very difficult, especially when also considering voter anonymity: not only do the authorities need to be convinced that each voter is running the correct voting protocol, but the voters must also be convinced that the authorities are behaving correctly.

It is very important that *revocable anonymity* in electronic voting—the ability to link a ballot back to its voter—be given adequate consideration. In the UK, it is a legal requirement that it should be possible for the election authorities to link a ballot to its voter [6, p. 106]. Only we currently consider this notion [30].

In this paper, we present a protocol which uses *trusted computing* to achieve assurances as to the state of the voter's (remote) machine, whilst also permitting revocable anonymity, and satisfying the other standard requirements of e-voting protocols. We use the Direct Anonymous Attestation (DAA) protocol [8] to provide a mechanism for cryptographically assuring the authorities of the state of a remote platform (run by a voter), whilst also assuring the voter that her vote is counted anonymously. No *remote* voting protocol has considered the state of a voting machine before, though the notion has been suggested at a high level, without implementation detail [9], and some 'polling station'-type protocols (not suitable for remote voting) exist [13]. Arguably, if a voter's machine can be made to display false statements to a voter, then there is simply no point in making the rest of the protocol secure: the user's machine is the 'weak link' in the chain. Indeed, if the voter's machine is compromised by a trojan (or such), then irrespective of the protocol being implemented, any remote voting protocol is

J.M. Alcaraz Calero et al. (Eds.): ATC 2011, LNCS 6906, pp. 187–202, 2011.
© Springer-Verlag Berlin Heidelberg 2011

inherently insecure. Use of the Trusted Platform Module (TPM) mitigates this risk.

1.1   Related Work

No work besides our own [30] provides revocable anonymity in electronic voting. Only a small amount of work provides coercion-resistant, remote electronic voting. Civitas [10] is a good example, based on the JCJ voting protocol [20]. However, it does not seem scalable—every encrypted vote requires several expensive plaintext equivalence tests, and credential generation requires the voter to contact every tallier. This complexity suggests that further modification to include revocable anonymity would be unwise.

Further, despite a discussion of using trusted computing and Direct Anonymous Attestation for peer-to-peer networks [4], and preliminary discussions of trusted computing in electronic voting [2,9,3,19], we found very few actual protocols: [13] give a protocol which uses the TPM to provide trustworthy 'polling station' DRE (Direct Recording Electronic voting) machines. Whilst their solution is interesting, we are interested in *remote* voting only, and find that the amount of trust placed in a number of entities by the authors is too high: the election authority, tallying authority and precinct judge all need to be fully trusted, and nothing is done to mitigate the possibility of a voter visiting the DRE machine multiple times in an election. The use of a single Platform Vote Ballot (PVB) key to sign the vote storage area also introduces a weak point for the security of all votes on a single DRE. [32] presents a discussion and high level, basic protocol for remote voting using the TPM. [25,26] also present high-level discussions of in-person polling station voting protocols using trusted hardware. It should be noted that the work of [25] is not receipt-free, and that of [26] places complete trust in the authorities.

Many electronic voting protocols [29,14,20] rely on anonymous channels, or anonymous and untappable channels [23], to satisfy some security properties. In our work, we require an anonymous channel in the voting phase. Many protocols use mix networks for this [10,27,29,7,17], which provide effective anonymity as long as at least one participant in the mix is honest. We deliberately do not specify the method of implementation for our anonymous channel, but suggest that a Tor/Onion Routing network [12], or any other protocol allowing *bidirectional* anonymous communication would be suitable.

We, like many previous protocols, use probabilistic homomorphic encryption and re-encryption to ensure universal verifiability and unlinkability of ballots (through decryption of a product of encrypted votes) [5,11,20,10], which naturally lends itself to threshold cryptography, affording us a greater level of assurance against corrupted talliers. These protocols require, for remote voting, that the voter is not observed at the "very moment of voting" [22].

We note that any protocol providing a list of voters' identities with encrypted ballots could provide revocable anonymity, given the collusion of all parties needed to perform decryption. However, such a list clearly evidences the fact that a voter *has voted successfully.* [20] and implementations thereof [10] involve talliers only keeping a list of votes at the end of the election (discarding the previous stage's encrypted credentials), thus severing the direct link between voter and vote. Not only does the protocol itself use several inefficient, expensive Plaintext Equivalence Tests throughout, but revocation of anonymity would require a further PET between the credential supplied with a vote and every credential on the voter list, followed by a collusion with the registrar. [22] would allow for revocation, *but* subject to collusion of the administrator, the entire mix and n talliers. The nature of usage of the bulletin board in the protocol also suggests that full coercion-resistance is not possible, as the fact that Alice has voted is plainly visible. Prêt à Voter [27] and similar schemes do not offer revocation at all, since Alice's choice of ballot paper is random, and as any identifying information is destroyed (by Alice), she cannot be linked to her ballot.

Revocable anonymity is a concept which has been considered at great length in other fields, such as digital cash [18,21]. In digital cash, it is particularly important that it should be possible to both link an electronic coin to the person who spent it once the transaction has occurred, and link a person's identity to all coins available to him. One manner in which this can be done is to encode an encrypted copy of the coin owner's identity into every coin. Requiring two or more parties to perform encryption, including a judge [18], ensures that a user's anonymity will not be revoked unless there is sufficient legal cause. In our work, we protect the voter's identity using a similar mechanism.

In [30], we present a coercion-free remote electronic voting protocol which permits the voter to vote anonymously, whilst maintaining coercion-resistance and voter verifiability, and the ability to revoke her anonymity should the need arise. One of the shortcomings of the protocol is that it requires a certain level of trust in the first set of talliers (*viz.*, that $\mathbb{T}_1$ does not reveal the link between a ballot and its reencryption, only encrypts Alice's identity correctly, and only posts valid ballots to the bulletin board), in order to assure that collaboration between both tallier sets could result in Alice being linked to her ballot only with the cooperation of a judge. The authors also assumed that the platform the Alice voted from was always trustworthy (as is common in remote voting).

It is possible to reduce the amount of trust required in the talliers if we reduce the amount of information that needs to be kept private. [30] also makes no use of Trusted Computing or the TPM: this limits the amount of trust that can be placed in any remote client. In our work, we present a new approach, which uses the TPM to enhance the trustworthiness of clients, further reducing the need for trust in the talliers.

1.2   Our Contribution

In this work, we introduce the first practical work on a *remote* electronic voting protocol which uses *trusted computing* (specifically, the TPM and Direct Anonymous Attestation protocol). As we have already mentioned, a number of existing works discuss the applicability of trusted computing and the TPM to electronic voting. We are the first to extend this to remote electronic voting whilst also providing a detailed protocol to do so, leading to several contributions:

- A remote voting protocol allowing authorities to be convinced of the state of the voter's machine, and allowing anonymity revocation via the TPM
- A protocol allowing Alice to remain anonymous, whilst satisfying her eligibility to vote via a novel use of the DAA protocol
- An extension to the protocol allowing a voter to be traced to her vote, should the legal need arise, but only with the co-operation of a judge.

Protocol Schema. We present a three-phase protocol, where voters do not need to synchronise between phases. In the first phase, our legitimate voter, Alice, registers *in person* to vote, In the next phase, she and her trusted platform module (TPM) execute the DAA *Join* protocol [8] and receive a certificate proving her eligibility to vote (the certificate is split into three parts, divided between Alice and her TPM).

In the final phase, Alice and her TPM execute the DAA *Sign* protocol in order to complete her vote, which is sent as an ElGamal encryption with a proof of its validity. Voting authorities execute the DAA *Verify* protocol, after which Alice's vote is re-encrypted, and she receives back a designated verifier proof of that re-encryption. Should Alice need to, she can request assistance from the Judge.

1.3   Structure

In §2, we define a number of preliminaries, and a number of primitives we make use of. In §3, we give the participants, trust model and threat model for our work. In §4 we present our protocol, and we give a brief list of the requirements that we have satisfied in §5. Finally we conclude.

2   Preliminaries

In this paper, we assume the availability of the following cryptographic primitives and protocols. Note that, like many papers in the field which adopt a standard Dolev-Yao model, we make the assumption that the cryptography in the primitives below is perfect.

2.1   Trusted Computing

A *trusted computer* is one that, through the use of a *trusted platform module* (TPM), and other technologies such as memory curtaining, sealed storage and *remote attestation*, removes reliance on the end user to prove that his computer is secure. The benefits of its use for remote applications requiring secure information flow and data handling are clear.

In the field of remote electronic voting (that is, voting from any internet-connected terminal), for example, we might require that a user can only vote from a machine that is running the correct voting software, for obvious reasons.

We could do this by providing each voter with a bootable operating system 'live CD'-type disc[1].

However, we naturally still require that the voter using the trusted machine remains *anonymous*, whilst still being able to demonstrate that the machine she is voting from is trustworthy.

For brevity we do not elaborate on the structure of, or commands of the TPM here. The reader is directed to [31] for further information. For our purposes, it is sufficient to state that actions performed by the TPM are trustworthy.

Direct Anonymous Attestation. *Attestation* in our context is the notion that some verifier wishes to be convinced that Alice is using a machine which contains a valid, permitted TPM. Later, this TPM can prove that Alice's machine is running the correct software, while allowing Alice to remain anonymous.

Direct Anonymous Attestation (DAA) is the solution currently built into the TPM specification. The protocol is complex, and we advise that the uninitiated reader consult [8] for a full explanation. On a high level, DAA is split into three sub-protocols: *join*, *sign* and *verify*. In the *join* protocol, a host and a TPM gain *attestation* (a Camenisch-Lysyanskaya signature) on a secret value, chosen by the TPM, demonstrating that the host's machine contains a valid TPM.

In the *sign* protocol, the host and TPM use a proof of knowledge of this attestation to anonymously prove that they gained this verification, possibly attesting to the state of their machine in the process, and producing a DAA Signature on some message (generally a key). This signature is verified in the final stage of the protocol.

2.2 Threshold ElGamal Cryptosystem

For encryption of actual votes, we use an exponential ElGamal encryption scheme under a q-order multiplicative subgroup $G_q = \langle g \rangle$ of $\mathbb{Z}_p^*$, generated by an element $g \in \mathbb{Z}_p^*$, where p and q are suitably large primes, and $q|(p-1)$. All agents a in the protocol have a private key s_a of which only they have knowledge. Each agent has a corresponding public key $h_a = g^{s_a}$ where g is a known generator of the subgroup. Public keys are common knowledge to all users. We detail in §4 how votes are encrypted, but also note that we use $\{m\}_k$ to denote encryption of m under key k, where the encryption scheme is unimportant. In parts of our protocol, we use a (t, n)-threshold decryption scheme analogous to that of [11], such that a majority t out of n key-share holders would have to collude to decrypt. For brevity we do not discuss this here.

We have selected our cryptosystem for the voting section of our protocol because of the ease of tallying that a multiplicative homomorphic cryptosystem provides. The use of an exponential encryption scheme permits simple tallying, but requires the solving of a discrete logarithm. Of course, this becomes

---

[1] We note that, as suggested by [13], security of any protocol that obtains software and private keys from removable media is vulnerable to compromise. This issue can be mitigated by having the TPM compare a publicly known signed hash of the intended executable code with a hash the TPM itself generates. In fact, the user could make this comparison.

more difficult with increasing exponent size. With modern computing power and methods such as the Index Calculus and Baby-step Giant-step algorithms for computation of discrete logarithms, we do not see this to be an issue, but it would also be possible to hold several smaller 'regional' elections, rather than one large election, with our protocol to alleviate this problem. We also note that alternative threshold cryptosystems, such as that of Paillier [24], could be used for very large, country-wide elections.

2.3   Threshold Signature Scheme

In order to ensure that eligibility and uniqueness are always satisfied in our protocol, we employ a (t, n)−threshold signature scheme during the voting phase of the protocol. A threshold signature scheme works in a similar way to a threshold decryption scheme: of n possible talliers, t must collude to generate a signature on a message. The scheme that we adopt is not of great consequence, but the one used by [15] has good verification properties and fits in well with the exponential ElGamal cryptosystem that we use.

2.4   Anonymous Channel

Due to the nature of our protocol, we require an anonymous, bidirectional channel, so that Alice can both send her vote anonymously, and receive proofs of her vote having been counted. We note that standard mix networks are not designed to receive replies, but onion routing-based networks are [12].

2.5   Strong Designated Verifier Signature Scheme

We adopt the designated verifier signature scheme of [28] due to its efficient nature, but others would be acceptable. We use designated verifier signatures to enable a prover (Bob, or any one of the first-round talliers in our case) to prove a statement to a verifier (Alice) by proving the validity of a signature. However, Alice is unable to prove the signature's validity to *anyone* else, on the grounds that she could have produced it herself [28, p. 43]. For brevity we do not discuss the scheme here, but direct the reader to [28] instead. We denote by $\mathsf{DVSign}_{\mathsf{a} \rightarrow \mathsf{b}}(m)$ a designated verifier signature on a message m produced by party a and intended for reading by party b.

2.6   Proof of Equality of Discrete Logarithms

In order to prevent an attack in our voting scheme (voting for several candidates or for one candidate multiple times with the same ballot), we require that the voter demonstrates to a verifier that her vote is of the correct form (without revealing what the vote is).

A voter's vote is of the form $(x, y) = (g^\alpha, h_{\mathbb{T}_v}^\alpha g^{M^{i-1}})$ where $\alpha \in_R \mathbb{Z}_q$, M is the maximum number of voters and i represents the position in the list of candidates of the voter's chosen candidate. Alice needs to prove, in zero knowledge, that she is sending to the bulletin board some value for y where the exponent of g is in

$\{M^0, \ldots, M^{L-1}\}$ where L is the number of candidates. If we did not have such a proof, any voter could spoil the election by adding spurious coefficients to the exponent, thereby voting several times.

We adopt our Generalised Proof of Equality of Discrete Logarithms (G-PEQDL) scheme [30, pp. 43-44] in order for Alice to provide such a proof (with the small change that the challenge value c is formed using Alice's TPM's public AIK, rather than h_{Alice}), and refer the reader to this paper.

2.7   Designated Verifier Re-encryption Proofs

The properties of the ElGamal encryption scheme allow re-encryption (randomisation) of ciphertexts. Given a ciphertext (x, y), another agent is able to generate a re-encryption $(x_f, y_f) = (xg^\beta, yh^\beta)$, where $\beta \in_R \mathbb{Z}_q^*$.

In our protocol, we use an ElGamal re-encryption to preserve the voter's anonymity. However, the voter needs to have some conviction that her vote has been counted (individual verifiability). We achieve this via a *Designated Verifier Re-encryption Proof* (DVRP) based on a fresh keypair that Alice selects: such a proof convinces Alice that a given re-encrypted ciphertext is equivalent to that she generated, whilst not convincing any third party. We adopt the scheme used by [22,16], such that the prover, P (the agent that does the re-encryption) demonstrates to Alice that (x_f, y_f) is equivalent to (x, y) in such a manner that the original message is not revealed, and this proof cannot convince any other entity. The reader is directed to the above papers for more details.

3   Protocol Model

3.1   Participants

Our protocol is modelled with four kinds of participants. All participants are able to communicate via a network, which is not untappable.

- **Voters.** The protocol allows M voters $v_i \in \{v_0, v_1, \ldots, v_{M-1}\}$ to vote. Alice is an honest voter who wishes to vote anonymously. She can vote an unlimited number of times, but must be able to vote *once* unobserved.
- **Administrator.** The (in-person) administrator $\mathbb{A}$ is a single entity, responsible for ensuring that Alice receives a random number of paper *validity cards* containing validity tokens δ_j. We expand upon this in the next section. $\mathbb{A}$ is responsible for identifying Alice, but not for determining her eligibility to vote.
- **Registrar.** The registrar $\mathbb{R}$ is a single agent, possessing a secret key $s_\mathbb{R}$. Note that we assume a bottleneck will *not* occur here, but we could equally use a group of identical registrar agents to mitigate such a problem. The registrar is responsible for ensuring, via the DAA *Join* protocol, that Alice is eligible to vote, and has not attempted to register already. The registrar will send Alice a voter group membership certificate, with which she can prove to the talliers that her vote is permitted.

- **Talliers.** The talliers, $\mathbb{T} = \{\mathbb{T}_1, \ldots, \mathbb{T}_n\}$, are a group of agents (disjoint from $\mathbb{R}$) who authorise the addition of each submitted ballot to the *bulletin board*, via the DAA *sign* and *verify* protocols. Each tallier has a copy of a secret key $s_{\mathbb{T}}$, with which he determines the validity of votes, and a *share* of a secret key $s_{\mathbb{T}_v}$, with which he collaborates with a quorum of $\mathbb{T}$ in order to decrypt the end tally, once the election is finished. These keys are unrelated—we use them to ensure that no single tallier has access to an individual vote. $\mathbb{T}$ are also responsible for re-encrypting votes, and sending proof of this to Alice.

3.2   Trust Model

We make the following assumptions in our protocol:

1. The TPM and the manufacturers of the TPM (the root of trust), are trusted to behave as intended by the protocol
2. All parties trust that $\mathbb{T}$ will not reveal the link between a ballot (x, y) and its re-encryption (x_f, y_f)
3. All voters trust that the validity of any given δ value will not be revealed by $\mathbb{A}$, *except* to members of $\mathbb{T}$ via a designated verifier signature
4. All parties trust that each voter will only be permitted to submit *one* validity card to the secured box for each election
5. All parties trust that $\mathbb{R}$ will not issue group membership certificates to ineligible voters, and will only do so once for eligible voters
6. All participants trust that the Judge will only authorise revocation of anonymity in appropriate circumstances
7. Alice trusts the Judge to honestly state whether votes have been counted

3.3   Threat Model

We now consider the potential threats that could affect our protocol, based on the attacker's capabilities. We address how these threats are managed in §4. Note that, as mentioned earlier, we assume perfect cryptography.

In our protocol, the attacker can assume the role of any entity, except the Judge or $\mathbb{A}$. He is able to corrupt up to $t - 1$ talliers where collusion is required to decrypt messages (and t is the threshold size for that quorum). All channels are public (the mix network is tappable, but anonymous), so the attacker can:

1. Read and intercept messages
2. Decrypt and read any message m, subject to having the correct decryption key s for an encrypted message $(g^\alpha, g^{\alpha s} m)$
3. Inject bad ballots in the voting phase, and spurious messages generally
4. Temporarily block messages (although we assume resilient channels for liveness)

4   Protocol

Our protocol has three stages. Diagrams, where necessary, are given in Figures 1, 2 and 3. We use a number of TPM commands in our protocol: these are denoted as such. We do not modify the TPM API in any way.

In-Person Registration (Fig 1).   In order to begin voting, Alice first has to apply *in person* to vote, with the administrator $\mathbb{A}$. This can be at any point before the election. Once her identity is confirmed by $\mathbb{A}$, Alice is observed selecting a number, r, of *validity cards* from a box. r is generated randomly by $\mathbb{A}$ when Alice's identity is confirmed. These cards are pieces of paper with a perforation down the middle, and the same value $\delta_j : j \in \{0, \ldots, r-1\}$ printed on each side. Alice selects (mentally) one of the cards, whose δ value, δ_A, will denote her intended vote. She separates the card along the perforation, and places half of it into a secure box, retaining the other half. The bin must be designed to accept only one card per voter. Note that Alice does <u>not</u> need to bring any device (viz., the machine containing her TPM) with her: she merely needs to select cards.

With the remaining cards, Alice separates each card and places one half of each card into a shredder. Again, we must ensure that Alice destroys half of each validity card that she has not chosen to denote her intended vote.

Alice leaves in-person registration with several halves of validity cards. She has a mental note of which is valid (and could, in fact, discard or hide that one), but cannot prove which is valid to any observer. As she took a random number of cards, an observer cannot force her to vote once with every card she selected. Note that only $\mathbb{A}$ has access to the secure box, and that the voter has no way to prove how many cards she selected.

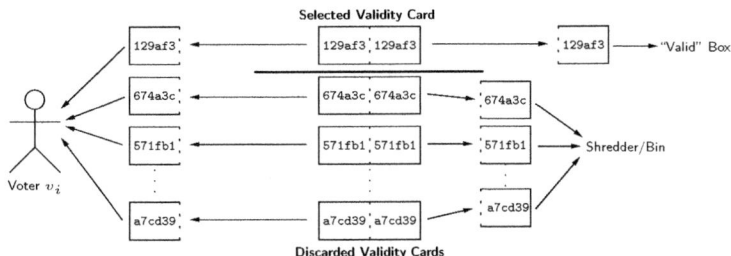

Fig. 1. In Person Registration

We note that our approach to voter registration is unconventional for a remote voting scheme. However, it removes the unrealistic requirement for an electronic untappable channel to the administrator (like that suggested by [10]), instead using a physical registration in which the voter can take part at any time before the election. This approach is clearly also more "user-friendly". Our design considerably reduces the trust we need to place in $\mathbb{A}$ (he now only knows which δ values are valid, not for whom, so we need only ensure that he does not release this information).

Join. Alice and her TPM, TPM$_{\text{Alice}}$, execute the DAA *Join* protocol: this is as with the DAA *Join* protocol [8], and so we do not provide a diagram to represent it. The only change that we make is that, before issuing a certificate to a voter, the registrar $\mathbb{R}$ must ensure that said voter is eligible to vote. The communication channel with $\mathbb{R}$ does not need to be anonymous. We however adopt the requirement of [8] that the channel must be 'authentic' between TPM$_{\text{Alice}}$ and $\mathbb{R}$: i.e., the registrar must be sure that it is communicating with the correct TPM. Such authenticity can be achieved using the TPM's *endorsement key* (EK) for initial communications [8].

The product of the Join protocol is a membership certificate generated by $\mathbb{R}$. With this certificate, Alice can prove that she is a member of the group of legitimate voters, and is therefore allowed to vote. She will have registered using a unique pseudonym, and will use a different pseudonym to vote, making her registration and voting unlinkable. We refer to [8] for more detail.

Voting (Fig 2). The protocol by which Alice and her TPM vote is shown in Figure 2. If we assume that Alice can be tracked by an attacker with a global view of the network (and thus, the ability to see the IP address Alice votes from), then we must use an anonymous channel to preserve Alice's coercion-resistance and privacy.

First, we begin with an execution of the DAA *Sign* protocol (denoted as such in Figure 2—again, we omit the detail of the DAA Sign protocol for brevity, and refer the reader to [8] instead).

The outcome of the *Sign* protocol is a signature σ which convinces the talliers $\mathbb{T}$ that Alice's machine contains a TPM, and that she is a certified, eligible member of the voters group. Alice's TPM generates an *attestation identity key* AIK$_{\text{Alice}}$ which is sent to $\mathbb{T}$ as part of the DAA signature, and will be used to prove authenticity of later messages. Note that this AIK is not linkable to Alice in any way, and the communication with $\mathbb{T}$ is similarly unlinkable [8].

With the *Sign* protocol complete, $\mathbb{T}$ can then query Alice's TPM as to the state of her machine. To do this, any member $\mathbb{T}_i$ of $\mathbb{T}$ begins an *encrypted transport session* between itself and Alice's TPM directly (note that Alice does not see the result of any transactions that occur here). $\mathbb{T}_i$ selects a challenge nonce c_v, and requests a hash of the current state of the TPM's registers, using the command TPM_QUOTE, and including the challenge. The TPM responds with the appropriate data. If $\mathbb{T}_i$ is satisfied that the machine is in the correct state, it requests that the TPM create a new keypair, bound to the correct TPM register (PCR) states. This means that, when a decryption is needed using this key, it can only occur if the TPM's PCRs are in the correct state. We denote the *handle* of this key as k_A, and note that the key is asymmetric, the private part being accessible only to the TPM.

Next, Alice generates a fresh ElGamal keypair, $(s_v, h_v = g^{s_v})$. She then sends a message votetoken to $\mathbb{T}$. votetoken contains Alice's vote, in the form of an exponential ElGamal encryption $(x, y) = (g^\alpha, h_{\mathbb{T}_v}^\alpha g^{M^{i-1}})$, where she is selecting the ith candidate, her chosen δ_A value (should she be voting according to her own wishes) or any other δ value (if she is being coerced), the public part of the aforementioned key h_v, and the **G-PEQDL** proof that her vote is for one valid candidate only. The tallier $\mathbb{T}_k$ that receives Alice's vote now checks whether it was sent under coercion. To do this, he sends $\delta, \text{sign}_\mathbb{T}(\delta)$ to $\mathbb{A}$. $\mathbb{A}$ checks whether the δ value received is in the secure box, and if so, sends a correct designated verifier signature of the value, $\text{DVSign}_{\mathbb{A}\to\mathbb{T}_k}(\delta)$. If the δ value is not found in the box (meaning Alice sent a vote under coercion), an incorrect designated verifier signature is returned to $\mathbb{T}$. Again, only $\mathbb{T}_k$ can determine this, and cannot prove this fact to an observer.

Once Alice's vote is determined to be non-coerced, her G-PEQDL proof is checked by $\mathbb{T}_k$. If this is invalid, her vote is discarded. If the G-PEQDL is correct, Alice's vote is re-encrypted using a re-encryption factor $\beta \in_R \mathbb{Z}_q$. If her vote was not coerced, Alice is sent a tuple of designated verifier proofs of re-encryption (DVRPs), produced using the public key h_v Alice generated earlier. One of these is valid for Alice's re-encrypted vote; the others are valid for other votes already on the bulletin board[2]. Each DVRP is separately encrypted using the public part of the key k_A which Alice's TPM generated. This means that Alice is free to have her machine generate re-encryption proofs herself (the nature of the proof is such that the entity for whom the proof is designated can use her private key—s_v in this case—to generate further DVRPs), to fool coercers.

The re-encrypted (x_f, y_f) is sent to a threshold of talliers in $\mathbb{T}$, along with the re-encryption factor and the G-PEQDL proof. If that threshold agree, they jointly generate a signature on (x_f, y_f), and the vote and its signature are placed on the bulletin board.

If Alice's vote _was_ coerced, she is sent several DVRPs as before. However, this time, $\mathbb{T}_k$ produces DVRPs based on re-encryptions of votes on the bulletin board that were <u>not</u> Alice's. Note that the DVRPs Alice receives use a key which she freshly generated (to prevent her being identified). Each DVRP is encrypted with a key for which only Alice's TPM has the private part. As a consequence, Alice needs to load the correct key into the TPM (using `TPM_LoadKey2`), and then requests the TPM to decrypt each DVRP ciphertext, using `TPM_UnSeal`.

At this point, it should be noted that the keypair k_A generated by the TPM was bound to a certain set of PCR states. If this set of states is not in place at the time of DVRP decryption with `TPM_UnSeal`, decryption cannot occur. This ensures not only that Alice still uses the same TPM, but also that no rogue software is executed after Alice casts her vote.

Alice can then check to see if any one of the DVRPs represent valid re-encryptions, checking the bulletin board. Note that _every_ re-encryption will be on the bulletin board, but only Alice can be convinced that any vote is hers. If she does not find her vote, Alice may contact the Judge, who will contact $\mathbb{T}$. The Judge may further allow Alice to vote again, under his supervision.

When voting is complete, the product of all encrypted votes is calculated by $\mathbb{T}$ as $(X, Y) = (\prod_{j=1}^l x_{f_j}, \prod_{j=1}^l y_{f_j})$. This product is calculable by any observer.

---

[2] Vote submissions are batched so that there are always enough votes on the bulletin board to do this: talliers can agree a policy beforehand as to how the first few votes are posted.

The final tally is calculated by a quorum (size t) of $\mathbb{T}$ colluding to decrypt this product, giving $g^{r_1 M^0 + r_2 M^1 + \ldots + r_L M^{L-1}}$, and $r_1, \ldots, r_L$ as the final tally. Note that since every vote is threshold-signed on the bulletin board, observers are convinced that every vote is genuine.

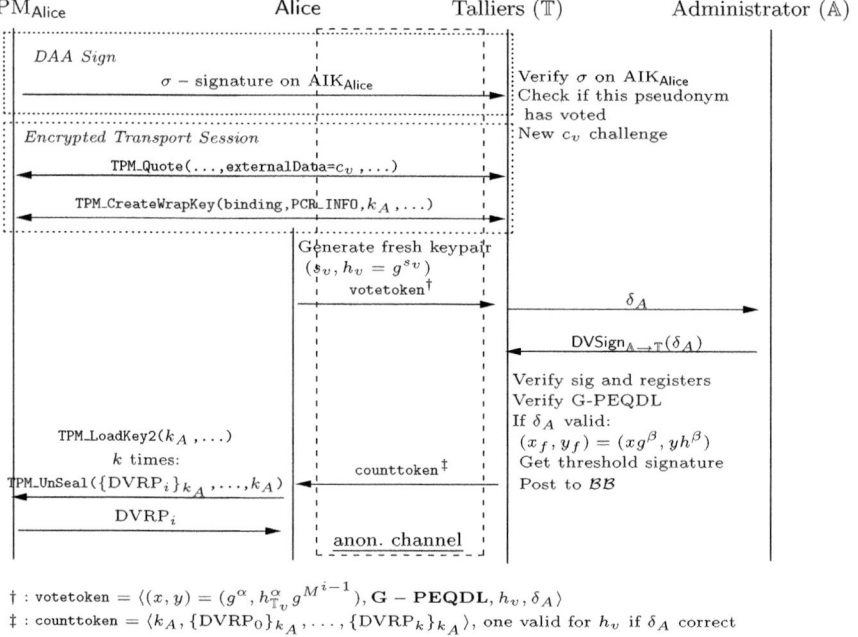

$\dagger$: votetoken $= \langle (x, y) = (g^\alpha, h_{\mathbb{T}_v}^\alpha g^{M^{i-1}}), \mathbf{G - PEQDL}, h_v, \delta_A \rangle$

$\ddagger$: counttoken $= \langle k_A, \{DVRP_0\}_{k_A}, \ldots, \{DVRP_k\}_{k_A} \rangle$, one valid for h_v if δ_A correct

Fig. 2. The Voting Protocol vote1 (without revocable anonymity). Ellipses suggest standard uses of unchanged TPM commands: only salient parameters are given.

Anonymity Revocation (Fig 3).   In [30], we introduced the notion of revocable anonymity in electronic voting: i.e., that a voter could be linked to his ballot when this link was authorised by a Judge. Being able to link a voter to his/her ballot is a legal requirement in the United Kingdom.

The changes that we make to the protocol in Figure 2 in order to provide revocable anonymity are quite simple. We begin with a small change to the registration protocol. Once the DAA *Join* part of the protocol is complete, the registrar $\mathbb{R}$ sends Alice an encryption of her ID with the Judge's public key, $\overline{id} = \{id\}_{\text{Judge}}$. $\mathbb{R}$ also sends a signature of this encryption, $\text{Sign}_{\mathbb{R}}(\overline{id})$ to Alice.

The voting protocol completes the DAA *Sign* protocol as before. Alice then sends the encryption and signature thereof to $\mathbb{T}$, who verify the signature and store the ciphertext. She then extends a TPM PCR with the value of $\overline{id}$ using **TPM_Extend** (this is equivalent to hashing the current value of the chosen register, concatenated with $\overline{id}$). $\mathbb{T}$ can ensure Alice has done this, by ensuring that the value received from **TPM_Quote** is that which would be expected for a correct machine state *concatenated with* the encrypted ID value.

Voting then proceeds as normal: Alice's identity is re-encrypted by $\mathbb{T}$ and printed on the bulletin board next to her vote. Should revocation be required, a member $\mathbb{T}_k$ of $\mathbb{T}$ sends the tuple $\overline{\text{id}}$ to the Judge, along with appropriate evidence justifying revocation. The Judge is then free to revoke Alice's anonymity and take further action against her. Note that in order to preserve Alice's anonymity, we add a trust requirement that $\mathbb{R}$ does not collude with $\mathbb{T}$ to reveal Alice's identity, and always provides the correct identity for a voter (since $\mathbb{R}$ is trusted to perform the DAA Join protocol correctly, this is not a large increase in trust). Note that Alice could later contact the Judge to determine whether her anonymity had been revoked or not. This does not, to us, constitute full auditability, as Alice needs to contact a third party to audit her vote. We discuss approaches to achieving auditable revocable anonymity in the conclusion.

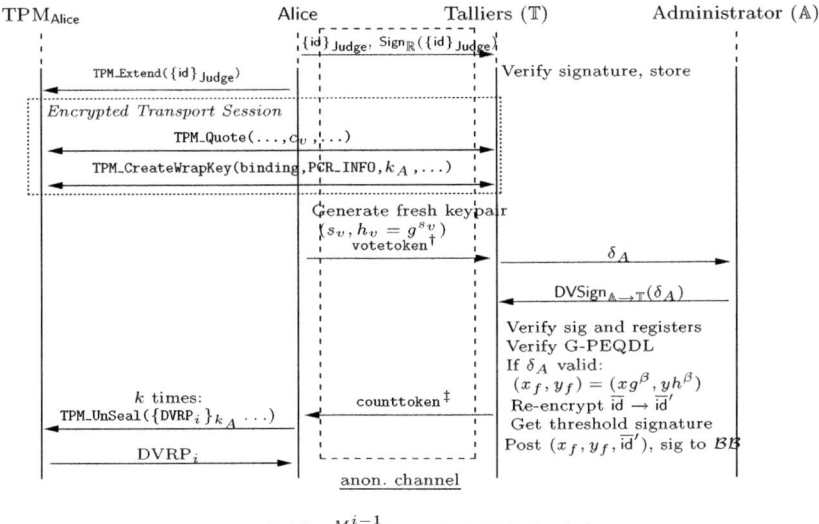

$\dagger$: votetoken $= \langle (x,y) = (g^\alpha, h^\alpha_{\mathbb{T}_v} g^{M^{i-1}}), \mathbf{G - PEQDL}, \delta_A, h_v \rangle$

Fig. 3. Changes to the Voting Protocol vote2 (with revocable anonymity)

5   Protocol Properties

For brevity, we do not go into detail about the properties achieved by this protocol (we aim to include a detailed, formal verification in a future version of this work). The protocol satisfies the following requirements:

- **Coercion-Resistance.** Voters cannot prove how they are voting, even if interacting with the voter during voting. The protocol prevents a coercer from determining even if a voter has voted, even when the coercer is physically present
- **Verifiability.** The protocol allows voters to determine that their vote was counted (individual verifiability), and allows all observers to determine that

the tally accurately represents all cast votes (universal verifiability). The ability to verify that one's vote is counted as cast is generally considered contradictory to one's vote being private (voter privacy) and being unable to prove how one is voting (coercion-resistance).

- **Fairness.** No-one gains any information about the tally until the end of the voting process.
- **Voter Privacy.** No participant can link a voter to their ballot, unless the revocation protocol has been invoked:
  - **Revocable Anonymity.** An authorised entity (or collection thereof) can link a voter to her ballot.
- **Remote Voting.** Voters are not restricted by physical location, providing they have a computer with a TPM and Internet access.

6   Conclusions and Future Work

We have presented an electronic voting protocol providing what the first scheme that uses trusted computing to guarantee the security of the remote voter's machine, whilst also allowing the voter coercion-free remote voting and verifiability, as well as legitimate-voter privacy, and enabling authorities to revoke a voter's anonymity under certain circumstances. Further, the remote nature of our protocol allows voters to cast their votes from any computer with a TPM even with a physically present coercer, providing they can vote unobserved once (a minimal requirement, as otherwise a coercer could always simulate the voter, or trivially suppress her ability to vote).

In the form described in protocol vote2, our protocol does not permit genuine *auditable* revocable anonymity. In an ideal scenario, we would like to supply $\mathbb{T}$ with a 'sealed envelope' containing Alice's identity. If the envelope is opened, Alice can see this later. A simple solution involves Alice remaining online throughout the election, her own TPM encrypting and decrypting her identity. In this manner, the TPM would know when Alice's identity was traced, and could inform Alice. If Alice wished for her vote to be counted, she would leave her machine on, rather than risk her TPM being unreachable. Of course, the problem is that a rogue Alice would rather risk turning her machine off and having her vote uncounted than being imprisoned for voting fraud. For us, this is not an acceptable implementation of auditability, and hence we leave this to future work. We note that preliminary work on the 'digital sealed envelope' problem has been recently considered by [1]. Our next step will be to build a prototype implementation of this work in Java, beginning with a TPM simulator.

References

1. Ables, K., Ryan, M.D.: Escrowed data and the digital envelope. In: Acquisti, A., Smith, S.W., Sadeghi, A.-R. (eds.) TRUST 2010. LNCS, vol. 6101, pp. 246–256. Springer, Heidelberg (2010)

2. Alkassar, A., Sadeghi, A.R., Schultz, S., Volkamer, M.: Towards Trustworthy On-line Voting. In: Proceedings WISSec 2006 (2006)
3. Arbaugh, W.A.: The Real Risk of Digital Voting? Computer 37(12), 124–125 (2004)
4. Balfe, S., Lakhani, A.D., Paterson, K.G.: Trusted Computing: Providing Security for Peer-to-Peer Networks. In: Proceedings of Fifth IEEE Conference on Peer-to-Peer Computing, pp. 117–124. IEEE, Los Alamitos (2005)
5. Benaloh, J., Tuinstra, D.: Receipt-Free Secret-Ballot Elections (Extended Abstract). In: Proceedings of 26th ACM Symposium on the Theory of Computing, pp. 544–553. ACM, Montreal (1994)
6. Blackburn, R.: The Electoral System in Britain. Macmillan, London (1995)
7. Boneh, D., Golle, P.: Almost Entirely Correct Mixing with Applications to Voting. In: Proceedings of CCS 2002, pp. 68–77. ACM, Washington DC (2002)
8. Brickell, E., Camenisch, J., Chen, L.: Direct Anonymous Attestation. In: Proceedings of CCS 2004, pp. 132–145. ACM, New York (2004)
9. Challener, D., Yoder, K., Catherman, R., Safford, D., Doorn, L.V.: A Practical Guide to Trusted Computing. IBM Press, Boston (2008)
10. Clarkson, M.R., Chong, S., Myers, A.C.: Civitas: Toward a Secure Voting System. In: Proceedings of 2008 IEEE Symposium on Security and Privacy, pp. 354–368. IEEE, Los Alamitos (2008)
11. Cramer, R., Gennaro, R., Schoenmakers, B.: A secure and optimally efficient multi-authority election scheme. In: Fumy, W. (ed.) EUROCRYPT 1997. LNCS, vol. 1233, pp. 103–118. Springer, Heidelberg (1997)
12. Dingledine, R., Mathewson, N., Syverson, P.: Tor: the second-generation onion router. In: SSYM 2004: Proceedings of 13th USENIX Security Symposium, pp. 21–38. USENIX Association (2004)
13. Fink, R.A., Sherman, A.T., Carback, R.: TPM meets DRE: reducing the trust base for electronic voting using trusted platform modules. IEEE Transactions on Information Forensics and Security 4(4), 628–637 (2009)
14. Fujioka, A., Okamoto, T., Ohta, K.: A Practical Secret voting Scheme for Large Scale Elections. In: Zheng, Y., Seberry, J. (eds.) AUSCRYPT 1992. LNCS, vol. 718, pp. 244–251. Springer, Heidelberg (1993)
15. Harn, L.: Group-Oriented (t, n) Threshold Digital Signature Scheme and Digital Multisignature. In: IEE Proceedings—Computers and Digital Techniques, vol. 141, pp. 307–313 (1994)
16. Hirt, M., Sako, K.: Efficient receipt-free voting based on homomorphic encryption. In: Preneel, B. (ed.) EUROCRYPT 2000. LNCS, vol. 1807, pp. 539–556. Springer, Heidelberg (2000)
17. Jakobsson, M., Juels, A., Rivest, R.L.: Making Mix Nets Robust for Electronic Voting by Randomised Partial Checking. In: Proceedings of 11th USENIX Security Symposium, pp. 339–353. USENIX Assoc., Berkeley (2002)
18. Jakobsson, M., Yung, M.: Revokable and Versatile Electronic Money (Extended Abstract). In: Proceedings of CCS 1996, pp. 76–87. ACM Press, New York (1996)
19. Jorba, A.R., Ruiz, J.A.O., Brown, P.: Advanced Security to Enable Trustworthy Electronic Voting. In: Proceedings of Third European Conference on E-Government, EJEG, Dublin, Ireland (2003)
20. Juels, A., Catalano, D., Jakobsson, M.: Coercion-Resistant Electronic Elections. In: Proceedings WPES 2005, pp. 61–70. ACM, New York (2005)
21. Kügler, D., Vogt, H.: Off-line Payments with Auditable Tracing. In: Blaze, M. (ed.) FC 2002. LNCS, vol. 2357, pp. 269–281. Springer, Heidelberg (2003)

22. Lee, B., Boyd, C., Kim, K., Yang, J., Yoo, S.: Providing receipt-freeness in mixnet-based voting protocols. In: Lim, J.-I., Lee, D.-H. (eds.) ICISC 2003. LNCS, vol. 2971, pp. 245–258. Springer, Heidelberg (2004)

23. Okamoto, T.: Receipt-Free Electronic Voting Schemes for Large Scale Elections. In: Christianson, B., Lomas, M. (eds.) Security Protocols 1997. LNCS, vol. 1361, pp. 25–35. Springer, Heidelberg (1998)

24. Paillier, P.: Public-Key Cryptosystems Based on Discrete Logarithms Residues. In: Stern, J. (ed.) EUROCRYPT 1999. LNCS, vol. 1592, p. 223. Springer, Heidelberg (1999)

25. Paul, N., Tanenbaum, A.S.: Trustworthy Voting: From Machine to System. Computer 42(5), 35–41 (2009)

26. Rössler, T., Leitold, H., Posch, R.: E-Voting: A Scalable Approach using XML and Hardware Security Modules. In: Proceedings of 2005 IEEE International Conference on e-Technology, e-Commerce and e-Service, pp. 480–485. IEEE, Los Alamitos (2005)

27. Ryan, P.Y., Schneider, S.: Prêt à voter with re-encryption mixes. In: Gollmann, D., Meier, J., Sabelfeld, A. (eds.) ESORICS 2006. LNCS, vol. 4189, pp. 313–326. Springer, Heidelberg (2006)

28. Saeednia, S., Kremer, S., Markowitch, O.: An Efficient Strong Designated Verifier Signature Scheme. In: Lim, J.-I., Lee, D.-H. (eds.) ICISC 2003. LNCS, vol. 2971, pp. 40–54. Springer, Heidelberg (2004)

29. Sako, K., Kilian, J.: Receipt-free mix-type voting scheme. In: Guillou, L.C., Quisquater, J.-J. (eds.) EUROCRYPT 1995. LNCS, vol. 921, pp. 393–403. Springer, Heidelberg (1995)

30. Smart, M., Ritter, E.: Remote electronic voting with revocable anonymity. In: Prakash, A., Sen Gupta, I. (eds.) ICISS 2009. LNCS, vol. 5905, pp. 39–54. Springer, Heidelberg (2009)

31. TCG: Trusted Computing Group: TPM Main: Parts 2 and 3, Version 1.2, Revision 116 (March 2011), http://bit.ly/camUwE

32. Volkamer, M., Alkassar, A., Sadeghi, A.R., Schulz, S.: Enabling the Application of Open Systems like PCs for Online Voting. In: Proceedings of the 2006 Workshop on Frontiers in Electronic Elections, FEE 2006 (2006)

A Survey of Security Issues in Trust and Reputation Systems for E-Commerce

Stefan Spitz and York Tüchelmann

Department of Electrical Engineering and Information Sciences
Research Group Integrated Information Systems
Ruhr-University Bochum, Germany
{stefan.spitz,york.tuechelmann}@iis.ruhr-uni-bochum.de

Abstract. Trust and reputation systems are always subject to attacks if an adversary can gain a benefit in doing so. The list of different attacks against them is extensive. Attacks like bad mouthing, newcomer, sybil, collusion and many more are subject to current research. Some of them present methods that allow to detect adversarial behaviour, hence providing protection against attacks. However, smart adversaries will adapt their behaviour strategies to the existing protection mechanisms and bypass some of the security methods.

In this paper, we discuss the options available to adversaries for achieving their goal: Gaining a benefit. For this, we analyse the well-known attacks and propose security methods which provide resistance or immunity against them at any time, hence independently from the cleverness or strategy of adversaries. Our second focus is to elaborate on the problem of reliably identifying an adversary amongst transacting participants and its influence on possible security methods.

Keywords: Trust model, adversary, security methods.

1 Introduction

Today's trust and reputation systems are widely used in the field of ecommerce. These systems are based on trust and reputation models with diverse mathematical approaches. The management of memberships and presentation of trust and reputation relations is usually the task of a trusted third party (TTP) in centralized systems. In the absence of a TTP, each member is responsible for managing the trust and reputation presentation by itself. This situation occurs in fully decentralized systems.

Rating based models represent the most commonly used basis for trust and reputation systems. They are used in ecommerce platforms such as eBay, amazon and many other online market or product review sites. More refined approaches such as Bayesian probability, fuzzy logic or models based on discrete values do exist, but have not yet been included widely in commercial systems. This is probably due to the fact that these models are too inconvenient to use for the average customer. One approach to lessen this inconvenience is given by Ries [10] providing a visualization for these customers.

J.M. Alcaraz Calero et al. (Eds.): ATC 2011, LNCS 6906, pp. 203–214, 2011.
© Springer-Verlag Berlin Heidelberg 2011

Some researchers [15], [3], [4], [14] included methods in their models to detect adversarial behaviour which did provide some form of protection against one or several attacks influencing the reputation of other members. These methods are based on discounting. Here, opinions of members which do not match the predominant opinion within the trust system are either ignored or reduced in their significance.

In our opinion, this should not happen because it is almost impossible to verify whether the discounted opinion is from an adversary or honest member. For example, in [15] fair ratings for flat panel tv's were used as basis for the evaluation. 50 adversaries were tasked to boost two flat panel ratings while reducing the rating of two others. The results showed, that the adversaries were identified and their influence on the ratings was neglegible. The problem is, that in another scenario the previous adversaries might now be honest raters. The result will be the exact same if we just switch the description "honest rater" with "adversary". Now, honest raters will be identified as adversaries.

Many security methods only work if the assumption is correct about who the adversary and who the honest member is. Consider two members, each rating a product. The rating of member A is high, stating that all expectations are met or surpassed. Member B gives a low rating, stating that the product is faulty and has a bad quality. If previous ratings of other members were high, then member B's rating could be considered malicious. With low previous ratings, member A might be identified as an adversary, damaging the reputation of the product or manufacturer. However, both members' ratings could be justified. Member A received a product which was perfectly fine, while member B was less lucky. The product had several manufactoring errors.

Without information about the complete transaction, communication and evaluation process, a correct decision about which member is the adversary is almost impossible. It is due to this problem that we advise that all opinions should be accepted as given. In this paper, we identify security methods which do accept all opinions without reducing their influence based on assumptions regarding malicious behavior.

2   Adversarial Goals

The prime goal of an adversary is to gain a benefit. Without benefit, there is no intention to attack members of a trust and reputation system or the system as a whole. This benefit can be diverse, depending on the intention of the adversary. We will analyse two main adversarial goals with different benefits for the adversary.

2.1   Exploit Victim

The most obvious adversarial goal is the exploitation of another member, the victim P_{Vic}. The benefit for an adversary P_{Adv} in exploiting P_{Vic} depends on the application the trust system is used for. In the field of online auctioning, the goal might be to convince P_{Vic} in buying something from P_{Adv}. As soon as the money transfer is executed, P_{Adv} disappears without sending the auctioned item. As provider of a cloud or grid, P_{Adv} builds a high reputation first and collects as much information as possible regarding the jobs from the customers. Then P_{Adv} sells these informations to other companies with a high profit.

Of course, many more possibilities to gain a benefit exist like first selling products using high quality resources to build up the reputation, then substitute the high quality resources with less expensive ones.

2.2 Destroy Victim Reputation

The incentive behind the destruction of a victim's reputation is given, if the victim offers the same goods as the adversary. This adversarial goal targets the competitors with the intention to lessen their reputation, consequently luring customers to P_{Adv}'s store. The effect of a good or bad reputation on sales in ecommerce is assessed in several papers ([2,1,8,9]). To negatively influence the victim's reputation, P_{Adv} needs to sow discontent among the victim's customers throughout the trust system. That is, distributing false accusations about the victim's products. If done right, the reputation of the competitor slowly declines and finally presenting P_{Adv} as a viable, and of course more trustworthy alternative.

In the upcoming sections we will identify means to pursue these goals. We do this by analysing attacks against trust and reputation systems as well as identifying protection mechanisms countering these attacks.

3   Attack Strategies

For the threat analysis of well-known attacks we need an adversarial model that defines which tools are available for achieving the adversarial goal.

- An adversary is a valid member of the system and only has access to tools or functions which are available for any other member as well.
- A third party is not able to distinguish between an adversary and a honest member if the adversary did not already misuse the system to gain a benefit.
- The opinion of a member, be it an adversary or not, can't be questioned without full access to all aspects of the regarding transaction including the evaluation process of a transaction.
- The communication channels between members are secure. Messages can not be modified, redirected or intercepted.
- Adversaries may cooperate with each other to increase the effect of an attack (collusion).

In a nutshell, an adversary is just like any other member of the trust and reputation system but with a hidden agenda.

In the following, we introduce the attacks against trust and reputation systems and analyse to which degree they help in achieving the adversarial goals.

3.1 Bad Mouthing (BM)

The bad mouthing attack is used to influence the reputation of another member P_i. Independently from the outcome of a transaction between P_i and P_{Adv}, a trust value is assigned by the adversary which aids in attaining the adversarial goal. This goal could be to either increase or descrease the reputation of P_i. In the first case, P_i could be a colluding adversary while being the victim in the second case. This unjustifiable opinion about the transaction is then distributed to other members in the trust system.

Opinions are usually deemed to be subjective which makes is extremely hard to identify an unfair opinion. Without access to all informations and influencing factors regarding the transaction and the evaluation process, noticing this attack reliably is impossible without further mechanisms in place.

3.2 Ballot-Stuffing (BS)

During a ballot-stuffing attack [7], a single adversary votes more often than allowed. In a trust and reputation system, this means distributing multiple opinions about the same member, even though no or only a single transaction between P_i and P_{Adv} took place. The value of the distributed opinion can vary, depending on the intention of the adversary.

The ballot-stuffing attack is a stronger version of the bad mouthing attack, due to the increased number of distributed opinions. If no countermeasures are present, the influence on the reputation of P_i is only limited by the number of opinions P_{Adv} can distribute to other members.

3.3 Sybil (SY)

A trust and reputation system allowing the creation of member accounts without identity verification is prone to the sybil attack [5]. The adversary is able to create several valid member accounts, which are under full control of P_{Adv}. If realizable, the need for colluding adversaries is no longer given. The adversary can create an own set of colluding adversaries which aid in achieving the adversarial goal.

3.4 Newcomer (NC)

A new member in a trust and reputation system, which did not yet transacted with another member is a newcomer. No records about the new member exist in the trust system. This is an ideal re-entry situation for any adversary which currently is subject to a bad reputation. By simply closing the current account and creating a new one, the previously bad reputation is cleared. This attack is most efficient in trust systems where the initial trust value of a newcomer is sufficiently high to be eligible to transact with other members. As soon as the adversary's trust level drops below the initial value of a newcomer, a new account is created.

3.5 On-Off (O^2)

The on-off attack is a behaviour strategy against the trust model's computation algorithm. This attack exploits the model's computation of a member's reputation in a way that an adversary behaves bad and good alternatively while maintaining an average, unsuspicious level of trust. While behaving bad, the adversary tries to benefit as much as possible. With good behaviour during a transaction, i.e. providing a good service or high quality products, the adversary increases his reputation which took a hit during the bad behaviour phase. Trust models, where a bad transaction is compensated by a good transaction, are especially susceptible to this kind of attack. Here, an adversary can exploit his victim during a transaction with high benefit, while compensating the resulting bad opinion using a transaction with low benefit.

3.6 Conflicting Behaviour (CB)

The conflicting behaviour attack [12] is a modified version of the on-off attack. An adversary executing this attack strategy behaves inconsistent towards several members within the trust and reputation system. While transactions to member subset S_1 are performed well, transactions to another subset S_2 are performed bad. Consequently, members from S_1 distribute good opinions regarding the adversary, while members from S_2 distribute bad opinions. Members from subset S_1 then receive bad opinions about the adversary, which do not match the own opinion (and vice versa). This attack poses a threat, if recommendation reputation is used in the trust model.

Recommendation Reputation is based on distributed opinions and the future behaviour of a member. If the opinions and the behaviour regarding a target member are consistent, the opinion distributing member's recommendation reputation rises, otherwise declines. The degree of the recommendation reputation influences the weight of the opinions. The higher the recommendation reputation of a member, the higher the weight of the member's opinion.

The conflicting behaviour strategy aims at reducing the recommendation reputation of members. In an ideal state for the adversary, the reputation recommendation of member subset S_1 perceived by subset S_2 is low. If this state is reached, another adversary joins the attack. Previously, this adversary behaved correct to all members. If members are exploited by our new adversary P_{Adv}, the exploitation of members in subset S_1 is nearly unnoticable in S_2 (and vice versa) because opinions from S_1 have minimal impact on the reputation of P_{Adv} in S_2.

4 Security Methods

We now discuss possible security methods for the aforementioned attacks and exploits. For this, we assume that the opinions from seemingly honest members are as influential as opinions from possible adversaries. This assumption is made, because (as stated in Section 1) we think that it is impossible to reliably identify adversaries only by analysing their distributed opinions.

Therefore, each distributed opinion influences the reputation of a member in the same manner. The rough estimate is, that the influencial power is about $\frac{1}{\sum \text{collected opinions}}$.

The precise analysis of an opinion's influence needs to be based on the mechanisms of the underlying trust model. For example, if opinions are weighted, a higher or lower influence is possible. Due to the numerous trust models we will use our rough estimate and refer to the influential power of a member's opinion as IP with $IP \in N^+$, where $IP = 1$ represents the influence of a single opinion, distributed within a trust and reputation system. For example, a system, which is immune to the sybil attack will have an $IP(\text{SY}) = 1$. This means that any member, including adversaries, can influence the reputation of a target member only with an influential power of 1 opinion.

We will state the IP of opinions in regard to the existance and absence of security methods.

4.1   Identity Verification

Identity verification allows a trust and reputation system to verify the identity of members. It is a very strong countermeasure, providing the trust and reputation system with immunity against the sybil attack and the newcomer attack. Sybils can no longer be created by the adversary, as is true for more than one account associated with an identity. This immunity is, however, bound to a certain requirement. The digital certificates which are used to verify the identity of members need to be issued by a certified authority (CA) such as VeriSign (USA) or AuthentiDate (Germany) with the following requirement. During the process of creating the certificate, the certified person has to provide a passport to verify the real identity. Hence, the real identity of a member is bound to the digital certificate and verifiable by contacting the certified authority. Certificates, which are not bound to the verification of the certified person's real identity, provide only minimal resistance against aforementioned attacks. An adversary could use fake names or aliases to obtain several certificates which are used to create new member accounts. Self-signed certificates are one example for insufficient protection against sybil or newcomer attacks.

The use of ID verification is not free. The costs for issuing a certificate varies, depending on the CA. The verification process has to be included in the system, resulting in additional costs and account maintenance. This could lead to customers being put off by the extensive account creation process, reverting to alternative systems without certificates.

However, the system will be immune to both the sybil and newcomer attack ($IP(SY) = IP(NC) = 1$), as long as an adversary has no means to obtain faked passports. Without identity verification, an adversary can gain access to an unlimited number of fake accounts, hence the influential power of one adversary is, in theory, unlimited ($IP(SY) = IP(NC) = x$), with $x =$ number of fake accounts controlled/created by an adversary.

4.2   Member or Transaction Specific Opinion

Trust models like the one used in the eBay system are based on transaction specific opinions. Each transaction within the trust and reputation system is evaluated and the resulting opinion is distributed. In such a system, the reputation of a member is based on the total of all opinions regarding transactions with this member. A monitoring instance is neccessary to prohibit the distribution of opinions which are not related to real transactions. Otherwise, the number of distributed opinions is theoretically unlimited, resulting in $IP(BS) = x$, with $x =$ the number of unjustly distributed opinions by the adversary.

The security issue of transaction specific opinions is, that a weaker type of ballot-stuffing is possible even if a monitoring instance is present. Adversaries which cooperate to increase the partner's reputation transact with each other several times. An opinion is distributed for each transaction, but without a provided service. Except transaction fees (if used), no costs arise for the involved adversaries in these empty transactions.

If the reputation of a member is not based on the number of transactions but on the current opinions of members regarding the target member, ballot stuffing is no longer possible. In this case, only one opinion from each member is considered in the reputation computation process. The influence, which an adversary can exert on the reputation of the victim, is reduced to that of a bad mouthing attack, hence $IP(BS) = 1$.

Aging and Signatures. The effect of member specific opinions against a negative badmouthing attack (reducing another member's reputation) can be increased if opinions are aged as presented in [11]. Instead of using the arrival rate of experiences such as [6], [13] or [14] for the application of the aging factor, time slots are used which continuously age them independently from the arrival rate. This method can easily be used for distributed opinions of members. Current opinions excert a stronger influence on the reputation of a certain member than old opinions. If a transaction is made, the evaluating member can now update his current opinion and distribute it to other members.

An additional technique needs to be used to reduce the effect of a negative badmouthing attack. The transaction between two members needs to be signed by both parties before being evaluated. In this case, the member distributing the updated opinion is able to prove that a transaction took place. Otherwise, this member would be able to continuously update the distributed opinions even if there was no new transaction that justifies the update. Without prove of a new transaction, the current opinion will now age over time. With this, the full influence of a negative badmouthing attack against another member is present only for the time length of the first time slot (i.e. 1 week). A positive badmouthing attack, on the other hand, is not limited by this because the two members can collude and sign a non-existing transaction as often a needed.

4.3   Recommendation Reputation

A trust model that utilizes the recommendation reputation is susceptible to the conflicting behaviour attack. Hence, without this trust modelling aspect, the conflicting behaviour attack can not be used. So, the recommendation reputation, as used in [12], is not a security method against attacks, but a security risk. In the mentioned model, the recommendation reputation is used to weight opinions against each other. As described in 3.6, an adversary can exploit this trust modelling aspect to sow recommendation distrust among the members of the trust system.

However, recommendation reputation can be used differently to identify discrepancies in distributed opinions. If repeated discrepancies between distributed opinions about a target member and the real behavior appear, a third authority is informed to examine and monitor the involved members. This includes the target member as well as the members, which distributed the discrepant opinions. In one case, the adversary might be the target member trying to exploit someone, which is why distributed positive opinions do not match the current behaviour. The opinion distributing members could be adversaries as well, trying to damage the reputation of the target member. If future transactions are to be monitored by a third authority, the adversary might be identified.

Recommendation reputation is no bad idea, but should be used as watchdog. This allows for identifying discrepant behavior or opinions within the system without influencing the weight of opinions in regard to the reputation of other members. In this case, the influence of the conflicting behaviour attack on opinions is non-existance, hence $IP(CB) = 1$.

4.4   Weighted Transaction Influence

Every transaction represents some form of value for the requestor and service provider. The higher the value of a transaction, the more influential the outcome should be. This weighting of a transaction result provides resistance against exploitation. The adversary can no longer increase the own reputation by using low-value transactions as fast as without weighted transactions. The low-value transactions exert a reduced influence on the adversary's reputation value, with high-value transactions exerting an increased influence. Moreover, an adversary that exploits a victim with a high-value transaction will be confronted with a strong negative impact on the own reputation.

Ideally, the influence of low-value transactions is balanced against high-value transactions. That is, for example, the processing of 10 positive transactions with value of -1 for the adversary (hence $+1$ for the victim) is balanced against 1 negative transaction with value of $+10$ for the adversary (-10 for the victim). If the adversary has to partake in 10 positive transactions before being able to exploit the requestor with a bad transaction, then in our example, the adversary has an effective transaction value of 0. If this transaction value translates into a net profit of 0 USD, adversaries will be discouraged to exploit a victim, like performed during the on-off attack.

The resistance against exploitation is only given, if two conditions are met. First, a trust and reputation system is used which monitors all transactions. In a system without monitoring instance, each member needs to have a database storing the received opinions about other members as well as own experiences with previous transaction partners. Received opinions, be they member or transaction specific, need to be weighted equally because the weighted transaction influence is based on the knowledge about the value of transactions. A member receiving an opinion about another member does not have this knowledge. Even if distributed opinions include the value of the transactions that they are based on, one can not be sure that the provided transaction values are correct. Adversaries could easily fake the value of transactions without a monitoring instance. It is therefore advisable to only use a weighted transaction influence if a monitoring instance is present. In this case, all transactions can be weighted against each other to compute a meaningful reputation.

Second, adversaries have no means to easily increase their reputation with the help of sybils, ballot stuffing or colluding adversaries. If any of these were possible, an adversary could partake in several empty but high value transactions with the transaction partner. Now, increasing the reputation is done even faster and with less transactions. Therefore, the use of a weighted transaction influence is only advisable, if the sybil attack as well as ballot stuffing is not possible. Furthermore, member based opinions should be used, to limit the influence of colluding adversaries performing empty high value transactions.

4.5   Opinion Discounting

Some trust model authors identified the problem of bad mouthing and included a method to prevent this attack from being successfull. This method, mostly referred to as *discounting*, ignores opinions which do not comply to the predominant opinion. In a nutshell, if 9 out of 10 members state, that the target member is trustworthy, the 10'th member's opinion is ignored if stating, that the target member is not trustworthy. Some authors reduce the impact of discounting by not ignoring but reducing the influence of differing opinions. At first glance, discounting seems like a good method to prevent the bad mouthing attack, hence counteracting the adversaries goal to destroy the victim's reputation.

At second glance, using this method is outright irresponsible. This method allows an adversary to exploit a victim without fear of repercussions. The adversary behaves correct to all members except the victim, hence all but the victim state, that the adversary is trustworthy. Due to discounting, the victim's opinion is ignored or reduced in it's influence.

Except for discounting, there currently seems to be no real countermeasure to bad mouthing. All methods use some form of censorship regarding the opinion of members. But without reliable means to distinguish between fair and unfair opinions, all have to be accepted as provided. Otherwise it is likely, that opinions of honest members are ignored as well.

4.6   Transaction Fee

The transaction fee, already mentioned in 4.2, is assigned to each successfully executed transaction between a service provider and requestor. The commercial aspect aside, the purpose regarding the security of the trust and reputation system is to reduce the intention of an adversary to use ballot stuffing or empty transactions. With a transaction fee in place, an adversary has to pay for influencing the reputation of a target member. If the costs of a good reputation exceed the expected profit made by exploiting a victim, the adversary is probably seeking other ways to influence the reputation of a target member.

The downside of transaction fees is, that honest members have to pay as well. The eBay trust system uses transaction fees, but they seem negligible considering a protection against empty transactions (see selling fees [16]). Consequently, the transaction fees need to have significance (be higher) for protecting against empty transactions or ballot stuffing. A high transaction fee would most likely discourage adversaries, but also honest service providers to offer their services, or they lead to increased prices which include the transaction fee. Here, one could argument that this is the fee for a secure trust system, but members could deliberate about whether to use another, less costly system. Transaction fees can be used to provide resistance against ballot stuffing and empty transactions. The negative side effect is, that these fees can also influence the prices of provided services and ultimately can lead to a decline in active memberships.

5   Reducing the Security Issues

A trust system without security methods is like a big playground for adversaries. The more security methods are in place, the more effort an adversary has to make to exploit a victim. In this section, we propose a combination of the aforementioned security methods reducing the number of attacks that can be performed efficiently against a member of a trust and reputation system. Table 1 shows the effect of the discussed security methods based on the influential power of a single adversary in regard to the influence on another member's reputation.

Table 1. Effect of Security Methods

IP(Attack Method)	No protection	ID Ver.	Opinion based	ID + Opinion
IP(BS)	n	n	1	1
IP(SY)	m	1	m	1
IP(NC)	o	1	o	1
IP(SY+BS)	m· n	n	m	1

Here, n represents the number of ratings that a single adversary is able to sumbit. The number of created sybils is denoted as m, while o is the number of times a single adversary can change to a new account.

The use of identity verification provides the system with immunity to the sybil and newcomer attack, hence $IP(SY) = IP(NC) = 1$. The inclusion of identity verification has no influence on the underlying trust model, hence it is usable in conjunction with any trust model. Member specific opinions provide an immunity against ballot stuffing, since each member, including adversaries, can only distribute the most current opinion for each target member. This results in $IP(BS) = 1$. However, member specific opinions do influence the choice of the trust model. Trust models such as the beta reputation system [6] or eBay's system are based on transaction specific opinions and can not be used without modifications.

Even with immunity to the ballot stuffing, newcomer and sybil attack, adversaries can still exploit other members. One of the possible strategies is the on-off attack. This exploitation strategy aims at gaining the trust of the victim to allow for a profitable exploitation. The strategy is similar to a playbook and the profit is the difference between the cost of achieving a high reputation, and the profit made by exploiting the victim due to the high reputation. By combining the weighted transaction influence and the transaction fee, the costs for achieving and retaining a high reputation rise. This results in less profit for the adversary. Sadly, this method is only feasible for a centralized trust and reputation system (see 4.4).

If the transaction fee and weighted transaction influence are bound to the transaction value, colluding adversaries can no longer use empty transactions to increase each other's reputation for free. A low-cost transaction of 1 dollar still has a minimal transaction fee, but also minimal influence on the reputation. Ideally, there is no difference between n 1 dollar transactions and a single n dollar transaction regarding the reputation influence and costs.

The combination of above mentioned security methods provides immunity or resistance against adversaries that want to influence the reputation of other members in addition to a reduced incentive to exploit them.

6   Conclusion

Trust and reputation systems are used to provide meaningful predictions about the future behaviour of participating members. These systems have to provide methods to protect against attacks, otherwise adversaries could easily manipulate reputation values or exploit their victims. In this paper, several security methods were introduced and discussed. We have shown, that it is very important to analyse all aspects of possible security methods, because a countermeasure to one attack can easily lead to a weakness against another attack.

The combination of verifiable identities, member specific opinions, transaction fees and weighted transaction influences will protect honest members from adversaries. Problems arise, if not all of these security methods can be included in the trust system. Especially ID verification is a strong security method, but costly to implement and maintain. And without ID verification trust and reputation systems are still vulnerable to the sybil and newcomer attack. Hence, our future research effort will be to identify other means to protect against adversarial behaviour in the absence of a TTP - i.e. in fully decentralized systems.

References

1. Anderson, S., Friedman, D., Milam, G., Singh, N.: Seller strategies on ebay. In: Industrial Organization 0412004, EconWPA (December 2004)
2. Brown, J., Morgan, J.: Reputation in online markets: Some negative feedback (February 2006)
3. Buchegger, S., Le Boudec, J-Y.: A robust reputation system for mobile ad-hoc networks. Technical report, Proceedings of P2PEcon (2003)
4. Dellarocas, C.: Immunizing online reputation reporting systems against unfair ratings and discriminatory behavior. In: EC 2000: Proceedings of the 2nd ACM Conference on Electronic Commerce, pp. 150–157. ACM, New York (2000)
5. Douceur, J.R.: The sybil attack. In: Druschel, P., Kaashoek, M.F., Rowstron, A. (eds.) IPTPS 2002. LNCS, vol. 2429, pp. 251–260. Springer, Heidelberg (2002)
6. Jøsang, A., Ismail, R.: The beta reputation system. In: Proceedings of the 15th Bled Electronic Commerce Conference (2002)
7. Kerr, R.C.: Toward Secure Trust and Reputation Systems for Electronic Marketplaces. PhD thesis, University of Waterloo, Diploma Thesis (2007)
8. Kotha, S., Rajgopal, S., Rindova, V.: Reputation building and performance: An empirical analysis of the top-50 pure internet firms. European Management Journal 19(6), 571–586 (2001)
9. Melnik, M.I., Alm, J.: Does a seller's ecommerce reputation matter? evidence from ebay auctions. Journal of Industrial Economics 50(3), 337–349 (2002)
10. Ries, S.: Extending bayesian trust models regarding context-dependence and user friendly representation. In: SAC 2009: Proceedings of the 2009 ACM Symposium on Applied Computing, pp. 1294–1301. ACM, New York (2009)
11. Spitz, S., Tüchelmann, Y.: A trust model considering the aspects of time. In: The 2nd International Conference on Computer and Electrical Engineering (2009); ISBN: 978-1-4244-5365-8
12. Sun, Y.L., Han, Z., Yu, W., Ray Liu, K.J.: A trust evaluation framework in distributed networks: Vulnerability analysis and defense against attacks. In: IEEE INFOCOM, pp. 230–236 (2006)
13. Wang, Y., Vassileva, J.: Bayesian network-based trust model. In: WI 2003: Proceedings of the 2003 IEEE/WIC International Conference on Web Intelligence, p. 372. IEEE Computer Society, Washington, DC, USA (2003)
14. Whitby, A., Jøsang, A., Indulska, J.: Filtering out unfair ratings in bayesian reputation systems (2004)
15. Yang, Y., Sun, Y.L., Kay, S., Yang, Q.: Defending online reputation systems against collaborative unfair raters through signal modeling and trust. In: SAC 2009: Proceedings of the 2009 ACM Symposium on Applied Computing, pp. 1308–1315. ACM, New York (2009)
16. Fees for selling on ebay. Ebay Homepage (2011)

Copyright Protection in P2P Networks by False Pieces Pollution*

Chun-Hsin Wang and Chuang-Yang Chiu

Department of Computer Science and Information Engineering
Chung Hua University, Hsinchu, Taiwan 30012, R.O.C.
chwang@chu.edu.tw

Abstract. In P2P networks, the typical methods of protecting copyright files are to distribute false files with similar key words, the same file size and so on as the copyright files or publish volumes of error messages to declare the location of nonexistent copyright files. These ways lead to the difficulty in getting the copyright files for abnormal users. But these methods does not work in P2P networks such as eMule and BitTorrent with commentaries on the shared files because users can sift the true files from the false files or error location of the shared files by the commentaries. In this paper, a new technology of copyright protection by polluting pieces of files is proposed. We distribute false pieces with the same authentication keys as normal pieces but their contents are different, which is called the false pieces with authentication collision. The abnormal users will keep sharing the false pieces of copyright files they have since the false pieces can not be identified. People may have fun to download the copyright files but they can not get the correct copyright files. Due to high cost of finding authentication collision for false pieces, the way of embedding the found authentication collisions in the copyright files is also proposed. Extend simulations show approximately 100 % protection of copyright files can be reached when the associated false pieces are distributed early in time once the sharing of copyright files happened.

Keywords: Copyright protection, P2P networks, false pieces pollution.

1 Introduction

Peer-to-Peer (P2P) technology is widely applied to integrate the resources of network nodes for network applications such as grid computing, files sharing, and so on. One of most popular P2P applications is file-sharing system, which is a good and simple way to share files in internet. The report [1] in 2004 shows that P2P file-sharing traffic occupied more than 60% in the USA and 80% in Asia are in a tier-1 ISP. It is out of control that users share the copyright files by P2P file-sharing system such as KaZaA [2], eMule [3], BitTorrent [4], and so on. The illegal sharing of copyright files in P2P systems results in huge finical lost. The Envisional research [5] reveals that 23.76% of internet traffic was estimated to be infringing due to the illegal sharing of copyrighted works. According the BASCAP research [6] of International Chamber of Commerce (ICC), the total global

---

* This research is supported by the National Science Council, Taiwan, R.O.C., under grant NSC 99-2221-E-216-017-.

J.M. Alcaraz Calero et al. (Eds.): ATC 2011, LNCS 6906, pp. 215–227, 2011.

economic and social impact of counterfeiting and piracy is 775 billion every year. ICC also predicts that these cost will reach 1.7 trillion by 2015 and put 2.5 million jobs at risk each year. How to protect copyright files from the P2P file-sharing systems is worth receiving much attention.

The difficulty of copyright protection is that no limits can be imposed on using P2P file-sharing systems for users. To protect the copyright files, the main idea proposed in the literatures is trying to interfere with the process of getting the copyright files in P2P file-sharing system. We classify them into three categories as follow.

- Decoy: In [7]-[8], the way of protection is to publish some false files which their names, file size, file types are similar with the copyright files. By keyword searching, users may confuse how to choose the correct copyright files from the searching result. The decision whether the selected files are correct or not will be delayed till the downloaded files are tested. This kind of protection method is referred to as "decoy". The companies [9] and [10] provide this kind of services for copyright protection.
- Index poisoning: In [11] and [12], the volumes of false indexes are published to make users finding wrong addresses where the copyright files does not exist. Users have to spend much time for communication to peers which they have no copyright files. The difficulty of getting correct copyright files is increasing.
- Unauthenticated false blocks: In [13-15], they try to protect the copyright files by sharing the false blocks. In BitTorrent-like systems, the shared file is composed of pieces and each piece can be divided into blocks. The blocks can be shared without any authentication, whereas pieces can be distributed only when they are authenticated by a SHA-1hash function [16]. By sharing false blocks, peers may get wrong pieces containing false block(s). But wrong pieces can be checked by authentication and then being discarded. Since blocks can not be identified, peers may retrieve wrong pieces again and again. To overcome this problem, the BitTorrent system retrieve all of blocks composed of a wrong piece from the same peer. Therefore peers can sure which peers are sharing false blocks finally. In [15], they report that the pollution of false blocks may postpone the time of getting the copyright files for peers but it can not stop the distribution of correct copyright files.

The first two classes of copyright protection described as above are trying to pollute the searching result. Since users can not distinguish which published information of the shared files are correct from the polluted searching result, they may pay much time to get the correct copyright files by trial and error. To filter bogus information which interferes with the copyright file sharing, the correct published information of the shared files is declared in communities [17] or forums from web sites, which can provide with commentaries on the shared files or reputation for peers. It does not work to protect the copyright files by publishing some false index information or false similar files of copyright files in these web sites. Because users can sift the true files from the false files or error location of the shared files by commentaries or reputation. We referred to this kind of searching for the published files-sharing information from communities as "*searching from communities*". Since the published files-sharing information by searching from communities can be verified, the performance of copyright protection for the first two methods will be seriously decreasing, even useless. Besides, the third class of copyright protection by distributing unauthenticated false blocks also can not prohibit the sharing of copyright files. Therefore, we have to reconsider how to protect the copyright files in P2P files-sharing system.

In this paper, a new protection mechanism for copyright files by polluting pieces composed of files is proposed. The main idea is to distribute false pieces with the same authentication key as normal pieces but their contents are different, which is called the false pieces with authentication collision. The abnormal users will keep sharing the false pieces of copyright files since the false pieces can not be identified. As a result, user may have fun to download the copyright files but they can not get the correct copyright files finally. To the best of our knowledge, we are the first to propose false pieces pollution for copyright protection. The idea is simple and effective.

The authenticated key usually are generated by well-known hash functions such as MD4 [18], MD5, SHA-1, and so on. That is the false piece and normal piece have to be hash collision. In cryptographic theory, there exists collisions in these hash functions and it's hard to find hash collisions. But Wang et. al made a big evolution of hash collision since their publications [19] in 2004. There are many hash functions are broken one after another such as MD4, MD5, HAVAL-128/192/224/256, RIPEMD, and SHA [20-25]. The need of cost and time for creating (or preparing) false pieces depend on what hash functions are used to generate authentication keys.

Consider high cost of finding hash collisions, the way of embedding the found hash collision(s) into the copyright files is proposed. The size of copyright files, the number of false pieces, and the number of nodes used to distribute the false pieces are simulated to study the performance of copyright protection. The timing of starting to distribute false pieces is also studied. Extend simulations show approximately 100 % protection of copyright files can be reached when the associated false pieces are distributed early in time once the sharing of copyright files happened.

The rest of paper is organized as follows. The preliminary is described in the next section. The methods of copyright protection by false pieces pollution are described in Section 3. Section 4 shows the extended simulation results. Finally, some concluding remarks and future work are given in Section 5.

2   Preliminary

In this paper, we focus on how to prepare false pieces associated with their normal pieces to pollute the sharing file instead of breaking hash functions. We only summarize results of finding collisions for hash functions adopted by some popular P2P applications such as eMule, BitTorrent, and so on.

1. MD4 is an early-appeared hash function and available on modern computers. Under the consideration of time to execute the hash function, MD4 is adopted by eMule for authentication. Wang et al. [19,20] propose a collision attack on MD4 with a success probability 2^{-2} to 2^{-6}. In 2005, Y. Naito [21] et al. improve the collision attack based on Wang's method with probability almost 1 (7/8) and the average complexity is upper bound by three times MD4 hash operations. In summary, the collision on MD4 can be found easily for modern computers.

2. SHA-1 is a strength version of MD4 and widely used for hash function. It is adopted by BitTorrent for pieces authentication. Although SHA-1 has still not been broken, recently many new collision attacks on it have been devised. The SHA-1 collision can be found in 2^{63} hash operations([22,23]). It is the fact that even supercomputer can't find the SHA-1 collision in practical time. But Satoh Akashi [24] propose a custom hardware architecture which can find a real SHA-1 collision in 127 days. The cost of building the hardware system needs $10 million. In [25], the method on the SHA-1 attacking hardware is improved, SHA-1 can be broken with a 1 million budget in 22 days.

3. There are many projects(ex. [26,27]) toward finding collisions for various hash functions. We try to make use of the found collisions to protect the copyright files.

Next we introduce the operation how does share files in P2P networks briefly. The publisher of sharing file is referred to as initial seeder. A peer which has not finished to get the whole sharing file is denoted "leecher". Leechers will become seeders when they own the whole sharing file. A joining node(i.e. leecher) will get a list of peers from the tracking server(s) in centralized P2P system or from other peer(s) in distributed DHT-based P2P system. The peers in the list are referred to as the local peers of the leecher. Then leecher will communicate with its local peers and exchange the information which pieces (or blocks) of the sharing file they have. Therefore, the distribution of pieces in its local peers can be statistical. To avoid the absent of the rarest piece, leechers will request the rarest piece first according to their statistical distribution in local peers. This is what is called the rarest-piece-first policy [28]. For example, leechers in eMule-like and BitTorrent P2P systems flow the rarest-piece-first policy.

3   Protection by False Pieces Pollution

In most of P2P applications, only the authenticated pieces will be shared continuously by peers. To realize the protection by false pieces pollution, the first thing we have to do is how to prepare the false pieces composed of the files and then make the false pieces spreading fast and widely in time. We discuss these two things as follows.

3.1   Preparation of False Pieces

According to the degree to what cost and time of finding hash collision is, three ways of preparing false pieces for polluting the sharing files are provided as follows.

1. Since MD4 hash collisions can be found easily with 3 times MD4 hash operations, the false pieces for MD4 hash function can be computed in time with high probability (7/8).

2. For SHA-1 hash function, the false pieces of the copyright files can be prepared in advance. Although the hardware cost of finding collisions is $1 million at least, the cost is much less than the loss of illegal P2P distribution. In addition, note the built custom hardware system can be reused to find hash collisions again and again. It is worth investing $1 million to build the hardware system of finding collisions to protect the copyright files. Some pollution companies like [9] and [10] may

set up this kind of hardware system to service the owner of copyright files for preparing false pieces. Therefore the difficulty of preparing false pieces for SHA-1 hash function can be reduced considerably.

3. The third way of preparing false pieces is to embed the found collisions in the copyright files. The set of collisions, say S_c, can be collected from the projects (ex. [26,27]) or hardware system in [25]. One collision in S_c contains a pair of messages at least. One message of a collision is used to be the false piece and another message is as the normal piece which will be embedded in the copyright file. The copyright file is encrypted by normal piece by symmetric encryption and then the normal piece is inserted in the encrypted copyright file at random boundary between any two pieces. To increase the degree of pollution, more than one normal pieces can be embedded into the copyright file. A simple way to approach this is to divided copyright file into several parts and one normal piece is used to encrypt each part of copyright file respectively. Beside that, the encrypted files can be designed to automatically decrypt by the embedded normal piece(s) when they are accessed. In this way, the copyright file can not be accessed once the embedded normal piece(s) is (are) polluted by the false piece(s).

Note the first two methods of preparing false pieces can be applied to any kind of sharing files because the original files are not needed to be changed. The third method is especially suitable to be applied to the class of execution files. Before the execution file with copyright is released, the found normal piece(s) could be embedded in it by the third method described as above. The protection of copyright files can be approached by spreading the prepared false pieces in P2P system.

3.2   Methods of Spreading False Pieces

If the false pieces of the file people want to download can be spread fast and wide in time, the probability of getting polluted files with false piece(s) will be increasing. To spread the false pieces, the owner of copyright files can setup one or more PC-based stations to be the peer(s) by joining the P2P systems which are found to distribute the copyright files illegally. We refer these stations to as *guardians*. Due to the complexity and cost of finding a collision such as SHA-1 is too complex to compute a collision in time, the guardians should prepare the false pieces in advance for BitTorrent. But the guardians can prepare the false pieces easily for eMule because they adopt MD4 hash function. The methods of spreading false pieces are considered as follows.

– Timing to start spreading false piece(s): The timing of guardians to start spreading false pieces will affect the performance of copyright protection. This method is to spread false piece(s) in different times by guardian. We investigate the effect of two different times when the guardian joins the P2P system on the performance of copyright protection. The first is the timing at the beginning when the copyright file is illegally shared and the second is at few hours after the copyright file is shared. The subscription of RSS news [17] and key words monitoring softwares ([7,11]) can help guardian to know the time when the copyright files are sharing and then start spreading false piece(s).

- Multiple IDs of a guardian: The guardian can join the P2P system more than once to get multiple IDs of peers. That is one guardian can spread more than one false pieces. This method is used to observe the effect of multiple IDs on copyright protection.
- The number of false pieces: This method is trying to increase the pollution by spreading number of false pieces. It is expected that the performance of copyright protection will be affected by how many number of false pieces are distributed to pollute the copyright files.

4   Simulation Results

The size of a piece for eMule is fixed to be 9.28MB. In our simulation, we assume the size of a piece for eMule is 10MB for convenience to divide the sharing file into integer number of pieces. The size of a piece for BitTorrent is 2 to the power. It can be configured by BitTorrent software automatically or by user manually. The default size of piece for BitTorrent is set to be 256 KBs. The default of uploading bandwidth is 256 $kbps$, which is the uploading bandwidth of ADSL in Taiwan popularly. The delay of sending one piece from one peer to another peer in the network is variant for many reasons such as the size of pieces, traffic load, and so on. We simply assume the end-to-end delays are to form an exponentiation distribution. Three different mean end-to-end delays are adopted to be observed the effect of pollution, namely 30 seconds, 60 seconds and 120 seconds. The default mean end-to-end delay is 30 seconds.

The peers are supposed to join the P2P system in Poisson distribution after the initial seeder have published the shared file. The mean of joining rate is 96 peers per hour. According the report in [17], peers which finish downloading the shared file will stay in P2P system for 24 hours and then leave. To simulate the worse situation of spreading false pieces, only fifty percentage of peers which own the error shared file are supposed to stay in P2P system. For each data point in our experiment, 30 sample runs are executed. Each sample run is starting by an initial seeder till the time when there are 3000 seeders which have finished downloading the shared file. The pollution ratio is defined as the average percentage of polluted seeders which own the false piece(s). It is measured to evaluate the performance of our proposed methods.

The number of local peers for a peer is set by the P2P software automatically or user manually. It is usually 50 or 100. A peer can ask more other peers to be its local peers from tracker server(s) when the wanted pieces are absent in its local peers. We simply set the number of local peers to be 100.

In our simulation, we assume the guardian can receive normal piece in eMule and then find its collision for MD4 hash function in time with $7/8$ probability [21]. Due to the high complexity and cost of finding a collision for SHA-1, the guardian is supposed to prepare only one false piece in advance for BitTorrent. One guardian with one default ID is supposed to execute the pollution. The time of guardian joining the P2P system to start spreading false piece(s) is denoted "GJT" (Guardian Joining Time), it is relative to the starting time when the shared file is published in P2P system. The time unit of it is hour. $GJT = 0$ means that the guardian almost starts spreading false piece(s) at the same time when the shared file is published.

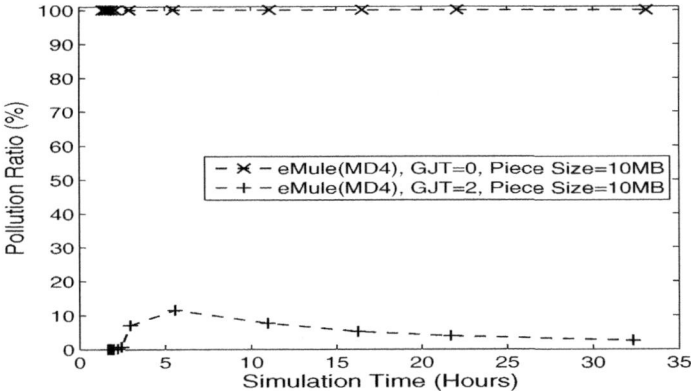

Fig. 1. GJT=0 versus GJT=2 in eMule

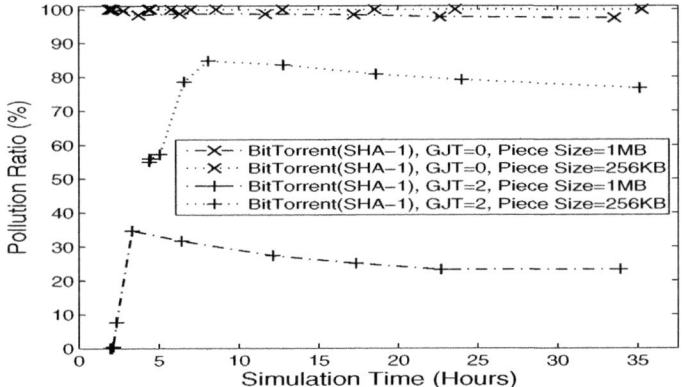

Fig. 2. GJT=0 versus GJT=2 in BitTorrent

Fig. 1 and Fig. 2 show the effect of times to start spreading false pieces. The shared file size is 100 MBs. With the piece size of 10 MBs, the shared file is composed of 10 pieces in eMule. In BitTorrent, it can be composed of 100 and 400 pieces with the piece size of 1 MBs and 256 KBs respectively. From these two figures, we can see that the pollution ratio almost approaches to 100% when GJT=0, whatever the eMule or BitTorrent is. It reveals that guardian can simple pollute the shared file for protection when the time to start spreading false piece is as soon as possible. This is because the false piece provided by guardian plus the same normal piece in the initial seeder will not be the rarest piece when only a guardian joins the P2P system. The pieces except that false piece in the initial seeder will become rarest pieces. It results in that the peers joining after the guardian will ask normal pieces except the prepared false piece from the initial seeder by the rule of rarest-piece-first. The initial seeder is always busy sharing the normal and rarest pieces and therefore its uploading bandwidth is occupied. The joining peers will get the false piece from the guardian with high probability and

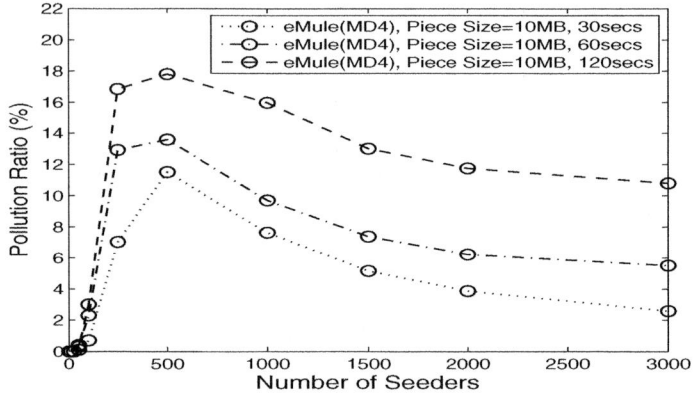

Fig. 3. The effect of network delay in eMule

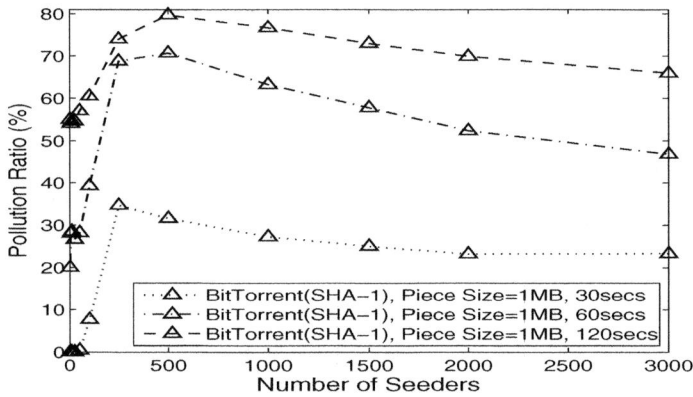

Fig. 4. The effect of network delay in BitTorrent, size of piece=1MB

keep spreading the false piece. If the guardian joins two hours after the shared file is published(i.e., $GJT = 2$), peers in the system have already gotten normal pieces from initial seeder or others peers. It will reduce the probability of spreading the false piece in the system seriously.

From Fig. 2, we can also observe that the performance with piece size of 256 KBs is better than it with piece size of 1MBs in BitTorrent when $GJT = 2$. This is because a large number of pieces will extend the time to spread all of normal pieces to other peers. There may exist some pieces which are not shared with any one peers or some pieces are only distributed to a few of peers when $GJT = 2$. The false piece provided at GJT=2 by guardian may have the probability to be the same with one of these rare pieces in initial seeder or other few peers. Therefore, the false piece still have high probability to be distributed to the upcoming peers. Simulation shows it has more than 75% pollution ratio.

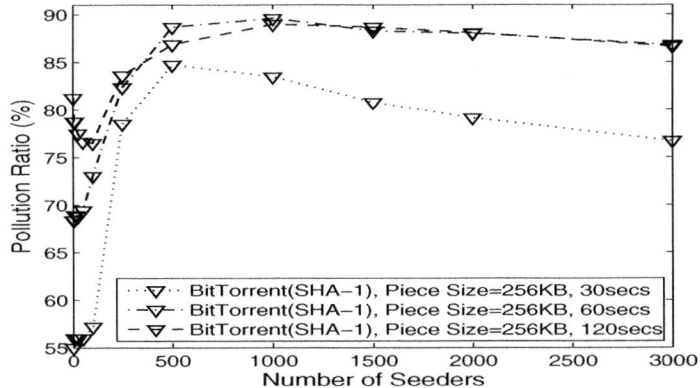

Fig. 5. The effect of network delay in BitTorrent, size of piece=256kB

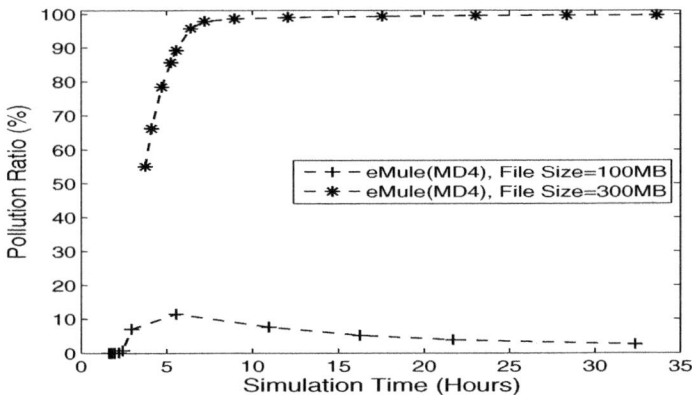

Fig. 6. The effect of file size in eMule

Next, we want to investigate the effect of pollution by the network traffic. To observe how the pollution is when pieces of the shared file have been distributed for a period time, we set $GJT = 2$ instead of $GJT = 0$. Three different mean end-to-end delays are adopted, namely 30 seconds, 60 seconds and 120 seconds. From Fig. 3 to Fig. 5, we can see that the pollution ratio for small size of pieces is much better than it for large size of pieces under the same network delay. The result is consistent with it in Figure 2. In addition, the pollution ratio for long end-to-end delay (60 and 120 seconds) is better than small end-to-end delay (30 seconds) in eMule and BitTorrent.

Note there exist some variations of pollution ratios for network delay 60 and 120 seconds in Fig. 5. It can be explained that the performance of pollution depends on how many peers have owned the normal piece being polluted and the time needed to spread pieces over peers. Since long network delay may take long time of spreading pieces, the number of peers owned the normal piece being polluted for end-to-end delay 120 seconds is less than it for end-to-end delay 60 seconds at two hours after system

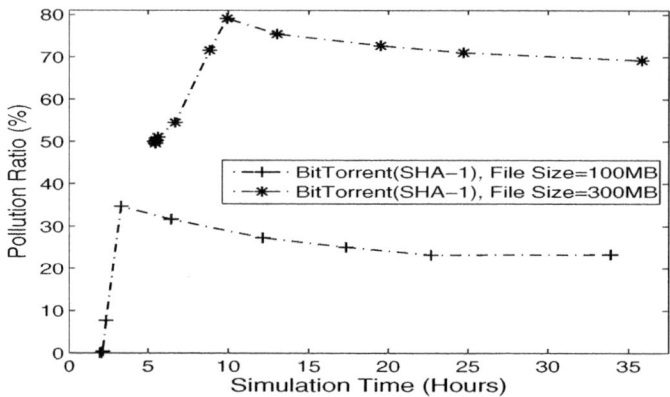

Fig. 7. The effect of file size in BitTorrent

initialization. Therefore, the false piece have high probability of being distributed to the peers without that normal piece in the environment with long end-to-end delay. The pollution ratio for end-to-end delay 120 seconds is better than it for end-to-end delay 60 seconds in the beginning when $GJT = 2$. But the growing of pollution ratio for end-to-end delay 60 seconds is faster than it for end-to-end delay 120 seconds due to the short time needed to spread the false piece for end-to-end delay 60 seconds. From Fig. 5, we can observe that the pollution ratio for end-to-end delay 60 seconds is gradually increasing, over and then equal to it for end-to-end delay 120 seconds. It's worthy noting that the pollution ratio can be larger than 85% even the pollution is starting at two hours after the shared files is published.

Fig. 6 and Fig. 7 show how the file size of the shared file does affect the pollution ratio. The size of piece is 10M bits for eMule and 1M bits for BitTorrent. The two different file sizes, 100MB and 300MB, are used to observe the effect on pollution ratio when $GJT = 2$. The simulation result shows that large file size has better performance in eMule and BitTorrent. Because large file is composed of more number of pieces comparing with the small file. A large number of pieces will extend the time to spread all of normal pieces from initial seeder to other peers. As the same reason described in Fig. 2, the false piece still has high probability to be distributed to the upcoming peers. Simulation shows it has more than 75% pollution ratio.

The guardian can join the P2P system more than once to get multiple IDs of peers. Fig. 8 shows the effect of pollution ratio on multiple IDs of a guardian in eMule. The shared file size equals 300MB and $GJT = 5$. One guardian with two IDs may spread the same false pieces to two peers. It's reasonable that a guardian with two IDs has better performance than a guardian with one ID. But the pollution ratio is less than 40% even the guardian with two IDs. This is because the time of starting pollution is too late. There are many peers owned the normal piece we want to pollute at 5 hours after the shared files is published by the initial seeder.

Fig. 9 shows the effect of pollution on multiple IDs of a guardian and multiple false pieces in BitTorrent. The shared file size equals 300MB, size of piece is 1MB and $GJT = 5$. The guardian with two IDs, distributing two different false pieces, has better

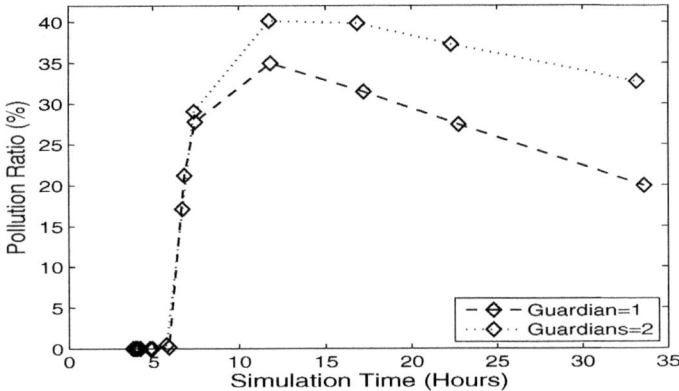

Fig. 8. Multiple IDs of a guardian in eMule.

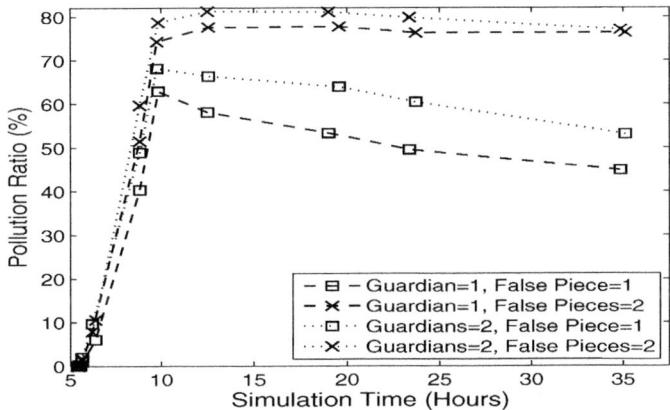

Fig. 9. Multiple IDs of a guardian and false pieces in BitTorrent.

performance than the others. Form Fig. 9, we can also find that the pollution ratio for the guardian with one ID and two different false pieces is better than it for the guardian with two IDs but one false piece. The main difference is that two different false pieces are distributed in the former but only one false piece is spreaded in the later. The guardian with two IDs and one false piece means that there exists two guardians for spreading the same false piece in the system. Since the shared file can be polluted by one of two different false pieces, the guardian with one ID and two different false pieces has better performance than the guardian with two IDs and one false piece.

5   Conclusion and Future Work

Typical methods of copyright protection by polluting the searching result does not work in modern P2P networks. A new method of copyright protection by false pieces pollution is proposed in this work. It's simple and effective because only one guardian distributing one false piece is needed and has good performance. The subscription of RSS news and key words monitoring softwares can help guardian to know the time when the copyright files are sharing and then start spreading false piece(s). Extend simulations show approximately 100 % protection of copyright files can be reached when the associated false pieces are distributed early in time once the sharing of copyright files happened. In future, the guardian will be implemented and real experiment on copyright protection will be tested in internet. The copyright protection for different types of files such as multimedia files will be developed.

References

1. CacheLogic Research: The True Picture of P2P File Sharing,
   http://www.readwriteweb.com/archives/p2p_growth_trend_watch.php
2. Offical KaZaA homepage, http://www.kazaa.com
3. Official eMule homepage, http://www.emule-project.net/
4. Official BitTorrent homepage, http://www.bittorrent.org/
5. Envisional Research,
   http://documents.envisional.com/docs/Envisional-Internet_Usage-Jan2011.pdf
6. BASCAP Research,
   http://www.iccwbo.org/uploadedFiles/BASCAP/Pages/Global%20Impacts%20-%20Final.pdf
7. Liang, J., Kumar, R., Xi, Y., Ross, K.W.: Pollution in P2P file sharing systems. In: Proc. IEEE INFOCOM 2005, Miami, FL (March 2005)
8. Christin, N., Weigend, A.S., Chuang, J.: Content Availability, Pollution and Poisoining in File Sharing Peer-to-Peer Networks. In: ACM Conference on Electronic Commerce, Vancouver, Canada (June 2005)
9. Viralg, a digital copyrights protecting company (February 2009),
   http://www.viralg.com/
10. MediaDefender (February 2009), http://www.mediadefender.com/
11. Liang, J., Naoumov, N., Ross, K.W.: The Index Poisoning Attack in P2P File Sharing Systems. In: INFOCOM 2006 25th IEEE International Conference on Computer Communications, Barcelona, Spain (April 2006)
12. Sun, X., Torres, R., Rao, S.: DDoS Attacks by Subverting Membership Management in P2P Systems. In: 3rd IEEE Workshop on Secure Network Protocols, Beijing, China (October 2007)
13. Liogkas, N., Nelson, R., Kohler, E., Zhang, L.: Exploiting BitTorrent For Fun (But Not Profit). In: Proc. 5th Itl. Workshop on Peer-to-Peer Systems (IPTPS), Santa Barbara, CA, USA (February 2006)
14. Locher, T., Moor, P., Schmid, S., Wattenhofer, R.: Free Riding in BitTorrent is Cheap. In: Fifth Workshop on Hot Topics in Networks. ACM, Irvine (2006)
15. Dhungel, P., Wu, D., Schonhorst, B., Ross, K.W.: A Measurement Study of Attacks on BitTorrent Leechers. In: Proc. 7th Itl. Workshop on Peer-to-Peer Systems (IPTPS), Tampa Bay, Florida, USA (February 2008)
16. RFC3174, SHA-1, http://tools.ietf.org/html/rfc3174

17. Andrade, N., Mowbray, M., Lima, A., Wagner, G., Ripeanu, M.: Influences on Cooperation in BitTorrent Communities. In: ACM SIGCOMM 2005 Workshops, Philadelphia, PA, USA (August 2005)
18. RFC1320, MD4, http://tools.ietf.org/html/rfc1320
19. Wang, X., Lai, X., Yu, H.: Collisions for Hash Functions MD4, MD5, HAVAL-128 and PIREMD, rump session. In: CRYPTO 2004 (2004) (e-Print)
20. Wang, X., Lai, X., Feng, D., Chen, H., Yu, X.: Cryptanalysis of the hash functions MD4 and RIPEMD. In: Cramer, R. (ed.) EUROCRYPT 2005. LNCS, vol. 3494, pp. 1–18. Springer, Heidelberg (2005)
21. Naito, Y., Sasaki, Y., Kunihiro, N., Ohta, K.: Improved Collision Attack on MD4. Cryptology ePrint Archive, Report 2005/151 (2005)
22. Wang, X., Yin, Y.L., Yu, H.: Finding Collisions in the Full SHA-1. In: Shoup, V. (ed.) CRYPTO 2005. LNCS, vol. 3621, pp. 17–36. Springer, Heidelberg (2005)
23. Cochran, M.: Notes on the Wang et al. 2^{63} SHA-1 Differential Path. Cryptology ePrint Archive, Report 2007/474 (December 2007)
24. Satoh, A.: Hardware Architecture and Cost Estimates for Breaking SHA-1, pp. 259–273. Springer, Heidelberg (2005)
25. Akashi, S.: Study on Architecture and Cost Estimates for SHA-1 Attacking Hardware. Transactions of Information Processing Society of Japan, 2182–2193 (2006)
26. SHA-1 Collision Search Graz, http://boinc.iaik.tugraz.at/
27. www.iaik.tugraz.at/content/research/krypto/sha1/
28. Mathieu, F., Reynier, J.: Missing Piece Issue and Upload Strategies in Flashcrowds and P2P-assisted Filesharing. In: Proceedings of the Advanced International Conference on Telecommunications and International Conference on Internet and Web Applications and Services (AICT/ICIW 2006). IEEE, Los Alamitos (2006)

Detection and Classification of Different Botnet C&C Channels

Gregory Fedynyshyn[1], Mooi Choo Chuah[2], and Gang Tan[2,*]

[1] Lehigh University. Bethlehem, PA 18015, USA
gef209@lehigh.edu
[2] {chuah,gtan}@cse.lehigh.edu

Abstract. Unlike other types of malware, botnets are characterized by their command and control (C&C) channels, through which a central authority, the *botmaster*, may use the infected computer to carry out malicious activities. Given the damage botnets are capable of causing, detection and mitigation of botnet threats are imperative. In this paper, we present a host-based method for detecting and differentiating different types of botnet infections based on their C&C styles, e.g., IRC-based, HTTP-based, or peer-to-peer (P2P) based. Our ability to detect and classify botnet C&C channels shows that there is an inherent similarity in C&C structures for different types of bots and that the network characteristics of botnet C&C traffic is inherently different from legitimate network traffic. The best performance of our detection system has an overall accuracy of 0.929 and a false positive rate of 0.078.

Keywords: Botnet detection, network security, host-based intrusion detection system.

1 Introduction

Botnets are organized networks of infected (zombie) machines running bot code, categorized by their use of a command and control (C&C) channel. Through the C&C channel, a central authority (i.e., the *botmaster*) may issue commands to his army of zombie machines and essentially take full control over the infected machines. These networked armies of zombie machines are typically used to carry out an array of malicious activities, including, but not limited to, engaging in spam campaigns, stealing personal or financial information, participating in click-fraud campaigns, initiating distributed denial of service (DDoS) attacks, and propagating bot code to other vulnerable machines. Due to the vast amounts of damage botnets can cause, detecting and mitigating infections are imperative.

---

* The authors would like to thank Alex Lanstein of FireEye for all around, general assistance, and Dezhao Song and Xu Li of Lehigh University for help in collecting some botnet data.

J.M. Alcaraz Calero et al. (Eds.): ATC 2011, LNCS 6906, pp. 228–242, 2011.

1.1   Background: C&C Channel Types and Fast Flux

Current botnet C&C channels follow a general model: first, a botmaster must issue a command to the botnet; second, the botnet performs activities in response to the command; and third, the botnet sends the results of performing its activities back to the botmaster. There are 3 types of C&C channels, namely (a) Internet Relay Chat(IRC)-Based C&C channels which use a *push-based* model, where the botmaster *pushes* new commands to the botnet, which then responds directly to the commands, (b) HTTP-based C&C channels which use a *pull-based* model where bots periodically poll the C&C server to request new commands, (c) Peer-to-peer (P2P) based C&C channels where peer-to-peer communication is used to proxy commands or to locate a C&C server. P2P-based C&C has the advantage of not having a single point of failure which is inherent to IRC-based and HTTP-based bots.

Many botnets use a DNS technique called *fast flux* to hide their central C&C server. The idea behind *fast flux* is to use an ever-changing array of compromised hosts to proxy messages between the central C&C server and the botnet. The botmaster continually changes the proxy to which a domain name points and bots find the C&C proxy by looking up the domain name instead of using hard-coded, static IP addresses. In the event a proxy is taken down, the central C&C server will remain intact and continue to issue commands through different proxies, adding a layer of resiliency and stealth to the botnet.

1.2   Botnet Detection Approaches

Most botnet intrusion detection systems (IDS) fall into three categories: host-based, network-based, and a hybrid of the two. Host-based systems, such as [1,2,3] focus on detecting bot infections on an individual host and typically use signature- or behavior-based methods to correlate network traffic or system events with known bot signatures or behavioral information. While host-based IDS's are able to detect single bot infections, some knowledge of the bot's behavior must be known in advance. Host-based approaches also benefit from being easy to deploy and from empowering the end-user directly.

Network-based methods, such as [4,5,6,7], attempt to detect bot infections by correlating similar behaviors among several different hosts on the monitored network. Network-based methods do not need prior knowledge of bot signatures or behavioral information as they rely on the intuition that hosts infected by the same bot will behave very similarly to one another whereas uninfected hosts will exhibit different network characteristics from one another. While network-based intrusion detection systems (IDS) may not require prior knowledge of a bot's behavioral patterns, they do require that multiple hosts in the same network become infected for the intrusion to be detectable. In addition, network-based approaches may require additional cooperation of the network administrator and care must be taken to protect the privacy of the network users.

1.3   Contributions

We adopt a host-based IDS in this paper. Our contributions to the field are:

1. Our system detects not only bot infections independent of packet payload content, but also types of C&C channels, as knowing the type helps with deploying appropriate defenses. To identify botnets and their types, our system identifies *persistent* connections (similar to [3]), however, unlike [3] our system can distinguish the type of C&C channel.
2. A domain-based approach is used to undermine the effectiveness of fast flux obfuscation techniques. The domain-based approach groups conversations using full domain names rather than IP addresses, allowing us to deobfuscate fast flux botnets.
3. A binary classifier to identify IRC-based traffic instead of examining packet payload content (which consumes much processing power and is not viable for encrypted IRC traffic) or using popular IRC port numbers (which may miss IRC traffic on non-popular IRC ports).

Our preliminary evaluation shows that there is a similarity inherent in the traffic produced in botnet C&C communications that is different from legitimate network traffic. Additionally, we show that each C&C style shares similarity across multiple botnet families. This inherent similarity implies that that, unlike many host-based IDS's, our model has the potential to discover infections of previously unknown bots.

The rest of the paper is organized as follows. In Section 2, we discuss related work. In Section 3, we discuss hypotheses, objectives, and the architecture of our IDS framework. In Section 4, we present the evaluation of our approach with the results presented in section 5. In Section 6, we provide some discussions of why our approach works and in Section 7, we conclude by discussing work that we intend to carry out in the near future.

2   Related Work

Much work has been done on botnet intrusion detection. Many IDS's make use of the observation that the characteristics of botnet network traffic differ greatly from those of normal network traffic. Many botnet detection systems rely on *anomaly detection* to discover bot infections. Anomaly detection simply aims to detect significant deviations from normal behavior and is typically applied to network behavior, such as the characteristics of network connections, or system-level behavior, such as CPU usage or modifications to the file system. The main advantage of anomaly detection is that it is good at discovering new infections, as infections are likely to cause changes in the monitored activity no matter what shape they take.

There are different types of botnet detection methods, e.g. host-based or network-based systems. The host-based IDS presented in [1] uses anomaly detection on aggregate network features to identify a deviation from normal activity.

Once identified, a snapshot of the network traffic surrounding the anomaly is taken. Using the intuition that snapshots containing similar anomalies are likely multiple instances of a bot responding to the same botmaster command, the packet payloads leading up to the anomaly are searched for common content to find the command. Once a suitable representation of the command is found, the IDS can build a profile which can then be used to detect future occurrences of the command/response pair. One drawback to this IDS is its need to examine packet payloads. Many current-day botnets use encryption to obfuscate their C&C messages. If the botnet uses a complex encryption algorithm for its C&C channel, this approach will not find any commonality in packet payloads containing botmaster commands.

Another host-based IDS presented by Giroire et al. [3] is based on the intuition that bots must contact their C&C server regularly to receive commands from the botmaster. Thus, unlike transient connections, the connections to C&C channels will appear to be *persistent*. This IDS first builds a whitelist of legitimate destinations that the monitored host contacts persistently. If any new connection is observed that exhibits high enough temporal persistence, an alarm is raised. If this connection is legitimate, a user can simply add it to the whitelist, otherwise, the connection is assumed to be malicious and is blocked. The success of such a system relies on the assumption that the whitelist is easy to maintain and that it does not need to be updated frequently. The system presented in this paper also uses the notion of observing persistent connections to detect botnet C&C channels.

The network-based IDS, BotSniffer [5] exploits the *spacial* and *temporal* similarity of botnet activity to differentiate between botnet network traffic and legitimate network traffic. The inspiration behind BotSniffer is that each bot in the network will receive a similar or identical command at similar times, and then perform similar activities in response to the command at similar times. Potential C&C messages are limited to incoming IRC and HTTP packets. Bot responses are categorized into two types: *message responses*, such as sending a message to an IRC chat room, and *activity responses*, such as scanning the network or sending spam emails. Botnet detection works as follows: if at any point in time a group of hosts is observed to be performing similar activities in response to similar messages from the same server, they likely belong to the same botnet.

Similar to BotSniffer, BotMiner is a network-based IDS [6]. BotMiner categorizes network activity into *communication activity* that corresponds to potential C&C communication and *malicious activity* that corresponds to scanning, spamming, or binary download events. BotMiner clusters hosts according to similar communication activities and according to similar malicious activities, then performs cross-cluster analysis to identify hosts that share both similar communication and malicious activities. While the BotMiner IDS had impressive results, it still falls prey to the same problem most network-based detection schemes do: that multiple hosts in the monitored network must be infected to be detected by BotMiner.

3   Methodology

The goal of our host-based IDS is to be able to detect the presence of botnet C&C traffic on the monitored host, as well as classify the style of C&C communication the bot is using, be it IRC, HTTP, or P2P. Furthermore, our detection system is completely independent of the content of the C&C messages, i.e., we do not examine packet payloads. The ability to locate and classify botnet C&C connections depends on a few hypotheses:

1. Botnet C&C communication can be differentiated from botnet non-C&C communication.
2. Botnet C&C communication can be differentiated from legitimate communication.
3. The characteristics of different styles of C&C are similar across different botnet families.

We will use the term *conversation* to refer to all network packets transmitted between two unique hosts, based on full domain name when available, otherwise IP address. We use full domain name to undermine fast flux techniques. As a botnet C&C channel may use several different servers in a fast flux network to perform the same service of issuing commands to the bot, we wish to capture the full C&C conversation, which an IP addressed based approach would fail to do. Unless otherwise noted, we will refer to a *conversation* as being between the monitored host and some destination host. We will also present the results when IP addresses are used rather than domain names to define conversations at the end of Section 5 for comparison. We use the observation that while humans and bots alike may connect to a vast quantity of different destination addresses during the course of any given day, the number of connections that exhibit long-term, continual two-way traffic is relatively small. We also use the observation that a bot must be in continual contact with its botmaster to effectively be a member of a botnet. Thus, the C&C channel must appear as a conversation that exhibits continual two-way network traffic over the course of time.

Instead of examining features of aggregate network activity on the monitored host, we examine features on a per-conversation basis. We begin by dividing the network traffic for each conversation into time slots of length t. Within each time slot, we track the total number of bytes and packets sent, the total number of bytes and packets received, the protocol and the ports used in the conversation. We then generate *instances* with which to train the classifier by examining statistical features contained within an *observation window* that is n time slots in length. Thus, the network features as calculated across the time slots in each observation window generate a single *instance* of a conversation. Note that a conversation that lasts longer than n time slots will generate more than one instance. Let W be the observation window such that $W = \{s_i, s_{i+1}, ..., s_{i+n-1}\}$ where s_i is the network traffic contained in time slot i. Figure 1 shows an example of the relationship between time slots to the observation window where the observation window consists of twelve time slots.

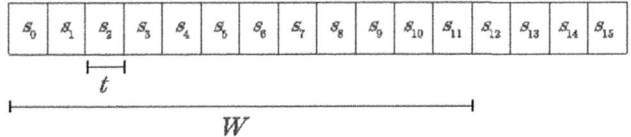

Fig. 1. Example showing time slots and observation window

3.1 Data Collection

In this section, we describe the data collection process. As we will eventually be training a classifier, we need a good set of network traces which are comprised of legitimate traffic as well as a set of network traces comprised of botnet traffic.

Normal Traces: To collect data with legitimate network traffic, we used a libpcap-based packet capture program to capture all network traffic on four hosts for a combined total of 29 days. We do not want to promiscuously capture network traffic for two reasons. First, we are implementing a host-based IDS, so we do not want to look at the network activity of other hosts on the network. Second, we know that the machines used to generate normal network activity are clean of malware but cannot be certain about other hosts on the network. An IDS is useless if it is not robust enough to work on any given host. To that end, we ensured our normal traces covered a wide range of legitimate activity, such as instant messaging, email communications, web browsing, video streaming, SSH, IRC, etc.

Botnet Traces: Collecting botnet traffic is a more challenging affair. Our requirements for running bot samples are: to make sure that the generated traffic is typical of the specific bot and to make sure the bot does not damage any other hosts on the network. To tackle the first requirement, we ran our bot samples on a virtual machine running Windows XP SP2 and recorded network traffic using a libpcap-based capture program. Virtual machines can be easily reverted back to their pre-infection state, which established a clean baseline from which to run the bot samples. As the host machine running the virtual Windows XP system is on the Lehigh University campus network, it is important to make sure it will not cause any damage to the network. For example, many botnets infect new users through worms and OS exploits, so outgoing traffic on known exploit ports was blocked. We believe that our measures were sufficient in avoiding any damage to the Lehigh University campus network. Table 1 shows a summary of the network data collected. In many cases, data for botnet families were generated using different variants of the bot. Botnet family identification was performed using the open source ClamAV antivirus tool [8].

Table 1. Summary of data collected

Trace Type	C&C Type	Number of Variants	Total Length
Normal	NA	NA	29 days
Ircbot	IRC	4	8 days
Agobot	IRC	3	18 days
Rustock	HTTP	2	5 days
Storm	HTTP	4	17 days
Bobax	HTTP	4	5 days
Waledac	P2P	2	6 days
UDP Storm	P2P	1	6 days

3.2 Data Processing

We define *persistence* in terms of the number of time slots in the observation window in which two-way communication occurs divided by the total number of time slots in the observation window. For example, if two-way communication is only observed in half of the time slots in the observation window, the *persistence* of the conversation in that particular observation window is 0.5.

Figure 2 provides a graphical representation of the steps taken to create instances which can then be sent to the Botnet Classifier for botnet detection:

1. Collect network traffic
2. Split network trace into conversations
3. Divide conversations into observation windows and extract feature values to create instances
4. Filter out impersistent instances
5. Pass final instance set to Botnet Classifier

Only instances that pass the persistence test are retained. For each retained instance, we compute the following features across the time slots contained within the instance:

- Standard deviation of bytes sent / byte received
- Standard deviation of packets sent / packets received
- Standard deviation of bytes sent / packets sent
- Standard deviation of bytes received / packets received
- Standard deviation of the number of source ports used
- Standard deviation of the number of destination ports used
- Average number of bytes sent
- Average number of bytes received
- Average number of packets sent
- Average number of packets received
- Average number of TCP packets transmitted
- Average number of UDP packets transmitted

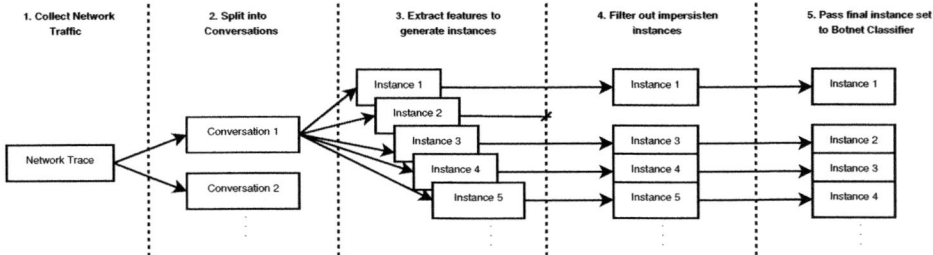

Fig. 2. Instance generation steps

- Average number of IRC packets transmitted
- Persistence value

Furthermore, let p be the *persistence threshold*. If the persistence value calculated for an instance of a conversation is less than the *persistence threshold*, the instance is considered to be transient, and therefore not a likely candidate for a potential C&C channel. A conversation that persists over time may produce some instances that do not exceed the persistence threshold. Such a situation may arise from a user shutting down her machine or losing her Internet connection. Thus, we decide to filter out these impersistent instances as they do not accurately reflect the true behavior of the conversation that our botnet classifier is concerned with.

Through experimentation, we found that $t = 600$ seconds (10 minutes), $n = 24$ time slots (4 hours), and $p = 0.6$ produces the best results. As our data clearly spans more than 4 hours, we can make use of a sliding observation window to generate multiple instances for a single conversation. Defining instances based on observation windows has some benefits. Conversations can theoretically persist indefinitely. Instead of having to store statistics regarding entire conversations in computer memory, we only need to keep track of a handful of observation windows. In addition, were there a situation where a legitimate site becomes hijacked and used for malicious purposes, the observation window would soon slide past the time slots encompassing the legitimate traffic and be able to detect the new, malicious behavior.

There are two approaches we can take when determining how far to slide the observation window, W, to generate the next instance: slide W a single time slot or slide W n time slots, such that no observation windows overlap. For an online IDS, it would make the most sense to slide W by one time slot at a time as overall detection time would decrease. On the other hand, sliding W by n time slots at a time ensures that there is no overlap from one instance to the next. Overlapping instances may skew the accuracy of the classifier favorably, so we present results based on a non-overlapping sliding observation window. Using a non-overlapping observation window with $t = 600$ seconds and $n = 24$ time slots, a 24-hour long conversation can generate at most 6 instances. Using an overlapping observation window with the same values for t and n, a 24-hour long conversation can generate at most 20 instances.

Table 2 shows the number of instances generated from the persistent conversations using the domain-based approach. Note the relatively low number of persistent conversations found in each trace compared to the overall number of conversations. As Table 2 shows, the number of persistent conversations in both normal and botnet traces is immensely smaller than the total number of conversations. By filtering out all transient conversations, we are left only with likely C&C conversations. In addition, by disregarding impersistent connections, we drastically cut down the amount of network traffic we need to analyze, leading to a more computationally efficient model.

During our evaluation, we split our 89 total days network traffic such that half (44 days) is used to build the training set and the other half (45 days) is used to build the testing set, where there is no overlap between the training and testing data. The number of instances generated for both training and testing are also shown in Table 2.

Table 2. Summary of instance generation

Trace Type	Total Convs	Persistent Convs	Training Instances	Testing Instances
Normal	8,662	98	95	128
Ircbot	377	31	57	89
Agobot	32	4	17	10
Rustock	181	7	15	21
Storm	433	18	12	155
Bobax	42,307	24	40	51
Waledac	705	16	60	59
UDP Storm	1341	126	116	194

3.3   IRC Binary Classifier

Calculating the value of the average number IRC packets requires that we know which conversations are IRC sessions and which are not. While typical IRC servers are run on ports in the 6667-6669 range, many botnets use other ports for IRC servers as a way to obfuscate their presence. We did indeed notice this behavior with several of the bot samples we ran, with one contacting an IRC server on port 65520. One can examine packet payload content for strings common to IRC sessions, however any approach that examines packet payload content would fail if the IRC session is encrypted. Thus, we need a scheme for detecting IRC sessions that satisfies the following criteria:

1. Must be port independent
2. Must be packet payload-content independent
3. Must be accurate

Our solution was to build a binary classifier to determine whether a conversation is an IRC session or not. The IRC binary classifier should not be confused with the botnet classifier, as its aim is to distinguish IRC sessions from non-IRC session regardless of whether they belong to a bot or a legitimate user. To build the IRC classifier:

1. Make a copy of our training and testing sets
2. Manually examined our network traces to locate IRC conversations
3. Manually remove encrypted conversations (i.e., unsure if IRC)
4. Set the class label of the instances corresponding to IRC conversations to be "IRC"
5. Set the class label of the instances not corresponding to IRC conversations to be "Non-IRC"

While manually examining network traces to locate IRC conversations is an expensive process, it only needs to be done once to build an appropriate training set for building the classifier. We found a J48 classifier to perform best at detecting IRC sessions. We performed sensitivity analysis on our full feature set to find a reduced feature set for the IRC classifier that gave the best performance:

– Standard deviation of bytes received / packets received
– Standard deviation of the number of source ports used
– Average number of bytes received
– Average number of packets sent
– Average number of packets received
– Average number of UDP packets transmitted

A single conversation can generate several instances according to our scheme, meaning that it is possible that our IRC binary classifier could classify some instances of a conversation as being IRC traffic and some instances as not being IRC traffic. Such a result is not reflected in reality as IRC sessions will continue to be IRC sessions. Rather than labeling single instances, we decided to label entire conversations as being IRC or not. Our approach begins by classifying the instances in each conversation as being instances of IRC traffic or non-IRC traffic. If the majority of instances in a conversation are labeled as being IRC traffic, we consider the entire conversation to be an IRC session and update all of its instances to be considered IRC instances. Similarly, if the majority of instances in a conversation are labeled as non-IRC instances, the entire conversation is considered not to be an IRC session and all of its instances are updated to reflect this. Figure 3 illustrates our IRC binary classification process. The results of our IRC binary classifier are presented in Table 3. For the IRC binary classifier, accuracy is defined as the number of correctly classified conversations divided by the total number of conversations. Using the IRC binary classifier, we are able to differentiate IRC sessions from non-IRC sessions with an accuracy of 0.977. Now that we can be fairly confident about which conversations are IRC sessions, we are able to determine the value of the "average number of IRC packets" feature.

Table 3. Results of IRC Classifier on conversations

Classified as →	NON-IRC	IRC
Non-IRC	151	2
IRC	2	17

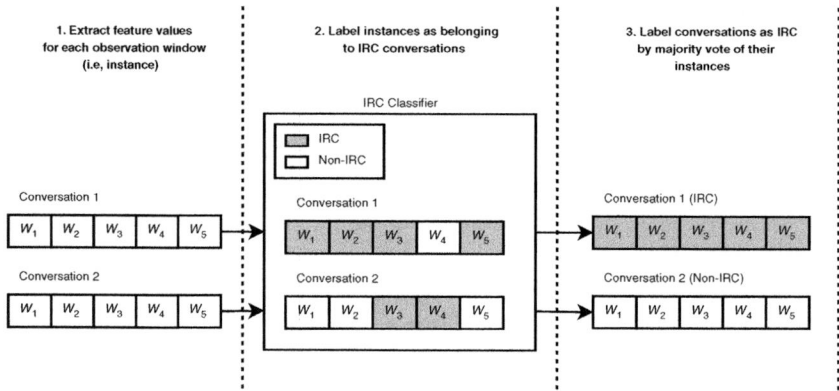

Fig. 3. Classification of IRC conversations: domain-based

4   Evaluation

We used the Weka Machine Learning Java library [9] to build our classifiers. During the training phase, all generated instances (see Table 2) are labeled with one of four class values indicating the type of C&C channel used: *NORMAL*, *IRC*, *HTTP*, *P2P*. Labeling is based on prior knowledge of the bots used to generate network traces. We examined the effectiveness of the two best performing classifiers, a J48 classifier and a Random Forest classifier [9]. As there was no overlap in destination hosts for persistent conversations between normal and botnet traces, testing the classifier on the generated test instances is equivalent to overlaying botnet traces on top of normal traces because the data processing stage would separate the individual conversations from the merged traces.

In addition, we performed sensitivity analysis on our feature set to select reduced subsets of features that produced the best overall accuracy. Trying all possible combinations of features from our total fourteen-feature set, the best set of features for the J48 classifier was found to be:

– Standard deviation of packets sent / packets received
– Average number of bytes sent
– Average number of bytes received
– Average number of TCP packets transmitted
– Average number of UDP packets transmitted
– Average number of IRC packets transmitted
– Persistence value

Similarly, the best feature set for the Random Forest classifier was found to be:

- Standard deviation of bytes sent / bytes received
- Standard deviation of the number of source ports used
- Average number of bytes sent
- Average number of bytes received
- Average number of packets sent
- Average number of UDP packets transmitted
- Average number of IRC packets transmitted
- Persistence value

5 Results

Accuracy is defined as the number of instances correctly classified divided by the total number of instances. False positive rate is defined as the number of instances of legitimate traffic classified as botnet traffic divided by the total number of instances of legitimate traffic. The results of running the classifiers on the reduced feature sets are shown for both the J48 classifier and the Random Forest classifier in Table 4. The J48 classifier had an overall accuracy of 0.926 with a false positive rate of 0.188. The Random Forest classifier had an overall accuracy of 0.929 with a false positive rate of 0.078.

Table 4. Results of Botnet Classifiers: domain-based

	J48				Random Forest			
Classified as →	NORMAL	IRC	HTTP	P2P	NORMAL	IRC	HTTP	P2P
Normal	104	0	21	3	118	0	5	5
IRC	0	99	0	0	0	99	0	0
HTTP	21	1	201	4	32	1	189	5
P2P	2	0	0	251	2	0	0	251

In the results we presented in Table 4, we chose to classify individual instances of conversations rather than entire conversations since we are hoping to produce an online detection system eventually. With an observation window of 4 hours long, our online IDS would potentially be able to detect the presence of a bot within 4 hours of the initial infection. However, it is more intuitive to think of botnet C&C detection in terms of detecting entire C&C conversations. Thus, we also report the accuracy rate of our detection method for classifying entire conversations using a majority vote of the classification results for the instances generated from a conversation. Our results for both the domain-based approach as well as the IP-based approach are shown in Table 5. On a per-conversation basis, accuracy is defined as the number of correctly classified conversations divided by the total number of conversations. False positive rate is defined as the total number of normal conversations classified as botnet conversations divided by the total number of normal conversations. For the domain-based approach, the J48 classifier correctly classified 169 out of a total of 181 conversations and the Random Forest classifier correctly classified 171 of 181 conversations. On a per-conversation level, the J48 classifier had an accuracy of 0.934 and a false positive rate of 0.173 and the Random Forest classifier had an accuracy of 0.945 and a false positive rate of 0.038.

Whereas the domain-based approach found a total of 19 IRC botnet conversations, the IP-based approach found 30. However, in many cases, multiple IP addresses of IRC servers corresponded to a single domain name. Though only 19 persistent connections to domain names were found in the domain-based approach for IRC-based botnets, they accounted for a total of 48 IP addresses, meaning that the IP-based approach missed 18 of the IP addresses associated with the IRC C&C channels. Thus, the results presented in Table 5 are adjusted to include the missed IP addresses. The IP-based approach only found 30 of 38 IP addresses associated with HTTP C&C channels. Both the P2P-based bots did not demonstrate multiple IP addresses associated with a single domain name. While the IP-based approach missed 8 IP addresses associated with persistent conversations to domain names for the instances generated from legitimate traffic, it does not make sense to count those additional IP addresses as misclassified when calculating false positives, as a missed conversation can not raise an alarm. Therefore, the number of normal conversations found by the IP-based approach is left at 48 in Table 5. The per-conversation accuracy of the J48 classifier using the IP-based approach is 0.752 with a false positive rate of 0.200 and the accuracy of the Random Forest classifier using the IP-based approach is 0.771 with a false positive rate of 0.042. Compared to the per-conversational accuracy and false positive rate achieved using the domain-based approach, it is clear that the IP-based approach has poorer performance.

Table 5. Results of Botnet Classifiers (entire conversations)

	Domain-based				IP-based			
	J48		Random Forest		J48		Random Forest	
Conversations	Total	Correct	Total	Correct	Total	Correct	Total	Correct
Normal	52	43	52	50	48	40	48	46
IRC	19	19	19	19	48	24	48	23
HTTP	34	31	34	26	38	24	38	23
P2P	76	76	76	76	76	76	76	76
Total	181	169	181	171	218	164	218	168

6   Discussion

We describe three hypotheses at the beginning of Section III that have to be true in order for our approach to work. The results we have presented in the previous section have shown that botnet C&C communication can be differentiated from botnet non-C&C traffic through the use of a persistence metric. The intuition that botnet traffic follows an inherent command-response pattern such that it can be differentiated from normal, legitimate traffic was shown to be true, as our classifiers were able to successfully distinguish between normal and botnet traffic. Furthermore, the thought that the characteristics of C&C styles across different botnet families would still contain inherent similarities was also shown to be true, as both of our classifiers were able to successfully differentiate the different C&C styles across multiple variants of bots in the same botnet family, and across bots from different bot families. We have also shown that, while IP-based approaches to botnet detection may appear to produce decent results, they run both the risk of missing connections to malicious IP addresses as well as the risk of not capturing the entire behavior of a C&C conversation in the presence of fast flux DNS techniques.

Ultimately, the Random Forest classifier produced the best results in terms of accuracy and false positive rate. For an online IDS, one could either prompt the user when a suspicious conversation is detected, asking her whether or not she wants to block the connection or could automatically block the connection. A high false positive rate would either annoy the user by raising prompts too frequently or would block legitimate connections, leading to further user annoyance. Thus, minimizing the false positive rate is imperative. Sometimes, a botnet conversation may not be detected when it first appears in an observation window but it is very likely that it will be detected in subsequent windows. We hope to quantify the detection time in the near future. As a single, persistent conversation will generate multiple classifiable instances as time progresses, even if the bot infection is not detected in the first observation window, it could certainly be detected in a future observation window. Furthermore, many bot samples initiated several persistent conversations. To successfully detect a bot infection, we only really need to discover one of the persistent conversations. To this end, our IDS was able to detect every bot infection even if it misclassified some of the instances generated from the multitude of bot conversations.

7   Concluding Remarks

Botnets are serious threats to computer networks. Malicious activities such as sending spam, stealing personal or financial information etc can be launched by botnets. In this paper, we present a host-based method for detecting and differentiating different types of botnet infections e.g. IRC-based, HTTP-based or P2P based bots. Our method includes a few unique features, namely (a) the ability to correctly identify the C&C style, (b) a binary IRC classifier that allows identification of IRC traffic without payload inspection, and (c) a domain-based approach that helps to deal with fast flux obfuscation techniques which are becoming more popular in botnet traffic that has been identified in recent months. Our detection scheme can achieve an accuracy of 0.929 with a false positive rate of 0.078 and a false negative rate of 0.033 using the Random Forest classifier. In the near future, we would like to extend our work to detect botnet infections on mobile devices as the growing popularity of smartphones is making them a growing target for hackers to exploit.

References

1. Wurzinger, P., Bilge, L.: Automatically Generating Models for Botnet Detection. In: European Symposium on Research in Computer Security (2009)
2. Vokorokos, L., Balaz, A., Chovanec, M.: Intrusion Detection System Using Self Organizing Map. Acta Electrotechnica et Informatica (2006)
3. Giroire, F., Chandrashekar, J., Taft, N., Schooler, E., Papaginnaki, D.: Exploiting Temporal Persistence to Detect Covert Botnet Channels. Recent Advances in Intrusion Detection (2009)
4. Ramachandran, A., Mundada, Y., Tariq, M.B., Feamster, N.: Securing Enterprise Networks Using Traffic Tainting. Special Interest Group on Data Communication (2008)
5. Gu, G., Zhang, J., Lee, W.: BotSniffer: Detecting Botnet Command and Control Channels in Network Traffic. Network and Distributed System Security (2007)
6. Gu, G., Perdisci, R., Zhang, J., Lee, W.: BotMiner: Clustering Analysis of Network Traffic for Protocol- and Structure-Independent Botnet Detection. In: Proceedings of the 17th Conference on Security Symposium (2008)
7. Chang, S., Daniels, T.: P2P Botnet Detection using Behavior Clustering & Statistical Test
8. Clam AntiVirus, http://www.clamav.net
9. Weka 3 Data Mining and Machine Learning Software, http://www.cs.waikato.ac.nz/ml/weka/
10. John, J., Moshchuk, A., Gribble, S., Krishnamurthy, A.: Studying Spamming Botnets Using Botlab. Network Systems Design and Implementation (2009)
11. Zeng, Y., Hu, X., Shin, K.: Detection of Botnets Using Combined Host- and Network-Level Information. In: International Conference on Dependable Systems & Networks (2008)
12. Stewart, J.: Inside the Storm: Protocols and Encryption of the Storm Botnet (2008), http://www.blackhat.com/presentations/bh-usa-08/Stewart/BH_US_08_Stewart_Protocols_of_the_Storm.pdf
13. Pitsillidis, A., Levchenko, K., Kreibich, C., Kanich, C., Voelker, G., Paxson, V., Weaver, N., Savage, S.: Botnet Judo: Fighting Spam with Itself. Network and Distributed System Security (2009)
14. Porras, P., Saidi, H., Yegneswaran, V.: A Multi-perspective Analysis of the Storm (Peacomm) Worm (2007), http://www.cyber-ta.org/pubs/StormWorm/report
15. Holz, T., Steiner, M., Dahl, F., Biersack, E., Freiling, F.: Measurements and Mitigation of Peer-to-Peer-based Botnets: A Case Study on Storm Worm. In: USENIX Workshop on Large-Scale Exploits and Emergent Threats (2008)

A Method for Constructing Fault Trees from AADL Models

Yue Li[1], Yi-an Zhu[1], Chun-yan Ma[2], and Meng Xu[2]

[1] School of Computer Science,
Northwestern Polytechnical University, Xian, P.R.C
[2] School of Software and Microelectronics,
Northwestern Polytechnical University, Xian, P.R.C
rogerlee0201@gmail.com

Abstract. System safety analysis based on fault tree has been widely used for providing assurance to the stringent safety requirement of safety-critical systems. Generating fault trees from models described in AADL, a promising standard language for modeling complicated embedded system, would realize the automation of system safety analysis which is traditionally performed manually. This paper proposes a whole method for constructing fault trees from AADL models, whose main idea is to extract fault information from AADL models by dynamically tracing the possible fault sources of the specified fault objective, store them into a proposed database structure, and then construct fault trees based on the extracted fault information in the database structure. Further, the challenge posed by the common problems of deadlock and fault tree sharing is resolved by one algorithm called Sharing_Label in our method. We prove the correctness of the whole method theoretically.

1   Introduction

Safety-critical systems are those whose failure would result in loss of life, significant property damage, or damage to the environment. System safety analysis provides assurance that the system satisfies certain safety constrains even in the presence of certain component failures. Safety engineers traditionally perform analysis manually based on information synthesized from informal design models and requirements documents. Unfortunately, these safety analyses are highly subjective and dependent on the skills of the engineers [1]. Fault tree is one of the most common techniques widely used in safety-critical systems by safety engineers. However, different engineers will often produce fault trees for the same system that differ in substantive ways [2]; moreover, constructing a fault tree is labor-intensive and time-consuming. Consequently, how to build fault trees for a safety-critical system effectively and consistently has become a vitally attractive and significant issue.

The key to resolve the foregoing problem depends on whether we can find a formal or standard model, on the basis of which we could construct fault trees that represent the components and their interactions in the context of the safety-critical system

J.M. Alcaraz Calero et al. (Eds.): ATC 2011, LNCS 6906, pp. 243–258, 2011.

architecture. This problem remains unresolved until 2004, when SAE (society of automotive engineers) released AADL (Architecture Analysis & Design Language) as a standard [3], which has inherent support for describing, binding various system components and modeling, analyzing the whole system in both functional and non-functional requirements through the core language. However, AADL itself provides no fault information to support the safety description of systems. Accordingly, AADL Error Model Annex [4] is published by SAE to complement the AADL standard with capabilities for dependability modeling through applying specification of error annotations on the original AADL architecture model. AADL and its error model annex can be regarded as appropriate formal models of most safety-critical systems, from which safety engineers could construct fault trees with consistency and effectiveness. By making full analysis of the fault trees built from AADL models of the system, safety engineers can modify and improve the reliability of the system in the early design stage of development progress iteratively.

Dehlinger et al. [5] proposes to construct DFT (Dynamic Fault Tree) from AADL models to solve the temporal sequence problem; nevertheless, DFT has much more complicated structures and the qualitative analysis results of the DFT would be questioned because there exists no definite qualitative analysis method towards DFT. This paper suggests using static fault tree with Priority-AND gate described in fault tree handbook [6] born with the capability to address the temporal sequence problem, for its simple structure and the relevant effective qualitative analysis methods [9-10]. Joshi et al. [2] describes a systematic approach to build static fault trees from AADL models in the view of system architecture; however, no detailed algorithm has been described in their paper. Their approach computes all the possible fault paths from AADL models with no necessity to identify any fault objective in advance. Accordingly, any fault tree with specified fault objective as its root node would be constructed directly through the computed fault paths. Commendably, the approach considers the reuse of the computed fault paths; however, when minor changes occur in AADL models, the construction of fault trees is forced to be executed again to achieve the correct and instant fault information no matter how complicated and time-consuming it would be. Besides, Guard_In, Guard_Out and Derived_State_Mapping attributes in AADL error models, regarded as the critical factors that determine the direction of fault propagation, are of significance discussed in [2,5], yet neither paper provides the detailed algorithm about the important attributes. In addition, Joshi et al. [2] concisely discusses the possible problems of deadlock and fault tree sharing when constructing fault trees from complicated AADL models; nevertheless, no algorithm has been described to address the two problems simultaneously. This paper proposes a whole detailed method to construct fault trees from AADL models, and describes some detailed algorithms to solve all the problems mentioned above.

The rest of the paper is organized as follows: Sect. 2 introduces the background about AADL and AADL error model. We present our method in Sect. 3 and explain the method through an example in Sect. 4. Correctness of the method is analyzed in Sect. 5. Finally, Sect. 6 concludes the paper.

2   Background

In this section, we will introduce a system example SimAADLSystem and its error model annex SimBasic, also the reference case in Sect. 4, to illustrate certain concepts about AADL and its associated error model respectively.

The SimAADLSystem is a simple system consists of both simple hardware and software components (see Fig. 1). SimHardware.Impl is the implementation of hardware component SimHardware consisting of two *processors* Pr1, Pr2 and one *bus* DataBus which connects Pr1 and Pr2. The software component in SimAADLSystem is composed of two *processes* P1, P2 and two logical *connections* Conn1, Conn2; data is transmitted through Conn1 from the *data port* Output in P1 to the *data port* Input in P2, and vice versa with Conn2. The *processes* of software are bound to the *processors* of hardware, and the logical *connections* of software are bound to the *bus* of hardware. AADL mainly describes the structure, rather than the fault propagation mechanism which is the duty of error model.

```
system SimHardware                          system implementation SimAADLSystem.Impl
end SimHardware;                               subcomponents
system implementation SimHardware.Impl           HW: SimHardware.Impl;
   subcomponents                                 SW: SimSoftware.Impl;
      Pr1: processor SimProcessor.Impl;       properties
      Pr2: processor SimProcessor.Impl;          Actual_Processor_Binding =>
      DataBus: bus SimBus.Impl;                     reference HW.Pr1 applies to SW.P1;
   Connections                                    Actual_Processor_Binding =>
      bus access DataBus -> Pr1.DataBus;            reference HW.Pr2 applies to SW.P2;
      bus access DataBus -> Pr2.DataBus;         Actual_Connection_Binding =>
end SimHardware;                                    reference HW.DataBus applies to SW.Conn1;
system implementation SimSoftware.Impl          Actual_Connection_Binding =>
   subcomponents                                   reference HW.DataBus applies to SW.Conn2;
      P1: process SimProcess.Impl;            end SimAADLSystem.Impl;
      P2: process SimProcess.Impl;
   connections
      Conn1: data port P1.Output -> P2.Input;
      Conn2: data port P2.Output -> P1.Input;
end SimSoftware.Impl;
```

Fig. 1. Snippet of a simple system in AADL

AADL error model mainly describes the fault information of systems. There are two implementations of error model SimBasic: SimBasic.Hardware and SimBasic.Software, which are defined in SimErrorLib error model library as shown in Fig. 2. SimBasic defines one *initial error state* which is also the initial state of certain component, two *error states* that possibly triggered by *error event* or *error propagation*, two *error events* and two *propagations*, prop1 and prop2 both of which can be regarded as *in* or *out propagation* at one time. *In propagation* is the propagation thrown from other components, and *out propagation* is the one that would be propagated to other components. Error model implementation describes the possible actions of fault information defined in error model. Take SimBasic.Hardware as example, assume that the component associated with SimBasic.Hardware error model implementation is in the *initial state* err_free currently, it would turn to *error state* failure1 when the *error event* fail1 occurs.

```
package SimErrorLib                          error model implementation SimBasic.Software
public annex error_model {**                   transitions
error model SimBasic                             err_free – [fail1] -> failure1;
  feature                                        err_free – [fail2] -> failure2;
    err_free : initial error state;             failure1 – [in prop2] -> failure2;
    failure1, failure2 : error state;           failure1 – [in prop1, out prop1] -> failure1;
    fail1, fail2 : error event;                 failure2 – [in prop2, out prop2] -> failure2;
    prop1, prop2 : in out propagation;        end SimBasic.Software; **}
    end SimBasic;                           end SimErrorLib;
error model implementation SimBasic.Hardware
  transitions
    err_free – [fail1] -> failure1;
    err_free – [fail2] -> failure2;
    failure1 – [fail2] -> failure2;
    failure1 – [in prop1, out prop1] -> failure1;
    failure2 – [in prop2, out prop2] -> failure2;
end SimBasic.Hardware;
```

Fig. 2. Specifications of AADL error model

Error model implementation can not work without associating itself to certain system component as shown in Fig. 3. The *annex error_model* block is defined in normal AADL component implementation, and the *Model* attribute associates the error model implementation with component. Now the component SimSoftware.Impl has its own error model information described in SimBasic.Software. Attribute such as *Derived_State_Mapping*, *Guard_In* and *Guard_Out* may alter the error propagation information defined in error model implementation.

```
system implementation SimSoftware.Impl        process implementation SimProcess.Impl
  annex error_model {**                          annex error_model {**
  Model => SimErrorLib::SimBasic.Software;       Model => SimErrorLib::SimBasic.Software;
  Model_Hierarchy => Derived;                    Guard_In => mask when Input[err_free],
  Derived_State_Mapping =>                          prop1 when Input[failure2],
    err_free when P1[err_free] and P2[err_free];    prop2 when Input[failure1]
    failure1 when P1[failure1] or P2[failure1];   applies to Input;
    failure2 when P2[failure2];                   Guard_Out => mask when Input[prop1]
  report => failure2; **}                         applies to Output; **}
end SimSoftware.Impl;                           end SimProcess;
processor implementation SimProcessor.Impl
  annex error_model {**
    Model => SimErrorLib::SimBasic.Hardware;**}
end SimProcessor.Impl;
```

Fig. 3. Associations of AADL error model

Take the component SimSoftware.Impl into consideration, only when one *subcomponent* of the component, either P1 or P2, is in *error state* failure1, will SimSoftware.Impl be in *error state* failure1 which is originally caused by the temporal combination of *error state* err_free and *error event* fail1 due to the function of *Derived_State_Mapping*. Likewise, the *in propagation* prop1 would be thrown when the connection or component connected with *data port* Input is in *error state* failure2 due to *Guard_In*, and the *out propagations* would be masked if the *in propagation* prop1 from *data port* Input is detected due to *Guard_Out*.

3   Method

3.1   The Overall Method

The overall method for constructing fault trees from AADL models can be divided into two phases as follows:

Phase I. Extract fault information from AADL and its associated error models, and store the extracted fault information into the database structure (see Sect. 3.2) by using algorithm Trace_Route (see Fig. 5). Since certain attributes such as Guard_In, Guard_Out, and Derived_State_Mapping have influence on the direction and content of fault paths, and the logical function of each attribute is independent, the attribute algorithms Guard_Out, Derived_State_Mapping and Guard_In (see Fig. 6, 7 and 8 respectively) are proposed to assist the implementation of Trace_Route algorithm.

Phase II. Construct fault trees by iterating and organizing fault information stored in database structure. Since the construction principle itself is simple due to the concise mapping rules (see Sect. 3.6), the key step of this phase depends on the strategy of addressing problems of deadlock and fault tree sharing which are the common phenomena of generating fault trees. Accordingly, Sharing_Label algorithm is proposed to resolve the problems of deadlock and fault tree sharing simultaneously.

3.2   Database Structure

We propose a database structure to store the fault information extracted from AADL error model as shown in Fig. 4. All *State* information of component is stored in *ErrorModel*. The *State* of component stores the possible *Paths* that might cause the *State*. *Path* is composed of *State* and *Condition*, and the temporal sequence between *State* and *Condition* indicates the logical relationship of Priority-AND in fault trees.

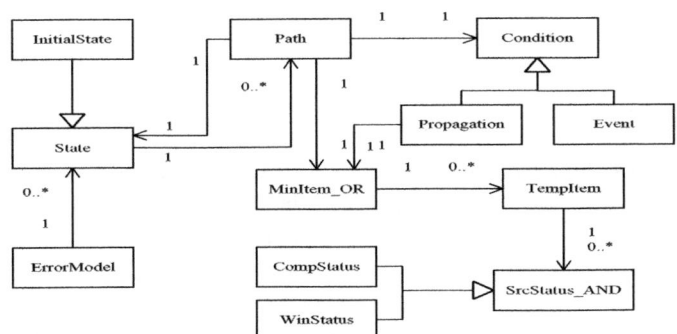

Fig. 4. Class diagram of database structure

Path associates *MinItem_OR* to resolve the ineffectiveness of paths in the original error model, which is caused by attribute Derived_State_Mapping. *Propagation* stores the information of *MinItem_OR* which indicates all the logical combination that might cause the *Propagation*. *MinItem_OR* stores the set information of *TempItem*, and the relationship between *TempItem* implies the logical relationship of OR which indicates all the probable combinations causing the *MinItem_OR*. The set information of *SrcStatus_AND* is stored in *TempItem*, and the relationship between *SrcStatus_AND* implies the logical relationship of AND which indicates the status that only all the *SrcStatus_AND* in set occur simultaneously could trigger one *TempItem*. *InitialState* represents the initial state of component which is beneficial to locate the end of search path quickly. *CompStatus* stores the information about the state of component and the component itself to locate the source of fault through Derived_State_Mapping. The combinations of features or component and the relevant state or propagation information are stored in *WinStatus*.

3.3   Related Definitions

Definition 1 (feature). Feature is the interaction point between components in AADL models which may be any one of the following: data port, event port, event data port, provide data access, require data access and server subprogram call.

Definition 2 (matching rule of name). In propagation of one component has the same name with the out propagation that causes it. The association way to search the same name of propagations is known as the matching rule of name.

Definition 3 (SI, SSI). Divide all the conditions after keyword in AADL error model into combinations split by logical operator OR. The set of combinations is called the Set of Simple Item (SSI). Each combination split by logical operator OR is called Simple Item (SI) and the SI consists of conditions which is in form of feature[propagation or state] and split by logical operator AND.

Definition 4 (constraint of "when others"). When conditions that may cause the specified error state or propagation are not in the combinations of conditions before keyword *when others*, the other combinations should be considered. The rule above is known as constraint of "when others".

3.4   Trace_Route Algorithm

The objective of algorithm Trace_Route is to find the fault paths which cause the top event (the root node of fault tree and also the specified error state in AADL error model) dynamically. Since the transfer of fault among components is delivered by error propagations and each propagation is triggered by the error state of the component involved, according to error propagations, trace towards the reasons of each error state in fault paths step by step until only the initial error states and error event remain, would extract all the possible fault paths from AADL models. The fault information stored in database structure after executing algorithm Trace_Route shown in Fig. 5 is the reason of causing the occurrence of specified top event.

Algorithm 1. Trace_Route
Input: AADL models and its error models. **Output:** modified database structure
 1: assure error state *S* and its associated component or connection *Comp* of top event according to
      keyword *report* in error model;
 2: **if** Derived_State_Mapping in *Comp* //*CompBD* as *Comp* here
 3:    execute **algorithm Derived_State_Mapping**;
 4: **else** find source path *P* cause *S* from implementation of error model and fill information of *P* in
      Path;
 5: **if** *InitialState* in *P*
 6:    turn to step 2;
 7: **if** *Propagation* in *P* {
 8:    **if** *Comp* has bounded component or connection *CompBD* {
 9:      find propagation *prop* of *CompDB* according to matching rule of name and find the error state
        S that causes *prop*;
10:    turn to step 2; }
11:    **for** each feature *F* of features in *Comp*
12:      if Guard_In applies to *F*
13:        execute **algorithm Guard_In** and turn to step 15; }
14: turn to step 28;
15: capture component or connection *Comp* associated with *F* according to AADL models;
16: **if** *Comp* is a connection {
17:    **if** direction of *Comp* points to component with *F* {
18:      **if** *Comp* has error model
19:        capture the error model of *Comp* and name *Comp* as *Cpt*;
20:      **else** capture the component *Cpt* of the other side of *Comp* and its associated error model;
21:      **if** *F* not executed by **algorithm Guard_In**
22:        capture the name of propagation in *Cpt* according to the matching rule of name;
23:      **else** turn to step 25;
24:    } **else** stop trace of current path and turn to step 28; }
25: capture feature *Fr* connected with *Cpt*;
26: **if** Guard_Out applies to *Fr*
27:    execute **algorithm Guard_Out**;
28: **if** switch of loop or recursion has *InitialState* or *Propagation*
29:    turn to step 2;
30: **else;** //no execution here, just go to next loop or judgment switch //under recursion that has not
        been iterated.
31: **if** no *InitialState* and *Propagation* exist
32: **end;**

Fig. 5. Algorithm Tace_Route

3.5   Attribute Algorithms

Each attribute algorithm could independently alter the fault paths that are to be extracted. Attribute Guard_Out makes regulation about which error propagation could go out of a component and where it goes. Algorithm 2 as illustrated in Fig. 6 describes the approach to find the error state or propagation that triggers the target propagation through the specified feature. Constraint of "when others" defined in Sect. 3.3 is a critical issue in all attribute algorithms. As shown in Fig. 6 and 7, algorithm 2 and 3 have the same process strategy when considering the constraint of "when others", because both algorithms have the similar application background and logical meaning, which is also the reason why Theorem 1 in Sect. 5 uses the same analysis method and test data to analyze the coverage rate of fault paths.

The responsibility of attribute Derived_State_Mapping is to define the fault information of subcomponents or connected components which differ from that in original error model. Algorithm 3 (see Fig. 7) provides the mapping rule to extract fault information under attribute Derived_State_Mapping.

The duty of attribute Guard_In is to guard the features of components and determine which error propagation could enter the component. In Fig. 8, algorithm 4 judges whether the specified *in* propagation could continue the fault path or just terminate in current component. The code statement in step 14 means that only when propagation reaches the feature applied by Guard_In could the combination condition be triggered, and the propagation might have any identity. The statement "only feature" in step 17 limits the matching rule, which means the feature alone that exists in SSI, would mask the specified *in* propagation.

Algorithm 2. Guard_Out.
Input: *WinStatus* in current *Path*. **Output:** modified database structure
1 : capture *feature* and *status* with propagation or error state;
2 : **if** *feature* not after keyword *applies to*
3 : execute as matching rule of name, then turn to step 27;
4 : **if** *status* is an error state {
5 : **if** *status* exists in condition *mask*
6 : set *WinStatus* as null, then turn to step 27;
7 : **else** set combination with current component and *status* to *WinStatus* and turn to step 27;
8 : } **else** { **if** *status* not matches any propagation in Guard_Out
9 : set *WinStatus* as null, then turn to step 27;
10 : **else** capture condition *C* after keyword *when* corresponded with *status*; }
11 : **if** *C* equals keyword *others* {
12 : split conditions above *others* into *SSI*;
13 : combine each *feature* and *subcomponent* declared in current component with error state and propagation of corresponding *feature* or *subcomponent* as a form of *Input[prop2]*;
14 : initial a set *tempSet* and store each combination in it;
15 : **for** each combination *comb* in *tempSet* {
16 : **for** each *SI* in *SSI* {
17 : **if** *SI* equals *comb*
18 : delete *comb* from *tempSet*; }}
19 : add *comb* of *tempSet* to *TempItem*;
20 : associate *TempItem* with *MinItem_OR*, *MinItem_OR* with *Path*;
21 : set combination with current component and *status* to *WinStatus* and turn to step 27
22 : } **else** { split *C* into *SSI*;
23 : add logical AND item of each *SI* to *SrcStatus_AND*;
24 : add logical OR item of *SSI* to *TempItem*;
25 : associate *SrcStatus_AND* with *TempItem*, *TempItem* with *MinItem_OR* and *MinItem_OR* with *Path* respectively;
26 : set combination with current component and *status* to *WinStatus*; }
27 : **end**

Fig. 6. Algorithm Guard_Out

Algorithm 3. Derived_State_Mapping.
Input: specified component and its state *S*. **Output:** database structure with filled *Path*
1 : **if** *S* in Derived_State_Mapping
2 :   capture condition *C* after keyword *when* corresponded with *S* ;
3 : **else** turn to step 18;
4 : **if** *C* equals keyword *others* {
5 :   split conditions above *others* into *SSI*;
6 :   combine each *feature* and *subcomponent* declared in current component with error state and
       propagation of corresponding *feature* or *subcomponent* as a form of *Iput[prop2]*;
7 :   initial a set *tempSet* and store each combination in it;
8 :   **for** each combination *comb* in *tempSet* {
9 :   **for** each *SI* in *SSI* {
10:       **if** *SI* equals *comb*
11:        delete *comb* from *tempSet*; }}
12:     add *comb* of *tempSet* to *TempItem*;
13:     associate *TempItem* with *MinItem_OR, MinItem_OR* with *Path*;
14: } **else** { split *C* into *SSI*;
15:     add logical AND item of each *SI* to *SrcStatus_AND*;
16:     add logical OR item of *SSI* to *TempItem*;
17:      associate *SrcStatus_AND* with *TempItem, TempItem* with *MinItem_OR* and *MinItem_OR*
            with *Path* respectively; }
18: **end**

Fig. 7. Algorithm Derived_State_Mapping

Algorithm 4. Guard_In.
Input: in propagation *inprop*. **Output:** modified database structure
1 : **if** *inprop* exists in list of propagation in Guard_In {
2 :   capture *feature* after keyword *applies to*;
3 :   capture condition *C* after keyword *when* corresponded with *inprop*;
4 :   **if** *C* equals keyword *others*
5 :   split conditions above *others* into *SSI* and turn to step 17;
6 :   **else** split *C* into *SSI*;
7 : } **else** turn to step 21;
8 : **for** each *SI* in *SSI* {
9 :   **if** *feature* not exists in *SI*
10:    turn to step 14;
11:   **else** { add logical AND item of *SI* to *SrcStatus_AND*;associate *SrcStatus_AND* with *TempItem*,
12:      *TempItem* with *MinItem_OR* and *MinItem_OR* with *Path* respectively; }
13: } turn to step 21;
14: add *feature* to *SrcStatus_AND* without fixed propagation;
15: add logical AND item of current *SI* to *SrcStatus_AND*;
16: associate *SrcStatus_AND* with *TempItem, TempItem* with *MinItem_OR* and *MinItem_OR* with
       Path respectively;
17: **if** *SI* with only *feature* exists in *SSI*
18:   turn to step 21;
19: **else** { add *feature* to *SrcStatus_AND* without fixed propagation;
20:    associate *SrcStatus_AND* with *TempItem, TempItem* with *MinItem_OR* and *MinItem_OR* with
          Path respectively; }
21: **end**

Fig. 8. Algorithm Guard_In

3.6   Construction of Fault Trees from Database Structure

The principle of construction is simple: first, target the top event presented as *State* in database structure, and then successively depth-first traverse the *Path* that causes *State* and *Propagation*, the *TempItem* that causes *Propagation*, and the *SrcStatus_AND* that causes *TempItem* (*SrcStatus_AND* or *TempItem* may store the new information of *State* that should be further traversed) until only *Event* and *InitialState* of database structure remain. When traversing each *State* or *Event*, construct the corresponding fault node with the same identity. The logical gate among fault nodes depends on the logical relation such as AND, OR and Priority-AND among defined classes as described in Sect.3.2.

Algorithm 5. Sharing_Label
Input: database structure. **Output:** fault tree
1:   push top event as root node into stack *S* and initial a set as *Set*;
2:   construct the first child node of specified node through iterating database structure;
3:   define current node as *N*;
4:   **if** *N* is a leaf node //*InitialState* or *Event*
5:   turn to step 19;
6:   **if** *N* not in *S*
7:   push *N* into *S*;
8:   **if** *N* in *Set*
9:   turn to step 12;
10:   **else** turn to step 2;
11:   capture the reference *Ref* of *N*;
12:   **for** each child node *CN* of *Ref* {
13:   **if** *CN* has no label and *CN* in *S*
14:   set label to *CN*;
15:   **if** *CN* has label and *CN* not in *S*
16:   remove label from *CN*; }
17:   substitute *Ref* for *N* and replace *N* in *S* by *Ref*;
18:   **if** *N* has brother node
19:   turn to step 3;
20:   **else while** *S* is not empty {
21:   pop top node of *S* and add it to *Set*;
22:   turn to step 18; }
23: **end**

Fig. 9. Algorithm Sharing_Label

Algorithm Sharing_Label serves to address the problems of deadlock and fault tree sharing when generating fault trees. Algorithm 5 as described in Fig. 9 utilizes a stack to record the visited nodes to detect deadlock, attaches labels to mark the deadlock node and uses a set to store the complete fault trees to be shared. The subtree under the deadlock node has no necessary to be cut down, because when algorithm encounters the deadlock node at the first time, it would ignore the subtree below the deadlock node. Codes from step 4 to 5 and 18 to 22 ensure the completeness of each fault tree stored in set, which enable the sharable feature of fault tree by removing the label of its node.

4   Example

This section illustrates the whole method in the context of an application introduced in Sect. 2. The AADL models of the example are descried in Fig. 1, 2 and 3.

4.1   Extraction of Fault Information from AADL Models

The top event of fault tree is the error state failure2 of SimSoftware P2 marked after keyword report as shown in Fig. 3. Before finding fault paths that might trigger failure2 of SimSoftware, we should store the identity information of top event in *State* of database structure. Algorithm 3 firstly finds the rules defined in attribute Derived_State_Mapping of SimSoftware, which indicates that the subcomponent P2 of SimSoftware at the error state failure2 would trigger the specified top event, shown in Fig. 3. Secondly, it adds failure2 of P2 into *MinItem_OR* of *Path* directly because the *Path* of *State* has no error event. Error model SimBasic.Software described in Fig. 2 shows that it would trigger failure2 of P2 in the following two situations: when P2 at state err_free and then event fail2 occurs; and when P2 at state failure1 and then propagation prop2 occurs. Therefore, add err_free:fail2 and failure1:prop2 as *CompStatus* to *TempItems* of *MinItem_OR* respectively, then initial *State* with its *Path* according to the information of *CompStatus*. Currently, the *State* of P2:failure2 should include two Paths: one associates *State* err_free and *Event* fail2, and the other associates *State* failure1 and *Propagation* prop2. Since the error model of SimProcess declares attribute Guard_In, as requirement of algorithm 1, we should refer the rules in Guard_In before tracing the fault sources of prop2. As defined in Guard_In, the in propagation prop2 is transferred from the other side of connection with feature Input, as described in Fig. 1. Besides, attribute Guard_Out of P1 fails to mask or change the propagation path according to algorithm 2, therefore failure 1 of P1 constitutes one of the causes of prop2. In addition, P2 is also bounded by Pr2 and hence another cause of prop2 would be the out propagation of Pr2. After tracing the causes of every non-initial State and Propagation and storing the identity information of them to the database structure as the way illustrated above, the fault information of triggering the top event failure2 of component SimSoftware would be extracted completely.

4.2   Construction of Fault Tree from Extracted Fault Information

After the process presented in Sect. 4.1, all fault information of triggering failure 2 of SimSoftware has been stored in database structure. Building fault nodes and associating logical gates among nodes from the fault information of database structure through the rule described in Sect. 3.6 would finish the task of construction. We will illustrate the construction of fault node with state failure2 of Pr2 in this example. Find the *State* in database structure with identity of Pr2:failure2, and then iterate the collection of *Path* in *State*. There are two *Paths* with *TempItem* including failure1:fail2 and err_free:fail2 both as a form of *CompStatus* respectively. Accordingly, build one fault node with identity of failure2 and one basic event node with identity of fail2, combine the two nodes by a Priority-AND gate and then associate the gate to one temp node A which serves as a connecting link with no practical sense. Likewise, another temp node

B with basic initial node err_free and basic event node fail2 would be combined by an OR-gate with the temp node A as the child nodes of fault node failure2 of Pr2. The fault tree with a top event of SimSoftware:failure2 is shown in Fig. 10. The case is too simple to involve deadlock and fault tree sharing; therefore this section would not apply algorithm 5 in this example.

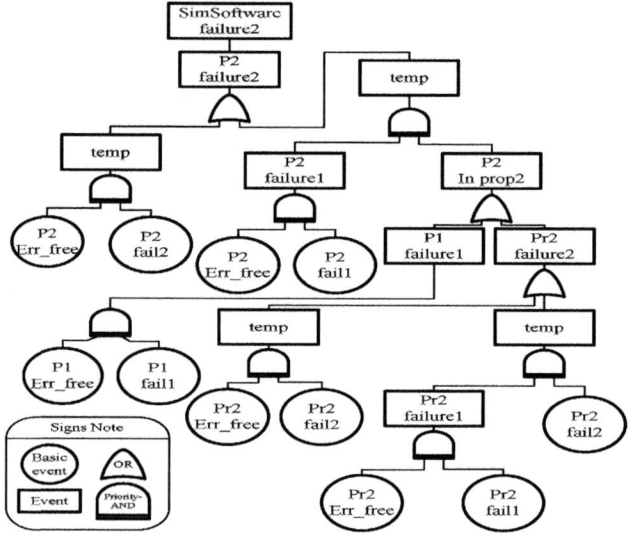

Fig. 10. Algorithm Sharing_Label

5   Correctness Analysis

The objective of the method for constructing fault trees from AADL models is to extract fault information from AADL models, process and organize them in a form of fault tree. Consequently, the problems that whether the fault information is extracted adequately from AADL models and whether the process of generating fault trees based on the fault information is correct constitute the key point.

The Algorithm Trace_Route serves to extract fault information from AADL models. Because the detailed rule of tracing fault sources of the specified error state is based on the attribute algorithms which might alter the direction and content of fault paths, the correctness of Trace_Route depends on the quality of three attribute algorithms. The three algorithms without constraint of "when others" (as defined in Sect. 3.3) can accurately cover all the paths which cause the specified error state according to the finite logical combinations. However, processing the constraint of "*when others*" precisely would introduce NOT-gate to fault tree, and the possible logical combinations related to *others* would be sizable and complicated. Three attribute algorithms under constraint of "when others" find the fault paths in simplification through simplified method of Boolean algebra and their own features, which reduces the accuracy by expanding search coverage; nevertheless, none of the three attribute algorithms omits the possible fault paths as proved in Theorem 1 and 2.

Theorem 1. *Algorithm 2 and algorithm 3 are able to cover all the fault paths under the constraint of "when others".*

Proof. The combination number of algorithm output is denoted as M. Let N be the number of all SI in SSI (defined in Sect. 3.3) before keyword *others*. Define L_j as the number of item with logical AND in current SI denoted as j. If current combination i in j, then define the value of K_{ij} as 0, otherwise the value of K_{ij} is 1. Let C1 be the number of feature and subcomponent (algorithm 2 without subcomponent). Let C2 be the number of error state and propagation that have ability to trigger the feature and subcomponent. Define P1 as the difference of percentage between results of algorithm and the ideal circumstance which satisfies the following equation:

$$P1 = \sum_{i=1}^{M} \sum_{j=1}^{N} \left(1/c1 \cdot c2\right)^{K_{ij} + L_j}$$

If there is no logical AND item in every SI before keyword *others* when computing P1, combine the combination of algorithm output with the logical OR item before keyword *others* by logical AND operation, which replaces the originally empty item of logical AND. The combinations with high probability in practical applications and the corresponding value of P1 are listed in Table 1. The accuracy difference values (D-value) are all equal or greater than zero, which means the fault paths are all contained in the results of algorithm by expanding the search coverage.

Table 1. Accuracy of algorithm 2 and 3 under constraint of "when others"

No.	Feature number	State number	Combina- tion number	AND items before keyword "others"	OR items before keyword"others"	Accuracy D-value:P1
1	2	1	2	A∩B	-	0.500
2	2	1	2	-	A|B	0.250
3	2	2	4	-	A1|...	0.281
4	2	2	4	-	(A1,A2)|...	0.313
5	2	2	4	A1∩A2,A1∩B1	B2	0.281
6	2	2	4	A1∩A2,A1∩B1,A1∩B2	-	0.297
7	2	2	4	A1∩A2	B1|B2	0.141
8	2	2	4	A1∩A2	B1,B2	0.125
9	2	2	4	A1∩A2	-	0.156
10	2	2	4	A1∩A2∩B1	-	0.051
11	2	2	4	A1∩A2∩B1	B2	0.047
12	2	2	4	A1∩A2∩B1∩B2	-	0.016
13	3	2	6	A1∩B1∩C1	-	0.016
14	3	2	6	-	A1|...	0.139

Theorem 2. *Algorithm 4 are able to cover all the fault paths under the constraint of "when others".*

Proof. The number of feature after keyword *applies to* is denoted as M. Let N be the number of all SI in SSI (defined in Sect. 3.3) before keyword others. Define L_j as the number of item with logical AND in current SI denoted as j. If current combination i in j, then let the value of K_{ij} be 0, otherwise let the value of K_{ij} be 1. Let C be the number of feature. If there exists SI in SSI that only has the current feature, let the value of W_i be 0, otherwise let the value of W_i be 1. Define P2 as the difference of percentage between results of algorithm and the ideal circumstance which satisfies the following equation:

$$P2 = \sum_{i=1}^{M} \left(W_i \cdot \sum_{j=1}^{N} \left(1/c \right)^{K_{ij} + L_j} \right)$$

If there is no logical AND item in each SI before keyword *others* when computing P1, combine every feature after keyword *applies to* with the logical OR item before *others* by logical AND operation respectively, which replaces the original empty item of logical AND. The combinations with high probability in practical applications and the corresponding value of P2 are listed in Table 2. The accuracy difference values (D-value) are all equal or greater than zero, which means the fault paths are all contained in the results of algorithm.

Table 2. Accuracy of algorithm 4 under constraint of "when others"

No.	Feature number	items after keyword "applies to"	AND items before keyword "others"	OR items before keyword "others"	Accuracy D-value:P2
1	2	A,B	A∩B	-	0.500
2	2	A|B	A∩B	-	0.250
3	2	A	-	B	0.250
4	2	A	-	A	0.000
5	3	A|B	A∩B	-	0.111
6	3	C	A∩B	-	0.037
7	3	A,C	A∩B∩C	-	0.074
8	3	C	A∩B	C	0.000
9	3	A|B|C	A∩B∩C	-	0.037
10	3	A|B|C	-	A,B,C	0.000
11	3	A,C	A∩B	-	0.148
12	3	A,C	A∩B	C	0.111
13	3	A|B	A∩B	C	0.222
14	3	B,C	-	A	0.222

As demonstrated in Theorem 1 and 2, all possible fault paths would be extracted even in the constraint of "when others", one condition that might omit fault information with a high probability; moreover, algorithm 1 traces the fault sources strictly through the precise description of propagation relationship among AADL components as shown in Sect. 3.4. So the method ensures the correctness of extraction of fault information from AADL models.

Because the relationship between fault node and the extracted fault information stored in database structure is one-to-one (see Sect. 3.6), the process of mapping fault information to fault node of fault tree would be correct. The factors that influence the correctness of generating fault trees from fault information are limited to the problems of deadlock and fault tree sharing in the construction.

Theorem 3. *By using algorithm 5, the problems of deadlock and sharing fault trees would be resolved simultaneously.*

Proof. Algorithm 5 adopts the strategy that it defines a set to store the complete fault trees or subtrees, and detects deadlock before sharing the tree with the same identity in set. As a result, all the possible locations of deadlock collision between the sharing fault tree and the fault tree under construction would be detected. Algorithm 5 avoids directly removing the node by attaching a label to the deadlock node, which keeps the completeness of sharing fault tree in set and has benefit for reuse of fault tree. When it finds a node in sharing tree with label and the node is not in the visited stack, the algorithm would remove the label from the node because the node may be a deadlock node before but not a deadlock node in the current path under construction; When it finds a node in sharing tree without label but the node is in the visited stack, the algorithm would attach a label to the node to show the fact that the node is a deadlock node currently, which avoid the possibility of implicit new deadlock. Since algorithm 5 can both remove the new deadlock nodes and avoid reusing the old deadlock nodes, it resolves the only two difficulties of keeping correctness, considering both deadlock and sharing fault trees.

6   Conclusion

This paper describes a method in detail for constructing fault trees from AADL models and proves the correctness of the whole method theoretically. The method is especially appropriate to be used in the early design stage of AADL models which needs to be modified frequently for system safety analysis based on fault tree.

References

1. Joshi, A., Whalen, M., Heimdahl, M.: Model-based safety analysis final report. NASA contractor report, NASA/CR-2006-213953 (2006)
2. Joshi, A., Vestal, S., Binns, P.: Automatic Generation of Static Fault Trees from AADL Models. Presented at Workshop on Architecting Dependable Systems of The 37th Annual IEEE/IFIP Int. Conference on Dependable Systems and Networks, Edinburgh, UK (2007)
3. SAE-AS5506. Architecture Analysis and Design Language. SAE (November 2004)
4. SAE-AS5506/1. Architecture Analysis and Design Language Annex vol. 1. SAE (2006)

5. Dehlinger, J., Dugan, J.B.: Analyzing Dynamic Fault Trees Derived from Model-Based System Architectures. Nuclear Engineering and Technology: An International Journal of the Korean Nuclear Society 40(5), 365–374 (2008)

6. Haasl, D.F., Roberts, N.H., Vesely, W.E., Goldberg, F.F.: Fault Tree Handbook, Systems and Reliability Research, Office of Nuclear Regulatory Commission, Washington, DC (1981)

7. Sun, H., Hauptman, M., Lutz, R.R.: Integrating Product-Line Fault Tree Analysis into AADLModels. In: Tenth IEEE Int. Symp. on High Assurance Systems Engineering (HASE 2007), pp. 15–22. IEEE Computer Society, Los Alamitos (2007)

8. Feiler, P.H., Rugina, A.-E.: Dependability Modeling with the Architecture Analysis and Design Language (AADL).Technical report, CMU/SEI-2007-TN-043 (2007)

9. Walker, M., Papadopoulos, Y.: Synthesis and analysis of temporal fault trees with PANDORA: The time of Priority AND gates. Hybrid Systems 2 (June 2008)

10. Walker, M., Papadopoulos, Y.: Qualitative temporal analysis: Towards a full implementation of the Fault Tree Handbook, Control Engineering Practice (November 2008) (in press) (available online)

Author Index